ENTERPRISE KNOWLEDGE MANAGEMENT

Related Titles for David Loshin's *Enterprise Knowledge Management:* **The Data Quality Approach.**

Joe Celko, *Joe Cleko's Data and Databases: Concepts in Practice.*
August 1999. 1558604324.

Jesse Feiler, *Database-Driven Web Sites.* February 1999. $44.95.
0-12-251336-3.

Jan L. Harrington, *Object-Oriented Database Design Clearly
Explained.* October 1999. $39.95. 0-12-326428-6.

Dorian Pyle, *Data Preparation for Data Mining.* March 1999.
01558605290.

ENTERPRISE KNOWLEDGE MANAGEMENT

The Data Quality Approach

David Loshin
Knowledge Integrity Incorporated

Morgan Kaufmann

AN IMPRINT OF ACADEMIC PRESS
A Harcourt Science and Technology Company

San Diego   San Francisco   New York   Boston   London   Sydney   Tokyo

ACADEMIC PRESS
A Harcourt Science and Technology Company
525 B Street, Suite 1900, San Diego, California 92101-4495, USA
http://www.academicpress.com

Academic Press
Harcourt Place, 32 Jamestown Road, London NW1 7BY, UK
http://www.academicpress.com

Morgan Kaufmann Publishers
340 Pine Street, Sixth Floor, San Francisco, California 94104-3205, USA
http://www.mkp.com

Library of Congress Catalog Card Number: 00-112074

International Standard Book Number: 0-12-455840-2

PRINTED IN THE UNITED STATES OF AMERICA
01 02 03 04 05 IP 9 8 7 6 5 4 3 2

CONTENTS

3
DATA QUALITY IN PRACTICE

4
ECONOMIC FRAMEWORK OF DATA QUALITY AND
THE VALUE PROPOSITION

5
DIMENSIONS OF DATA QUALITY

6

STATISTICAL PROCESS CONTROL AND THE IMPROVEMENT CYCLE

7

DOMAINS, MAPPINGS, AND ENTERPRISE REFERENCE DATA

8

DATA QUALITY ASSERTIONS AND BUSINESS RULES

9

MEASUREMENT AND CURRENT STATE ASSESSMENT

10

DATA QUALITY REQUIREMENTS

11

METADATA, GUIDELINES, AND POLICY

12

RULE-BASED DATA QUALITY

13
METADATA AND RULE DISCOVERY

14
DATA CLEANSING

15
ROOT CAUSE ANALYSIS AND SUPPLIER MANAGEMENT

16

DATA ENRICHMENT/ENHANCEMENT

17

DATA QUALITY AND BUSINESS RULES IN PRACTICE

18
BUILDING THE DATA QUALITY PRACTICE

PREFACE

While data quality problems are widespread, it is rare for an event to take place that provides a high-profile example of how questionable information quality can have a worldwide business effect. The 2000 US Presidential election and the subsequent confusion around the Florida recount highlights the business need for high quality data. The winner of this election is in a position to influence economies around the world. The uncertainty associated with the lack of a clear winner had an immediate effect the day after the election when stock prices plummeted. Whether it is unintuitive data presentation, questions about the way information is aggregated, or the method by which information policy regulates the use of data, valuable information quality lessons regarding at least six data quality issues that can be learned from the election.

POOR DATA REPRESENTATION

A poor decision with respect to data presentation resulted in voter confusion. The use of the butterfly ballot in Palm Beach County, FL is an example how the presentation of information did not correlate to users' expectations, leading to a large number of voting errors. In fact, many voters later claimed that they were dismayed to learn they may have voted for Pat Buchanan, a right-wing Conservative candidate, instead of Al Gore, the Democratic party candidate.

DATA VALIDATION

With no built-in mechanism to validate the data before it enters the system, the use of punch cards and the "butterfly ballot" leads to problems with vote validation. When using a punch card ballot, (which, according to the LA Times was used by more than 37 percent of registered nationwide voters in 1996), the voter selects a candidate by poking out the chad—the perforated section that should be ejected when the hole is punctured. The cards are read by a tabulation machine, which counts a vote when it reads the hole in the card.

The validation issue occurs when the chad is not completely ejected. The automated tabulation of both "hanging chads" (chads that are still partially attached) and "pregnant chads" (chads that are bulging but not punched out) is questionable, and so it is not clear whether all votes are counted. What constitutes a valid vote selection is primarily based on whether the tabulation machine can read the card. In the case of recounts, the cards are passed through the reader multiple times. In that process some of the hanging chads are shaken free which leads to different tallies after each recount.

In addition, if someone mistakenly punches out more than one selection, the vote is automatically nullified. It is claimed that 19,000 ballots were disqualified because more than one vote for president had been made on a single ballot. This is an example where a policy to pre-qualify the ballot before it is sent to be counted could be instituted. Since the rules for what constitutes a valid vote are well described, it should be possible to have a machine evaluate the punch card to determine whether it is valid or not, and notify the voter that the ballot would be invalidated before it is cast.

INVALID ANALYTICAL MODELS

For many people on election eve, it is customary to sit in front of their televisions and watch as their favorite newscasters predict the allocation of electoral votes. These predictions are based on the results of exit polls and election results provided by an organization called the Voter News Service (VNS), which is jointly owned by a coalition of news companies in order to cut the cost of data collection. Typically, the VNS feeds both vote counts and winner predictions to all the news media simultaneously, which is why all the different broadcasters seem to predict the winners all around the same time.

In the case of the 2000 election, the networks were led to predict the winner of Florida incorrectly, not just once, but twice. The first error occured because predicting elections is based on statistical models generated from past voting behavior that 1) were designed to catch vote swings an order of magnitude greater than the actual (almost final) tallies and 2) did not take changes in demographics into account. This meant that the prediction of Gore's winning Florida was retracted about 2 hours after it was made.

CONFLICTING DATA SOURCES

By 2:00AM the VNS (and consequently, the reporting organizations) switched their allocation of Florida's electoral votes from Gore to Bush, and declared Bush to have enough electoral votes to win the election. However, a second retraction occured when actual vote tallies were disputed. While the VNS report indicated that Bush led in Florida by 29,000 votes, information posted on the Florida Board of Elections web site indicated that Bush's lead was closer to 500 votes, with the gap narrowing quickly. A computer glitch in Volusia County led to an overestimation of Bush's total by more than 25,000 votes.

EXPECTATION OF ERROR

According to Title IX, Chapter 102 of Florida law, "if the returns for any office reflect that a candidate was defeated or eliminated by one-half of a percent or less of the votes cast for such office...the board responsible for certifying the results of the vote...shall order a recount of the votes..."

This section of the law contains data-accuracy implication that there is an expected margin of error of one-half of one percent of the votes. The automatic recount is a good example where the threshold for potential error is recognized and where there is defined governance associated with a data quality problem.

TIMELINESS

Timeliness is an important aspect of information quality. We have come to expect that the results of a national election are decided by the time we wake up the next day. Even in a close election when the results are inconclusive, there are timeliness constraints for the reporting and certification of votes.

DATA QUALITY ON THE PERSONAL LEVEL

My personal connection to data quality began at a very early age, although I did not realize the connection until recently. My parents, through family coercion, decided to give me the first name "Howard," although they had wanted to give me the name "David." So David became my middle name, but even though they named me Howard, I have always been called — by my parents and, subsequently, everyone else — David.

Hence the source of the problem. This fixed-field database-oriented world is ill prepared to deal with a person who is called by his middle name. Everywhere you go, you are asked for your first name and middle initial. So, officially, I am Howard, but I always go by the name David. At school, at camp, at college, at work, filling out applications, opening bank accounts, filing tax returns, and so on, I fill out my name in its official form.

People try to bend the rules: "Put down David as your first name and H as your middle initial." "Just use David." "Scratch out first name and change it to middle name." Unfortunately, these ideas are too radical for the poor data entry people, so I either end up as David H. Loshin or I am stuck with being called Howard.

This really happened: At a doctor's office recently, the receptionist insisted that if my name were officially Howard D. Loshin on my insurance card, they were only going to call me Howard. I have three different credit cards, all with different names on them. Not only that — my last name, Loshin, sounds the same as "lotion," and I find my last name is consistently misspelled: Lotion, Loshen, Loshion, Loshian. When it comes to how my mail is addressed, I never know what to expect — except for one thing: I *will* get at least two of every direct marketing sales letter.

Despite my inherited data quality connection, it was not until a few years ago that I found a new motivation with data quality. I was associated with a securities processing group at a large financial services company, who were analyzing their accounts database. What was interesting was that up to that point they had considered their accounts as just that: accounts. Over a period of time, however, some people there became convinced of the benefits of looking at the people associated with those accounts as customers, and a new project was born that would turn the accounts database inside out. My role in that project was to interpret the different information paradigms that appeared in the accounts database name and address field. For it turned out that a single customer might be associated with many different accounts, in many different roles: as an owner, a trustee, an investment advisor, and so forth.

I learned two very interesting things about this project. The first was that the knowledge that can be learned from combining multiple databases was much greater than from the sum total of analyzing the databases individually. The second was the realization that the problems that I saw at this organization were not limited to this company — in fact, these problems are endemic and not only within the financial industry but in any industry that uses information to run its businesses.

The insight that brought full circle the world of data quality was this: Every business process that uses data has some inherent assumptions and expectations about the data. And these assumptions and expectations can be expressed in a formal way, and this formality can expose much more knowledge than simple database schema and Cobol programs.

So I left that company and formed a new company, Knowledge Integrity Incorporated, (*www.knowledge-integrity.com*) whose purpose is to understand, expose, and correct data quality problems. Our goal is to create a framework for evaluating the impacts that can be caused by low data quality, to assess the state of data quality within an enterprise, to collect the assumptions and expectations about the data that is used, and recast those assumptions and expectations as a set of data quality and business rules. In turn, these rules are incorporated as the central core of a corporate knowledge management environment, to capture corporate knowledge and manage it as content.

This book is the product of that goal. In it, we elaborate on our philosophy and methods for evaluating data quality problems and how we aim to solve them. I believe that the savvy manager understands the importance of high-quality data as a means for increasing business effectiveness and productivity, and this book puts these issues into the proper context. I hope the reader finds this book helpful, and I am certainly interested in hearing about others' experiences. Please feel free to contact me at Loshin@knowledge-integrity.com and let me know how your data quality projects are moving along!

I have been collecting what I call "Data Quality Horror Stories" and placing them on our corporate Web site (*www.knowledge-integrity.com/horror.htm*). If you have any interesting personal experiences, or if you see news stories that demonstrate how poor data quality has serious (or comical) effects, please e-mail them to me at Loshin@ knowledge-integrity.com.

I would like to thank the people who have helped make this book possible. First and foremost, my wife, Jill, and my children, Kira and Jonah, are always there when I need them. Ken Morton acted as acquisitions editor and general enabler. Thomas Park, who took over the project from Ken, was invaluable in helping me get this project completed. I thank Thomas Redman, with whom I worked for a short period of time and consulted on some of the concepts in this book. Thank you to Mary O'Brien, who read through early drafts of the proposal and was a big supporter.

Thanks also go to Bob Shelly, whose experienced eye validated my content, and to the rest of the Morgan Kaufmann staff involved in this project. Sheri Dean and Julio Esperas also provided significant help in the preparation of the book.

I also must thank Justin Kestelyn of *Intelligent Enterprise* magazine, who has vetted some of my ideas by publishing abridged versions of a few chapters. Thanks also go to Dennis Shasha at New York University, who gave me the opportunity to teach this material as a special topic graduate class at the Courant Institute. I also thank my wife's parents, Marty and Phyllis Fingerhut, who are two of my biggest supporters. Last, I want to thank and remember my mother, Betty Loshin, who was a source of inspiration and who passed away earlier this year.

1

INTRODUCTION

Without even realizing it, everyone is affected by poor data quality. Some are affected directly in annoying ways, such as receiving two or three identical mailings from the same sales organization in the same week. Some are affected in less direct ways, such as the 20-minute wait on hold for a customer service department. Some are affected more malevolently through deliberate fraud, such as identity theft. But whenever poor data quality, inconsistencies, and errors bloat both companies and government agencies and hamper their ability to provide the best possible service, everyone suffers.

Data quality seems to be a hazy concept, but the lack of data quality severely hampers the ability of organizations to effectively accumulate and manage enterprise-wide knowledge. The goal of this book is to demonstrate that data quality is not an esoteric notion but something that can be quantified, measured, and improved, all with a strict focus on return on investment. Our approach is that knowledge management is a pillar that must stand securely on a pedestal of data quality, and by the end of this book, the reader should be able to build that pedestal.

This book covers these areas.

- Data ownership paradigms
- The definition of data quality
- An economic framework for data quality, including steps in building a return on investment model to justify the costs of a data quality program
- The dimensions of data quality
- Using statistical process control as a tool for measurement

- Data domains and mappings between those domains
- Data quality rules and business rules
- Measurement and current state assessment
- Data quality requirements analysis
- Metadata and policy
- Rules-based processing
- Discovery of metadata and data quality and business rules
- Data cleansing
- Root cause analysis and supplier management
- Data enhancement
- Putting it all into practice

The end of the book summarizes the processes discussed and the steps to building a data quality practice.

Before we dive into the technical components, however, it is worthwhile to spend some time looking at some real-world examples for motivation. In the next section, you will see some examples of "data quality horror stories" — tales of adverse effects of poor data quality.

1.1   DATA QUALITY HORROR STORIES

1.1.1   Bank Deposit?

In November of 1998, it was reported by the Associated Press that a New York man allegedly brought a dead deer into a bank in Stamford, Connecticut, because he was upset with the bank's service. Police say the 70-year-old argued with a teller over a clerical mistake with his checking account. Because he was apparently unhappy with the teller, he went home, got the deer carcass and brought it back to the branch office.

1.1.2   CD Mail Fraud

Here is a news story taken from the Associated Press newswire. The text is printed with permission.

> Newark — For four years a Middlesex County man fooled the computer fraud programs at two music-by-mail clubs, using 1,630 aliases to buy music CDs at rates offered only to first-time buyers.

David Russo, 33, of Sayerville, NJ, admitted yesterday that he received 22,260 CDs by *making each address — even if it listed the same post office box — different enough to evade fraud-detection computer programs.*

Among his methods: adding fictitious apartment numbers, unneeded direction abbreviations and extra punctuation marks. (Emphasis mine)

The scam is believed to be the largest of its kind in the nation, said Assistant U.S. Attorney Scott S. Christie, who prosecuted the case.

The introductory offers typically provided nine free CDs with the purchase of one CD at the regular price, plus shipping and handling. Other CDs then had to be purchased later to fulfill club requirements. Russo paid about $56,000 for CDs, said Paul B. Brickfield, his lawyer, or an average of $2.50 each. He then sold the CDs at flea markets for about $10 each, Brickfield said. Russo pleaded guilty to a single count of mail fraud. He faces about 12 to 18 months in prison and a fine of up to $250,000.

1.1.3 Mars *Orbiter*

The Mars *Climate Orbiter,* a key part of NASA's program to explore the planet Mars, vanished in September 1999 after rockets were fired to bring it into orbit of the planet. It was later discovered by an investigative board that NASA engineers failed to convert English measures of rocket thrusts to newtons, a metric system measuring rocket force, and that was the root cause of the loss of the spacecraft. The orbiter smashed into the planet instead of reaching a safe orbit.

This discrepancy between the two measures, which was relatively small, caused the orbiter to approach Mars at too low an altitude. The result was the loss of a $125 million spacecraft and a significant setback in NASA's ability to explore Mars.

1.1.4 Credit Card Woes

After having been a loyal credit card customer for a number of years, I had mistakenly missed a payment when the bill was lost during the move to our new house. I called the customer service department and explained the omission, and they were happy to remove the service charge, provided that I sent in my payment right away, which I did.

A few months later, I received a letter indicating that "immediate action" was required. Evidently, I had a balance due of $0.00, and because of that, the company had decided to revoke my charging privileges! Not only that, I was being reported to credit agencies as being delinquent.

Needless to say, this was ridiculous, and after some intense conversations with a number of people in the customer service department, they agreed to mark my account as being paid in full. They notified the credit reporting agencies that I was not, and never had been, delinquent on the account (see Figure 1.1).

1.1.5   Open or Closed Account?

Three months after canceling my cellular telephone service, I continue to receive bills from my former service provider indicating that I was being billed for $0.00 — "Do not remit."

1.1.6   Business Credit Card

A friend of mine is the president of a small home-based business. He received an offer from a major charge card company for a corporate charge card with no annual fee. He accepted, and a short time later, he received his card in the mail. Not long after that, he began to receive the same offer from the same company, but those offers were addressed differently. Evidently, his name had been misspelled on one of his magazine subscriptions, and that version had been submitted to the credit card company as a different individual. Not only that, his wife started to receive offers too.

Six months later, this man still gets four or five mail offers per week in the mail from the same company, which evidently not only cannot figure out who he is but also can't recognize that he is already a customer!

1.1.7   Direct Marketing

One would imagine that if any business might have the issue of data quality on top of its list, it would be the direct marketing industry. Yet, I

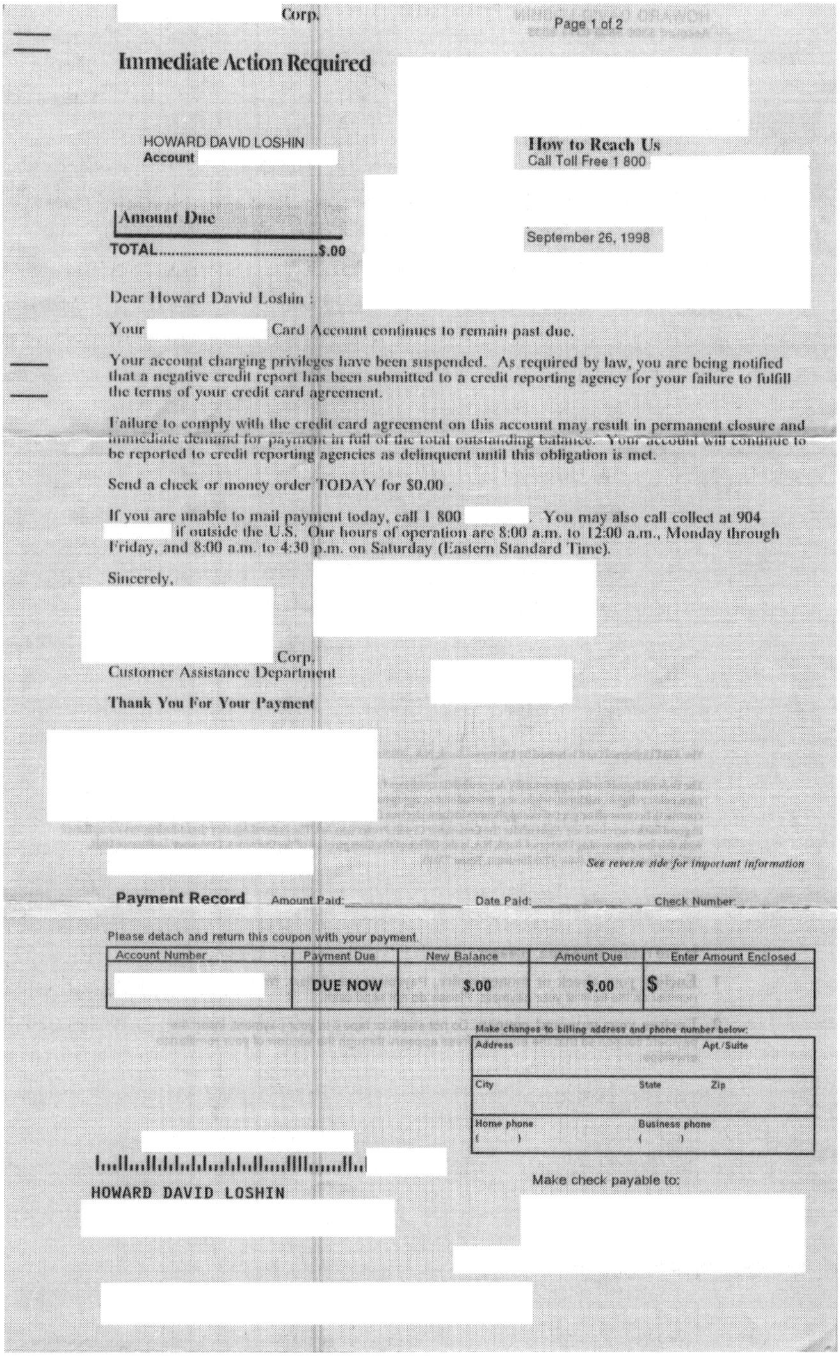

Corp.

Immediate Action Required

Page 1 of 2

HOWARD DAVID LOSHIN
Account

How to Reach Us
Call Toll Free 1 800

Amount Due

TOTAL.......................................$.00

September 26, 1998

Dear Howard David Loshin :

Your   Card Account continues to remain past due.

Your account charging privileges have been suspended. As required by law, you are being notified that a negative credit report has been submitted to a credit reporting agency for your failure to fulfill the terms of your credit card agreement.

Failure to comply with the credit card agreement on this account may result in permanent closure and immediate demand for payment in full of the total outstanding balance. Your account will continue to be reported to credit reporting agencies as delinquent until this obligation is met.

Send a check or money order TODAY for $0.00 .

If you are unable to mail payment today, call 1 800   . You may also call collect at 904   if outside the U.S. Our hours of operation are 8:00 a.m. to 12:00 a.m., Monday through Friday, and 8:00 a.m. to 4:30 p.m. on Saturday (Eastern Standard Time).

Sincerely,

Corp.
Customer Assistance Department

Thank You For Your Payment

See reverse side for important information

Payment Record   Amount Paid:_____   Date Paid:_____   Check Number:_____

Please detach and return this coupon with your payment.

Account Number	Payment Due	New Balance	Amount Due	Enter Amount Enclosed
	DUE NOW	$.00	$.00	$

Make changes to billing address and phone number below:

Address		Apt./Suite
City	State	Zip
Home phone ( )	Business phone ( )	

HOWARD DAVID LOSHIN

Make check payable to:

Figure 1.1   Mysterious bill

recently received two identical pieces of mail the same day from the local chapter of an association for the direct marketing industry. One was addressed this way.

David Loshin
123 Main Street
Anytown, NY 11787

Dear David, . . .

The other was addressed like this

Loshin David
123 Main Street
Anytown, NY 11787

Dear Loshin, . . .

1.1.8   Tracking Backward

I recently ordered some computer equipment, and I was given a tracking number to follow the package's progress from the source to my house. If you look at the example in Table 1.1 (which has been slightly modified from the original), you will see that the package was scanned at the exit hub location in a specific state on June 26, was (evidently) scanned in Nassau county, NY, at 12:30 A.M. the following day but was scanned as a departure from the airport in the same state as the exit hub at 1:43 P.M., which is practically 11 hours later. The rest of the tracking makes sense — from the XX airport to an airport local to my area, then onto my locality, and finally to the delivery point.

Obviously, the June 27, 12:30 A.M. scan in Nassau has either the incorrect location or the incorrect time. It is most likely the incorrect time, since packages are scanned on entry to a location and on exit, and this scan appears between the location scan at EXIT HUB and the departure scan at ANYTOWN INTL, same state.

1.1.9   Conclusions?

These are just a few stories culled from personal experience, interactions with colleagues, or reading the newspaper. Yet, who has not been subject to some kind of annoyance that can be traced to a data quality problem?

TABLE 1
Tracking history for the equipment I ordered.

	PACKAGE PROGRESS		
Date	Time	Location	Activity
June 28, 2000	5:25 P.M.	NASSAU-HICKSVILLE, NY US	DELIVERED
	3:42 A.M.	NASSAU, NY	DESTINATION
	3:31 A.M.	NASSAU, NY US	LOCATION SCAN
June 27, 2000	11:21 P.M.	NEWARK INTL, NJ	DEPARTURE SCAN
	4:45 P.M.	NEWARK INTL, NJ	ARRIVAL
	1:43 P.M.	ANYTOWN INTL, XX	DEPARTURE SCAN
	12:30 A.M.	NASSAU, NY US	ARRIVAL
June 26, 2000	11:29 A.M.	EXIT HUB, XX US	LOCATION SCAN
June 23, 2000	9:11 P.M.	ADDISON, IL US	LOCATION SCAN
	1:38 P.M.		SHIPMENT DATA RECEIVED

1.2 KNOWLEDGE MANAGEMENT AND DATA QUALITY

Over the past 30 years, advances in data collection and database technology have led to massive legacy databases controlled by legacy software. The implicit programming paradigm encompasses both business policies and data validation policies as application code. Yet, most legacy applications are maintained by second- and third-generation engineers, and it is rare to find any staff members with firsthand experience in either the design or implementation of the original system. As a result, organizations maintain significant ongoing investments in daily operations and maintenance of the information processing plant, while mostly ignoring the tremendous potential of the intellectual capital that is captured within the data assets.

1.2.1 What Is Knowledge Management?

An organization's data collection is a valuable business resource that until now has been largely underutilized. In the past, when data were mostly locked up in databases, ferociously guarded by organizational overlords, the ability to share and benefit from enterprise knowledge was limited. Today, as technology evolves to unlock and distribute these databases, a procedural methodology has evolved in tandem to help integrate the technical, organizational, and behavioral issues associated with enterprise knowledge. This methodology is referred to as "knowledge management."

According to Karl Erik Sveiby, knowledge management is "The art of creating value by leveraging the intangible assets." The Gartner Group states it in a more down-to-earth way: "Knowledge management is a discipline that promotes an integrated approach to identifying, managing, and sharing all of an enterprise's information assets. These information assets may include databases, documents, policies and procedures as well as previously unarticulated expertise and experience resident in individual workers."[1]

In other words, knowledge management is a strategic process meant to capture the ways that an organization integrates its information assets with the processes and policies that govern the manipulation of those intellectual assets. The desired goal of knowledge management is the determination and the harnessing of the value of the information resources within the enterprise.

While knowledge management encompasses many disciplines, such as document management or e-mail technology, our goal is to focus on the embedded knowledge in data sets that can be expressed as a set of business rules. Having expressed these rules, we can then validate our expectations of the information that we use by testing it against the business rules.

1.2.2   What Are Business Rules?

A business rule is an assertion about the state of a business process. All business processes and data sets have rules. Unfortunately, these rules are frequently expressed as "lore" instead of being properly documented, passed from one "generation" of managers or technicians to another by word of mouth. Even worse, sometimes these rules are forgotten over time, having been implemented in software and then left to happily chug away until a crisis strikes.

---

1.   http://cestec1.mty.itesm.mx~laava/sdsites/cursos/pqg_base/definicion1.htm

Business rules are likely to be expressed in a natural language. An example of a business rule for an employee database might be "No employee makes more than five times the salary of the lowest-paid employee." An example for an electronic data interchange system might be "If the header of an incoming message includes the symbol #, then the message is routed to the accounts payable office." A business rule might govern the way operations proceed. An example for a sales office might be "No customer is pitched for a new sales transaction within 10 days after the customer's last sales transaction."

When business rules are undocumented, the chances are high that the meanings or implications of these rules will be lost within a short period of time. Knowledge is lost when employees leave the company or change positions internally, when managers have too much control over information, and when there is entropy in communication protocols. When business rules are lost, the opportunity to take advantage of the information resources is squandered as well.

1.2.3   Why Data Quality Is the Pivot Point for Knowledge Management

The opportunity to take advantage of the data and information resource can only be enabled if there is an understanding of the structure and knowledge about the collections of information. The critical point is that a formal method is needed for collecting, documenting, and validating business rules. This methodology revolves around ensuring that the information that is present in the system meets or beats the expectations of what is in the system. Ensuring data quality is a process of stating information requirements followed by a process of validating that those requirements are being met.

A significant effort is made today to bring data out of the transactional framework and into an operational data store that can be used for analytical processing. These operational data stores are embodied in data marts and data warehouses, which are useful knowledge management tools when used effectively. A major component of the data warehouse process is the extraction and transformation of data from source and legacy data systems into the target data warehouse. This extraction process is an inflection point at which business rules can both be discovered and used for ensuring enterprise-wide data quality.

Based on the growing awareness of data quality as an enterprise responsibility, there is a burgeoning need for inline data quality policy management. According to the Gartner Group, "It is critical for enterprises to develop a data quality program and ensure that it is carried out. Key to this effort is identifying data stewards[2] in end-user areas where data ownership is clearly defined. . . . Enterprises can minimize these data inconsistencies by better understanding the parameters governing the meaning and movement of data."[3]

The use of data quality management as a tool for knowledge management along with these definitions are the initial motivators for this book. But we won't stop at that! The next section gives nine reasons for caring about data quality.

1.3   REASONS FOR CARING ABOUT DATA QUALITY

The data quality problem is pervasive in organizations across all industries. Bad data cost money and reduce productivity — time spent diagnosing and fixing erroneous data is time not spent productively. Low data quality eventually leads to reduced customer satisfaction. For example, customers exposed to incorrect reports or statements are less likely to trust the organization providing those reports. Finally, strategic decisions based on untrustworthy information are likely to result in poor decisions.

1.3.1   Low Data Quality Leads to Operational Inefficiency

The use of a manufacturing chain assumes that multiple stages are associated with the final product, and at each stage there is an expectation that the partially completed product meets some set of standards. Information processing is also a manufacturing chain — pieces of information flow into and out of processing stages where some set of operations are performed using the data.

To continue this analogy, when a product developed on a manufacturing chain does not fit the standards required at a specific stage, either the product must be thrown away or fixed before it can continue down the manufacturing line. Information is the same way: When a data

---

2.   Explored later in this book.
3.   J. Hill, and S. Laufer, *Data Transformation: Key to Information Sharing,* Gartner Group Strategic Analysis Report, September 29, 1998.

record is found to be incorrect, the record needs to be deleted or fixed before the processing can continue. Sometimes this "break" means the delay of the entire processing stream, although it is more likely that the records will be shunted aside and the stream continued on the next set of records, with the erroneous records being dealt with at a later time.

As the level of data quality decreases, the more frequent the breaks in operation. As more employees are allocated to fixing and reconciling incorrect records, the rate at which information is processed decreases — in other words, operational inefficiency. This inefficiency is manifested as error detection, error correction, and rework. We will look at these issues more closely in Chapter 4.

1.3.2   Low-Quality Data Constrains Decision Making

Information production can be used for either operational processing or analytical processing. The same information can be used for both purposes. Yet, if the data are used for analytical processing or decision support, the quality of the data can affect the analysis. If senior managers rely on the results of the analysis, they may rely on conclusions drawn from faulty assumptions. If these same managers are aware of the low quality of the input data, they may choose to delay making decisions until better information can be collected or until the same information can be improved.

The same factors that cause delays in decision making can also produce constraints. When one unit of an organization depends on the results of analytical processing or decision support analysis from another unit, the level of quality of the source information will affect the first unit's ability to take action on the analysis and may cause an erosion of trust between the two units.

For example, an airline may use an online reservation system as an operational process as well as the basis for analytical processing. The information may be targeted for use in determining what kinds of frequent flyer promotions to create and to which sets of customers to make these offers. If the data is of low quality, the conclusions presented by an analysis may not be trustworthy, and managers making any decisions about the new promotions may be hesitant if they cannot rely on those conclusions.

1.3.3   Good Data Enhances Data Warehouse Utility

According to an article presented by the Data Warehousing Institute,[4] a survey conducted by survey.com ("Database Solutions III") estimates that the worldwide data warehousing market is growing at the rate of 43% a year, and will reach $143 billion by 2003, with sharp growth outside of North America. Additionally, it is commonly recognized (and attributed to Data Warehousing pioneer Bill Inmon) that 80% of the effort of a data warehousing project is spent in extracting, cleansing, and loading data.

Considering this significant investment as well as the fact that data warehouses are used for analytical processing, anything that improves the customer's ability to analyze data increases the value of the data warehouse. A major component of the data warehouse solution process is the extraction and transformation of data from a legacy source before the warehouse is populated. If the information in the warehouse is of poor quality, a significant amount of time is spent in tracking and removing errors. And since many warehouses are populated on a short period basis (such as completely reloaded daily, with hourly sweeps), if the error correction time frame exceeds the refresh period, the warehouse would be nothing but a white elephant.

This stage of data population is the best opportunity to include data quality validation and standardization, since good data in the warehouse enables its use. We will focus on the data warehouse certification process that uses a data quality rules engine in Chapters 7, 8, and 12.

1.3.4   Bad Data Leads to Incorrect Conclusions

Just as a house built on a weak foundation cannot stand, conclusions based on incorrect input will not withstand scrutiny. As more and more data warehouses are being built for critical business analytical applications, the criticality of ensuring data quality increases. Analytical results based on bad data will be bad results — period.

Not only that, operational decisions that rely on poor data can cause inefficiencies in application systems. For example, load-balancing accesses to a database based on a distribution of data in one attribute can lead to skewed balancing if half of the records referenced have an empty index field!

4.   http://www.dw-institute.com/whatworks9/Resources/warehousing/warehousing.html

1.3.5 Bad Data Lead to Customer Attrition

Have you ever been billed for service that you have not received? Or have you been threatened with being reported to a credit bureau for being late on a payment on a balance due of $0.00? Many people have some nightmare experience with which they can relate, always associated with some incorrect information that causes pain in the pocketbook. These stories always seem to end with the customer ending his or her relationship with the vendor or product provider over the matter.

These errors are typically due to some mistake on behalf of the service or product provider, whether it is in customer records, customer billing, product pricing, or during data processing. No matter what, the problem is worsened by the fact that it is apparent that the organization at fault has no evident means of proactive error detection in place. This conclusion may be drawn because it is the customer who is doing the error detection. We can claim that while a significant expense is made to acquire new customers, it is worthwhile to invest the time and money into improving the data collected on the current customers, since customer attrition may be tied directly to poor data quality.

1.3.6 Good Data Enhances New Customer Acquisition

Just as poor data foster mistrust among current customers, it also can cast doubt in the minds of potential customers. When a potential customer is presented with an offer backed by high-quality data, the image of the seller is enhanced, which can improve the opportunity to turn a potential customer into a real customer.

As an example, consider this real-life pitch we recently received in the mail. My wife and I recently took a trip with our 5-month-old baby. We purchased a seat for our child at a discount rate because of her young age. About a month after our trip, our baby received a letter from the airline and a major long-distance carrier, offering her 10,000 frequent flyer miles if she switched her long-distance service. Clearly, this cooperative sales pitch, cobbled together between the airline and the long-distance carrier (LDC), may be effective some of the time, but consider this: The airline knew that we had bought a discount seat for our baby, and typically babies don't have authority to make purchasing decisions in a household. In addition, both my wife and I have received the same pitch from the same airline-LDC combination — on the same day! Because we saw that the long-distance carrier was unable to keep their records straight about who we were, we weren't sure that we could trust them to handle our telephone records correctly either.

1.3.7   Poor Data Quality Leads to Breakdown in Organizational Confidence

On behalf of both customers and employees, when an organization displays an inability to manage simple information management issues, it sows a seed of doubt that the organization can manage critical processes. When customers lose faith in a provider's ability to provide, it leads to customer attrition. When employees no longer believe in the company's ability to do business, it leads to employee turnover and loss of strategic business knowledge.

1.3.8   Bad Data Restricts System and Data Migration Projects

Having been involved in some legacy migration projects, I can say from direct experience that the most frustrating component of a migration project is the inability to accumulate the right information about the data and systems that are being migrated. Usually, this is due to the tendency of implementers to program first, document later, if at all. But as systems age, they are modified, broken, fixed, or improved but without any updates to documentation.

This situation forces the integrators to become information archaeologists to discover what is going on within the system. Naturally, undirected discovery processes will increase costs and delay the actual implementation, and the amount of time needed to determine what is going on cannot be predicted ahead of time.

1.3.9   Good Data Increases ROI on IT Investment

When we have assessed the data quality requirements of our system and put in place the right kinds of processes to validate information as it passes through the system, we can limit the downtime and failed processes based on low data quality. In turn, this means that without having to diagnose and fix data quality problems, processing can proceed with a greater bandwidth, which subsequently allows for an increase in processing volume without an increase in resources. In a company whose business depends on increasing processing volume without increasing overhead (such as securities processing or order fulfillment), this can increase the return on information technology investment.

1.4   KNOWLEDGE MANAGEMENT AND BUSINESS RULES

Business operations are defined using a set of rules that are applied in everyday execution. When the business depends on the correct flow of information, there is an aspect of data quality that intersects the operational specification.

In essence, in an information business, **business rules are data quality rules.** This implies that data quality is an integral part of any operational specification, and organizations that recognize this from the start can streamline operations by applying data quality techniques to information while it is being processed or communicated. This in turn will prevent bad data from affecting the flow of business, and denying the entry of incorrect information into the system eliminates the need to detect and correct bad data. Because of this, a "data quality aware" operation can execute at lower cost and higher margin than the traditional company.

1.4.1   Competition in Knowledge-Intensive Industries

Businesses that traditionally rely on the leverage of timely information (retail securities sales, market data providers, analytical market analysis) suddenly have competition from players whose barrier to entry is low. For example, in the retail securities investment business, the combination of low-cost "electronic" securities trading combined with the widespread availability of financial and investment recommendations demonstrates that margins on securities transactions can be lowered, but businesses can still profit.

As the availability of online analysis increases, there will be a decrease in the need for a large sales staff as a distribution channel for standard financial products. In the future, the perceived value of the information provided by an investment analyst will not necessarily be based on "brand name," but instead, the business rules will focus on presentation, accuracy and timeliness, which are critical data quality dimensions.

1.4.2   Micromarketing

Businesses that traditionally rely on marketing analysis will find that "micromarketing" analyses will provide opportunities for micromarket penetration. Businesses that have not traditionally relied on marketing analysis are beginning to use information gleaned from online transactions. The rules for accumulating and merging these data sets are managed as business rules. The capability provided by desktop access to data sources (such as consumer databases) allows more information to enhance the analysis. This strategic analysis can only be trusted if the data on which it is based are of high quality.

1.4.3   Cooperative Marketing Arrangements

With increasing frequency, organizations from different industries join forces in cooperative or cross-linked marketing programs. A common example is an offer of frequent flyer miles coupled with a change in long-distance service. Because of the potential disparity between different organizations' data models and the currency of their stored data, these arrangements provide strong opportunities for data quality improvements. The rules for value-added information merging, which incorporates both known data and inferred information, can be encapsulated as business/data quality rules.

1.4.4   Deregulation in the Communications, Energy, and Financial Services Industries

The recent consolidation of the insurance and brokerage industries in anticipation of deregulation and the (expected) waves of deregulation in the communications and the energy industries pave the way for consolidation of multiple business entities. When two (or more) independent organizations merge their operations, their combined data resources need to be combined as well. A streamlined data merging, migration, and quality assurance methodology will uncover synergistic opportunities when combining data sets. Leverage in affecting the organizational bottom line can be obtained through the qualified merging of data resources by decreasing operational costs (for example, error detection and correction) and by increasing customer response and customer satisfaction.

1.4.5 The Internet as a Knowledge Transport Medium

The rapid ascension of the Internet as a business medium has created opportunities for industries based on information and knowledge. When the business relies on the use of information, the quality of that information suddenly takes on a much higher visibility. This is an entirely different dimension of applicability for the data quality business, since the growing boom of "e-commerce" cuts across all major industries.

The World Wide Web can be can be seen as the largest uncoordinated database service in the world. All Web sites can be characterized in terms of some database service. Some sites act primarily as data presentation systems, others act as data collection systems, and some act as database query systems. Success in the arena of electronic commerce will be largely dependent on customer-focused micromarketing and automated customer relationship management and sales force automation. We will provide guidelines for both the acquisition of valid data over the Internet, as well as guidelines for accurate, customer-focused data presentation.

1.5 STRUCTURE OF THIS BOOK

1.5.1 Chapter 1: Introduction

This chapter is an introduction to the ideas behind enterprise knowledge management and the importance of data quality in this endeavor. In this chapter, we enumerate the most important issues regarding information quality, how business is aversely affected by poor data quality, and how business can be improved when data quality is high.

1.5.2   Chapter 2: Who Owns Information?

Because the data quality problem ultimately belongs to the data consumer, it a good idea to start out by establishing ownership and boundaries. Chapter 2 focuses on the issues of data ownership. The chapter begins by discussing the data processing activity as a manufacture of information. The final product of this factory is knowledge that is owned by the data consumers in a business enterprise.

Who are the data producers and data consumers in an enterprise? We look at internal data producers (internal processes like account opening, billing, marketing) and external data producers ("lead lists," consumer research, corporate structure data). We also look at the enterprise data consumers, ranging from the operational (customer service, billing, resource planning), the tactical (middle management, scheduling), and strategic consumers (directional management, strategists).

There are complicating notions with respect to data ownership. The means of dissemination, collecting data from the public domain, as well as acquiring data from data providers confuse the issues. Therefore, a set of ownership paradigms are introduced, including decision makers, sellers, manipulators, guardians, and workers. These paradigms bound the "social turf" surrounding data ownership. Finally, Chapter 2 focuses on a finer granularity of ownership issues, including metadata ownership, governance of storage and repositories, and accountability for data policies.

1.5.3   Chapter 3: Data Quality in Practice

In Chapter 3, the notion of data quality is introduced, loosely defined through the term "fitness for use." Background in traditional quality systems is provided. Chapter 3 also provides some insight into information theory as it can be applied to data quality. Finally, statistical process control is discussed as critical to improving data quality.

1.5.4   Chapter 4: Economic Framework for Data Quality and the Value Proposition

The rationale for designing and building data quality systems seems logical, but an economic framework that can be used to measure the effects of poor data quality while highlighting its benefits is needed to demonstrate the value of improving poor data quality. Chapter 4 reviews the knowledge hierarchy and the knowledge manufacturing process, then defines a set of impact domains that can be used to model the costs and missed opportunities that result from bad data. The chapter focuses on strategic, tactical, and operational impacts, followed by a description of a way to model these impacts.

1.5.5   Chapter 5: Dimensions of Data Quality

In Chapter 5, a number of dimensions of data quality are discussed. These dimensions are grouped into quality of the data model, quality of data values, quality of data presentation, and other data quality dimensions.

1.5.6   Chapter 6: Statistical Process Control and the Improvement Cycle

In Chapter 6, we look in detail at the notion of control and how that idea can promote predictability of the quality of the product being produced. Statistical process control is a method for measuring the quality of the product while its process is in operation, instead of relying on measuring the product after it has been completed. SPC is a process of gathering measurements during processing in order to identify special causes of inconsistencies and variations that lead to a flawed product. We will focus in particular on the notion of control charts and how these charts are used to look for processes that are in control and processes that are out of control. In addition, we will look at how control charts are used for setting up an improvement cycle with respect to conformance with data quality specifications.

1.5.7   Chapter 7: Domains, Mappings, and Enterprise Reference Data

In this chapter, we begin to explore the ideas revolving around data types and how data types are related to the notion of sets. We then describe our definition of data domains, both descriptive and enumerated. Next, we discuss the relations between domains, how those relations exist in databases, and the power of abstracting these mappings as reference metadata. Finally, we propose a publish/subscribe model for the management and use of enterprise reference data.

1.5.8   Chapter 8: Data Quality Assertions and Business Rules

In this chapter, we really begin the investigation of the kinds of rules that can be applied to the measurement of data quality. With respect to any tabular data (such as database tables), we will look at these classes of rules: (1) data value rules, (2) attribute rules (rules for data values associated with a particular attribute), (3) domain rules, (4) tuple rules (rules associating different attributes within a tuple), and (5) table rules. We identify a number of rules that can be characterized by a measurable method.

1.5.9   Chapter 9: Measurement and Current State Assessment

We look at measuring conformance to the rules described in Chapter 8 in two different ways. The first way is a static measurement, which involves looking at the data after it has been delivered into its target location. The second way is in-process (dynamic) measurement, which is consistent with the notions of statistical process control as described in Chapter 6. This way involves integrating the measurement of the conformance to the data quality rules while the data is in transit.

The goal of the initial measurement is to gauge the degree of any data quality problem as well as use the economic framework to measure the effects of any poor data quality. The current state assessment is a report that focuses on the important dimensions of data quality, the degree on conformance, and how the lack of conformance affects the bottom line. The result of the CSA is a characterization of the state of data quality and what needs to be done to improve it.

1.5.10   Chapter 10: Data Quality Requirements

How do we determine data quality requirements? We use a technique borrowed from object-oriented design called use-case analysis, which is used to specify the system in terms of actors, use-cases, and triggers.

Actors represent the roles that users play, use-cases represent what the actors do with the system, and triggers represent events that initiate use cases. We then select from the list of data quality dimensions from Chapter 5 those dimensions that are of greatest importance to the actors and define data quality rules, as described in Chapter 8. We can choose thresholds for conformance to the data quality rules as a baseline for acceptance of the data. These baseline thresholds are defined so that when met, the data set consumers can be confident of the levels of data quality.

1.5.11   Chapter 11: Metadata, Guidelines, and Policy

When defining data quality rules and requirements, it is necessary to build a central repository for the collection of all metadata, which is information about the data. All data processing systems maintain some form of metadata, whether it is explicit using a DBMS system's data dictionary, or implicit, such as the methods and inheritance embedded in a C++ class definition.

The traditional view of metadata includes mostly static information about the data, such as data types, sizes, and perhaps some rudimentary rules such as enforcing a primary key or indexing. Metadata, though, could and should encompass much more, including data quality and business intelligence rules that govern the operational manufacture and use of data. This is not to say that this kind of metadata isn't being maintained now — because a lot of it is! This metadata, however, is maintained in a format unsuitable for easy access and understanding by the actual data consumer.

1.5.12   Chapter 12: Rules-Based Data Quality

Having defined an assertional framework in Chapter 8, how would data integrity assertions be defined and validated? The answer is through the use of rule-based systems that a user employs to both define and test rules. In Chapter 12, we describe rule-based systems: definitions of "rule" and rule-based system and how we incorporate our assertion system from Chapter 8 into an information integrity language. Last, we describe how a rules engine can use these validation specifications to provide a test framework for both data integrity validation and the data for statistical process control, all within the context of the data consumer's constraints.

1.5.13   Chapter 13: Metadata and Rule Discovery

Chapter 12 presents a rule system for defining and testing information validity. In Chapter 13 we discuss what we learn from the rule definition and rule-testing process. Included is domain discovery, association rules, map discovery, functional dependencies, overlapping and intersecting domains, and attribute splitting. These all form a link in a feedback chain in the metadata analysis and data quality improvement process.

1.5.14   Chapter 14: Data Cleansing

Understanding data quality rules, assertions, and validity checks is one thing; actually "fixing" the problems is another! Chapter 14 focuses on techniques for cleansing data to the point where it meets or exceeds the conformance thresholds and is therefore acceptable. We start with metadata cleansing — identifying and documenting what we know about our data. We look at using our assertions to form information filters that prevent bad data from entering the system.

When identifiability constraints specify uniqueness, it is worthwhile to eliminate duplicate entries. This takes on two faces: absolute duplicates and near-match duplicates. To address the latter, we discuss approximate searching and matching techniques. These techniques are also useful in householding, a special kind of duplicate elimination process that looks to accumulate information about individuals sharing a single residence.

When there is a standard form for an information set (as specified by a structured domain or such as the United States Postal Service standard), we use a technique called standardization to make our data to look the way we want it to. We will discuss issues surrounding the opportunity for cleansing data during a data migration process.

1.5.15   Chapter 15: Root Cause Analysis and Supplier Management

One technique not yet discussed is using the results of the information validity exercise to prevent the continuation of low data quality events.

When using the rule-based system for validity checking, we can use the information in the reports to look for root causes of the occurrences of bad data quality. This technique is the last link in our improvement chain, since fixing the sources of bad data will directly improve overall data quality.

1.5.16 Chapter 16: Data Enrichment and Enhancement

Data enrichment is a process of enhancing the value of a pool of information by combining data from multiple sources. The goal of enrichment is to provide a platform deriving more knowledge from collections of data. A simple enrichment example is the combination of customer sales data with customer credit data to build a data mart that can be used to make special offers to preferred customers (customers with high purchasing profiles and good credit profiles). Other examples would be merging health insurance claim information with professional billing information to search for insurance fraud and the enrichment of financial electronic data interchange messages to enable straight-through processing.

In any case, data quality is critical to successful enrichment. In Chapter 16, we discuss how data standardization, clustering techniques, and the use of data quality rules can be used to express enrichment directives. We also look at some enrichment examples and how they can be affected by poor data quality.

1.5.17 Chapter 17: Data Quality and Business Rules in Practice

In Chapter 17, we review our data quality rules in a context that demonstrates ways to actually make use of these rules. Specifically, we talk about the way these rules partition the data into two sets, the set of conforming records and the set of nonconforming records. There is already a means for specifying set partitions in databases — the query language SQL, which is not just used for performing operations on databases — but to show how to turn the rules into executable queries. The rest of this chapter is designed to show how the implementation of a data quality rules process can add significant value to different operating environments.

1.5.18   Chapter 18: Building the Data Quality Practice

Our final chapter is basically a "run book" for building a data quality practice. We walk step by step through the issues in building the practice, starting with problem recognition, followed by the way to gain senior-level support, adopting a methodology, and creating an education program as well as actual implementation.

2

WHO OWNS INFORMATION?

Before we delve into the details of what data quality means and how it relates to knowledge management, we should establish where the responsibility for data quality falls within a company. Without a clear assignment of accountability, it is almost impossible to measure the quality of data, much less effect improvements.

This chapter examines the question of data ownership as the first step in establishing a knowledge-oriented organization. We begin by discussing data processing activity as a manufacture of information, and knowledge, which is owned by the data consumers in a business enterprise and is the final product of this factory.

Who are the data producers and data consumers in an enterprise? We look at internal data producers (internal processes like account opening, billing, marketing) and external data producers ("lead lists," consumer research, corporate structure data). We also look at the enterprise data consumers, ranging from the operational (customer service, billing, resource planning), the tactical (middle management, scheduling), and strategic consumers (directional management, strategists).

There are complicating notions with respect to data ownership. The means of dissemination, collecting data from the public domain, as well as acquiring data from data providers confuse the issues. Therefore, a set of ownership paradigms is defined, including decision makers, sellers, manipulators, guardians, and workers. These paradigms bound the "social turf" surrounding data ownership.

Finally, we try to resolve some of these issues by investigating data policy paradigms. This includes metadata ownership, governance of storage and repositories, and accountability for data policies.

2.1   THE INFORMATION FACTORY

A relatively simple analogy for processing data that we use throughout the book is the information factory. Any information processing activity can be viewed as a small factory that takes some data as raw input, processes that input, and generates some information result, potentially generating data by-products and side effects in the process. Inside the factory there may be smaller subfactories, each with its own input/output production activity. The raw input data are provided by data suppliers external to the organization or by data manufacturers within the organization. The ultimate data customers may be internal or external consumers.

2.1.1   Actors in the Information Factory

To be more precise, let's look at the different roles that exist in the context of the information factory. These roles may represent real people or automated proxies within the system.

1. *Suppliers:* Data suppliers provide information to the system.
2. *Acquirers:* Acquirers accept data from external suppliers for provision into the factory.
3. *Creators:* Internal to the factory, data may be generated and then forwarded to another processing stage.
4. *Processors:* A processor is any agent that accepts input and generates output, possibly generating some side effects.
5. *Packagers:* A packager collates, aggregates, and summarizes information for reporting purposes.
6. *Delivery Agents:* A delivery agent delivers packaged information to a known data consumer.
7. *Consumer:* The data consumer is the ultimate user of processed information.
8. *Middle Manager:* The people responsible for making sure the actors are correctly performing their jobs.
9. *Senior Manager:* The senior manager is responsible for the overall operation of the factory.
10. *Deciders:* These are senior-level managers associated with strategic and tactical decision making.

Each of these actors plays a well-defined role in the data processing operation, and each is responsible at some level for quality assurance within each activity domain. In a perfect world, these responsibilities will all propagate up to the enterprise level, providing some degree of quality assurance overall, but in reality there are complicating factors that may prevent this from happening. It is clear, though, that at any stage of processing, it is difficult to specifically assign ownership to the information being created or processed.

2.1.2 Processing Stages

In any data processing system, it is helpful to be able to break down the entire information flow into a series of processing stages, most of which relate directly to the activity associated with one of the previously enumerated actors. Ultimately, we would like to be able to precisely identify all input and output information streams, as well as all affected data stores associated with each processing stage, and then associate responsibility with a particular actor.

When truly decomposed, the information manufacturing process contains many different stages, each of which in itself might represent an entire instance of an information factory. We end up with a hierarchical description of the information processing chain.

2.1.3 Data Producers

Data producers are those organizations that create, compile, aggregate, package, and provide information to be inserted into an information processing system. This includes organizations that generate internal data (audit data, workflow messages, intermediate processed data for incorporation into other processing stages) or external information, such as marketing data, sales reports, invoices, corporate structure data, credit reports, and so forth.

2.1.4 Data Consumers

Data consumers can be categorized into three groups: operational data consumers, tactical and strategic data consumers, and external customers. Operational data consumers are manifested as the role of processors described in Section 2.1.1. They are any internal processing stage that requires input to operate, including any transaction processing activity, message passing or routing, or workflow activities.

The tactical and strategic data consumers are those who use processed information to make tactical and strategic decisions. This includes sales management, marketing, enterprise resource planning, mergers and acquisitions, and so on.

The external customers are those who receive information processed by the information factory. The kinds of information in this category include invoices, customer billing, sales teams data, geographic data, and data provided by government agencies.

2.2   COMPLICATING NOTIONS

What complicates the ownership question is that there are factors orthogonal to data creation or consumption that create real or artificial boundaries around information. The ownership issue is essentially a control issue — control of the flow of information, the cost of information, and the value of information.

Here is an example of how control over the flow of information can have a major impact. Some government interest rate financial data was mistakenly released early, prompting trading associated with selling bonds on the market before the official release time. The same traders, by buying back the same bonds at a discount after the official release time, made a huge profit. In this case, one party's loss of control over the flow of information allowed other parties increased control over the value of that same information!

A few of the many issues that complicate the notion of data ownership are value, privacy, turf, fear, and bureaucracy. This list is by no means inclusive, and we make no attempt to resolve them — only to expose them.

2.2.1   Value

The value of information drives a particular wedge into the question of ownership. In any environment where there is shared data ownership, how does the degree of ownership relate to the responsibility of care of that same information? Presumably, the degree of ownership may be related to more mundane aspects of the system, such as who initially created the database or what silo currently manages the system. But at the core, the degree of ownership (and by corollary, the degree of responsibility) is driven by the value that each interested party derives from the use of that information.

2.2.2 Privacy

The issue of privacy as a complicating notion could take up an entire volume, if not more. What information should remain private, and under what circumstances? If a party willingly releases private information under one set of conditions, does that allow the receiving party the right to use that information in other situations? Consider credit information. The fact that someone applies for any particular credit card might be considered private information, although in order to receive that credit, a credit bureau must be consulted. At that point, the fact that the credit card application has been taken is now added to the credit record.

And once information is released from one party to another, who exercises control over that information? For example, if a pharmacy fills an individual's medicine prescription, can the pharmacy report back to the pharmaceutical company the information regarding which doctors prescribed the medication, which patients filled the prescriptions, and which came back for refills?

When private knowledge can be inferred from public data, does this violate any privacy constraints? For example, the amount of money one borrows on a mortgage to pay for a house might be considered a private matter between the borrower and the bank, but in fact this information is lien information that is frequently filed under various state codes and is not private information at all.

2.2.3 Turf

On a different level, the question of data ownership within an enterprise is often complicated because of the notion of "turf." In many organizations, the control of the flow of information is regarded, as are many other forms of control, as a means of job security. "As long as I am in charge of this report," thinks the middle manager, "and no one else has access to the data, I can't be fired!" Being in charge of creating, packaging, and distributing the report naturally leads one to the conception of owning the data that makes up the report.

2.2.4   Fear

As organizational employees carve out their little fiefdoms of control, the overall ability of the organization to react to inconsistencies flowing out of these fiefdoms decreases. Any suggestion that there is a reason for an "outsider" to assess or analyze the current state of the data is taken as an attack on the fiefdom's turf and therefore can be construed as a direct challenge to the data controller's job.

An even worse fear is that any closer viewing of what goes on within one's organization will reveal that what appeared to be stellar work is actually mediocre, or worse. People can be so desperate to conceal their own mistakes that they will sabotage any attempt to uncover them. Of course, this is a prime example of conflict within the enterprise — what is good for the individual is terrible for the organization, and vice versa.

2.2.5   Bureaucracy

Another major issue that complicates data ownership is institutional bureaucracy. As organizations grow, the intermediate management structure grows as well, thereby diluting the responsibility for information as it passes from one subsystem to another. When issues regarding data quality problems arise, typically there tends to be a lot more finger pointing than problem solving.

This may be due to the fact that organizations become divided along project or system lines. Because of this, attribution of problems associated with information that passes through individually managed processing stages is hard to pin down, since each manager will pass the buck further upstream.

Another bureaucratic issue involves decisions associated with upgrades, renovations, and changes in the existing data processing infrastructure. With a highly hierarchical organization, the ability to make a decision hinges on building consensus among all interested parties both across vertical departmental lines as well as up and down the management hierarchy. Obviously, the effort involved is significant and, combined with the turf and fear factors, may account for the failure of many enterprise infrastructure renovation projects.

2.3 RESPONSIBILITIES OF OWNERSHIP

What do we mean when we talk about ownership of data? The essence lies in the control of information as an enterprise asset. That control includes not just the ability to access, create, modify, package, derive benefit from, sell, or remove data but also the right to assign these access privileges to others. In this section, we discuss in greater detail some of the responsibilities associated with data ownership.

2.3.1 Definition of Data

In any data environment, the data owner is responsible for understanding what information is to be brought into a system, assigning the meanings to collections of data, and constructing the data model to hold the collected information. In addition, any modifications to the data model and any extensions to the system also fall under duties of the data owner.

2.3.2 Authorization of Access and Validation of Security

A major concern for any data system is the coordination and authorization of access. In a system that contains data that is in any way sensitive, whether it is confidential information, human resource data, or corporate intelligence, it is necessary to define a security and authorization policy and to provide for its enforcement.

2.3.3 Support the User Community

When information is provided to a user community, there is a responsibility to provide support for those users. This includes providing accessibility to new users, granting them access rights, providing documentation, training, and addressing technical needs and questions. This also includes

defining and maintaining a service level agreement, which may entail
measuring system performance, and scaling or rebalancing resources to
provide the agreed upon level of service.

2.3.4   Data Packaging and Delivery

In addition to standard user support, the owner also holds the responsibility for providing the data to the data consumers. This may include
data preparation, packaging and formatting, as well as providing a
delivery mechanism (such as a data portal or a publish/subscribe mechanism).

2.3.5   Maintenance of Data

Aside from the maintenance of the system itself, there is also the maintenance of the information. This includes managing the data input
process, instituting gauges and measurements associated with the data,
and creating data extraction and loading processes.

2.3.6   Data Quality

The data owner is also accountable for maintaining the quality of the
information. This may include determining and setting user data quality expectations, instituting gauges and measurements of the levels of
data quality, and providing reports on the conformance to data quality.
This also includes defining data quality policies for all data that flows
into the system and any data cleansing, standardization, or other preparation for user applications.

2.3.7   Management of Business Rules

All data processing operations have business rules. Whether these rules
are embedded in application code, abstracted into a rules format, or
just documented separately from their implementation, the data owner
is also responsible for managing business rules.

2.3.8   Management of Metadata

Managing metadata involves the data definitions, names, data types, data domains, constraints, applications, database tables, reference repositories, and dependence rules associated with different tables and databases, users, access rights, and so forth.

2.3.9   Standards Management

Whenever information is shared between two or more parties, there must be some agreement as to a format for that data. When multiple parties agree to a representation format, that format is defined as a data standard. The owner is also responsible for making sure that all relevant data sets conform to their standard form, as well as negotiating standards on behalf of the users.

2.3.10   Supplier Management

When data sets are built as a composition of supplier-provided data, the data owner is also responsible for supplier management. This involves negotiating arrangements with each supplier, determining data delivery agreements, defining sets of data quality criteria, and enforcing these requirements and arrangements with each supplier.

2.4   OWNERSHIP PARADIGMS

We can enumerate owner responsibilities, but that does not solve the problem of assigning (or declaring) data ownership. Instead of trying to proactively dictate an ownership model, it is more helpful to explore different existing ownership paradigms. In each one of these paradigms, we will look at the question of value and how it relates to the claim of ownership.

2.4.1   Creator as Owner

In this paradigm, the party that creates or generates the data owns the data. It represents a speculative investment in creating information as a prelude to recognizing value from that information in the future.

An example of this is a geographic data consortium that analyzes geographic regions, collects latitude/longitude measures, and enters that information into a geographic database. The measurements in isolation are essentially useless; it is the collection of all the measurements that forms a useful data set. The consortium creates the information, and most likely claims ownership of that data as well.

2.4.2   Consumer as Owner

This ownership paradigm indicates that the party that consumes the data owns that data. This is a relatively broad ownership spectrum, covering all aspects of data acquisition. In this paradigm, any party that uses data claims ownership of that data. When the consumer requires a high level of confidence in the data input into a process, this ownership paradigm is very logical, since the party that cares most about the value of the data claims ownership (and thus, responsibility). In this case, the consumer derives the value from the data.

An example of this is a sales organization that uses information provided from different organizations within a company. Once the data lands at the sales staff's door, though, the information becomes integral to the proper operation of the sales team, and so the sales team will claim ownership of the data that it consumes.

2.4.3   Compiler as Owner

The operation of selecting information sources and compiling information from these different sources constitutes an ownership model. By combining data sets, the compiler is adding value and may expect to reap the benefits of ownership.

A good example of data compilation is a news item retrieval company that provides, as a service, a search for newspaper articles. By collecting and providing search capability, the data compiler has created a body of information that is more valuable than the individual pieces making up that body.

2.4.4 Enterprise as Owner

In larger corporate information technology organizations, there is a notion that all data that enter the enterprise or are created within the enterprise are completely owned by the enterprise. In effect, the company makes use of all input and generated data as fuel for its ongoing data processing needs, and therefore the value derived from the information resides with the organization as a whole.

The investment banking industry demonstrates this ownership model when it accumulates information from external market data vendors as well as data generated from internal sales and securities processing. All data are absorbed into a single operational data center that then redistributes the data, potentially with added value, out to data consumers within the organization as well as individuals (such as clients and customers) external to the enterprise.

2.4.5 Funding Organization as Owner

In this paradigm, the user that commissions the data creation claims ownership. Here there are two parties involved: the one that pays for the creation of data and the one that actually creates the data. In this case, the patron claims ownership, since the work is being done on his or her behalf.

An example is a company that commissions a research organization to prepare a competitive intelligence report covering a particular industry. The company may stipulate that the company is the sole owner of the provided data.

2.4.6 Decoder as Owner

In environments where information is "locked" inside particular encoded formats, the party that can unlock the information becomes an owner of that information. The cost of the decoding process and implementations is an investment in the value to be derived from the information.

A good example of this is embodied in the results of decoding DNA sequences to isolate specific genes. The value of decoding the DNA structure can be expressed in terms of any improvement in the discovery, prevention, or treatment of certain hereditary diseases. Bio-informatics companies that decode genetic material can then sell the data that they decode to the medical and pharmaceutical industries.

2.4.7   Packager as Owner

As opposed to the compiler ownership paradigm, the packager paradigm focuses on the party that formats information for a particular use. There is value added through formatting the information for a particular market or set of consumers.

An example of this is authors who publish public domain information packaged as a book. The compilation process is most likely straightforward — the value added is in formatting the material to make the collected data useful.

2.4.8   Reader as Owner

This is an interesting paradigm in that it implies that the value of any data that can be read is subsumed by the reader, and therefore the reader gains value through adding that information to an information repository. The investment is in the reader's selection and consumption of data.

For example, consulting firms establish expertise practices in particular areas. In order to become a principal in one of these practices, an individual must acquire knowledge in the practice area by absorbing as much information about that area as possible. Going forward, remaining an expert requires active information gathering.

2.4.9   The Subject as Owner

This paradigm revolves around the subject data ownership issues, such as personal privacy or image copyrights. In this view, the subject of the data claims ownership of that data, mostly in reaction to another party claiming ownership of the same data.

As an example of the privacy issue, consider a pharmacy filling prescriptions. Drug companies are interested in knowing which doctors are prescribing their medicines, and doctors like to know which of their patients are refilling prescriptions as a tool to see how well their patients follow instructions. Recently, it was revealed that a national pharmacy chain was providing to both health care providers and drug companies detailed information about who was filling which prescriptions at each of their sites. When this practice became public, naturally their customers were incensed. In effect, the individual patients were claiming ownership of personal information and insisting that the pharmacy chain had no right to sell it.

Another example is the issue of corporate image and branding. Companies will make a significant effort in establishing a connection between the quality of the products or services that it provides and a corporate image or logo. In this case, representations of the image are equated with the company, and any misrepresentation or other unauthorized use could affect the branding, so the company claims complete ownership of the image (or logo) as well as protects the use of that image.

2.4.10   Purchaser/Licenser as Owner

Similar to the funder paradigm, the individual or organization that buys or licenses data may stake a claim to ownership. In this paradigm, the purchaser assumes that the investment made in acquiring the data yields ownership. This holds for licensing as well, even if the terms of the license specify some restrictions on use.

A good example is the sale of mailing lists for direct marketing campaigns. One organization may own the lists and license their use, but once the lists are sold, the purchaser or licenser considers the data its own.

2.4.11   Everyone as Owner

The final paradigm is the model of global data ownership. Some feel that monopolization is wrong and data should be available to all with no restrictions. Clearly, in the business world, this is a radical view, and it has its benefits as well as detriments.

This ownership model is often in operation, to some degree, in scientific communities, where experimentation, following by the publishing of results, is common practice. In this situation, a common goal is the increase in the global knowledge of a particular subject, and results are subject to other experts' scrutiny.

2.5   CENTRALIZATION, DECENTRALIZATION, AND DATA OWNERSHIP POLICIES

This section explores the issues regarding the distribution of ownership across an enterprise. The question of centralization versus decentralization is orthogonal to the responsibilities of ownership, yet it is distinctly intertwined with it as well. As in our ownership model, the critical point revolves around value.

In a centralized ownership model, there is a single entity (person or group) responsible for all data ownership for the entire enterprise. Centralization implies that all ownership activities are coordinated from a single point of control, as well as coordination of metadata, information sourcing, and so forth. Centralized ownership yields the benefit of the value added — and whether the costs associated with centralization are offset by it. The costs include the increased management overhead, bureaucracy, and system integration, among others. The benefits include enterprise standardization for data and systems, the ability to make use of merged data for additional knowledge discovery, and increased leverage when dealing with external data suppliers.

In a decentralized model, the ownership roles are allocated to separate areas of interest. A decision to opt for decentralization implies that the value added from centralized control is more than offset by its associated costs. On the other hand, most organizations do not explicitly opt for decentralized control; instead, organizations evolve into it. Therefore, the real question is whether migrating from a decentralized ownership model to a centralized ownership model will increase the value of the enterprise knowledge base.

Finding the answer to this question is not simple. It involves a process of identifying the interested parties associated with all data sets, determining each party's interest, identifying the different roles associated with all data sets, and assigning roles and responsibilities to the right parties. All of these activities are embodied in an organization's **data ownership policy**, which incorporates all governance rules regarding data ownership and usage within the enterprise.

2.5.1   Creating a Data Ownership Policy

A data ownership policy is a tool used by the enterprise to establish all roles and responsibilities associated with data ownership and accountability. The goal of a data ownership policy is to finesse the kinds of complications discussed in Section 2.2, as well as hash out the strict definitions of ownership as described in Section 2.4. The data ownership policy specifically defines the positions covering the data ownership responsibilities described in Section 2.3. At a minimum, a data ownership policy should enumerate the following features.

1. The senior level managers supporting the enforcement of the policies enumerated
2. All data sets covered under the policy
3. The ownership model (in other words, how is ownership allocated or assigned within the enterprise) for each data set
4. The roles associated with data ownership (and the associated reporting structure)
5. The responsibilities of each role
6. Dispute resolution processes
7. Signatures of those senior level managers listed in item 1

A template for describing the ownership policy for a specific data set is shown in Figure 2.1.

Data Set Name				
Primary Owner				
Data Set Location				
	Owner	Responsible Party	Reports to	Notes
Data Definition				
Access/Security				
User Support				
Data Packaging				
Data Delivery				
Maintenance				
Data Quality				
Business Rules				
Metadata				
Standards Management				
Supplier Management				

FIGURE 2.1   Template for data ownership policy

These are the steps for defining a data ownership policy.

1. Identify the interested parties or stakeholders associated with the enterprise data. This includes identifying the senior level managers that will support the enforcement of the policy.
2. Catalog the data sets that are covered under the policy.
3. Determine the ownership models in place and whether these are to continue or will be replaced.
4. Determine the roles that are and are not in place. Assign the responsibilities to each role, and assign the roles to interested parties.
5. Maintain a registry that keeps track of policies, data ownership, roles, responsibilities, and other relevant information.

2.5.2 Identifying the Stakeholders

All stakeholders in the information factory, including all the actors delineated in Section 2.1.1, should be considered interested parties. A stakeholder is anybody who expects to derive some benefit or value from the data, whether it is through the use of the data, the sale or license of the data, or beneficially through association with the data. For example, a business customer who uses the reports gets value through the data, receives monetary compensation through the sale or license of the data, and benefits from the jobs that may be dependent on continued data center operations and application development.

In a small enterprise, stakeholder identification can be relatively simple, but as the enterprise grows, the process can become extremely complex due to the degrees to which information is processed and disseminated. A good heuristic is to begin from the outside of the enterprise and work in. In other words, figure out who the end users are, look at the data they are using, and follow it backward through the information chain. While some business users may be outspoken in terms of staking their claim, others may be blind to the fact that there is any organizational process that generates the paper reports that land on their desks. Also, just because people receive the reports, they may never look at the data provided on a periodic basis.

The process of identifying the stakeholders will likely reveal areas of conflict with respect to data ownership. This is a particularly valuable part of the process, as it provides a guide to deciding how the ownership responsibilities are assigned.

2.5.3   Cataloging Data Sets

Once the stakeholders have been identified, the next step is to learn what data sets should fall under the ownership policy. The stakeholders should be interviewed to register the data sets with which they are associated and the degree to which each believes his or her stake in the data is. The goal of this step is to create a create a metadatabase of data sets to use in the enforcement of the data ownership policies. This catalog should contain the name of the data set, the location of the data set, and the list of stakeholders associated with the data set. Eventually, the catalog will also maintain information about data ownership and responsibilities for the data set.

2.5.4   Identifying and Assigning Roles

The next step is to determine the roles that are associated with each set of data in the enterprise and describe the responsibilities of each role. Here are some examples, although this list is by no means meant to be exhaustive.

Chief Information Officer   The CIO is the chief holder of accountability for enterprise information and is responsible for decisions regarding the acquisition, storage, and use of data. He or she is the ultimate arbiter with respect to dispute resolution between areas of ownership and is the ultimate manager of the definition and enforcement of policies.

Chief Knowledge Officer   The chief knowledge officer is responsible for managing the enterprise knowledge resource, which dictates and enforces the data sharing policies, as well as overseeing the general pooling of knowledge across the organization.

Data Trustee   The data trustee manages information resources internal to the organization and manages relationships with data consumers and data suppliers, both internal and external.

Policy Manager   The policy manager maintains the data ownership policy and negotiates any modifications or additions to the data ownership policy.

Data Registrar   The data registrar is responsible for cataloging the data sets covered under the policy as well as the assignment of ownership, the definition of roles, and the determination of responsibilities and assignments of each role. The data registrar also maintains the data policy and notifies the policy manager if there are any required changes to the data ownership policy.

Data Steward   The data steward manages all aspects of a subset of data with responsibility for integrity, accuracy, and privacy.

Data Custodian   The data custodian manages access to data in accordance with access, security, and usage policies. He or she makes sure that no data consumer makes unauthorized use of accessed data.

Data Administrator   The data administrator manages production database systems, including both the underlying hardware and the database software. The data administrator is responsible for all aspects related to the infrastructure needed for production availability of data.

Security Administrator   The security administrator is responsible for the creation of and the enforcement of security and authentication policies and procedures.

Director of Information Flow   The director of information flow is responsible for the management of data interfaces between processing stages, as well as acting as an arbiter with respect to conflicts associated with data flow interfaces.

Director of Production Processing   The director of production processing manages production processing operations, transference of data from one production source to another, scheduling of processing, and diagnosis and resolution of production runtime failures.

Director of Application Development   The director of application development manages requirements analysis, implementation, testing, and deployment of new functionality for eventual turnover to the production facility.

Data Consumer   A data consumer is an authorized user that has been granted access rights to some data within the enterprise.

Data Provider   A data provider is an accepted supplier of information into the system.

These roles will then be integrated into a reporting structure where there are clear lines of responsibility corresponding to degrees of ownership. Note that some responsibilities are assigned to multiple roles, causing "role overlap," whose governance must be integrated into the reporting structure as well. At this point, the senior manager responsible for information (typically a chief information officer) will then assign ownership roles and responsibilities to the different organizational stakeholders.

2.5.5   Maintaining the Ownership Registry

The ownership registry is created from the data catalog and the assign-ment of roles. It is the enterprise log that can be queried to determine who has the ultimate responsibility for each data set. The ownership registry should be accessible by all interested parties, especially when new data requirements arise or there is a conflict that needs resolution.

Management of the ownership registry requires keeping a pulse on the organization, as it is not unusual for employee turnover to affect the data management structure. In addition, as new data sets are added to the governance by the data ownership policy, the decisions regarding the new data must be added to the registry.

2.6   OWNERSHIP AND DATA QUALITY

This brings us back to the issue of data quality. Once we have estab-lished a chain of command for the ownership of data, we can look at how the responsibility for data quality falls with respect to the policy. A major factor is the relationship between ownership and care, which is explored in this section, along with the enforcement of data policies and an introduction to data quality rules.

2.6.1   Ownership and Care

This may seem pretty obvious, but a person demonstrates a greater amount of care for an object that he or she owns than for something that belongs to someone else. To this end, it is important to consider the ownership stake associated with the parties in the enterprise responsible for the quality of an organization's data. It is less likely that the quality of data will be high when it is entrusted to someone who has no stake in the value of the data.

To be more precise, there are two ways to incorporate the owner-ship ideal with data quality: (1) Assign some degree of ownership to those entrusted with the data quality, or (2) assign the responsibility of data quality to the party with the highest degree of ownership.

In the first case, a person has been assigned the responsibility of maintaining the integrity of a data set but does not feel any personal attachment to the information in his or her trust. By allocating some ownership role to that person, such as creating some kind of bonus compensation structure tied to maintaining or increasing the overall value of the data, an organization can infuse the employee with a renewed interest in data quality.

The second case reveals another common ownership issue where the end users (in many cases, business users) rely on the quality of the data but have no stake in ensuring that quality. This can be remedied by forcing the business users to get involved in the definition and assurance of data quality. This includes understanding the data that is being used, defining data quality rules that are the basis for acceptability, and enforcing data policies and data quality rules.

2.6.2   Enforcing Data Policies

It is not enough to have a set of data policies. Without a process for enforcement, the policy has no "teeth" and will be useless. It is incumbent on the drafters of a data ownership policy to incorporate the methods for enforcement as well as the process for conflict resolution. Enforcement takes the form of a means for validating that the policies are being followed and actions to be taken if it is determined that the policies are not being followed. It is the role of the policy manager to ensure that the policies are being enforced.

Validating policies is a making sure that all parties are living up to their responsibility agreements and are not overstepping the bounds of their responsibility. This involves periodic reviews by the policy manager, under the authority of the CIO, of whether each assigned role is being performed adequately. If the parties are not doing their job, it may be necessary to give them further training or decrease their responsibility (and authority) and possibly remove them completely from the position of responsibility.

No organization is immune to conflicts, and there should be a dispute resolution process in place. Typically, this will involve bringing the dispute to the next level in the management hierarchy with responsibility over the particular area of conflict (we will call this person the dispute manager). If the parties dispute an ownership role or whether the responsibilities of an ownership role have not been fulfilled properly, the dispute manager should consult the ownership policy along with the ownership registry and use that information to establish a ruling for the dispute. If the issue is not covered in the data ownership policy, then the policy needs to be modified to incorporate the issue.

2.6.3   Data Quality Rules

As we move toward an organization with negotiated ownership roles, part of the responsibility of the management is to ensure that any data that is shared across the enterprise lives up to a standard of use. Ensuring this implies a few notions.

- There is a notion of data quality that is well defined throughout the enterprise.
- There is a means to describe data quality requirements.
- There is a means to measure conformance to the data quality requirements.
- There is an enterprisewide agreement as to the expected levels of data quality.
- There is a mechanism for improving data quality.

The concept of a definition of data quality is complex and important and will be covered in Chapter 3, and details of data quality ideas are discussed in Chapter 5. Ways to measure ongoing performance are examined Chapter 4. A large part of this book is devoted to defining and validating data quality rules.

2.6.4   Education and Training

When using data ownership policies to regulate the movement and management of information across an enterprise, it is critical that all participants understand the policies and how they work. This means that the managers defining the data ownership policy must also arrange for the education and training of staff members who are expected to use it. Data ownership training should cover at least these items.

1. An overview of data ownership, including ownership paradigms, ownership value, and data ownership responsibilities
2. A survey of the enterprise knowledge system covering the system architecture, the data architectures, the data set catalog, and all management, delivery, and presentation applications

3. An overview of the data ownership hierarchy describing the different roles involved, the responsibilities of each role, the reporting structure, and the conflict resolution process
4. A session covering enterprise metadata
5. A training session on the value of enterprise data quality, including an overview of data quality, a discussion of continuous measurement for improvement, and the definition and use of data quality and business rules

2.7 SUMMARY

This chapter introduced the concept of data ownership as a management issue. Because information is bought, used, created, modified, propagated, and sold throughout an organization, the enterprise data processing function can be contrasted to a factory where individuals or automated processes play specific roles.

Complicating notions in the enterprise make data quality management a difficult task, especially due to issues such as differing views of the value of data, privacy issues, turf wars, or standard bureaucracy. A list of the responsibilities of data ownership was provided for clarity.

There are different kinds of data ownership paradigms, and, depending on the organizational point of view, different ownership rules may apply in different situations. Ultimately, though, the management of the organization must choose between tight, centralized control or loose, decentralized control of data. These decisions are incorporated into a data ownership policy where the stakeholders, data sets, responsibilities, and dispute resolutions are all clearly defined. As stakeholders agree to subscribe to the data ownership policy, a more ordered environment enables better knowledge management overall and data quality management in particular.

3

DATA QUALITY IN PRACTICE

In this chapter, we explore what data quality means and how it can be effected in the enterprise. Without a definition for data quality, how can we ever hope to improve it? And since everybody has a different idea as to what data quality means, how can we level-set the members of an organization so that an improvement in data quality can be measured and recognized?

With the simple definition of data quality as "fitness for use," we can start to plan how to improve data quality across the organization. We first outline our procedure for a data quality improvement program, which incorporates the gaining of senior management consensus, training, analysis, and implementation in a way that allows for a continuous improvement program to build on each individual success.

We will also spend some time discussing what data quality means within certain implementation domains — operations, databases, data warehousing, data mining, electronic data interchange (EDI), and the Internet. In each of these domains, we will explore the importance of data quality and how a data quality program can be integrated into the domain as an integral component.

3.1 DATA QUALITY DEFINED: FITNESS FOR USE

What does data quality mean? In practicality, almost everyone has a different view of data quality. To the mailing list manager, data quality means cleansed delivery addresses and deduplication. To the account manager, data quality means accurate aggregation of customer activity.

To the medical industry, data quality may mean refined ability for record linkage. Clearly, each definition is geared toward the individual's view of what is "good" and what is not. This leads to the conclusion that there is no hard and fast definition of data quality. Rather, data quality is defined in terms of how each data consumer desires to use the data.

In the most general sense, we will use a qualitative definition of data quality and refine that definition on a case-by-case basis. In essence, we define data quality in terms of fitness for use — the level of data quality determined by data consumers in terms of meeting or beating expectations. In practice, this means identifying a set of data quality objectives associated with any data set and then measuring that data set's conformance to those objectives.

This is not to say that the tools used for static data cleansing of names and addresses or products that link data records based on specific data fields are not useful. It is true, however, that the use of these tools is not a solution to the data quality problem. Instead, the best way to get a handle on an organization's data quality is to define a set of expectations about the data, measure against those expectations, and continuously improve until those expectations are satisfied.

What has proven to be difficult up until now is that because everyone's data sets are different, there are no well-defined means for defining data quality expectations. In this book, we address this need by developing all the tools needed to determine if there is a data quality problem, to measure the cost effect of low data quality, to assess the current state of the organization's data, and to develop data quality rules that can be used for measurement. But the first step in any of these processes is to understand the notions of data quality and getting senior-level management support for the assessment and improvement of enterprise data quality.

3.1.1   Freedom from Defects

If we want to refine the definition of fitness for use, the first area of focus is limiting the "badness" of the data. We can refer to this aspect as "freedom from defects," where a defect is any situation where data values are not accessible or do not correspond in accuracy to an established frame of reference. While we will explore the areas where defects can crop up in Chapter 5, here is a short list of the kinds of defects we want to avoid.

- Inaccessibility
- Inaccuracy
- Out-of-date information
- Unmanageably redundant information
- Inconsistency with other sources
- Incomplete data
- Incomprehensible data

3.1.2 Possesses Desirable Characteristics

The flip side of freedom from defects is that the information has the characteristics of a high-quality environment. Again, we will explore these characteristics in Chapter 5, but here is the short list.

- The information is timely.
- The data model completely and accurately models its real-world counterpart.
- The information is presented in a way that is easy to understand.
- The appropriate level of detail is maintained.
- The information captured is meaningful in its proper context.

3.2 THE DATA QUALITY IMPROVEMENT PROGRAM

In any improvement process, there are a number of steps that must be taken to get to the point of a demonstrable, measurable improvement. In this section, we review some of the steps, although we treat this in much greater detail in Chapter 18.

3.2.1 Senior-Level Endorsement

A data quality improvement project will not be successful if there is no senior-level management endorsement. Because of the kinds of complicating ideas about data ownership that we discussed in Chapter 2, the successful data quality engineer must first have in place a data ownership policy and a process for conflict resolution within the organization. Additionally, the conflict resolution process must take the value of the data quality improvement into account in a way that does not decrease the effectiveness of the data quality team.

Gaining senior-level management endorsement may prove to be a more difficult task than one might imagine. Unfortunately, we have often seen that data quality is like the weather — everybody talks about it, but no one ever does anything about it. There are some interesting reasons for this.

No Mea Culpa Syndrome   No one wants to admit that there might be mistakes in their work. Low data quality implies that there are errors somewhere in the system. This is especially true in environments where employees are rewarded for a job well done, particularly when it reflects well on the management chain. Rarely do employees admit their own mistakes or call attention to those of their subordinates.

"The Emperor's New Clothes"   People often assume that the diktats of a person in a senior authority position are naturally correct and appropriate and it would be folly to challenge the status quo. In this case, a comment about actually trying to find and fix poor data quality problems might be more of a job security risk.

Denial of Responsibility   The natural response when a mess is discovered is to point the finger at someone else. Few are willing to accept that the existence of poor data quality might be due to their *own* misjudgment, and so the DQ "ball" gets bounced from desk to desk, but it never lands anywhere.

Lack of Understanding   Too often data quality is confused with "data cleansing," "deduplification," or name and address standardization. While all these items are an integral part of a data quality program, a periodic run of a data cleansing application is not a replacement for an ongoing knowledge management program integrated with continuous data quality improvement.

Dirty Work   There is a feeling that looking for problems and cleaning up data "messes" are dirty work and no-glory activities. Therefore, involvement in data quality activities is viewed as a "career-limiting move."

Lack of Recognition   Building on our last point, there is always some expectation (by data consumers, customers, etc.) that things should be right, and this implies that making things right is expected. The employees who toil at making sure that everything looks correct are viewed as just doing their job and are not recognized for performing an extremely important knowledge management task.

The conclusion is that there must be an enlightenment among the senior-level managers that breaks the negative connotations associated with data quality and shows how an integrated set of data quality solutions can add value to the organization. This enlightenment can be effected through a number of steps, including initial training in knowledge management and data quality, followed by the creation and endorsement of a data ownership policy, along with the analysis that demonstrates the economic impact of low data quality and the economic value of measurable high data quality.

3.2.2   Data Quality Training

Training on data quality begins with understanding the principles of what quality means in the context of information. A training program in data quality should incorporate overviews and discussions of at least these concepts.

1. Creation and usage of information
2. Storage of information
3. Data ownership
4. Quality concepts and the quality improvement cycle
5. Understanding the economic impact of data quality issues
6. Dimensions of data quality
7. Aspects of reference data domains
8. Data quality and business rules
9. Metrics for measuring and assessing data quality
10. Metadata
11. Data quality requirements analysis
12. Data cleansing and standardization
13. Error detection, correction, and root cause analysis using data quality rules
14. Data enhancement

3.2.3   Data Ownership Policy

As we discussed in Chapter 2, a data ownership policy governs the responsibility over the collections of information used in an enterprise. Without a policy, there is no process for accountability, so before any further steps can be taken, the endorsing senior managers must draft, accept, and publicize a data ownership policy, as well as define and incorporate the procedures for enforcing the policy.

3.2.4   Build an Economic Model of Low Data Quality

Once the policy and its enforcement procedures are in place, the next step is to identify those areas in greatest need of improvement. (Chapter 4 presents a framework for finding those areas.) In our economic model of low data quality, we provide a mechanism characterizing the actual impact of data quality both within and external to the organization. This is done by taking these steps.

1. Looking for the signs of data quality problems
2. Mapping the flow of information into, through, and out of the enterprise
3. Characterizing the impacts of low data quality at particular stages in the information chain
4. Measuring the cost impact of low data quality
5. Building the data quality scorecard

The data quality scorecard is a tool used to focus on the locations in the information chain where there are data quality problems that have the greatest impact on the organization. The scorecard can be used as input to the next step, current state assessment.

3.2.5   Current State Assessment and Requirements Analysis

Finding areas of high impact is one thing, but figuring out how to address them is another. Before we can fix a problem, we have to know how bad the problem is. That is where the current state assessment comes in.

At each location of impact, we select some of the dimensions of data quality covered in Chapter 5 and measure the level of data quality. These levels are correlated to the degrees of economic impact determined by the scorecard analysis. We then use the current state analysis to discover which areas of data quality account for the largest economic impact and for a baseline measurement of the overall data quality of the enterprise.

The baseline numbers coupled with the degree of impact allow us to both determine what needs to be fixed and the levels needed to demonstrate improvement. This is all determined during the requirements analysis stage. Requirements analysis will assign target levels of data quality that need to be met in order to relieve the problems uncovered during the economic impact analysis and current state assessment.

3.2.6 Project Selection

With the data quality scorecard, the current state assessment, and the requirements analysis, there is enough data to select a project for improvement. With senior management support, a team is assembled and assigned a specific goal: to bring up the level of measured data quality to the target level determined during the requirements analysis.

Selecting a single project for execution is important. Unfortunately, many data quality improvement projects are subject to failure because the scope encompassed is way too large. It may be impossible to demonstrate overall improvement if there is no particular focus. Remember that the overall success of the program is determined by small successes in small steps. Selecting a high-profile but small project for improvement, and successfully completing that project, accomplishes three things.

1. It provides a measurable (both in hard metrics and in economic benefit) improvement in the quality of information in the enterprise.
2. It gains positive association within the organization for accomplishment, which in turn builds more senior-level buy-in and general consensus.
3. It opens the possibility for additional improvement projects.

3.2.7 Implement and Deploy the Improvement

The implementation of the improvement is the critical denouement of the data quality drama. The improvement team must be empowered to take these steps.

1. *Architect a solution*   This means determining what actual steps must be done to address the data quality problem.
2. *Implement the solution*   This incorporates the acquisition of a development platform, access to the environment in which the solution is needed, and access to the resources needed to perform the implementation.
3. *Deploy the solution*   This means being able to integrate the solution with the production systems and move the new solution into production.

3.3   DATA QUALITY AND OPERATIONS

Business operations are defined by a set of rules that are applied in everyday execution. When the business depends on the correct flow of information, there is an aspect of data quality that intersects the operational specification.

In essence, in an information business, business rules are data quality rules. This implies that data quality is an integral part of any operational specification, and organizations that recognize this from the start can streamline operations by applying data quality techniques in process. This in turn prevents bad data from affecting the flow of business and stops incorrect information from entering the system, eliminating the need to detect and correct bad data. Thus, a "data quality aware" operation can execute at lower cost and higher margin than the traditional company.

Data quality and business rules can be used to incorporate a rule-based execution engine that can validate information as it passes through an organization (see Figure 3.1). Rules are defined that specify

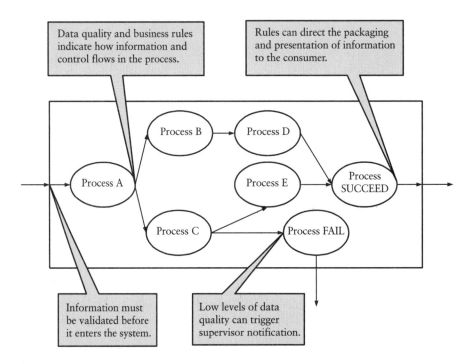

FIGURE 3.1   The need for data validation in the operational environment

what information must look like before it can enter a specific process, as well as validate the information as it passes from producer to consumer. In addition, data validation and business rules can be used as triggers for particular events within an operational environment. For example, threshold limits can be set for operational efficiency based on the amount of invalid information in the system. When these thresholds are encountered, an event is triggered that notifies a supervisor of the presence of a problem and the location of the problem.

3.4   DATA QUALITY AND DATABASES

Of course, the concept of data quality pervades the world of databases. Our lives are touched by databases every day, ranging from direct marketing mailings that bombard us, utility and credit card bills that distress us, exasperating health insurance provider services and down to taxes, our driving history, and those videos we rent.

It is unusual, though, for anyone to be untouched by bad data sitting in one of these databases. Though these can be due to machine errors, more often they are the result of human error. Data quality is integral to the proper use of databases.

3.4.1   Databases and Data Quality

There has been longstanding recognition of the importance of data quality within the world of databases. Databases are in fact designed with certain safeguards for data quality, although they are often overridden in practice. Processes such as embedded null testing, functional dependence, data normalization, and referential integrity are all testaments to the need for DBMS providers to include some degree of data validation within the database system.

Databases are often meant to represent a model of the real world, and their quality can be measured by their conformance to the real-world entities that they are designed to model. As a database ages and no longer has the input of "positive energy," the real world tends to diverge from what is represented in the database.

There are a number of data quality areas associated with database systems, such as static cleansing applications that will examine data and attempt to put it into some canonical format. Standardization can be applied to name and address data, and deduplification is a process to remove duplicate entries from a database. See Figure 3.2.

Rule-based data quality can be used to direct the entry of information into a database (see Figure 3.3). If there are dependencies between values in certain attributes, that information can be used to direct the process of collecting the information. An example of this might be in automated screen generation based on data dependence rules. The data entry process would then be guided by the staged accumulation of data values targeted to specific attributes. As the values are seen, they may have some impact on the types and sets of attributes that must be filled next. For example, consider an online medical history form, which should only ask about a patient's most recent pregnancy only if the

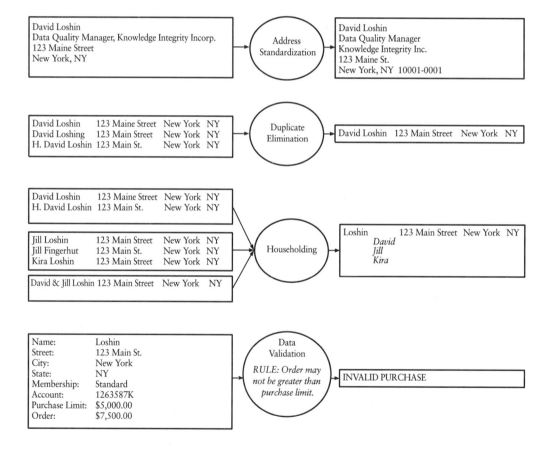

FIGURE 3.2   Data quality applications

patient is determined to be female. We explore this in greater detail in Chapter 17.

3.4.2 Legacy Databases

Legacy databases pose interesting data quality questions, since it is likely that the people originally involved in the creation and development of the database have long since left the organization. Legacy databases hold more than just data — they hold secrets about embedded business rules folded into the way the information is stored, viewed, manipulated, and so on.

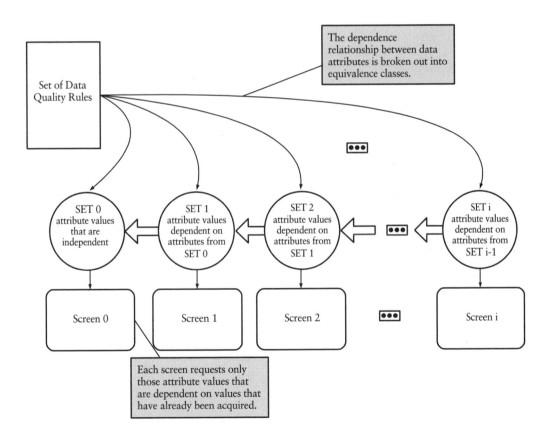

FIGURE 3.3 Data directed input screen generation

An interesting data quality issue surrounding legacy data is in discovering the data quality rules and business rules embedded both in associated application code and in the data itself. As systems evolve, there is a growing reluctance to handle or modify any piece that is working in production, so as time passes, many changes are applied "around the edges" in ways that create new application execution dependencies that are artificial.

For example, in some mainframe execution systems, the job scheduler must know exactly what the job execution dependencies are in order to arrange an execution schedule. Lore regarding the completion time associated with certain jobs was passed down as an imperative to defining those dependencies. This stricture was imposed because of an assumption that a certain processing phase must be finished before another could begin. This did affect the completion time of the cycle of processing, which by industry regulation had to be completed within a prespecified time.

In reality, the actual dependence between jobs was much less rigid. The actual set of rules showed a less restrictive dependence between the initiation of the jobs (one had to wait until the other started, not finished). That discovery, along with an increase in the available technology associated with database locking, had obviated the original dependence. By removing the dependence and logging the interaction rules between the two jobs, a much more efficient schedule could be produced.

The benefit of a more efficient job schedule was a decrease in the critical path of execution, which also decreased the completion of the production cycle. The processing time freed by optimizing the job schedule enabled an increase in processing volume as well as a decrease in the per-item cost of processing. The result: an increase in cost margin for the company!

Another interesting feature about legacy data is that while technology has advanced, legacy systems are bound by their implementation platform. Systems developed before the introduction of relational database systems are limited to the power provided by the original system. This can have two effects: (1) Many things that can be implemented easily with today's technology, are impossible in older technology, which can be an argument for a database renovation project, and (2) clever tricks that had been used in older systems to get around implementation deficiencies become albatrosses, which prevents improving the system in its current implementation. The innovators of these tricks move on to other positions, and these secrets are lost, but the constraints remain.

3.4.3   Data Migration

An issue complementary to legacy databases is the migration of legacy data to new databases. There are similar data quality issues involving implementation decisions and how they affect overall information quality.

We could say that in the migration environment, we really want to perform information archaeology. We want to understand the historical use, manipulation, and storage of information in the transactional system and then characterize that knowledge in a way that eases the movement of data from the legacy system to the new system. Since a lot of knowledge is likely to be embedded in the data and in supporting application code, we will need to document what we learn about the data (that is, metadata) and maintain the learned metadata in a metadata repository.

What are the reasons for data migration? Here are a few.

1. The underlying database management system (DBMS) is obsolete.
2. There is no longer enough support personnel for the transaction system.
3. The company making the application code has gone out of business.
4. There are better DBMS systems available.
5. There are system requirements that can be better met using a new system.
6. The current DBMS is not supported on high-performance hardware.
7. There are better ways to manage data in a new DBMS.

In any case, the reasons for migration yield insight into what kind of metadata must be collected. This metadata can be used for the data migration process followed by any transformations that must be performed before loading it into the destination database. Both data quality rules and business rules will govern the extraction and transformation process. This is shown in Figure 3.4.

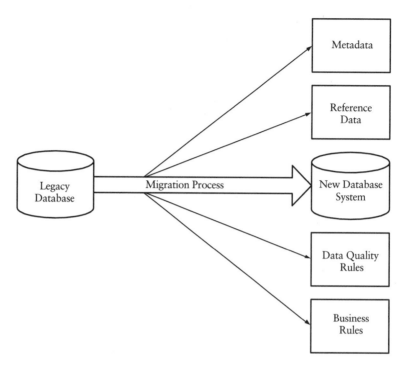

FIGURE 3.4   Learning from the migration process

3.4.4   Data Extraction, Transformation, and Loading

The data extraction, transformation, and loading process (referred to as ETL) is almost completely governed by data quality rules. The processes of extracting data from a set of data sources, combining that data, perhaps applying some changes, and then loading that data into a target database all comes under the category of the data quality rules we will discuss in Chapters 7 and 8.

Many tools are designed specifically for the ETL process. These tools often use a visual interface to define a mapping between the original source data sets and the target data set. A library of transformation functions, combination or aggregation functions, or insert user-defined operations can be used to apply to data. The tools order the set of operations (data extractions, transformations, etc.) and then automatically generate the application code needed to extract the data from the source databases, perform the transformations, and insert the result into the target. The result is a packaged application from end to end to perform the ETL.

3.5   DATA QUALITY AND THE DATA WAREHOUSE

Data marts and data warehouses are used for an analytical environment. It is often said that the bulk of the work performed in implementing a data warehouse is in the data extraction, cleansing, and transformation phases of moving information from the original source into the warehouse. Nevertheless, many data warehouse projects fail because not enough attention is spent on either understanding the data quality requirements or on the validation and quality assurance of information imported into the warehouse.

3.5.1   Flawed Data = Flawed Results

Analyses performed using data warehouses with flawed information will produce flawed strategic decisions. Many organizations report that as much as 70 percent of their effort goes into supporting the data cleansing and transformation process. This effort is split between data auditing and data cleansing.

Ensuring that high-quality data enters a data warehouse decreases the potential for flawed strategic decision making. What distinguishes the approach presented here in data warehouse design and implementation is that our philosophy revolves around the idea of building data quality into the product at the time of design. Instead of relying on data cleansing tools that statically clean a database, this methodology presumes the validation of data items upon insertion into the database.

It is necessary to work with data consumers to understand, identify, and abstract data quality requirements, to determine the data quality rules, and to integrate tools to test and validate data items at the insertion point. The methods described here allow the user to integrate in-process qualification into the information manufacture and processing chain to both measure and validate data quality. At the same time this will provide feedback for the identification of root causes of data quality problems.

3.5.2   Example: Data Warehouse Certification

As an example, you can use data quality and business rules for what we call "data warehouse certification." Certification is a means of scoring the believability of the information stored in a data warehouse. A data warehouse is considered fit for use when the data inside conforms to a set of data quality expectations embodied in a set of rules. Given these rules, we assign a score to the quality of the data imported into a data warehouse for certifying warehouse data quality (see Figure 3.5).

The first step is to define a set of rules that will qualify the data. Again, we can use the rules framework that is described in Chapters 7 and 8. The next step is to import those data quality rules into a rules engine. Each rule will have an associated validity threshold (as a percentage) based on the users' expectations of quality.

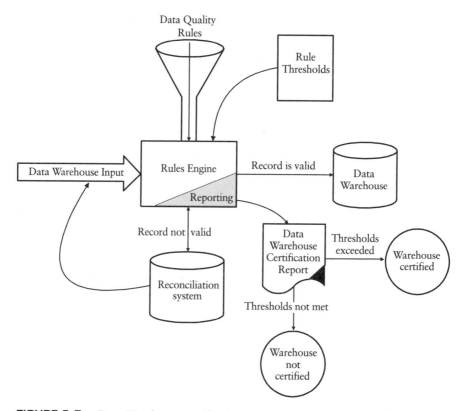

FIGURE 3.5   Data Warehouse certification

As records are fed into the engine, any relevant rules (that is, any rules that refer to values of attributes defined within the record) are tested. If no rules fail, the record is said to be valid and is successfully gated through to the warehouse. If any rules fail, the record is enhanced with information about which rules were violated, and the record is output to a reconciliation system. The violating record can also be passed through to the warehouse, but now it is marked as having not conformed to the users' expectations, and this information can be used when performing analysis. The count of failures and successes is maintained for each rule.

After the data is imported, each rule's validity value is computed as the ratio of valid records to the total of records. A data quality certification report delineating all validity percentages is generated. If all validity percentages exceed the associated thresholds, the warehouse is certified to conform to the users' data quality requirements. Otherwise, the warehouse is not certified, and until the percentages can be brought up to the conformance level, the warehouse cannot be said to meet the data quality requirements.

To qualify the warehouse after a failed certification, the records output to the reconciliation system must be analyzed for the root cause of the failures. This analysis and correction is part of a business workflow that relies on the same set of data quality and business rules used for validation. After reconciliation, the data is resubmitted through the rules engine, and the validity report is generated again. The root cause information is used to return to the source of problems in the legacy data and to correct those bad data at the source, gradually leading to certification.

Data warehouse and data mart certification is an ongoing process, and the certification report needs to be aligned with the ways that data records are inserted into the warehouse. For example, if a data mart is completely repopulated on a regular basis, the certification process can be inserted as a component to the reloading process. Alternatively, if a data warehouse is incrementally populated, the results of the certification engine must be persistent.

3.6 DATA MINING

Data mining, or knowledge discovery, is the process of looking for patterns or anomalies in large data sets. Data mining is really a compendium of algorithms meant to discover knowledge embedded in data. This includes decision trees, neural networks, genetic algorithms, and association rule discovery, along with other statistical and correlation techniques.

It is well known that the bulk of the work associated with data mining is in preparing the data for analysis. This data preparation can be broken down into these phases.

Data Characterization   Data miners will typically know how the data is put together — the base data types, the size of each attribute, and other elements, but data characterization takes this to a higher level. Characterization involves describing the nature of the content of the data as opposed to just the format or the structure of the data.

Consistency Analysis   Although we expect to use the same name all the time, inconsistencies can creep into data that indicate different names for the same entity — for example, "IBM," "International Business Machines," or "Int'l Bus. Mach." There can also be inconsistencies on a broader scale, such as different terms used as attribute names in several tables that model the same domain.

Domain Analysis   In order to make sure the data values are valid, the data types are subtyped into more restrictive domain descriptions.

Data Enrichment   This involves incorporating more than one data source into the data set used for analysis.

Frequency and Distribution Analysis   Sometimes the value of certain data values is related to the number of times the values occur. Frequency analysis can capture some of this information.

Normalization   Normalization involves transforming data values within one domain into values within another domain. For many purposes it is desirable to relate data values drawn from a continuous domain into a narrowed range. For example, for many neural network applications, all continuous values should lie between 0 and 1.0.

Missing and Empty Value Analysis   Missing data values potentially skew analytical models, so there must be some mechanism for detecting, characterizing, and dealing with missing values.

Data mining and knowledge discovery are particularly valuable when in tandem with the data quality and business process because data mining can be both a consumer and a producer of data quality and business rules. Data quality techniques must be used to prepare the data for the knowledge discovery process. In turn, the data mining will expose data quality and business rules that can be used for further knowledge discovery.

3.7   DATA QUALITY AND ELECTRONIC DATA INTERCHANGE

Electronic Data Interchange (or EDI) is the term used for any standardized format for representing business information for the purposes of electronic communication. EDI is enabled through a process of cooperative data standardization within a particular business environment. It is used in many industries today, such as the health care and financial industries, and is firmly entrenched in interactions with the federal government.

EDI is used to eliminate manual processing when executing routine business operations such as purchase orders, product orders, invoicing, securities trading transactions, shipping notices, and so forth. This increases efficiency and volume, thereby lowering the overall cost per transaction.

EDI is more than just forwarding purchase orders and invoices via e-mail or through Intranet postings. It is designed to use standards for formatting and transmitting information that are independent of the hardware platform. EDI enables a process known as straight-through processing, (STP), which is the ability to completely automate business operations with no manual intervention.

Any STP or EDI activity is almost by definition one that is based on data quality. Because EDI is defined as a standard form for transmitting information, there are rules about validation of the both the format and the content of EDI messages. Precisely because STP is meant to replace well-defined operational processes, there are specific business rules that guide the STP applications in how to process the transaction.

What is more relevant is that not only must an STP application be able to execute operations based on a set of predefined business rules, it must also be able to distinguish between valid and invalid EDI messages. Validity is more than just structural conformance to the EDI format — it must also include validation of the content as well. STP systems often will only perform the structural validity checks, and not the content validity, which may account for slips in actual complete automation.

3.7.1   XML

A good example of this can be seen in XML (Extensible Markup Language) for EDI. XML is both a structure definition framework (for the definition of data standards) and a well-defined set of rules for validating based on defined standards. XML syntax imposes a structure on the form of a document through the use of tags for markup — metadata directives describing the data in the document. These are the six kinds of markup that can occur in an XML document.

- *Elements,* which are delimited by angle brackets and denote the kind of information they surround. There are two kinds of tags that are used for elements: start tags, (denoted with <item>) and end tags (denoted with <item>).
- *Entity references,* which are alternate ways of expressing special characters or symbols as well as frequently used text within a document.
- *Comments,* which are delineated text items that are not part of the document.
- *Processing instructions,* which include pieces of information that are to be passed to a processing application but are not part of the document.
- *Marked sections,* which section off areas from being parsed by an XML parser (that is, all characters are taken verbatim).
- *Document type declarations,* which is a set of declarations and specifications for creating well formed documents.

A DTD can be used to define a data format standard for EDI, and XML is a nice framework because there are inherent notions of "well formed" and "valid."

3.7.2   XML: Well Formed

In the context of XML, a document is well formed if it conforms to the syntax of XML. This means that an XML parser can successfully parse the document. Also, in order to be well formed, a document must meet a number of other conditions. For example, no attribute (a name-value pair that attributes a tag) may appear more than once on the same start tag, all entities must be declared, and nonempty tags must be nested properly. Another condition is that neither text nor parameters may be directly or indirectly recursive. Other conditions are beyond the scope of this discussion. Suffice it to say, an XML parser can determine whether a document is well formed or not.

3.7.3   XML: Valid

An XML document is valid if it is well formed and contains a DTD and the document obeys the rules specified in the DTD. This means that element sequence and nesting conform to the DTD, all required attribute values are present, and their types are correct.

3.7.4   Structure vs Content

While there are notions of both well-formedness and (structural) validity, note that there is no notion of content validation. Thus, even when the format of an EDI message conforms completely to the syntax rules, the data inside the message can still cause problems down the line.

As an example, consider a financial securities trading application. The EDI format may specify that any trade must include the name of the security, the security type, and the quantity traded. But if a message came through with an invalid security in the security name field, the message may still be gated through to the trade processing application, where it will most likely create a failure in processing. The structure of the message was valid, but the content was not. We will explore ways to specify content validation rules that add additional insurance against incorrect messages causing failure in straight-through processing.

3.8   DATA QUALITY AND THE WORLD WIDE WEB

As an information forum, it is hard to fully understand the impact of the World Wide Web. One feature that permeates the Internet is the complete lack of organization of the available information. Another is the temporal quality of the information presented.

The Internet can be seen as the largest uncoordinated database in the world. Here technology enables the use of information available over the World Wide Web as a large data repository, with data collection and aggregation scripts acting as a "view-generator" for any particular user application. All Web sites can be characterized in terms of some kind of data service. Some sites act as data presentation systems, some as data collection systems, and some as database query systems.

The plethora of information that can be accessed and viewed by a web user provides great potential for simulating a data warehouse or business intelligence repository viewed through a "virtual portal." This portal can aggregate collected information sources (both internal and external) into a single business intelligence console coupled with "intelligent agents" that seek out the desired data and deliver it directly to the desktop.

3.8.1   What Is Missing from the Data Warehouse Analogy

The data warehouse analogy partially breaks down when it comes to the actual aggregation and presentation of information at the presentation site. A critical value that can be derived from the aggregation of information is its coagulation, enrichment, and presentation in terms of critical business intelligence that is meaningful to the user.

The obvious reason for this is that similar types of information available across the Web are represented in different ways. Whether using different storage formats, different names, or different visual representations, the data presented at different Web sites and collected and delivered to the client location can be made much more valuable when that data is massaged into business intelligence guided through client-defined requirements.

Another reason for the breakdown in the analogy has to do with governance (or more clearly, the lack thereof). Anyone can publish anything on the Internet, yet there is no governing body that oversees the quality of any information published. Therefore, it is up to the user to characterize his or her data quality requirements to which the information should conform before the information is presented.

3.8.2   The Web as a Transaction Factory

Another aspect of the use of the Internet is the growth of both business-to-consumer (B2C) and business-to-business (B2B) EDI frameworks for executing transactions. Whether we talk about amateur day traders, competitors in online auctions, or B2B order processing and fulfillment, there is an increase in the use of the Internet as a distributed transaction factory.

3.8.3   Data Presentation

Both commercial sites for presenting information about a company's services or products and personal Web sites for presenting personal information are data presentation systems. A single Web page peppered with text statements is the simplest form of data presentation.

As Web sites expand, they are frequently fragmented into different presentation paradigms, including frames, tables, and pages. At some point, there is too much information for a single Web page, so the information is broken up into multiple pages. The presenter might also want to use frames to allow more controlled navigation throughout the Web site. Within a single page (or frame), tables are used both for data aggregation and data presentation.

Another presentation device is the use of hyperlinks. Hyperlinks are embedded references to other Web site addresses that can be considered "canned" information queries. Each hyperlink represents a request to provide more information about a particular subject.

3.8.4   Internet Data Queries

There are at least five different data query paradigms over the Internet.

1. *Hyperlinking*   As we said, hyperlinks can be seen as canned queries that lead to (relatively) static data sets. As Web pages evolve, sets of hyperlinks are grouped under distinct headings to further refine and classify the virtual query.
2. *Local data searching engines*   A local search engine that has indexed the information present in a Web site's set of Web pages can produce a set of references to Web pages that matches a user's specific query.
3. *Service queries*   This allows the web page to act as a front end to an actual database service that is connected to the Web site, although it may act independently of the Web site. Many e-commerce sites operate in this manner. An example is a query through an online catalog site as to the number of requested items currently in stock and ready to be shipped.
4. *Web-wide search engines*   These are web search engines that front to databases of indexed Web pages. This can be considered an extension to the localized Web searching.

5. *Meta-Web-wide search engines*   These are Web sites that front to other Web search engines.

3.8.5   Data Collection

Another primary database activity includes data collection. Anytime the browsing user is required to submit some set of information, either to gain access to a site, to register as a site user, to gate to more secure sites, or just for informational purposes, a Web site acts as an update mechanism to a database. The database may consist of customer information, statistical information, or even simple logging information.

3.8.6   Example: Poor Data Collection

Once when I was using the Internet to collect information for a report I was preparing on some data management tools, I visited a number of Web sites for companies that provided those tools. At one particular corporate site, I found a menu of white papers that were clearly relevant to my task, but in order to download the papers, I was required to fill out a form with pertinent contact information — name, mailing address, phone number, e-mail address, and so forth.

After submitting the form, I was gated through to the Web site to download the white papers, at which point I made my selection and downloaded the paper. After reading the paper, I realized that there had been another paper at that site that I also wanted to read. I repointed my browser at the site, only to find that I was required to fill out the form again. Only after resubmitting all the same information was I able to download the other white paper.

About two days later, I was called by a company representative who introduced himself and asked if I had successfully downloaded the white paper (not papers!) and inquired about my interest in their product. I replied that I had gotten the papers, but that I had to fill out the form twice. I asked him if my filling out the form twice meant that I would appear in their database twice. He said it would. I then asked if that was a problem, considering that if I were called more than once about the product, I might get annoyed. The salesman answered that while I would appear in the database more than once, he was aware of the problem and usually was able to mentally keep track of whom he had already called. We briefly talked about data quality and duplicate record elimination, but he seemed convinced that this was not a serious dilemma.

About four hours later, I found a message on my voice mail. Who was it? It was the same salesman, calling to introduce himself and to see if I had successfully downloaded the white paper! What was ironic is that the salesman not only completely exposed his inability to keep track in general, he completely forgot our earlier conversation focusing on this exact problem!

The simple practice of collecting sales lead information through Web-based forms is a compelling idea as long as the operational aspects don't backfire. We can see at least three ways how the absence of a data quality program associated with this Web site can diminish the effectiveness of the process.

Across one dimension, by filling out that form I expressed interest in the area associated with the products being sold. As a potential customer, filling out the form is a proactive action, exposing me as a qualified sales lead. Yet, by registering a visitor in the database more than once, the system dilutes the effectiveness of this sales lead qualification.

Across a second dimension, a measurable cost of customer acquisition is increased each time the salesman makes a telephone call. Associated with each call is some expectation of converting the lead into a sale. By calling the same person twice, however, the salesman is not only performing rework but preventing himself from getting real work done, such as following up on other sales leads.

Across a third dimension, there is a strategic weakening of the targeted sales process. When targeting a potential customer, it is in the salesman's best interest to foster a good working relationship with that customer. Interrupting a decision maker once during a day to gauge interest is probably bearable, but someone might be irritated by having his or her work routine interrupted twice in the same day by the same person. I would probably make the assumption that the company is not very organized, which would make me question their ability to provide a good product.

3.9   SUMMARY

In this chapter, we examined the definition of data quality in terms of fitness for use and how understanding the measure of data quality may be very dependent on the context and domain in which the data is scrutinized. We looked at the development of a data quality improvement program and what it takes to get the ball rolling. We determined that there are seven phases to the program.

1. Gaining senior level endorsement
2. Training in data quality
3. Creating and enforcing a data ownership policy (as discussed in Chapter 2)
4. Building the economic model (will be discuss in Chapter 4)
5. Performing a current state assessment (as will be described in Chapter 9)
6. Selecting a project for improvement
7. Implementing and deploying the project

Of course, with each successful project implementation and deployment, there are opportunities to select new improvement projects, which turns phases 6 and 7 into a cycle, although the entire process may need to be repeated.

We also looked at different contexts for data quality — namely, data quality in an operational context, data quality in the database world, data quality and the data warehouse, data mining, electronic data interchange, and the Internet. While there is a distinct need for data quality in each of these contexts, the actual work that is done with respect to data quality is understated but will grow in importance.

4

ECONOMIC FRAMEWORK OF DATA QUALITY AND THE VALUE PROPOSITION

The key to understanding the importance of quality data lies with an examination of the costs and benefits associated with data quality. Without an economic framework to measure the detrimental effect of poor data in an organization, it is difficult to make an argument for the investment in a knowledge management program.

Most frequently, poor data quality is measured by anecdotes or descriptions of hazy feelings of difficulty in implementation, as well as by tales of customer dissatisfaction. While these somewhat vague measurements seem to verify that *something* is wrong, they give no clear indication of the severity of this "wrongness," nor do they offer solutions.

If there is a more concrete means of measuring the impact of poor data quality on an economic basis, we can then determine the extent to which the bottom line is affected by bad information. This is a good time to discuss a framework for categorizing the costs and benefits in economic terms. There are five interrelated steps to evaluating the *cost-effect of low data quality*, or COLDQ. The first step involves charting the flow of data through the organization. The second is categorizing the costs associated with bad data. The third is identifying and estimating the actual effect of the presence of poor data quality. The fourth step is determining the cost of fixing the problems, whether by a static operation or a continuous improvement program. The fifth and final step is the calculation of a return on investment to help senior-level management make a decision as to the level of commitment to a data quality program.

In this chapter, we abstract the flow of information from original source to final information product, whether the ultimate consumer of that product is an operational process, a decision process, or customer.

We then develop a taxonomy of data quality cost categories. We look at how to identify "break points" along the data flow/information chain where data quality problems might arise. This is followed by a description of the analysis used to measure the actual costs of poor data quality. The economic framework outlined in this chapter combined with the more detailed qualification of data quality problems as described in Chapters 5 through 8 and the current state assessment process described in Chapter 9 will compile a complete "data quality score card" that can guide an organization's path to better knowledge management.

4.1 EVIDENCE OF ECONOMIC IMPACT

How do we know that there is an economic impact on a company due to poor data quality? Most likely, there will be evidence of an impact. Let's look at some common issues that might be related to poor data quality.

4.1.1 Frequent System Failures and Service Interruptions

An information-based system that experiences frequent system failures or systems interruptions may be highly sensitive to poor data quality. Failures may be caused by irregular or unexpected data values cropping up in processing. Time spent searching for errors and fixing them before restarting the processing will account for service interruptions.

4.1.2 Drop in Productivity vs Volume

As the volume of processing (transactions, data input) increases, a system should scale appropriately and be able to handle the increased volume and meet the need with only an adjustment of the base resources (processor power, storage, bandwidth). Any significant increase in other resources (support staff, programmers, diagnosticians) may indicate an inability to scale properly, which in turn might be associated with inability to tolerate higher levels of bad data. If productivity decreases as volume increases, this may be an indication of low data quality.

4.1.3   High Employee Turnover

While it is a stretch to claim that high employee turnover is related to poor data quality, there is certainly frustration associated with enterprise-wide employee mistrust. When the senior management is stymied (due to insufficient or incorrect input assumptions) in its ability to set and execute strategic initiatives on behalf of the company, the staff loses faith in the core management's ability to get things done. This loss of faith translates into a more mobile staff eager to bolt for more promising opportunities.

4.1.4   High New Business/Continued Business Ratio

It is said that the best new customers are your current customers. In other words, you are more likely to sell something to your current customer base than to new customers. So when your organization is always focusing on new business and not closing deals with current customers, this may be evidence of customer dissatisfaction, which can be related to poor data quality.

4.1.5   Increased Customer Service Requirements

A high demand for customer service indicates that problems are leaving the enterprise and making it to the customers. When the customer service budget increases — especially when the customer service department mostly attends to billing problems — this is likely indicative of a data quality problem.

4.1.6   Decreased Ability to Scale

Small data sets with problems result in small sets of errors, but as data sets grow, so do the size of the error sets. In some cases the growth of the error sets is linear, but it can increase exponentially compared to the source data. If the number of errors multiplies rapidly, the organization will not be able to scale its systems to address those problems.

4.1.7   Customer Attrition

When customers stop being your customers, it is even stronger evidence that some area of dissatisfaction has not been successfully resolved. This is a more serious indication of data quality problems and shows how much impact low data quality can have on an organization.

4.2   DATA FLOWS AND INFORMATION CHAINS

Although it is clear that data are used in both operational processing and decision-making processes, outside the implementation arena, these processes are often considered "black boxes" that take input data as "raw material" and generate value-added information as output. This output then proceeds to another processing operation (or another black box), or it is summarized as a report as input to a decision-making process.

The first step in understanding the effect of low data quality is peering inside the black box to identify the steps through which the input data is converted into usable information. For simplicity, let's divide the world into one of two data flow models: the strategic data flow, used for decision-making, and the operational data flow, used for data processing. Either model represents a data processing system, and, also for simplicity, let's reduce the number of processing stages to an abstract minimum. Note that there are, of course, exceptions to these generalizations, but we'll use them as the generic model for determining the COLDQ.

4.2.1   Processing Stages

These are the processing stages that we will work with.

1. *Data supply*   Data suppliers forward information into the system.
2. *Data acquisition*   This is the processing stage that accepts data from external suppliers and injects it into the system.
3. *Data creation*   Internal to the system, data may be generated and then forwarded to another processing stage.
4. *Data processing*   Any stage that accepts input and generates output (as well as generating side effects) is called a data processing stage.

5. *Data packaging*   Any point that information is collated, aggregated, and summarized for reporting purposes is a packaging stage.
6. *Decision making*   The point where human interaction is required is called a decision-making stage.
7. *Decision implementation*   This is the stage where the decision made at a decision-making stage is executed, which may affect other processing stages or may affect a data delivery stage.
8. *Data delivery*   This is the point where packaged information is delivered to a known data consumer.
9. *Data consumption*   Because the data consumer is the ultimate user of processed information, the consumption stage is the exit stage of the system.

4.2.2   Directed Information Channels

An information channel is essentially a pipeline for the flow of information from one processing stage to another. A directed information channel is attributed with the direction in which data flows. The delivery of supplier data to an acquisition stage is performed through an information channel directed from the supplier to the acquisition stage. It is preferable to make information channels directed because there may be bidirectional communication between any two points, and it is possible to differentiate between data flowing in the different directions.

4.2.3   Information Chain Map

A map of an information chain is represented by the combination of the processing stages connected by directed information channels. Because we need to analyze each location in the information chain where a data quality problem might occur, we need a naming scheme for the sites on the map. Each processing stage should be labeled with a name and attributed with its stage type. There may be multiple information channels between any pair of processing stages, which indicates multiple communications between those stages. Information channel names may either be a combination of the source and target processing stages, separated by a hyphen, along with a distinguishing number (such as "Customer-Hotel Agent 1"), or (as seen implicitly in Figure 4.1) tagged with the name of

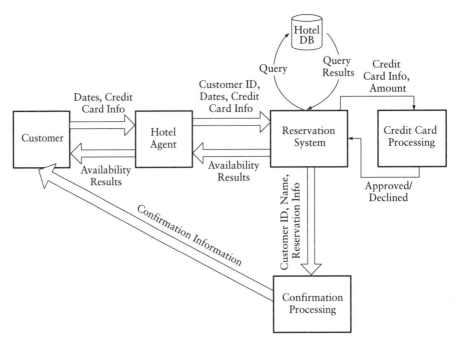

FIGURE 4.1　Sample information chain

the source and the target processing stage as well as the data items that are communicated through that channel.

4.2.4　Representing the Information Chain

The information chain can be represented in a pair of data tables as reference metadata. There are two types of objects that must be represented: processing stages and communications channels. For each processing stage, we must keep track of what type of processing stage it is and a unique name. The stage type refers to an enumerated list of known processing stages.

```
create table stages (
    stageID         integer,
    description     varchar(1000),
    stageType       integer
);
```

For communications channels, we need the source and the target of the channel. The stage identifiers for the source and the targets are indicated.

```
create table channels (
    channelID          integer,
    description        varchar(1000),
    source             integer,
    target             integer
);
```

4.2.5   Strategic Data Flow

A strategic data flow represents the stages used for the decision-making process, as shown in Figure 4.2.

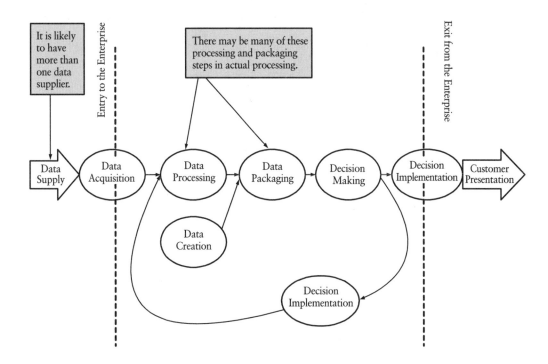

FIGURE 4.2   A strategic data flow

4.2.6   Operational Data Flow

An operational data flow represents the automated repeated process of transaction processing or result-oriented computing (that is, applications that return specific requested results). In this case, the system is the operationalization of a known process (or set of processes), and as long as the input data are correct, the data that pass through the system are, to some extent, irrelevant to the process, instead acting as "grease" to the system mechanism. The operational data flow is shown in Figure 4.3.

4.3   EXAMPLES OF INFORMATION CHAINS

4.3.1   Order Fulfillment

In a traditional direct marketing order fulfillment process, orders are received, payments are processed, and products are packed and shipped. The order fulfillment business is one of economy of scale — the business

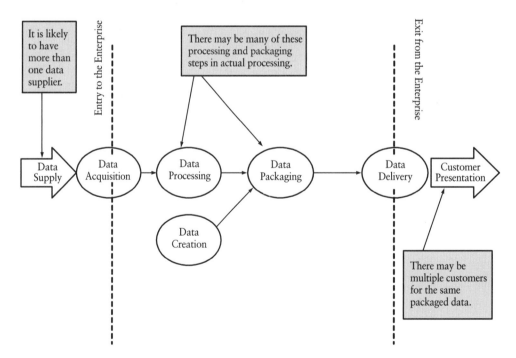

FIGURE 4.3   An operational data flow

thrives when larger volumes of orders can be handled, and it therefore fits into our category of an operational data flow, since the process is well defined and tangential to the actual data received.

There are a relatively small number of processing stages. The data suppliers are typically agents who will outsert (open envelopes) and sort mail. Alternatively, orders may be taken by telephone. Either way, an electronic version of orders is forwarded to a data acquisition stage, which can be called "order reception." The next stage is a data packaging stage, where orders being paid for by credit card are extracted, followed by a data delivery stage where those records are passed to the bank (a data consumer). Payments that are declined are returned as supplied data, held temporarily (a processing stage), and then resubmitted to the bank. Orders that have been paid for and can be filled are packaged again and sent to another department — shipping preparation — where the actual products purchased are plucked off the shelf and put into boxes for shipping.

If the ordered items are out of stock, the orders are placed in a back-order location, and an order to refill stock is generated and sent to the supplier. When back-ordered items arrive, the back-orders are examined to see if they can be filled, in which case they are then sent to the picking and packing process for shipping. Figure 4.4 shows this entire process.

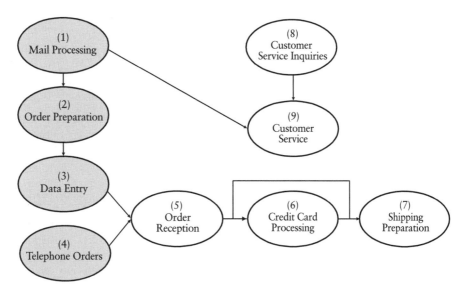

FIGURE 4.4   Order fulfillment

4.3.2   Credit Approval

Any organization that is in the business of extending credit will have a process that, based on a set of inputs associated with an applicant, will determine whether the credit request is approved. Basically, this is an information chain that will ultimately provide a single yes-no answer based on the input values and some internal determination application and therefore falls into the class of a strategic data flow.

In the process, data is supplied from both the applicant and external agencies that collect data associated with creditworthiness. A data acquisition stage merges the data from the two sets of sources and forwards those records to a data processing stage, where the values of the records determine an answer. If the answer is yes, the answer is packaged and forwarded to another department, where the applicant is provided with the details of the approval (a credit card is imprinted with the applicant's name). An additional data packaging stage prepares a report detailing the credit application that is forwarded to an external data consumer, who may be the same data agent that originally supplied the process with data (see Figure 4.5).

4.3.3   Consumer-Directed E-Commerce

Interestingly, Web-based businesses combine aspects of the two data flows. We can focus on the user-oriented component of Web browsing. The browsing process is relatively mechanical but involves the user as data supplier, either through direct data acquisition interfaces or more directly through the user's clickstream. At the Web server location, the supplied data is acquired, then fed into a process to determine the next set of information to deliver to the user's browser. That information is packaged according to the http protocol and is delivered through the protocol back to the user's browser. At this point, the user faces a decision stage, where the choice is made as to the next set of pages to request from the server. Ultimately, the entire process is geared toward leading the user to make a decision to purchase a product.

A different aspect of the information chain occurs when the user decides to purchase a product. At that point the service must acquire information from the user. At that acquisition stage, the order is broken into the product order component, which is sent to a processing stage to determine if the product is in stock, and a payment component, which

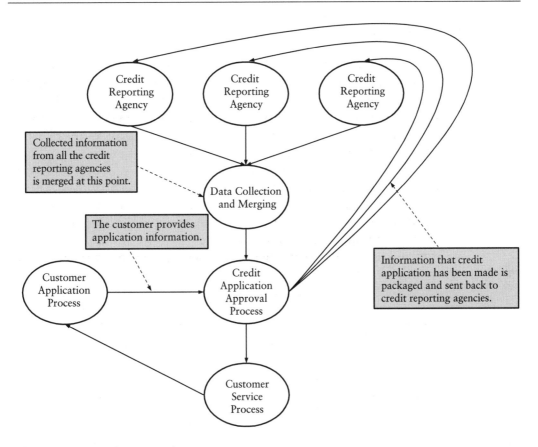

FIGURE 4.5 Credit Approval

is injected into a payment processing flow similar to the order fulfill-ment flow described in Section 4.3.1.

4.4 IMPACTS

We'd like to assume that if there are no data quality problems, either of the data flows described in Section 4.1 will operate smoothly. It is reason-able to rely on decisions based on valid data and that an operation system will function smoothly as long as no invalid data items gum up the works.

Issues appear when the information chains involve low quality data. The effects of low data quality propagate through the systems, ultimately leading to poor decision making, tactical difficulties, increased costs, reduced revenues, and lowered customer satisfaction. Similarly, improvements in data quality can lead to reduced costs, increased revenues, streamlined and effective decision making, and increased customer satisfaction.

Impacts can be divided into *soft* impacts, which are clearly evident but still hard to measure, and *hard* impacts, whose effects can be estimated and measured. Ultimately, the level of data quality rolls up to the company's bottom line: Allowing low levels of data quality to remain will lower profits, while improving data quality should increase profits.

4.4.1   Hard Impacts

Hard impacts are those whose effects can be estimated and/or measured. These include the following.

- Customer attrition
- Costs attributed to error detection
- Costs attributed to error rework
- Costs attributed to prevention of errors
- Costs associated with customer service
- Costs associated with fixing customer problems
- Time delays in operation
- Costs attributable to delays in processing

4.4.2   Soft Impacts

Soft impacts are those that are evident and clearly have an effect on productivity but are difficult to measure. These include the following.

- Difficulty in decision making
- Costs associated with enterprise-wide data inconsistency
- Organizational mistrust
- Lowered ability to effectively compete
- Data ownership conflicts
- Lowered employee satisfaction

4.5   ECONOMIC MEASURES

Simply put, how do we measure a cost or a benefit? Since we are trying to figure out the total economic benefit of improved data quality as compared to the economic detriment of poor data quality, each impact must relate to some quantification that goes directly to a company's bottom line. Again, for simplicity's sake, we boil down these measures into these categories.

1. *Cost increase*   This measures the degree to which poor data quality increases the cost of doing business.
2. *Revenue decrease*   This measures how low data quality affects current revenues.
3. *Cost decrease*   This measures how an improvement in data quality can reduce costs.
4. *Revenue increase*   This measures how improving data quality increases revenues.
5. *Delay*   This measures whether there is a slowdown in productivity.
6. *Speedup*   This measures the degree to which a process's cycle time can be reduced.
7. *Increased satisfaction*   This measures whether customer satisfaction, employee satisfaction, or shareholder satisfaction is increased.
8. *Decreased satisfaction*   This measures whether customer satisfaction, employee satisfaction, or shareholder satisfaction is decreased.

In each of these categories it is possible to measure with precision the actual economic impact, but because some impacts are difficult to tie down to precise dollar amounts, they must be estimated at orders of magnitude.

4.6   IMPACT DOMAINS

Low data quality has an impact on the operational domain, the tactical domain, and the strategic domain. Within each domain, the different kinds of cost measures and their effect on the economic model must be evaluated. Note that in all three domains relying on incorrect or unfit data will have a noticeable impact.

4.6.1   Operational Impacts

The operational domain covers the aspects of a system for processing information and the costs of maintaining the operation of that system. Operational issues typically are characterized as short-term issues, discrete in scope and reactive by nature. These impacts can be characterized as "immediately reactive."

As an example, fixing a broken pipe is operational because the action is in reaction to some event (the bursting of the pipe), it is limited in scope (does not represent a major investment in capital improvement but is meant to treat a problem), and it can be fixed using a short-term solution. Operational issues revolve around "how to do" or "when to do" something, and they are usually delegated to operations employees. Data quality problems that escape detection within the operational domain manifest themselves internally to the operational system (in other words, they gum up the works) and frequently find their way to customers.

4.6.2   Tactical Impacts

The tactical domain covers the aspects of "what to do" as opposed to how or when. Tactical issues are typically medium-term decisions made to address system problems before they arise. In other words, we can refer to these impacts as "reactive proactivity." Continuing with our pipe example, the decision to replace the plumbing infrastructure because of a burst pipe is a tactical decision. These kinds of decisions are usually made by those responsible for making sure things run smoothly, such as middle-level managers.

4.6.3   Strategic Impacts

The strategic domain stresses the decisions that affect the longer term. Strategic issues are proactive, less precise decisions that address "where to be" along a long time period. The burden of strategic decisions falls to the senior executives of an organization.

4.7   OPERATIONAL IMPACTS

The nature of the operational domain makes it easy to focus on hard impacts associated with low data quality. Data quality problems may be propagated from a supplier of data at the acquisition stage, can be introduced during any number of internal data creation stages, or can be introduced at the time of data packaging. We can associate these problems into cost categories: detection, correction, rollback, rework, prevention, and warranty costs.

As errors propagate out of the enterprise to the customer base, there is a risk of customer dissatisfaction, leading to lost revenues. We can classify risk areas for lost revenue as: spin, reduction, attrition, and blockading.

4.7.1   Detection

Detection costs are those incurred when a data quality problem provokes a system error or processing failure, and a separate process must be invoked to track down the problem. Error detection only happens when the system has the ability to recognize that an error has occurred. Sometimes this is implied by a total system failure, such as an incorrectly provided divisor of 0 that causes a system interrupt for dividing by zero. Sometimes this is implied by an abnormal end during transaction processing because of an invalid data record.

The cost of error detection is mostly associated with three activities: determining where the failure occurred, determining what caused the system failure, and determining the seriousness of the problem. This cost is mostly attributable to employee activity, although there are also costs associated with the purchase and maintenance of diagnostic tools.

4.7.2   Correction

Correction costs are associated with the actual correction of a problem as well as the restarting of any failed processes or activities. The amount of time associated with the activity that failed and extraneous employee activity are all rolled up into correction costs.

The critical point of correction is the earliest location in the information chain where the effect of fixing bad data is the expected execution of the process. Correction involves figuring out what the incorrect item should have been and then searching for the critical point of correction. Correction may require a modification to data, a modification to processing (software or operations), or both. The cost of correction encompasses all these activities.

4.7.3   Rollback

When work that had been performed needs to be undone, rollback costs are incurred. Rollbacks may be a straightforward undoing of a number of transactions or a complicated full restoration from backup.

4.7.4   Rework

When a processing stage must be repeated because of an error and the required correction, there are rework costs. Rework represents all work that was additionally performed before the successful run took place.

We expect that all system processes will run correctly each time they are invoked. When a process must be restarted to complete a successful run, the work that was already performed must be accounted to rework.

4.7.5   Prevention

Prevention costs arise when a new activity is designed, implemented, and integrated to identify data quality problems and to take the necessary actions to prevent operational failure due to unexpected data problems.

Frequently, prevention design and implementation costs can be amortized over a period of time as long as the prevention system is still in effect.

4.7.6   Warranty

Data quality problems that affect customers incur costs associated with both fixing the problem as well as compensation to customers for damages. These are warranty costs. Any risks and costs associated with legal action are also rolled up as warranty costs.

4.7.7   Spin

Spin control is a reaction to bad events that "makes them better." As errors propagate to the customers, more and more complaints will filter back to the organization. This in turn creates an increased need for customer service — improving the customer service systems, increases in personnel, telephone costs, and so on. Since customer service needs are directly tied to the quality of the product, a decrease in data quality will cause an increase in the costs of customer service.

A very simple, yet measurable, example of this is in telephone charges. Let's assume that a company has set up a toll-free telephone number for customer support. Because it is a toll-free number, the company pays the costs on a per-minute basis. If the average on-hold time for a customer increases from 5 to 10 minutes, that extra 5 minutes per person translates into an increased per-call cost, and as the number of complaints increases, so does the average on-hold time.

4.7.8   Reduction

Reduction occurs when a customer chooses to do less business with an organization because of its data quality problem. When a customer loses faith in a company's ability to properly conduct business, he or she will avoid the company until its performance improves or until the next revenue-reduction impact — attrition — is established.

For example, let's say we hire a billing agency to outsource our customer billing. This agency bills us on a monthly basis based on the volume of service that the agency provides. If we begin to see errors in the agency's monthly invoices, we would naturally doubt its ability to do a good job.

4.7.9   Attrition

Attrition occurs when a customer's reaction to poor data quality results in the customer no longer patronizing the business. This can be reflected in the business-to-business world, as illustrated in the example in Section 4.7.7, or in the consumer world.

It is not unusual to see errors on service or utility bills, requiring frequent calls to customer service departments. As the customer service requirements increase, this should be a signal that there may be a data quality problem that is escaping the confines of the organization.

4.7.10   Blockading

Blockading is the result of customer dissatisfaction so pervading that it alienates potential customers of the organization or causes current customers to leave. Occasional data quality problems that are exposed to customers may be tolerated overall, but the inability to resolve them will result in customer attrition. These former customers will also discourage others from doing business with the company.

This class of impact is prevalent in many places, including complaints to a better business bureau. Many good examples of this can be gleaned by reading Netnews postings complaining of billing errors or service interruptions. Very often a consumer reports a bad experience with some company and advises others to not patronize it. The speed and breadth of distribution of information on the Internet can only magnify this ability to spread negative opinions.

4.8   TACTICAL AND STRATEGIC IMPACTS

Enterprises collect data about the operation and effectiveness of the organization. This information can be relevant to the internal operations as well as external activity. These data are often used as input to decision-making processes. When information is incorrect or suspect, that can lead to delays in decision making or the preemption of a decision process. Delays in decision making at a senior level lead to delays in production — called idling — as well as increased difficulty in getting things done. On the other hand, a high level of data quality will enhance the decision-making process and prevent delays.

Other aspects of the tactical and strategic impact arenas include lost opportunities, organizational mistrust, and cross-business unit misalignment. There are also tactical maintenance costs associated with low data quality. We can classify these costs as acquisition overhead, decay, and infrastructure costs.

4.8.1   Delay

If data are not accessible, or the timely availability of the data is constrained, the decision-making process becomes delayed. A delay in making a decision will spread to the operational arena as well, causing productivity delays.

4.8.2   Preemption

If data are deemed untrustworthy, managers may decide to defer the decision making until the right information is available or choose to not make a decision at all. If the data are untrustworthy and the management is not aware of any problems, a spurious decision based on faulty data may be made, and it may ultimately affect the bottom line.

4.8.3   Idling

Idling takes place when delays in the decision-making process extend the amount of time needed to complete a project. When productive team members are waiting for executive decisions to be made, they cannot take the steps that must be taken to implement those decisions.

4.8.4   Increased Difficulty

Increased difficulty occurs when the information needed to assess a process, create a data warehouse, or reengineer a process is incorrect or unavailable. Additionally, increased difficulty can be encountered when team members implement incorrect or suboptimal decisions.

4.8.5   Lost Opportunities

As in the operational realm, data quality impacts of reduction, attrition, and blockading can have a serious impact on strategic initiatives.

4.8.6   Organizational Mistrust

Because managers encounter inconsistencies in the data they solicit to make decisions, they often choose to implement their own information acquisition and maintenance systems, frequently using the same data from the same data sources. This decision leads to redundant work when multiple teams build and maintain the same data. This also leads to inconsistency across the organization as entropy sets in.

The redundancy of data ownership eventually exacerbates territoriality in the company. The bunker mentality expressed in terms of "my data is better than your data" or the bottlenecks created when an employee no longer knows whom to contact to get a report all lead to decreased productivity and increased costs.

This kind of mistrust also can explode past the corporate boundary. A company's inability to set and execute business strategies leads to shareholder mistrust as well, resulting in decreased valuation of the business as a whole.

4.8.7   Misalignment

The issue of organizational mistrust compromises the ability to keep different business units aligned. Delays in decision making and silo mentalities divert executive management attention and allow a decentralization of organization and a decrease in corporate agility as the mistrust grows.

4.8.8   Acquisition Overhead

This is the cost associated with modifying or manipulating supplied data in order to make it usable within the system. This cost is incurred in two situations. The first is when supplied data do not conform to the specific needs internally and must be modified, merged, joined, or otherwise manipulated to prepare it for processing. The second is when the quality of the data supplied does not meet the internal expectations and additional processing is performed to bring the level of quality up to a usable point.

4.8.9   Decay

Information that is kept and never used or updated is subject to a degree of decay. Any activity that is used to keep stagnating information up to date, as well as the overhead of maintaining the information (storage, backup, etc.) is classified as a cost of decay.

4.8.10   Infrastructure

The costs of developing and maintaining an enterprise-wide shared data repository, as well as creating and maintaining redundant databases, are associated with infrastructure. This includes the construction of any reference databases or data warehouses, distribution data marts, information packaging, information delivery, and information display.

4.9   PUTTING IT ALL TOGETHER — THE DATA QUALITY SCORECARD

Now that we have all the pieces for our economic model, let's look at the actual steps involved in building it.

1. Map the information chain to understand how information flows within the organization.
2. Interview employees to determine what people are doing with respect to data quality issues.
3. Interview customers to understand the impacts on customers.
4. Isolate flawed data by reviewing the information chain and locating the areas where data quality problems are manifested.
5. Identify the impact domain associated with each instance of poor data quality.
6. Characterize the economic impact based on the ultimate effects of the bad data.
7. Aggregate the totals to determine the actual economic impact.
8. Identify opportunities for improvement.

The result is what we can call a data quality scorecard, shown in Figure 4.6. This scorecard summarizes the overall cost associated with low data quality and can be used as a tool to find the best opportunities for improvement.

4.9.1   Mapping the Information Chain

The first step in the analysis is mapping the information chain/data flows. Before assessing the impacts, the locations of the sources of those

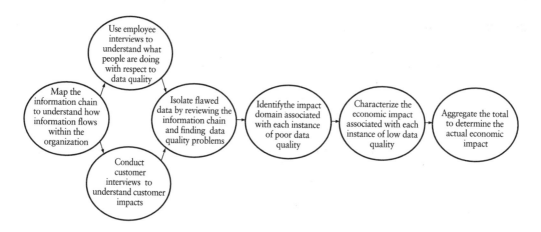

FIGURE 4.6   Steps in the Data Quality Scorecard

impacts within the system must be pinpointed. The information chain is a map composed of the processing stages connected by directed information channels. Each stage is annotated with its designation from Section 4.2.1.

4.9.2   Identifying the Data Flow

Once we have an information chain, the next step is to determine what data is being used within the system and at which information channel source and target points the data pass through. If possible, the record or message structure should be detailed, so that we can directly associate any error conditions with the specific data set in which the error occurs.

4.9.3   Employee Interviews

To understand the impact of flawed data within the organization, employees are interviewed. For each stage in the information chain, interview the people doing the actual work to determine the amount of time spent associated with each area of impact. The time for all employees can be aggregated into one time value.

4.9.4   Customer Interviews

To assess the impact due to decreased customer revenue, current and former customers are interviewed to determine the reasons for any decrease in business or attrition and blockading.

4.9.5   Isolating Flawed Data

With the results from the interviews in hand, it is time to start annotating the information chain. At each point where a data set is sent, received, or manipulated, any locations of a source of a data flaw are noted, along with a list of the activities attributable to those flaws.

4.9.6   Identifying the Impact Domain

With an information chain annotated with the list of both data flaws and the activities associated with each of those flaws, it is time to start attributing the flaws and activities to impact domains. For each source of low data quality, the impact domains are selected, and each activity is classified according to the classifications described in Sections 4.7 and 4.8.

4.9.7   Characterizing the Economic Impact

We can now build a matrix associated with each data quality problem. The first axis identifies the problem and its location in the information chain. The second axis represents the activities associated with each problem. The third axis denotes the impact areas for each activity. In each cell in this matrix, we insert the estimated cost associated with that impact, using the economic measures from Section 4.5. If no estimate can be made, an indication of the order of magnitude of the impact should be used.

Note that this matrix does not distinguish between hard and soft impacts. The values assigned to each cell can represent actual dollar values or coded indications of level of impact. Figure 4.7 shows the data quality scorecard matrix.

Reference ID	Data Quality Problem	Information Chain Location	Activity	Impact	Cost
1	Malformed credit card Numbers	Node 5	Credit Card Processing	Detection	$ 12,000.00
			Contact Customer	Correction	$ 7,000.00
				Rework	$ 20,000.00
2	Invalid addresses	Node 0	Direct Marketing	Detection	$ -
				Correction	$ 20,000.00
			Reduced Reach	Acquisition Overhead	$ 4,500.00
				Lost Opportunity	$ 9,000.00
3	Incorrect pick lists	Node 7	Shipping Processing	Detection	$ 25,000.00
				Correction	$ 21,000.00
			Customer Service	Warranty	$ 43,000.00
				Spin	$ 12,000.00
				Attrition	$ 50,000.00

FIGURE 4.7   The Data Quality Scorecard matrix

4.9.8   Aggregating the Total

The matrix described in Section 4.9.7 can be superimposed on a spreadsheet from which an aggregation model can be built. The costs can be tallied and summarized in different ways and can be used as input to the next stage, improvement.

4.9.9   Identify Opportunities for Improvement

The last component of this framework is using the model to look for the biggest "points of pain." Having categorized the location and the impacts of the different data quality problems, the next logical step is to find the best opportunities for improvement, where the biggest value can be gotten with the smallest investment.

4.10   ADJUSTING THE MODEL FOR SOLUTION COSTS

The final piece of the puzzle is computing a return on investment for improvement projects. Since there are costs associated with any improvement project, it must first be shown that the cost of the project is justified overall. We do this by adjusting our spreadsheet model to include the costs of the improvement projects but offset by the value yielded by the improvement project. The result is an environment for calculating return on investment (ROI) or break-even points for improvement project implementation.

For any suggested improvement, the cost of designing and implementing the improvement is added to the model, along with a time frame for the implementation of the improvement. Each improvement must correspond to the elimination of at least one cost impact. ROI is calculated based on the decrease in costs (or alternatively, increase in revenues) versus the cost associated with the improvement project. This analysis completes the economic framework.

4.11   EXAMPLE

As an example, consider our information chain example of order fulfillment from Section 4.3.1. One problem frequently occurs during the payment processing stage, when credit card numbers and their expiration dates are forwarded, along with the charges, to the merchant bank. There are two common, significant errors: invalid credit card numbers and invalid expiration dates. In either case, the charge will not go through successfully, with the result that (1) the payment cannot be processed and (2) the fulfillment center must analyze the mistake to determine the source of the problem.

Both of these activities have cost impact. So to determine the benefit of inserting a validation application before the payments are sent to the bank to check for those data quality violations, we must examine the actual impacts and how the improvement affects the impacts.

In this case there are detection, correction, rollback, and rework impacts. The detection occurs at the merchant bank site, as well as internally once the errors have been found. The correction may involve actually contacting the customer to get the correct information. The rollback is associated with any revenue booking policies that need adjustment because the payments did not actually go through. The rework is associated with any fulfillment processing performed on the unpaid orders.

Instituting the prevention application will have an effect on the detection, rollback, and rework impacts. The detection now takes place earlier in the process than after the data is sent to a data consumer (the merchant bank). Since the detection can be done before any other processing is performed, we can eliminate the rollback and rework costs, since they are preempted through early detection. On the other hand, the correction impact remains the same — if the card number or expiration date is incorrect, it is still necessary to contact the customer for the correct information.

Hopefully, our analysis will have told us how much time is being spent on rollback and rework associated with this set of data flaws. Our conclusion must be based on the cost of development and implementation of an error detection application, the time frame in which it can be implemented, and the break-even point based on the costs eliminated by the new application.

4.12   SUMMARY

In this chapter, we developed a framework for establishing the value proposition behind a data quality improvement process. Our main thrust is that there are real economic impacts of data quality problems, and the first step in addressing these problems is to build a data quality scorecard evaluating the cost of low data quality (COLDQ).

First, we looked at the factors indicating the existence of an economic impact, including frequent system failures, service interruptions, high employee turnover, customer attrition, and increased customer service requirements, among others. Using these indicators, we can begin to build the economic model.

The model itself consists of an information chain describing the flow of data throughout a system, which is later attributed with details about potential sources of data quality problems. An information chain consists of a set of processing stages connected by information channels. These building blocks allow us to describe both operational data flows and strategic data flows. We saw examples of different kinds of data flows.

The next step in building our framework is the delineation of impacts and impact domains. We characterize hard impacts as those that can be easily measured and soft impacts as those that are demonstrable but hard to measure. These impacts correlate to one of a number of economic measures, representing increase or decrease in cost, increase or decrease in revenue, increase or decrease in productivity, or increase or decrease in satisfaction. The impact domains include the operational, tactical, or strategic domains.

The last part of this chapter focused on putting the framework together into a real scorecard, which itemizes all areas of the data flow where poor data quality can affect the bottom line. This involved mapping the information chain, understanding the points of impact, characterizing the actual cost, and identifying opportunities for improvement. The value statement for each improvement can then be calculated in terms of a return on investment that can map directly to known areas of economic impact.

5

DIMENSIONS OF DATA QUALITY

The definition of poor data quality is similar to Justice Potter Stewart's definition of obscenity: We know it when we see it. If we truly want to improve data quality, however, we must find a way to measure it, and the first step in measuring something is to define what that something is. In this chapter, we try to define that "something" by listing the many dimensions of data quality.

Good data quality is frequently defined in terms of "fitness for use." Yet, it is difficult to delineate fitness when there are no metrics against which to measure it. Therefore, before we discuss how to improve data quality, let's first look at ways to measure it. The assessment of any data set's levels of data quality — whether data in a data warehouse or a stream of related messages in an inline processing system — can be done in the context of what are referred to as the dimensions of data quality. It is through the process of classifying requirements and setting measurement goals that data quality can be improved, and the action of defining this set of data quality dimensions is the beginning of this process.

The concept of data quality dimensions has been explored by Richard Wang and the Total Data Quality Management group at the Massachusetts Institute of Technology and is included in the book *Data Quality for the Information Age* by Thomas Redman. These dimensions can be used to identify users' data quality requirements, to delineate a product's data quality feature requirements, to measure the levels of data quality, and to identify the gaps and opportunities for data quality improvement.

The dimensions can be grouped by categories, distinguishing, for example, aspects of data models from the aspects of data presentation.

For our purposes, we use the categories that include these collections of data quality dimensions.

- Data models
- Data values
- Information domains
- Data presentation
- Information policy

We will use an example data application for illustrative purposes. First we will discuss the application of this data set, and the rest of the chapter will examine what issues come into play when building the data management system for this application.

5.1   SAMPLE DATA APPLICATION

The sample application will be a customer sales database consisting of two parts: current customers and potential customers. For each customer, name and contact information will be recorded. Sales information about current customers will be kept on file.

5.2   DATA QUALITY OF DATA MODELS

Any information-based application is built on top of a logical information framework called a data model. The data model describes the objects represented within the application, the attributes those objects take on, and the relationships between different objects within the application. Therefore, before talking about the levels of quality of the values in a data set, we must first talk about the suitability of the data model to represent the information that the user needs. The crux of the issue is understanding that while an application may mimic the real world, a "data model" is just that — a model.

Because of this, these data quality dimensions relate to ways of characterizing and measuring the data model's correspondence to the real world set of objects being modeled. In other words, adhering to the issues described in this section drives the definition of data quality requirements on the conceptual view of a data set, although most users are usually only vaguely aware, if at all, of these requirements.

The data model determines the ultimate usability of the information being represented. Assuming the data are accurate and there are appropriate mechanisms for capturing and presenting information, the data model must support the users' needs transparently. The data quality dimensions of data models clarify what we look for when discussing the data quality aspects of the representation of data.

5.2.1 Clarity of Definition

Clarity of definition refers to the nomenclature assigned to tables, fields, and relations within the system. When describing the components of the data model, the meanings of the names assigned to tables and fields should clearly reflect the sets of information they represent. This clarity should be reflected as unambiguous labels, as well as distinctive naming of similar attributes.

In our example, we may have an attribute in the customer table called "telephone number." Today, however, a telephone number may have many different meanings as part of a customer account. It could be a home number, an office number, a mobile telephone number, a personal toll-free number, a voice-mail system, or a fax number, among others. In our case, we might only be interested in the telephone numbers where the customer can be reached during telemarketing hours. For business customers, this may be during "business hours," while for residential customers, this may be during "evening hours." In our case, we would have an attribute named "marketing telephone number," which could then be distinguished from the other contact telephone numbers.

5.2.2 Comprehensiveness

When designing a data model, it is important to determine a scope that accommodates all the information pertinent to current users, as well as that of future users. Comprehensiveness is a measure of how well that scope has been covered.

There are two aspects to this dimension. The first is whether enough information is being modeled to adapt to future uses of the application, which implies that the users have thought about both their current and future needs. The second aspect is whether enough information is being modeled to support all the applications that might draw from that data set, which implies that all stakeholders in the application suite have had their say in the design of the model. If users are sharing information that serves different purposes, there may be other comprehensiveness requirements. Is the model comprehensive enough to allow the users to distinguish data based on their independent needs?

In our example, we are using both contact information and sales figures when representing our current customers. But with that same information, the billing department can also run its applications, although it may be more important to the billing department that there be a set of attributes indicating if the product has been shipped, if the customer has been billed, and if the customer has paid the bill. Therefore, the data model must be comprehensive enough to support both sets of requirements as well as enable the collection and support of extracting only the information that each data consumer needs.

5.2.3   Flexibility

A data model's flexibility reflects the capacity to change in reaction to new user requirements. Flexibility is similar to comprehensiveness, the difference being that comprehensiveness addresses what is planned a priori, whereas flexibility addresses those situations that crop up but were not part of the original plan. Restrictions on flexibility include situations where the form of a data attribute's value carries extra information about the attribute or where denormalization is built into the data model.

We can see an attribute carrying extra information in our example if we designate an attribute for an account number for our customers. If this attribute held seven-digit account numbers, where the first digit of the account number indicates the region in which the customer lives, that would be a restriction on flexibility. This would allow for 10 regions. If one region is split, making 11 regions, the account numbers can no longer maintain the region indicator in the first digit.

5.2.4   Robustness

Robustness represents the ability to reflect changes in the modeled world without excessive changes to the data model. Robustness includes the foresight to build a model that can adapt to changes, as well as the definition of attribute types and domains to hold the possible values that each attribute might contain in the future. Robustness also involves defining attributes in ways that adapt to changing values without having to constantly update the values.

In our example, we might want to keep track of how many years a customer has been associated with our organization. A nonrobust way to do this is with an attribute containing the number of years that the person has been a customer. Unfortunately, for each customer this attribute will need to be updated annually. A more robust way to maintain a customer's duration is to store the date of initial contact. That way, the number of years that the customer has been retained can be computed correctly at any time without having to change the attribute.

The Year 2000 problem (Y2K), for example, evolved because of a lack of robustness in many data models: a date attribute that has four digits to hold the year is more robust than a date attribute with only two digits.

5.2.5 Essentialness

On the other hand, a data model should not include extra information, except for specific needs like planned redundancy or the facilitation of analytical applications. Extraneous information requires the expense of acquisition and storage, and unused data, by nature of its being ignored, will have an entropic tendency to low data quality levels. In addition, redundant information creates the problem of maintaining data consistency across multiple copies.

Another potential problem with unessential attributes is the "overloading" effect. With applications that have been in production, it becomes very hard to modify the underlying data model without causing a lot of stress in the application code. For this reason, when a new attribute needs to be added, a behavioral tendency is to look for an attribute that is infrequently used and then overload the use of that attribute with values for the new attribute. This typically is manifested in program code with conditional statements with tests to make sure that the overloaded attribute is treated in the right manner (see Figure 5.1).

These kinds of conditionals are one basis for hidden business rules that get buried in program code and/or are passed along as "lore" within the information technology groups. The issue becomes a problem once the application has been in production for many years and the original application implementers are long gone.

Name	Current Customer	Total Yearly Sales
John Smith	G	$1,200.00
Jane Jones	N	
Robert Kalmer	M	$200.00
Brian Kahn	N	
Ellen Fitzpatrick	N	
Jason Balder	G	$1,564.00
Kathy Knowles	P	$10.00
Jacob Jansen	N	
Errol Smythe	G	$1,295.00

Note that in this attribute, instead of just using "Y" and "N" to indicate whether the party is a customer or not, if the value is not "N," the attribute is used to indicate the customer classification as either "G" for good, "M" for mediocre, or "P" for poor.

This attribute is overloaded, actually representing two different attributes.

FIGURE 5.1   An overloaded attribute

5.2.6   Attribute Granularity

Granularity refers to the number of objects used to represent one notion. If a data field can take on more values, it is said to be of a fine granularity. If it can take on fewer values, it is said to be of coarse granularity. In a table, more attributes may be used to convey finer granularity. While fine granularity can provide more detailed information because of the extra information being stored, there are added costs for storage, and there is a greater possibility for introducing errors.

In our example, consider a table called "Customer Sales." Customer sales may be measured by the day, week, month, quarter, or year. Representing customer sales by quarter, the data model may look like this.

Customer Sales = (customer id, product, Q1, Q2, Q3, Q4)

To gain a finer granularity, we can represent customer sales by month instead.

Customer Sales = (customer id, product, Jan, Feb, Mar,
Apr, May, Jun, Jul, Aug, Sep, Oct, Nov, Dec)

5.2.7   Precision of Domains

As opposed to granularity of attributes, precision refers to the degree of granularity that may be applied to an attribute's value. While the number of attributes in a set of attributes characterizes attribute granularity, precision refers to the number of values that can be taken by a single attribute. The precision is partially determined by the data type of the attribute, but is also predicated on subtyping that is applied to the domain.

In our example, consider when we maintain a tally of the total sales revenues generated from a certain customer. If we use a packed decimal or fixed-size sales column along with a country code and a currency code indicating the country and currency, we may allow acceptable precision when the currency is U.S. dollars but will not allow an acceptable precision when the currency is Turkish lira.

Another case would be if we create a ZIP code field in the address with five places. This may be sufficient for pre ZIP+4 United States addresses, but it will not be able to accommodate Canadian or British postal codes.

5.2.8   Homogeneity

Overloaded attributes were introduced in Section 5.2.5 with respect to the overloaded use of nonessential attributes. Here we see the overloading of value classes within a used attribute. Often, while a data model is intended to maintain a single class of entities, the use of the model evolves to overload the data set to maintain multiple classes of entities within the same database.

In our example, this might occur when we want to be able to distinguish between different classes of customers, such as high-yield customers who generate greater than $1,000 a month in sales versus maintenance customers whose monthly sales are less than $200. In this case, we have two different kinds of customers that are being maintained within a single attribute.

Usually, this subclassing is evidenced by "footprints" in the accompanying application code. These conditional statements and extra support code are representative of business rules that are actually embedded in the data and are only unlocked through program execution. As this happens more and more, the application code will become more and more convoluted and will require some sort of reverse engineering to uncover the business rules. The evolution of subclassing of attribute values will eventually necessitate the insertion of new attributes by the database administrator to allow distinction between entities in each subclass.

5.2.9 Naturalness

Naturalness is a qualification of the relationship between what is being modeled and the model's representation, meaning that each represented attribute should pair with a natural object in the world being modeled. Also, each attribute should represent a single fact about the object and pull its values from a meaningfully natural (in other words, not artificially restricted) domain.

This is not to say that restricted domains are not a good idea. On the contrary, natural value domains may be defined as a subset of a "base" type. In our example, consider the account number (used above in the flexibility dimension) to illustrate this dimension. Having assigned the first digit of the seven-digit account number to represent the sales region, we have an unnatural representation of account number. Should a new sales region be opened, bringing the total to more than 10 regions, the representation will no longer be sufficient to represent all possible accounts. Additionally, should more than 999,999 accounts be opened in any region, there will also be a problem. These problems, due to the fact that one attribute is overloaded for information, can be fixed by having a more natural representation, breaking out the region from the account number and keeping it as a separate attribute.

5.2.10 Identifiability

In relational database systems, as well as in most data set collections, where there is a presumption that each entity (used in the generic sense, not the relational database sense) is unique, there must be some absolute means for distinguishing between any pair of entities. If not, there is a possibility that there are multiple records representing the same individual entity. Therefore, each entity type must allow for unique identification.

Identifiability is maintained via the presence of a primary key to the data set. A primary key is a set of (one or more) attributes that, when composed, form a unique reference into the data set. Because identifiability is contingent on the uniqueness of the primary key, this dimension drives an obvious data quality requirement that all primary key values be unique, which, surprisingly, is not always the case. In our example, we might assign a new attribute called "customer id" to each customer, and we will make sure that any newly assigned customer id is unique.

Data sets whose models are not built with a specific primary key must be checked for some kind of identifiability (perhaps through a combination of attributes, if no single attribute will work). In Chapter 13 we will discuss how to determine a unique primary key if one is not defined from the beginning. Once a primary key is discovered and the user chooses to maintain that set of attributes, the primary key constraint must be established as a business rule and maintained as the data set evolves.

5.2.11 Obtainability

Obtainability is a dimension that qualifies whether the information to be modeled can be collected and stored. This obtainability may be characterized by a measure of the ease and feasibility of collection and storage, as well as more obtuse issues such as legality of information collection or storage. Building a model to represent values that are difficult (or impossible) to obtain will probably result in having attributes that will remain mostly empty.

In our example, an attribute totaling each customer's assets might be useful when trying to determine the customer's ability to afford our products, but it is unlikely that any customer will willingly provide that information, and without a significant investment on our part, it will be relatively hard to obtain. As a good example of a legal constraint on obtainability, consider a Human Resources department database on hiring and employee information. An attribute representing candidate age is probably an unobtainable attribute.

5.2.12 Relevance

Obviously, it is important that the information being stored is relevant. An irrelevant attribute is one that, if it were removed, would have no effect on either the application as it is being run today or on any of the planned features of the application.

In our example, maintaining a list of addresses associated with an account is important, but if there is no additional attribute that indicates the reason for each address's association with the account, then those extra addresses are irrelevant. It is conceivable that with some additional attributes, or with better definition clarity, what appears to be irrelevant can be made useful. For example, if we have two address attributes but one is called "billing address" and the other is called "shipping address," there is some distinction between the two addresses and therefore some relevance.

5.2.13 Simplicity

The simplicity dimension refers to the complexity in the data model. Complexity in a model, whether it is due to extra attributes or a complicated relationship between attributes, can lead to errors. Complexity in the data model manifests itself over time in terms of complications in the associated application code. Another way of looking at complexity is looking at how easy it is to understand the model. Simplicity is hard to quantify, but, fortunately, its opposite — is not so problematical (although it's not that easy either!).

An example of complexity in a data set is if the account type attribute is set to a value within one range, there must be a set of associated addresses for delivery of a product, but if the account type falls within a different range, alternate delivery instructions must be specified. A "model normalization" might break the account types into more homogeneous object classes and then specify the rules for attributes within each object class separately.

5.2.14 Semantic Consistency

Semantic consistency refers to consistency of definitions among attributes within a data model as well as similarly named attributes in different data sets. Semantic consistency is a dimension that characterizes the degree to which the meanings and the names of objects within the data set are consistent. One aspect of semantic consistency involves the meanings of similarly named attributes in different data sets. The meanings of these attribute names should be distinguished, or the attributes should be assigned different names.

In our example, we are maintaining two tables, one for current customers and one for potential customers. In each table, there is an attribute for the name of the party. If both tables have that attribute named "customer name," we could claim there is a semantic consistency problem, since the potential customer database really does not contain customers but only *potential* customers. This is a subtle difference, but the meanings are different and the distinction should be noted.

Another example would be if that same customer name attribute were meant to represent the name of a single party. Sometimes composite names appear in data sets, such as "DBA" names ("Doing Business As") or trust accounts. What does it mean to have a composite name entered in that field? Semantic consistency would require that if the attribute represents a single party's name, then composite names are not to be allowed. In fact, this particular issue is a very common occurrence in customer and account databases (see Figure 5.2).

Another aspect of semantic consistency involves definitions of relations between tables. Data models contain many tables, and as applications mature, the size of the encompassing database grows. When this happens, new relations between tables appear, whether planned or by chance. Foreign key relations between tables based on a set of attributes belonging to the two tables are very common. If two attributes are assumed to be related, the definition of that relation should be made clear.

5.2.15   Structural Consistency

Structural consistency refers to the consistency in the representation of similar attribute values, both within the same data set and across the data models associated with related tables. Structural consistency is a characterization of the care taken by the database modelers, administrators, and stewards in guaranteeing "strong-typing" of similar attributes. This dimension can be measured across two axes. The first regards how different attributes of the same virtual type are represented, and

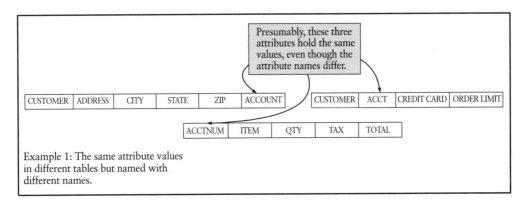

Example 1: The same attribute values
in different tables but named with
different names.

Example 2: This attribute is supposed
to refer to customer name, but in these
records, we see that the field often
represents more than one customer.

FIGURE 5.2   Breaks from Semantic Consistency

the second regards the degree to which there are different representations for the same value.

The first axis can be shown by this example: If our model has attributes for date of first contact and date of last sale, it is preferable to use the
same representation of dates in both attributes, both in structure (month,
day and year) and in format (American dates vs European dates). An
example of the second axis is measured by enumerating the different ways
that dates are maintained within the system. We will examine these issues
in the discussion of domains and mappings in Chapter 7.

5.3   DATA QUALITY OF DATA VALUES

Because low levels of quality of data values are the most obvious to observers, when most people think of data quality, they think of these most easily understood data quality dimensions. Low levels of data value quality are likely to be recognized by both the users (as well as customers!) and are most likely to lead the user to conclusions about the reliability (or lack thereof) of a data set. In an environment where data are not only being used to serve customers but also as input to automatic knowledge discovery systems (that is, data mining), it is important to provide high levels of data quality for the data values. Relying on bad data for decision-making purposes leads to poor strategic decisions, and conclusions drawn from rules derived from incorrect data can have disastrous effects.

Data value quality centers around accuracy of data values, completeness of the data sets, consistency of the data values, and timeliness of information. Most data quality tools are designed to help improve the quality of data quality values. In Chapter 8, we build a framework for describing conformance to dimensions of data value quality as a set of business rules that can be applied to the data set and used to measure levels of data value quality.

5.3.1   Accuracy

Data accuracy refers to the degree with which data values agree with an identified source of correct information. There are different sources of correct information: a database of record, a similar, corroborative set of data values from another table, dynamically computed values, the result of a manual workflow, or irate customers. Inaccurate values don't just cause confusion when examining a database — bad data values result in increased costs. When inaccuracies reach the customers, costs can increase due to increased pressure on customer service centers, searches for the inaccuracies, and the necessity to rework the process.

In our example data set, an inaccurate shipping address will result in errors delivering products to the customers. The repercussions may be great: A customer will delay payment, cancel the order, and even cease to be a customer.

5.3.2   Null Values

A null value is a missing value. However, a value that is missing may provide more information than one might think because there may be different reasons that it is missing. A null value might actually represent an unavailable value, an attribute that is not applicable for this entity, or no value in the attribute's domain that correctly classifies this entity. Of course, the value may actually be missing!

Even though databases may provide a default representation for the null value, there may be times when a specific internal representation of a null value is needed. An example of a poor design for null value representation is the use of 99/99/99 as a null date.

5.3.3   Completeness

Completeness refers to the expectation that certain attributes are expected to have assigned values in a data set. Completeness rules can be assigned to a data set in three levels of constraints.

1. Mandatory attributes that require a value
2. Optional attributes, which may have a value
3. Inapplicable attributes (such as maiden name for a single male), which may not have a value

We will see that completeness can be prescribed on a single attribute or can be dependent on the values of other attributes within a record or message. We can also discuss completeness with respect to a single attribute across all records or with respect to a record.

In our example, we decide that a record is considered incomplete if the daytime telephone number attribute is missing. There are two implications: No entry in the "daytime telephone" column is empty and no record may be inserted into the database if the daytime telephone attribute is missing.

5.3.4   Consistency

Consistency can be curiously simple or dangerously complex. In its most basic form, consistency refers to data values in one data set being consistent with values in another data set. But what does consistency really mean? If we follow a strict definition, then two data values drawn from separate data sets may be consistent with each other, yet both can be incorrect. Even more complicated is the notion of consistency with a set of predefined constraints. We may declare some data set to be the "database of record," although what guarantees that the database of record is of high quality?

More formal consistency constraints can be encapsulated as a set of rules that specify consistency relationships between values of attributes, either across a record or message, or along all values of a single attribute. These consistency rules can be applied to one or more dimensions of a table — or even across tables.

In our example, we can express one consistency constraint for all values of a ZIP code attribute by indicating that each value must conform to the U.S. Postal Service structural definition. A second consistency constraint declares that in every record, the ZIP code attribute's value must be consistent with the city attribute's value, validated through a lookup table. A third consistency constraint specifies that if the ZIP code represents an area within a qualified geographic region, the account specified by the account number field must be associated with a salesman whose territory includes that geographic region.

The first consistency constraint applies to a single attribute. The second applies to a relationship between two attributes within the same record. The third constraint applies to values in different tables. Consistency constraints can be arbitrarily complex — as shown by these three examples — and they frequently reflect business rules inherent in the applications using the data.

5.3.5 Currency/Timeliness

Currency refers to the degree to which information is current with the world that it models. Currency can measure how up to date information is and whether it is correct despite possible time-related changes.

Timeliness refers to the time expectation for accessibility of information. Timeliness can be measured as the time between when information is expected and when it is readily available for use.

In our example, we like to maintain customer addresses, but because we live in a mobile society, many of our customers move each year, leaving our address data slightly less than current. An example of a timeliness issue deals with publishing our product price list on a Web site. To make sure that we do not charge a customer the wrong price, we need to guarantee that the time lag between a product price change and the new price's appearance on the Web site is minimized!

5.4   DATA QUALITY OF DATA DOMAINS

A data domain, which will be discussed in greater detail in Chapter 7, is a collection of values that are related somehow, by definition, and represent a recognized authority for data sourcing. Data domains are restrictions on larger sets of values. A data domain can either be descriptive, which means that the set of values can be derived from some prescription applied to the larger set of values, or enumerated, in which all the values are explicitly listed.

A mapping exists between two domains when we express a relationship that associates any selected value in the first domain with one or more values in the second domain. As with domains, mappings may be descriptive or enumerated.

An example of a descriptive domain is the format definition for valid Social Security numbers. An example of an enumerated domain is a list of currencies accepted for payment for our products.

Domains and mappings are ubiquitous in databases. It is through domain discovery and analysis that denormalized tables can be normalized, and many data quality rules and business rules can be expressed in terms of relations between domains and mappings. The data quality dimensions associated with data domains include enterprise agreement of usage, stewardship, and ubiquity.

5.4.1   Enterprise Agreement of Usage

The notion of abstracting information into a data domain implies that there are enough users of the same set of data that it makes sense to manage that data set separately as a resource instead of having separate groups manage their own versions. The dimension of enterprise agreement of usage measures the degree to which different organizations conform to the usage of the enterprise data domain of record instead of relying on their own data set.

In our example, a usage agreement that we might make is to decide to use a shared ZIP code database to fill in the ZIP code field of customer addresses.

5.4.2   Stewardship

A dimension of data quality is the degree to which responsibility has been assigned for the stewardship of information domains. Since a data domain represents a collection of data values that are recognized as a data source of record, it is advisable to appoint a steward to be responsible for the upkeep and maintenance of the data domains. The degree of stewardship should increase as the agreement of usage across the enterprise grows.

5.4.3   Ubiquity

As a data quality–oriented organization matures, the agreement of usage will move from a small set of "early adopters" to gradually encompass more and more of the enterprise. Ubiquity measures the degree to which different departments in an organization use shared reference data.

5.5   DATA QUALITY OF DATA PRESENTATION

Data quality does not only apply to the way that information is represented and stored. On the contrary, there are dimensions of data quality that are related to the way that information is presented to the users and the way that information is collected from the users. Typically, we would like to measure the quality of labels, which are used for naming or identifying items in a presentation; classification categories, which indicate specific attributes within a category; and quantities, which indicate the result of measurement or magnitude of quantitative values.

We also want to look at formats, which are mappings from data to a set of symbols meant to convey information. The format for representing information depends on the application. As an example, in our application, we might want to report on sales activity within certain geographical ranges. We can take a dry approach and deliver a report of numbers of sales by product within each region, sorted by dollars, or we might take a different approach in providing a map of the region with color-coding for each product with intensities applied to indicate the sales ranges.

Formats and presentations can take many different attributes. Color, intensity, icons, fonts, scales, positioning, and so forth can all augment the presentation of text or numbers stored in a data set. Even though data may be stored in a traditional format, the presentation to the user is one that gives a multidimensional view of what information is inherent in the data.

5.5.1   Appropriateness

Appropriateness is the dimension we use to categorize how well the format and presentation of the data match the users needs. In our example, there is a difference between a high-level monthly sales report that is supplied to senior management and the daily product manifests that are handed to the shipping department for product packaging.

A data presentation is not appropriate if its intended users never look at it. There is an apocryphal story that revolves around a company's enterprise-wide system renovation. Each day, thousands of reams of paper reports were generated, and an entire department was dedicated to the collation and dispersal of these reports. Because the company wanted to reduce the amount of generated reports, the question arose as to how to determine which reports could be eliminated.

Because of the size of the system, it was difficult to see which reports depended on which other reports, so no decision was made until eventually this idea was proposed: Delay the daily delivery of the printed reports by one hour and wait to see who complained. That would be a clear indication that those who did not complain did not consider the reports critical, and these would be the first candidates for elimination.

5.5.2   Correct Interpretation

A good presentation provides the user with everything required for the correct interpretation of information. When there is any possibility of ambiguity, a key or legend should be included.

In our example, consider an attribute that represents priority of customer service calls, with the domain being integer values from 0 to 10. While it may have been clear to the data modeler that 0 represents the highest priority and 10 the lowest, the presentation of that attribute in the original integer form may confuse the user if he or she is not familiar with the direction of the priority scale. The presentation of the information, therefore, should not display the integer value of the priority, which might be confusing. Instead, providing an iconic format, such as incremental intensities of the color red, to indicate the degree of importance of each particular call. This is shown in Figure 5.3.

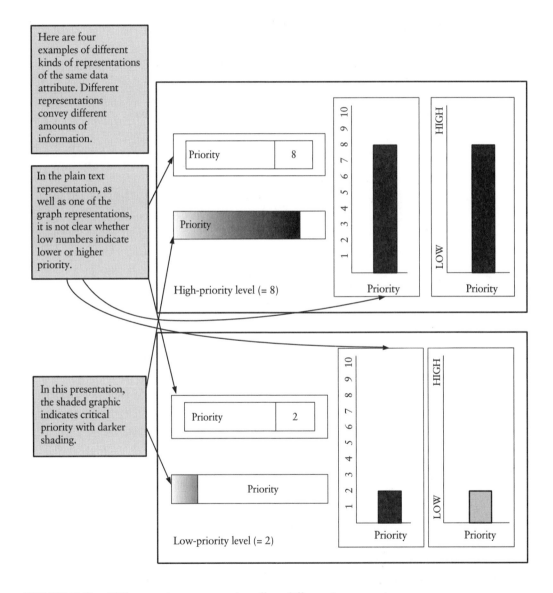

FIGURE 5.3 Differences in representation allow different interpretation

5.5.3   Flexibility

Flexibility in presentation describes the ability of the system to adapt to changes in both the represented information and in user requirements for presentation of information. For example, a system that displays different countries' currencies may need to have the screen presentation change to allow for more significant digits for prices to be displayed when there is a steep devaluation in one county's currency.

5.5.4   Format Precision

The degree of precision of the presentation of an attribute's value should reasonably match the degree of precision of the value being displayed. The user should be able to see any value the attribute may take and also be able to distinguish different values.

In many older systems, there was a limit on the number of significant digits that could be shown for floating-point values. In these systems, the screen display of a value with more significant digits than the allowed limit showed either a truncated or rounded value, neither of which represented the actual value. If the value were too large or too small, the value might be either displayed incorrectly or not appear at all.

5.5.5   Portability

In an environment that makes use of different kinds of systems and applications, a portable interface is important so that as applications are migrated from one platform to another, the presentation of data is familiar to the users. Also, when dealing with a system designed for international use, the use of international standards as well as universally recognized icons is a sign of a system designed with presentation portability in mind.

5.5.6   Representation Consistency

This dimension refers to whether instances of data are represented in a format that is consistent with the domain of values and with other similar attribute values. For example, the display of time in a nonmilitary

(12-hour) format may be confusing if all other instances of times in the system are displayed in the 24-hour military format.

5.5.7 Representation of Null Values

When the null value (or absence of a value) is required for an attribute, there should be a recognizable form for presenting that null value that does not conflict with any valid values. This means that for a numerical field, if the value is missing, it is not an indication that it may be represented to the user as the value 0, since the presence of any number there may have different meaning than the absence of the value. Also, if there are ways of distinguishing the different kinds of null values (see Section 5.3.2), then there should also be different ways of presenting those null values.

5.5.8 Use of Storage

Over the past few years there has been an incredible reduction in the cost of disk storage to the point where it seems silly to think about conserving disk space when building and using a database. Yet, just as the interstate highway system encouraged travel by automobile, the high availability of inexpensive disk space encourages our penchant for collecting and storing data.

It is important to remember that even though disk space is inexpensive, it is not unlimited. A dimension of data quality, therefore, is in the evaluation of storage use. This is not to say that the only issue is to squeeze out every last bit. Instead, it is in investigating how effectively the storage requirements are offset by other needs, such as performance or ease of use. For example, the traditional relational database is assumed to be in normal form, but in some analytical databases, databases are specifically denormalized to improve performance when accessing the data.

5.6   DATA QUALITY OF INFORMATION POLICY

5.6.1   Accessibility

The dimension of accessibility refers to the degree of ease of access to the information. This includes both how easy it is to access the information in the system and whether all the information can be accessed. This also includes determining if the presentation allows for the display of all expected information and whether the presentation is in a form that allows the user to absorb it as well. This dimension refers only to that information that is allowed to be presented to any selected subset of users. Privacy and security are separate dimensions of data quality.

In our example, it is important that senior managers have easy access to all sales data for each of the sales representatives for the past 18 months. This not only means that an 18-month sliding window of the database must be kept available at all times, but that there should also be application code to retrieve and display that information.

5.6.2   Metadata

Metadata is data about the data in the system. The dimension of data quality policy regarding metadata revolves around whether there is an enterprise-wide metadata framework (which differs from a repository). Is it required to maintain metadata? Where is it stored, and under whose authority? Metadata is particularly interesting, and we cover it in Chapter 11.

5.6.3   Privacy

If there is a privacy issue associated with any data set, there should be a way to safeguard that information to maintain security. Privacy is an issue of selective display of information based on internally managed permissions. It involves the ways unauthorized users are prevented from accessing data and ensures that data are secured from unauthorized viewing. Privacy is a policy issue that may extend from the way that data is stored and encrypted to the means of transference and whether the information is allowed to be viewed in a nonsecure location (such as on a laptop while riding on a train).

5.6.4   Redundancy

Data redundancy refers to the acquisition and storage of multiple copies of equivalent data values. Planned redundancy is desirable in that it provides fault-tolerance and may improve the accessibility of information. It may even ease political issues of ownership. But redundancy becomes unwieldy when organizations have a dozen or more copies of the same data. This leads to the opportunity for copies to become unsynchronized and for data to become stale. Unplanned redundancy increases costs and increases the opportunities for consistency flaws to creep into the enterprise system.

5.6.5   Security

The dimension of security is the protection of data from harm, unauthorized modifications, or unwanted destruction. Security is similar to privacy, except that privacy deals with protecting the entities being modeled by the system, whereas security protects the data itself.

5.6.6   Unit Cost

The costs incurred to obtain values, maintain levels of data quality, store data, and so on all comprise the cost of maintaining information. The cost of building data quality into an information product must be weighed against the cost of not having data quality. This includes both tangibles costs, such as the cost of rework and failed applications due to bad input, and intangible costs, such as low customer satisfaction, decrease in reputation, and loss of revenues.

5.7   SUMMARY: IMPORTANCE OF THE DIMENSIONS OF DATA QUALITY

In this chapter, we have looked at the dimensions of data quality that correspond to data models, data values, data domains, data presentation, and data policy. Understanding the notion of data quality dimensions gives us a starting point to a set of variables that we can start to measure, probe, and attempt to improve.

An interesting characteristic is that the different dimensions of data quality take on different levels of importance to different organizations. For some companies, just ensuring that data values are correct may be the most important issue, while other companies care more about the way that their information is presented. The critical point is that before we can improve the quality of data, we must first choose those dimensions that we care about most. It is at that point that we can begin to define our expectations and then measure how the data meet those expectations. Only then can we begin to improve data quality overall.

The list of dimensions of data quality is extensive, yet it is never really finished. As we continue collecting information and trying to make use of that information, we will find more and more ways in which that information may yield unexpected surprises. Maybe you already know an area of data quality that could be added to this list!

6

STATISTICAL PROCESS CONTROL AND THE IMPROVEMENT CYCLE

In Chapter 5, we looked at the different dimensions of data quality, with the understanding that in any system, there are a number of specific aspects of data quality that may be important to the users. In this chapter, we see how we can use those well-defined dimensions and specifically quantify the levels of data quality. We establish the tools used for initiating the measurement and for determining at a gross level the degree of conformance to data quality standards. In Chapters 7 and 8, we will define a framework for defining data quality rules, and in Chapter 9 we will discuss ways to measure the data quality dimensions discussed. Together, the next four chapters constitute the measurement gauges we use in the evaluation and measurement of data quality.

In the early 1920s, Walter Shewhart at Bell Laboratories performed a number of sampling studies that led to the development of a quality tool known as Statistical Process Control. By evaluating the occurrence of faults, defects, and errors in the manufacturing process, Shewhart discovered that, just as in nature, there are all sorts of variations that can occur during a manufacturing process. He determined that by studying the different kinds of variations (that is, the ones that generate unusable end products) and evaluating the root causes behind them, the occurrences of poor quality can be identified and the processes causing those irregularities can be improved.

These notions don't just apply to product manufacture. They also apply to data quality, and in this chapter we look at the use of Statistical Process Control (SPC) as a way to provide a context for a continuous data quality improvement cycle. SPC is a process of instituting measurements during a manufacturing process to both control quality and detect variations in quality as items are being produced, instead of finding them during inspection after production.

In this chapter, we first explore the notions of variation and control, followed by a discussion of the tools used for evaluating SPC. We look at the construction of control charts and the use of the Pareto Principle for identifying the variables that most affect the system. We then explore control charts in greater detail, looking at some of the different kinds of charts that can be used for analyzing SPC in the context of data quality.

6.1   VARIATION AND CONTROL

Variation occurs in many contexts, but in any quality program, we must be able to distinguish between those variations that are meaningless and those that have an adverse effect on the stability of the system. In other words, how can we differentiate between normal, expected variations and those that are business critical? And given the fact that different business environments have different characteristics, it may be possible that the same set of variations may be meaningless in one area and very critical in another!

To bring these questions into focus, we must look at the different kinds of variation within a system and the concept of a process in control. In any quality process, the goal is to narrow the possibility for unexpected and unwanted variation in the manufacturing process. In the data quality sense, since we consider the provision of information as a manufacturing process, we can use the notion of quality control as a means for monitoring data quality throughout a system. Statistical Process Control is a tool used to monitor control, but before we explore SPC, we must first understand the nature of variations and control.

6.1.1   Causes of Variation

Shewhart's studies focused on distinguishing between expected variations that occurred within a manufacturing process and any significant fluctuations that indicated a problem with the manufacturing process. He isolated two main causes of variation.

1. *Chance, or common, causes.* These are minor fluctuations or small variations in the end product that do not have to be fixed.

2. *Assignable, or special, causes.* These are specific causes of variation, resulting in significant fluctuation in the level of quality.

While specific variations from common causes are not predictable in their own right, their occurrences are likely to form a pattern, and Shewhart's observation was that they formed a normal distribution. Because of this, we expect that when we measure variation in a process, there are limits to the number of variations due to chance causes. The implication is that when we see fluctuation in the process that exceeds those limits, it is probably due to a special cause, which should then be investigated.

An example might be tracking the on-time performance of a railroad line. The train's departure and arrival times can be recorded daily and variations from the scheduled times measured. We would expect that from day to day, the train will likely be a little early, on time, or a little late. The times that the train is slightly early or late are due to common causes. But one day, a large electrical storm knocked out power from the third rail, causing systemwide delays. On that day, the train arrived an hour late, due to an assignable cause.

As another example, let's consider a simple information collection process and look at the different kinds of variations that might occur. Say we have several people transcribing names and addresses from hard-copy lists into a computer sales database. We can expect that, overall, most of the transcribers will make some kind of typographical error, perhaps substituting one letter for another. These errors are all due to common causes. Now let's say all of a sudden the "e" key on one of the keyboards breaks, creating consistent errors from that computer. This is an example of errors due to a special cause.

6.1.2 Statistical Control

According to the ANSI/ISO/ASQC standard A3534–1993 (*Statistics — Vocabulary and Symbols*), the state of statistical control is the state in which the observed sampling results can be attributed to a system of chance causes that does not appear to change with time. A process is in control (that is, it is *stable*) if each of its quality measures is in a state of statistical control.

What this means is that, having selected a set of variables or attributes of a process to measure based on random sampling, we expect that if the system is in control, there will be a normal distribution of variations and that the specific occurrences of variations will be random. If we observe that this is not the case, there must be some special cause to which this pattern or variation can be attributed, which then must be further explored.

6.2   CONTROL CHART

To determine whether an information process is in control, we must sample data to see how well it conforms to our expectations of data quality. We can sample data at predesignated points or at different points in the information chain. In addition, samples must be taken over a period of time to see whether there are any significant changes. The data samples can be integrated into a simple tool to record data quality measures over a certain time period that will highlight the differences between chance causes and assignable causes of variation. This tool is called a *control chart,* which is a graphical representation of the variations produced from a process.

Simply, a control chart plots the values of a time series or a sample series along with upper and/or lower control limits. A central line can be shown to display the typical (or mean) behavior of the system and to detect trends toward either of the control limits. Control limits are plotted lines above and below the central line to bound the space in which expected variations will occur.

Control limits are not defined by the customer but instead are determined by observing behavior over the series. Because the common causes form a normal distribution, we first need to determine how that distribution is reflected within the normal expectations. A process is said to be stable as long as all the points fall between the control limits. Figure 6.1 shows an example of a control chart.

6.3   THE PARETO PRINCIPLE

In any systems with causes and effects, the bulk of the effects are caused by a small percentage of the causes. This concept, called the Pareto Principle, has been integrated into common parlance as the "80–20 rule" — 80 percent of the effect is caused by 20 percent of the causes. This rule is often used to establish the degree of effort that must be

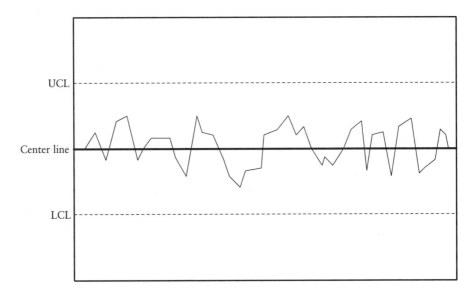

FIGURE 6.1   Control chart

expended on a particular project. If the rule of thumb is that 80 percent of the benefit can be achieved with 20 percent of the work necessary for completion, then the project will go forward, at least until the 80 percent benefit has been achieved.

In fact, the Pareto Principle has a more interesting application in that we use Pareto analysis to determine what aspects of a system (or in our case, data quality) are to be incorporated into the SPC process. A Pareto chart is a bar chart representing the measurement of specific aspects of a system. The presentation of the chart is based on cumulative frequency measurements of particular metrics, ordered from the greatest to the least frequency. The chart highlights the areas responsible for the greatest percentage of a problem and the variables involved in those areas (see Figure 6.2).

Another interesting corollary to the Pareto Principle is that as the larger problems are solved, there is a diminished opportunity for subsequent improvements. In other words, once we have attacked and conquered the first three or four problems, it is not likely that we will achieve significantly more improvements from attacking any additional problems. This is actually quite reassuring, since it means that we can limit the amount of effort to be expended on improving a particular area!

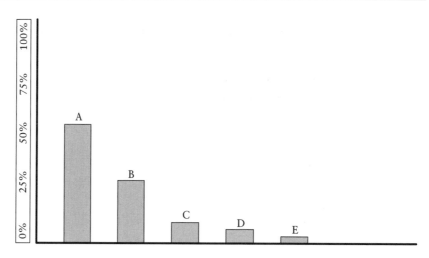

FIGURE 6.2   Pareto chart

Pareto analysis is used in performance improvement. A computer program that is not running up to speed is subjected to a series of profiling processes that gauge the time spent in each individual functional component. The professional performance technician then looks at the function in which the most time was spent, with an eye toward improving the performance of that function. Let's say we had these data points.

Function	Total Seconds
Foo	56
Bar	26
Baz	8
Boz	6
Raz	4
Faz	2

Together, these six functions account for 100 percent of the runtime of the program, totaling 102 seconds. If we can speed up function Foo by a factor of 2, we will have reduced the runtime of the entire application by 28 percent (half of the time of function Foo), making the total time now 74 seconds. A subsequent improvement in the function Bar of a factor of 2 will result in only an additional 13 percent improvement over the original runtime (actually, the effect is 18 percent of the current runtime, due to the previous reduction in runtime from improving Foo).

If we then focus on improving the runtime of function Baz by a factor of 2, the best speedup we can achieve is now a mere 4 seconds, which will only slightly improve our performance from 61 seconds to 57 seconds. The same improvement in function Boz only reduces the speed by another 3 seconds. As you can see, the same amount of effort expended on making improvements results in a rapidly decreasing benefit.

By performing a Pareto analysis, we can use the results to focus attention on the areas that are contributing the most to the problem. The variables that contribute to these areas become the variables or attributes that are to be incorporated into the control chart.

6.4   BUILDING A CONTROL CHART

Our next step is to build a control chart. The control chart is made up of data points consisting of individual or aggregated measures associated with a periodic sample enhanced with the center line and the upper and lower control limits.

These are the steps to building a control chart for measuring data quality.

1. Select one or more data quality dimensions to be charted. Use the Pareto analysis we discussed in Section 6.3 to determine the variables or attributes that most closely represent the measured problem, since trying to track down the most grievous offenders is a good place to start.

2. If the goal is to find the source of particular problems, make sure to determine what the right variables are for charting. For example, if the dimension being charted is timeliness, consider making the charted variable the "number of minutes late," instead of "time arrived." When trying to determine variables, keep in mind that the result of charting should help find the source and diagnosis of any problems.

3. Determine the proper location within the information chain to attach the measurement probe. This choice should reflect the following characteristics.

    a. It should be early enough in the information processing chain that detection and correction of a problem at that point can prevent incorrectness further along the data flow.

b. It should be in a location in the information chain that is easily accessed and retooled, so as not to cause too much chaos in implementing the charting process.

c. It should not be in a place such that observation of the sample can modify the data being observed.

4. Decide which kind of control chart is to be used.

a. A *variables chart* measures individual measurable characteristics. A variables chart will provide a lot of information about each item being produced.

b. An *attributes chart* measures the percentage or number of items that vary from the expected. An attributes chart provides summary information about the entire process, focusing on cumulative effects rather than individual effects.

5. Choose a center line and control limits for the chart. The center line can either be the average of past measurements, the average of data that has not yet been measured or collected, or a predefined expected standard. The upper control limit (UCL) is set at 3 standard deviations $(+ 3\sigma)$ above the center line, and the lower control limit (LCL) is set at 3 standard deviations $(- 3\sigma)$ below the center line.

6. Choose the sample. The sample may consist of measuring individual data values or measuring a collection of data values for the purpose of summarization. It is important that the sample be taken at a point in the process or a point in time where it has a significant effect.

7. Choose a method for collecting and logging the sample data. This can range from asking people to read gauges and recording the answers to having an integrated mechanism for measuring and logging sample results.

8. Plot the chart and calculate the center line and control limits based on history.

6.5　KINDS OF CONTROL CHARTS

There are many different varieties of control charts.[1] Since our goal is to measure nonconformance with data quality expectation, we will concentrate on particular control chart attributes for measuring noncon-

---

1.　For a detailed list of different control chart types, see *Juran's Quality Handbook, 5th edition,* edited by Joseph M. Juran and A. Blanton Godfrey (New York: McGraw-Hill. 1999).

formity. Our statement of the data quality requirements will be using the rules and assertions system we develop in Chapters 7 and 8. Our sample measurements will be based on defining the granularity of the data item being observed (record vs data attribute), defining a set of data quality rules, and then testing the data items against those rules. Each sample will consists of a number of measured items.

6.5.1   Percentage Nonconforming

The first type is a "Control Chart for Percentage Nonconforming" and is also known as a p chart. A p chart is an attributes chart whose data points represent a percentage of the data items that do not conform to our requirements.

The distribution of this data set is a binomial distribution if we assume that the process is constant. Most data points should fall within 3 standard deviations of the mean. For binomial variables, the standard deviation is computed as

$$\sigma_p = \sqrt{\frac{p(1-p)}{n}}$$

where p is the probability of occurrence, and n is the sample size.

To set up a p chart, a small sample size is collected over a short period of time (in most cases, 25 to 30 time points will be enough) and the average P is computed by counting the number of nonconforming items in each sample, totalling the number of items in each sample group, and dividing the total number of nonconforming items by the total number of sampled items. For p charts, the control limits are calculated using the binomial variable standard deviation; the UCL is computed as $P + 3\sigma_p$, and the LCL is computed as $P - 3\sigma_p$. If the LCL is computed to be a negative number, we just use 0 as the LCL.

6.5.2   Number Nonconforming

In this chart, instead of plotting the percentage of nonconforming data objects, we will plot the number of nonconforming items. In the p chart, the percentage p is equal to the number of nonconforming items divided by the number of observed items, n. Clearly, the number of nonconforming items is equal to np, and therefore, this chart is called an np chart.

For an *np* chart, the UCL is computed as $nP + 3\sqrt{nP(1-P)}$, and the LCL is computed as $nP - 3\sqrt{nP(1-P)}$ where P is the average of the number of nonconforming items, and n is the size of the sample.

6.5.3   Number of Nonconformities

It is not out of the realm of possibility that each data item being observed may have more than one error! In this case, we may not just want to chart the number of nonconforming data items but the total of all nonconformities. This kind of attributes chart is called a *c* chart, and the UCL is calculated as $C + 3\sqrt{C}$. The LCL is calculated as $C - 3\sqrt{C}$, where C is the average number of nonconformities over all the samples.

6.5.4   Number of Nonconformities per Item

If our samples consist of multiple observed data errors, then we might want to look at not only the number of nonconformities but the number of nonconformities per item. This chart is called a *u* chart, and the UCL is computed as $U + 3\sqrt{U/n}$. The LCL is computed as $U - 3\sqrt{U/n}$, where U is the average number of nonconformities, and n is the number of items.

6.5.5   Defining the Control Limits

Thus far, we have discussed the calculations of the upper and lower control limits as a function of the statistical distribution of points in the data set. This is not to say that we can only define these limits statistically.

In reality, as quality overseers, it is our duty to specify the acceptable limits for data quality. For example, when it comes to the acceptable level of incorrect values in certain kinds of databases, we can specify that there is no tolerance for error. In this case, the UCL for errors would be 0. In many cases of examining data quality, there is no need for a lower control limit either. Ultimately, it is up to the users to determine their tolerance for expected variations and errors and use that as a guideline for setting the control limits.

6.6 EXAMPLE: INVALID RECORDS

In this example, each day a number of records are passed through an automated data validation system, where each record is compared against a number of data validation rules. If the record fails any of the rules, it is tagged as an invalid record and a count is taken. This process was repeated for a period of 24 days, yielding the following table.

Day	Number of Records Processed	Number of Bad Records	Bad Ratio
1	10,000	300	0.03
2	10,000	600	0.06
3	10,000	532	0.0532
4	10,000	476	0.0476
5	10,000	620	0.062
6	10,000	546	0.0546
7	10,000	665	0.0665
8	10,000	331	0.0331
9	10,000	337	0.0337
10	10,000	328	0.0328
11	10,000	345	0.0345
12	10,000	358	0.0358
13	10,000	403	0.0403
14	10,000	341	0.0341
15	10,000	347	0.0347
16	10,000	395	0.0395
17	10,000	342	0.0342
18	10,000	334	0.0334
19	10,000	346	0.0346
20	10,000	347	0.0347
21	10,000	378	0.0378
22	10,000	365	0.0365
23	10,000	351	0.0351
24	10,000	432	0.0432

Over the period of time, the overall average ratio of bad records was computed to be 0.0409, which we use as the center line. The UCL and LCL were computed in accordance with the computation for the p

chart, to be 0.0469 and 0.0349, respectively. The corresponding control chart is shown in Figure 6.3.

Since we are trying to limit the error percentage to below a certain point, we can essentially ignore the lower control limit; the fewer errors, the better. As we can see, early on in the history, the process was not in control because there were a number of days (days 2 through 8) in which the upper control limit for errors was exceeded. At that point, the number of errors each day begins to move into a more predictable pattern, even sometimes moving below the lower control limit. Near the end of the measurement period, the process displays errors well within the acceptable limits.

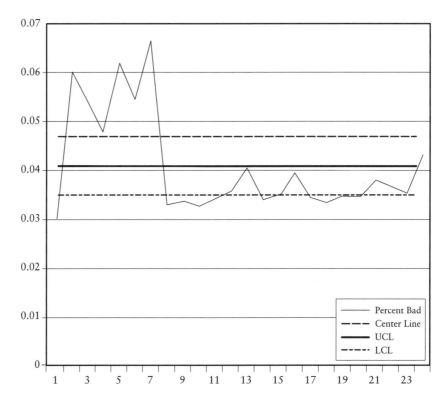

FIGURE 6.3   Control chart for invalid records

6.7   THE GOAL OF STATISTICAL PROCESS CONTROL

Statistical process control is a tool that makes use of measurements of certain aspects of quality of a process or a product over time to gain insight into the differences between expected, common variations and unexpected, special variations. The use of the control chart to represent the behavior of a process over time is not just used as a means for locating anomalous events; the ultimate goals of SPC are stability and predictability.

Let's look at stability first. By definition, when there are a large number of data points in the control chart outside the control limits, it means that the process is very unstable. This instability is more than just points plotted against a handful of parallel lines on a graph — it reflects different causes working at cross-purposes to affect the way the system acts. It is the role of the quality specialist to analyze the results of the SPC process to determine whether the instability is due to common or special causes.

As we identify the special causes associated with each set of out-of-control data points, we gradually improve the process, making it more stable. This will be reflected in the control graph moving forward because as the data points move closer to the mean, they will also begin to fall within the control limits. This exhibits the stabilizing effect that SPC can have on a process.

Another effect is that as the points fall closer together, the standard deviation becomes smaller as well, and since the control limits are defined as a function of the standard deviation, they will also begin to move closer to the center line. This is a different kind of stability, one that focuses on a tightening band within which we expect to see defective information — the narrower the band between the UCL and the LCL, the fewer expected errors! This kind of stability of a system also implies predictability: If for the past 30 days, there were fewer than 10 errors every day, we can expect that tomorrow there will also be fewer than 10 errors.

This notion of predictability is a significant benefit of SPC. By using the SPC tools to understand the nature of problems within a system and the selected variables measured to help locate the source of the problem and by eliminating the problems, we gradually bring a system where we can predict day-to-day behavior and confirm that anomalous activity is due to special causes.

6.8   INTERPRETING A CONTROL CHART

Our next step in the SPC process is interpreting a control chart. Now that we have collected and plotted the data points, how can we make sense out of the resulting control chart? When a process is stable, we can expect that all the points in the control chart will reflect a natural pattern. The data points on the chart should be randomly distributed above and below the center line, and the chart should have these characteristics.

- Most of the points are close to the center line.
- Some of the points are near the UCL and LCL.
- There may be some points above the UCL or below the LCL.
- The distribution of points on the chart should not have any non-random clustering or trending.

In the interpretation of control charts, our goal is to determine whether a process is stable, and if it is not stable, to find and eliminate special causes. So, what do we look for in a control chart?

6.8.1   Unnatural Patterns

The first thing to look for is any departure from what we expect to see. Any apparent patterns that belie the expected randomness in the chart should be a signal for further investigation. Here are some examples.

- Many points that lie outside of control limits. This clearly indicates that the system is out of control. Note that when the control limits are user-defined, there is a much greater possibility of this happening than if we rely on the equations prescribed for calculating the control limits.
- Unnatural clusters of points. Clusters most likely represent patterns in which special causes lurk.
- Shifts in levels seen in the control chart. In other words, is there a sequence of points within one standard deviation, followed by a sequence of points between one and two standard deviations?
- Any trends up or down probably indicate some deterioration in quality.

6.8.2   Zone Tests

Another aspect of unnaturalness in the distribution of data points can be uncovered using what is called a zone test. A zone is an area of the chart where there are unlikely distributions of data points on the chart, such as 2 or 3 successive points outside 2 standard deviations, 4 or 5 successive points outside 1 standard deviation, or 8 successive points on the same side of the center line. All these occurrences are equally likely to occur when the process is stable, and if any appear in a way that is not consistent with our expectations, this is an indicator of a special cause.

6.8.3   Rebalancing

After the root cause of a problem has been identified and corrected, we can claim that at least one aspect of an out-of-control situation has been resolved. In this case, it may be interesting to recalculate the points and control limits on the control chart, ignoring the data points associated with the identified cause. This should help strengthen the control limit calculations and point out other locations to explore for special causes.

6.8.4   Refactoring the Data

Let's say we collected several days' worth of data on the number of errors that occurred in the data each day as a function of the total number of records with errors in them. By aggregating the errors by record instead of by error we may have obscured the fact that many records failed more than one data validation test. As a result, the appearance of a special cause may have been overlooked.

Instead, we can rechart the data points by collecting the data as the number of records that failed due to a specific validation test failing. We might find out that a large number of records are erroneous due to failing more than one test or that several of the erroneous records have failed one test during the first half of the measurement period and failed a different test during the second half.

By separating data points by attribute or remeasuring based on a finer granularity, we may be able to identify occurrences of variations due to special causes that the standard charting method fails to highlight.

6.9   FINDING SPECIAL CAUSES

We have collected our data, built our control chart, plotted data points and control limits, and analyzed the chart for anomalous behavior. The last step in the SPC process is to identify the special causes that are echoed in the control chart.

Hopefully, we will have selected the areas of measurement in a way that will point us in the right direction. While we discuss this process in greater detail in Chapter 15, we can briefly introduce it here.

Assuming that we have translated our data quality expectations into a set of data quality rules, we can use those rules for validating data records. If we log the number of times a record is erroneous due to failing a particular test, we can use those logs to plot the daily conformance for each specific rule.

At the end of the measurement period, we can construct a control chart consolidating data from each of the data quality rules. Because each rule describes a specific aspect of the users' data quality requirements, the problem of identifying a special cause reduces to determining which of the data quality rules accounted for the anomalous behavior. This provides a starting point for the root cause analysis process described in Chapter 15.

6.10   MAINTAINING CONTROL

In Section 6.7, we discussed the goals of statistical process control as being stability and predictability. Once a process has been brought under control, it is beneficial to continue making use of the SPC process to make sure that the process remains under control.

As long as the data points continue to fall between the control limits, the process is stable. Attempts can be made to improve the process on a continuous process, either by making the control limits closer or by introducing new variables or attributes to be measured.

6.11   SUMMARY

In this chapter we discussed the use of an analysis tool called Statistical Process Control (SPC) as a method for measuring and charting the conformance of information to a set of data quality rules. The SPC methodology is based on the analysis of variation in a system and that some variations are due to chance or common causes, whereas others are due to special causes. It is those due to special causes that can be highlighted by SPC, since the occurrence of variations due to common causes form a normal distribution.

Because of this, we can build a chart called a control chart, which integrates data taken from a sample with control limits (both upper and lower). When the data points appear above the upper or below the lower control limit, it is an indication of a special cause. Other unnatural patterns also indicate the appearance of variations due to a special cause.

We looked at different kinds of control charts that can be used to analyze conformance to a set of data quality rules. We also looked at the issues involved in interpreting a control chart. Finally, we introduced the notion of root-cause analysis, which is discussed in greater length in Chapter 15, and maintaining control, which consists of continuing to collect and chart data for the control charts.

7

DOMAINS, MAPPINGS, AND ENTERPRISE REFERENCE DATA

Because a data type is assigned to each data attribute in a database table, it draws its values from a specific value set. The same goes for information embedded in a transmitted message: The value in each field in the message should conform to the expected type for that field. In a way, it is taken for granted that any value stored in a field is taken from a value class (or set) that has some structural (or syntactic) rules as well as some explicit connotative (or semantic) rules that govern the correctness or validity of those values. Either way, these expectations actually boil down into a set of restrictions on the values that the attribute may take.

The syntactic rules cover restrictions on the form of the value. A field that has an integer data type cannot take a value that has alphabetic characters. The semantic rules are additional restrictions on the set of valid values for an attribute that are expressed as a subset of the allowed structural values. When we can define an explicit set of restrictions on a set of values within a type, we call that a domain.

A simple example is a U.S. Social Security number. A Social Security number has a data type (character(11)), but it also has both structural and semantic restrictions. The structural restriction is on the form: three digits (0–9) followed by a hyphen (-), followed by two digits, a hyphen, then four digits. The semantic restrictions specify rules about the number itself. The first three digits denote the state (or area) where the application for the number was filed. The next two digits are called the group number, and they are issued in a particular order, namely odd numbers from 01 through 09, followed by even numbers from 10 though 98. After those groups have been allocated come even numbers from 02 through 08, followed by odd groups numbers from 11 through

99. Each month, the Social Security Administration (SSA) publishes high group numbers for each area. The final four digits, called the serial number, are allocated consecutively for each group. And, according to the SSA, "Alleged Social Security numbers containing area numbers other than those found on that table are impossible."

These rules define what is and is not a valid Social Security number. A program can be written to determine whether a proffered Social Security number is valid or not, but, as we will see, a framework can be developed that will allow us to express the validation of a Social Security number as a business rule that can be captured and documented and from which a validation script can be automatically generated.

There are two major benefits to formalizing business and data quality rules with respect to domains. The first is knowing the means of value restriction for a field can help in generating a test for validation. Knowing an attribute's domain is useful for prescriptive validation of data quality of data values. In other words, if we know what values the field cannot have, we can make sure that any value that is inserted is permissible. It is even better if we have a formal shorthand for describing those sets, if that formality can be turned into a validation test.

The second benefit is that accumulating metadata about the sets of values that are used throughout the enterprise adds to collective knowledge about how information is used and shared. By abstracting the sets of values used and documenting their use and subscribers, we begin to comprehend enterprise reference data, and then we can build a centralized enterprise reference data and metadata repository.

In this chapter, we explore the ideas revolving around data types and how data types are related to the notion of sets. We then describe our definition of data domains, both descriptive and enumerated. Next, we discuss the relations between domains, how those relations exist in databases, and the power of abstracting these mappings as reference metadata. Finally, we propose a publish/subscribe model for the management and use of enterprise reference data.

7.1   DATA TYPES

We begin our exploration with a discussion of data types. What is a data type, how is it used, and what are the mechanics of predefined data types?

7.1.1   Apples and Oranges

We are often reminded when we make questionable comparisons that we should not compare apples and oranges. What does this really mean? Usually, it implies that the basis for comparison of the two objects is flawed and the comparison is basically meaningless. Formally, the classification "apple" and "orange" are types, and it is meaningless to compare objects of different types.

This is true in the data world as well, where each object is associated with a data type. In many computer programming languages, intertype comparisons are illegal, whereas in others, there is implicit-type conversion if it is possible. In the data world, depending on the system, intertype comparisons will either be flagged as being illegal or worse yet, ignored, yielding a garbage answer.

A data type provides a complete specification of the values that can be stored in an attribute, such as the kind of value it holds, the rules for allocating physical storage space for the value, and the operations that may be applied to the values. For example, integers are whole numbers, they take up limited space if they can be stored in a long word, and they are subject to both arithmetic and conditional operators. Character strings, on the other hand, consist of sequences of symbols, may require explicit space allocations, and are not typically subject to arithmetic operations.

It is useful to look at the possible data types that occur frequently in database systems. In the next sections, we will build up an overview of data types, starting with simple data types and building up to more complex ones.

7.1.2   Base Types

The following are base data types.

- **Whole Number Types**   Whole number types are for storing integers. Integer types may be categorized within ranges, based on the amount of storage required.
- **Character and String Types**   The character type is used to hold alphanumeric and symbol characters. Character types are either fixed length or variable length, and there are frequently options for specifying national character sets (for example, Kanji).

- **Decimal**   Decimal types refer to exact numeric representation, based on a precision, which is the total number of digits on both sides of the decimal point, and a scale, which is the number of digits to the right of the decimal point. This is sometimes referred to as numeric.
- **Floating Point**   Floating point numbers are approximate representations of real numbers. The precision of floating point numbers is dependent on representation and the system that is used.
- **Dates or Times**   A date or time (or datestamp or timestamp) is used to store dates or times or combinations thereof.
- **Binary Types**   A binary object can hold data that may not conform to other predefined types, such as graphics, executable code, or representations of data structure objects.

7.2   OPERATIONS

We will build on the notion of data types in a moment, but first, let's look at the operations that are valid between data values within a data type and between data values in different data types.

7.2.1   Arithmetic Operations

The operations that can be applied to the numeric data types (integers, decimals, floating point, etc.) are the standard arithmetic operations.

- Addition (+)
- Subtraction (−)
- Multiplication (*)
- Division (/)
- Modulo (%)

Note that division of integers may by definition yield an integer result. Some systems may add it other numeric operations.

- Floor (returns the largest integer less than a real)
- Ceiling (returns the next integer greater than a real)

7.2.2   Conditional Operations

These are the operators used for making comparisons.

- less than (<)
- less than or equal to (<=)
- greater than (>)
- greater than or equal to (>=)
- equal to (==)
- not equal to (!=)

7.2.3   Logical Operators

These are the operators used for forming logical expressions.

- AND
- OR
- NOT

7.2.4   String Operations

These are operations that can be performed on character strings.

- Concatenation (composing two strings together)
- lpad, rpad (pad strings with blanks)
- ltrim, rtrim (removes a given substring from the left or right of a string)
- Lower, upper (conversion to lower case or upper case)
- Length (returns the length of the string)
- Substring (returns a substring of a given string starting at a specific location for a specific number of characters)

7.2.5   Aggregate Operations

Aggregate functions are those that can be used to summarize information across a set of values. These include the following.

- SUM, which sums up the values in a set
- AVG, which computes the average of the values in a set

- COUNT, which gives the number of values (there is also a DISTINCT classifier for this operator)
- MAX, which returns the highest value
- MIN, which returns the lowest value

7.2.6   Date and Time Operations

Dates are usually stored in a special format, but the conditional operators listed should work on dates. In addition, there are special versions of some of the arithmetic operators.

- Addition (add a number of days to a date to get a new date)
- Subtraction (subtract a number of days from a date to get a new date)

7.2.7   Conversion Operations

When dealing with strictly typed systems, operations between values with different types are not allowed. In the real world, though, we frequently have occasion to try to manipulate data values with different types. In order to accommodate this, there are conversion operators that change the data type (and possibly representation) of a data value.

Sometimes these conversions are implicit (such as multiplying a real value by an integer value to yield a real value — the integer is implicitly converted). Sometimes these conversions are explicit, such as transforming a string representation of a date to a date representation.

7.3   DOMAINS

In this section, we look at the ways to collect data values that can take on intuitive meanings. When it becomes clear that a single collection of values is used for the same meaning throughout different data repositories in the enterprise, a special status should be assigned to that collection as a data domain that can be shared by the users in the enterprise.

7.3.1   Data Types and Sets

A set is a collection of items that can be perceived as a whole, where each item in the collection is distinguishable from all the others, and where it can be clearly determined whether an item is a member of the collection. A data type is a way of classifying data values into sets: the set of whole numbers, the set of character strings of length 5, or the set of decimal numbers that have 10 significant digits, with 3 of them following the decimal point.

Data types differ from sets in that each data type has a set of operations on values that have that data type. This concept is explicit in object-oriented programming languages, where classes, which are really abstract data types coupled with intrinsically defined operations, are defined.

Alternatively, there are certain operations that can be applied to sets. Set union represents the combination of the values of two sets into one larger set. Set intersection as applied to two sets represents those values that reside in both sets. The difference between two sets represents those values that are in the first set but not in the second. There are also set comparison operators. We can compare two sets to see if one is a subset of the other, if two sets are equal to each other, and if two sets are not equal to each other.

7.3.2   The Descriptive Power of Sets and Domains

We can think about sets in two different ways: (1) through enumeration, listing all the elements in the set, and (2) through description. One nice thing about sets is that all the values in the set can frequently be described in a few short terms. A very simple example is the positive whole number — the integral values that are greater than 0. In that one small phrase we can categorize an infinite number of values that intuitively belong to the same collection.

When you think about it, the use of databases is very much driven by the idea of sets. All the records in a table in a database represent a set. An SQL SELECT query into a database is a definition of a subset of the records in the database.

In turn, when we look at the relationship between data attributes and data types, we can see that many attributes draw their values from a subset of the values allowable under the data type. For example, an attribute called *STATE* may have been defined to be CHAR(2). While there are 676 distinct two-character strings, the values populating that attribute are limited to the 62 two-letter United States state and possession abbreviations. This subset restriction can be explicitly stated as "All values in the attribute STATE must also belong to the set of recognized USPS state and possession abbreviations."

We call a set of values that is described as a restriction or subset of the values allowed within a base type a *domain*. There are two different kinds of domains: enumerated domains, which are likely to draw focus because of their relationship to preexisting business set definitions, and descriptive domains, which are defined through constructive rules such as "All three character strings where the first character is A and the third character is a digit."

Because domains represent additional restrictions on the values within a data type, they play an important role in data quality. Every explicitly stated restriction can be automatically transformed into a validation test. All the domains discussed in this book have these properties.

- A base type
- A name with intuitive meaning
- An enumeration list
- A description rule

7.3.3 Enumerated Domains

An enumerated domain is useful when there are a finite number of elements in the set or the set members cannot be described easily. An enumerated domain is a list of values all associated with a particular base type. Domain values are unique within a domain.

To continue our example from the previous section, we can define a domain entitled *USPS State Abbreviations* with a base type of CHAR(2) and an enumeration list of {AL, AK, AS, AZ, AR, CA, CO, CT, DE, DC, FM, FL, GA, GU, HI, ID, IL, IN, IA, KS, KY, LA, ME, MH, MD, MA, MI, MN, MS, MO, MT, NE, NV, NH, NJ, NM, NY, NC, ND, MP, OH, OK, OR, PW, PA, PR, RI, SC, SD, TN, TX, UT, VT, VA, VI, WA, WV, WI, WY, AE, AP, AA}.

7.3.4 Enumerated Domains

It is worthwhile to look at a number of examples of enumerated domains to appreciate how frequently they are used. We can even describe classes of enumerated domains without explicitly listing all the values.

- Geographic domains: comprehensive listings of countries, regions, continents, states, provinces, cities, and so on

- Code values
- Colors
- Employment categories and titles
- National Holiday dates
- Catalog items
- Telephone area codes
- Product suppliers
- Currency Codes

7.3.5   Descriptive Domains

A descriptive domain is defined using a base type and a descriptive rule. The rule specifies a restriction on the values within that data type, using operations that are allowed on values within that data type. A descriptive domain that is based on an integer data type can be defined using the standard integer arithmetic and conditional operations.

A descriptive domain can be used to describe data values that have an explicit format. Descriptive domains can also refer to other domains. Descriptive domains are often (unknowingly) used when there is some embedded information in the data value (see Figure 7.1).

7.3.6   Examples of Descriptive Domains

Here are some well-known examples of descriptive domains.

- **ZIP + 4 Code**   Has a base type of CHARACTER(10) where characters 0–4 must be numeric digits, the fifth character is a hyphen, and the last four digits must be numeric digits.
- **Corporate E-mail Address**   An alphanumeric string concatenated with an "at" sign (@) concatenated with an alphanumeric string followed by the string ".com."
- **Male Name**   The composition of two VARCHAR strings, separated by a blank, where the first is taken from the **male first names** domain, and the second is taken from the **last names** domain.
- **Passing Grade**   An integer value that is greater than or equal to 65 and less than or equal to 100.
- **Valid Password**   A character string whose length is at least 4 and not greater than 9 and has at least one character that is not alphabetic.

ZIP + 4 Code	DDDDD-DDDD
Telephone Number	1-(DDD)DDD-DDDD

Credit Card Number	DDDD DDDD DDDD DDDD
	
	and the digits, when alternately multiplied by 1 or 2, and then truncated to the units position, when summed, is divisible by 10. This is embodied in this psuedocode:
	
	multiplier := 1; sum := 0;
	for i := length(cardnumber) downto 1 do
	  begin
	  char := cardnumber[i];
	  if digittype(char) then
	    begin
	    product := digitvalue(char) * multiplier;
	    sum := sum + (product div 10) + (product mod 10);
	    multiplier := 3 - multiplier; // 1->2, 2->1
	    end
	  end;
	if (sum mod 10) = 0 then ok

E-mail Address	<String1>@<String2>.COM
ATM PIN	Alphanumeric string, whose length is greater than or equal to 4 and less than or equal to 8
Bank Account Number	CC-DDDDDDDD

FIGURE 7.1   Examples of some data domains

7.3.7   Operations on Domains

Our domains are restrictions on value sets, and so we allow the same operations for domains that we allow for sets. Figure 7.2 shows how domains are similar to sets.

- **Union**   The union of domain *A* and domain *B* yields a new domain that contains all the unique values of domain *A* and domain *B*.
- **Intersection**   The intersection of domain *A* and domain *B* yields a new domain that contains the values that are in both domain *A* and domain *B*.

- **Difference**   The difference of domain *A* and domain *B* yields a new domain that contains those values in domain *A* but not in domain *B*.
- **Membership**   A value *a* is a member of domain *A* if *a* is a value in domain *A*.
- **Subset**   A domain *A* is a subset of domain *B* if all the values in domain *A* are in domain *B*.
- **Equality**   A domain *A* is equal to domain *B* if all the values in domain *A* are in domain *B* and all the values in domain *B* are in domain *A*.
- **Inequality**   A domain *A* is not equal to domain *B* if there is a value in domain *A* that is not in domain *B* or there is a value in domain *B* that is not in domain *A*.

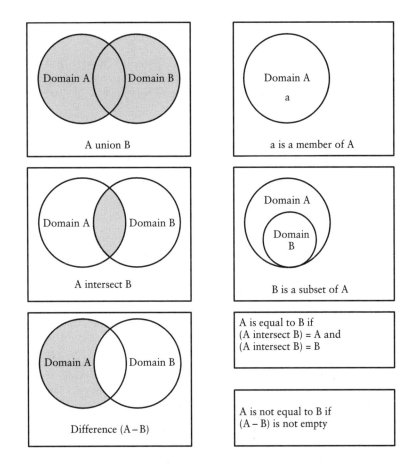

FIGURE 7.2   Domains are like sets

7.3.8   Composed Domains

A composed domain is a domain of values constructed through the composition of values selected from two or more domains.

7.3.9   Knowledge Management and Cataloging Domains

The first steps toward enterprise knowledge management are conceptually small ones, but they can be some of the more important ones.

- Identify those values that can be characterized as domains.
- Extract them and store them in a central repository.
- Manage them as explicit content.

Let's look at each one of these in turn. Identifying domains can be done two ways. The first is through expert interaction — asking the users if there are any sets of values that are commonly used. The second way is through automatic means by exhaustively analyzing the values that reside in enterprise data systems. We will explore these in Chapter 13.

Extracting domains and putting them into a central repository is relatively straightforward as long as the mechanics for representing domains and managing them is available. We will look at one way to do this in greater detail in Chapter 17.

Managing domains as explicit content is easier said than done. The reason is more political than technical: Convincing stakeholders to release their authority over a "staked-out claim" will probably be the biggest hurdle. An important factor is convincing senior management to take an active role.

7.4   MAPPINGS

Now that we have domains, we can start to see how relationships between domains become important. While relational database systems take relations across sets of values as tuples in a database table, there are more concrete relationships that appear frequently in an enterprise. Recognizing both the existence and the business value of one of these relationships is the next step in creating a knowledge-based enterprise.

7.4.1   What Is a Mapping?

The natural progression in discussing data values, data types, and domains is looking at relationships between data values that have already been assigned into different domains. Simply put, a mapping is a relationship between two domains. More formally, a mapping between domain A and domain B is a set of pairs of values $\{a, b\}$ where a is a member of domain A and b is a member of domain B such that there is an intuitive understanding of the relationship between the values a and b.

A familiar example of a mapping is the relationship between ZIP code and city. Every ZIP code belongs to a named area covered by a small post office or postal zone (see Figure 7.3).

7.4.2   Characteristics of Mappings

As with domains, all mappings have some intuitive meaning, which we can capture in its name. In addition, each mapping will have these features.

- A source domain
- A target domain
- An enumeration list
- A mapping rule

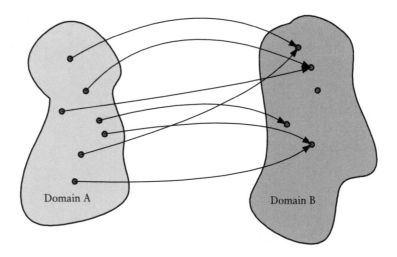

FIGURE 7.3   Definition of a mapping

The domain of a mapping itself is the same as the target domain.

Mappings may be *one-to-one*, in which for a value in domain X, there is one and only one value mapped to domain Y; *one-to-many*, in which for a value in domain X, there may be one or more values mapped in domain Y; *many-to-one*, in which there may be one or more values in domain X mapped to one value in domain Y; and *many-to-many*, in which there may be one or more values in domain X mapped to one or more values in domain Y.

If you recall mathematical terms, a one-to-one mapping can also be referred to as a *function*, and the other mappings can also be referred to as *relations*. By identifying a relation as a mapping, and by classifying the mapping and managing it as knowledge, we can clearly define validation rules for relationships between values in different domains. Figure 7.4 shows the four types of mapping.

7.4.3 Enumerated Mappings

A simple form of a mapping is the enumerated list of pairs. Per the definition in Section 7.4.1, a mapping between domain A and domain B is a

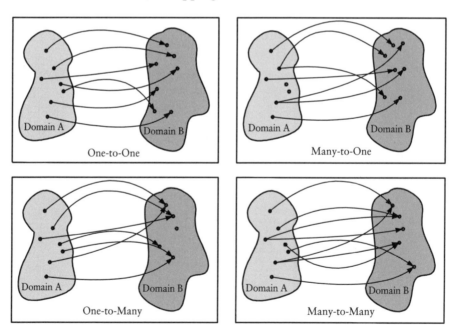

FIGURE 7.4   Different kinds of mappings

set of pairs of values {*a, b*} such that *a* is a member of domain A and *b* is a member of domain B. For an enumerated domain, the collection of {*a, b*} pairs is listed explicitly. Note that all the *a* values must be validated as belonging to domain A, and all the *b* values must be validated as belonging to domain B.

In Section 7.3.3, we encountered the domain of USPS state abbreviations. Presuming that we have another domain called *USPS State Names,* which has base data type VARCHAR(30), we can define a mapping from state abbreviations to state names, as shown in Figure 7.5.

(AA, Armed Forces—The Americas)	(MO, Missouri)
(AE, Armed Forces—Europe)	(MS, Mississippi)
(AP, Armed Forces—Pacific)	(MT, Montana)
(AL, Alabama)	(NC, North Carolina)
(AK, Alaska)	(NE, Nebraska)
(AS, American Samoa)	(NH, New Hampshire)
(AR, Arkansas)	(NJ, New Jersey)
(AZ, Arizonia)	(NM, New Mexico)
(CA, California)	(NV, Nevada)
(CO, Colorado)	(NY, New York)
(CT, Connecticut)	(ND, North Dakota)
(DC, District of Columbia)	(MP, Northern Mariana Islands)
(DE, Delaware)	(OH, Ohio)
(FL, Florida)	(OK, Oklahoma)
(FM, Federated states of Micronesia)	(OR, Oregon)
(GA, Georgia)	(PA, Pennsylvania)
(GU, Guam)	(PR, Puerto Rico)
(HI, Hawaii)	(PW, Palau)
(IA, Iowa)	(RI, Rhode Island)
(ID, Idaho)	(SC, South Carolina)
(IL, Illinois)	(SD, South Dakota)
(IN, Indiana)	(TN, Tennessee)
(KS, Kansas)	(TX, Texas)
(KY, Kentucky)	(UT, Utah)
(LA, Louisiana)	(VA, Virginia)
(MA, Massachusetts)	(VI, Virgin Islands)
(MD, Maryland)	(VT, Vermont)
(ME, Maine)	(WA, Washington)
(MH, Marshall Islands)	(WI, Wisconsin)
(MI, Michigan)	(WV, West Virginia)
(MN, Minnesota)	(WY, Wyoming)

FIGURE 7.5

7.4.4   Examples of Enumerated Mappings

Here are some examples of enumerated mappings.

- Geographic codes to geographic regions
- Part number to part description
- Radio station call letters to radio frequency
- Job title to maximum salary
- Currency code to country

7.4.5   Descriptive Mappings

A descriptive mapping is a mapping that is defined using a rule, similar to the way that descriptive domains use rules. A descriptive mapping is specified with a source domain, a target domain, and a rule for deriving the mapped value from the source value. Because the rule specifically maps a single value to a single value, a descriptive mapping must be a one-to-one mapping. Descriptive mappings are used when there is a simple way to describe the relationship.

7.4.6   Examples of Descriptive Mappings

These are some frequently encountered descriptive domains.

- Numeric scores to grades
- Currency to Currency Conversion
- Telephone call duration to charge

7.4.7   Composed Mappings

A composed mapping is a mapping that incorporates the use of a composed domain.

7.4.8   Operations on Mappings

The following are types of operations on mappings.

- **Membership**   A value pair $\{a, b\}$ is a member of mapping $M(A, B)$ if a is a value in domain A and b is a value in domain B.

- **Subset** A mapping $M(A, B)$ is a subset of mapping $N(C, D)$ if all the value pairs in mapping M are in mapping N.
- **Equality** A mapping $M(A, B)$ is equal to mapping $N(C, D)$ if all the value pairs in mapping M are in mapping N and all the value pairs in mapping N are in mapping M.
- **Inequality** A mapping $M(A, B)$ is not equal to mapping $N(C, D)$ if there is a value pair in mapping M that is not in mapping N or there is a value pair in mapping N that is not in mapping M.

7.5 EXAMPLE: SOCIAL SECURITY NUMBERS

To round out the examples, let's go back to the example discussed in the beginning of the chapter — the U.S. Social Security number. Our earlier discussion focused on the structure of a valid Social Security number. Now we'll look at constructing a domain definition for valid Social Security numbers.

Our first step is to note that the Social Security number is composed of five parts: the area denotation, a hyphen, the group number, a hyphen, and the serial number. We can start our domain definition by describing a Social Security number as a CHARACTER(11) string that is a composition of these five domains, ordered by simplicity.

7.5.1 Hyphen

Simply enough, the *hyphen* domain is a one-character domain consisting solely of the "-" character.

7.5.2 Geographical Code

The issued *geographic code*[1] domain GC has a base type of CHARACTER(3), and based on information collected from the Social Security Administration, is defined using this expression.[2]

1. The term *geographical code* is misleading, since according to the SSA, it is not meant to be any kind of usable geographical information. It is a relic of the precomputer filing and indexing system used as a bookkeeping device.

2. There are other number ranges that are noted as being "new areas allocated but not yet issued." We are using this to mean that for testing to see if a Social Security number is valid, it must have one of the issued geographical codes.

```
((GC >= '001') AND (GC <= '586')) OR
((GC >= '700') AND (GC <= '728'))
```

These ranges are based on the information in Figure 7.6, which is from the SSA Web site, indicating the mapping between geographic codes and U.S. location.

7.5.3   Group Number

The *group number* domain is actually more complicated, since the number is restricted based on both the order of issuance and the monthly report of high group numbers by geographic code, which can be accessed via the Internet at *http://www.ssa.gov/foia/highgroup.htm.*

The monthly issuance report is actually a mapping from geographic codes to high numbers. To properly create the rule for the group number, we must introduce a new operation on a CHARACTER(2) strings of digits X.

```
ODD(X) is TRUE if CONVERT(X, INTEGER) MOD 2 = 1
ODD(X) is FALSE if CONVERT(X, INTEGER) MOD 2 = 0
```

The defining rule for group number (GN) is conditional on the value mapped by the monthly issuance map *HGN* for the geographic code (GC) and reflects the convoluted logic described earlier in this chapter.

```
(ODD(HGN(GC)) AND (HGN(GC) < '10') AND (ODD(GN) AND GN <
  '10'))
OR
(NOT ODD(HGN(GC)) AND (HGN(GC) >= '1') AND ((ODD(GN) AND
  GN < '10') OR (NOT ODD(GN) AND GN < HGN(GC)))
OR
(NOT ODD(HGN(GC)) AND (HGN(GC) < '10') AND ((GN < '10')
  OR (NOT ODD(GN))
OR
(ODD(HGN(GC)) AND (HGN(GC) >= '10') AND (GN < HGN(GC))
```

7.5.4   Serial Number

The *serial number* domain is a CHARACTER(4) string where each character must be a digit between 0 and 9, and the number must be between '0001' and '9999'.

7.5.5 Putting It Together

We can finally describe the domain of valid Social Security numbers as a composite domain. *Social Security Number (SSN)* has the base type CHARACTER(11), where SUBSTR(SSN, 0, 3) belongs to the geographic code domain, SUBSTR(SSN, 4, 1) belongs to the hyphen domain, SUBSTR(SSN, 5, 2) belongs to the group number domain, SUBSTR(SSN, 7, 1) belongs to the hyphen domain, and SUBSTR(SSN, 8, 4) belongs to the serial number domain.

7.6 DOMAINS, MAPPINGS, AND METADATA

We have concentrated on a formal definition of domains and mappings because they are the basis for consolidating enterprise knowledge and experience in one knowledge repository. Once we begin to identify known collections of data and assign meanings to them, we begin to get a better understanding of what information is being used in the organization, who is using it, and how that information is being used.

7.6.1 Domains and Mappings as Reference Data

We differentiate between different flavors of information based on their derivation. *Transactional data* is generated from standard online transaction processing systems (OLTPs). *Reference data* is information used for reference, no matter where it came from. *Reference data sets* contain frequently used information, but the information is moderately static. It is updated infrequently compared to OLTP systems.

Domains and mappings are types of reference data. While the values that make up the domains and the mappings may have actually been derived from transactional data, once the data sets are categorized as domains and the relationships as mappings, and especially when we ascribe some meaning to the collections, those sets can be moved into the reference data arena.

As data sets cross the border into enterprise reference data, there will be a convergence of data users of the reference data. It is this process that leads to an increase in the three dimensions of data domain data quality: agreement of usage, stewardship, and ubiquity, discussed in Section 7.7.

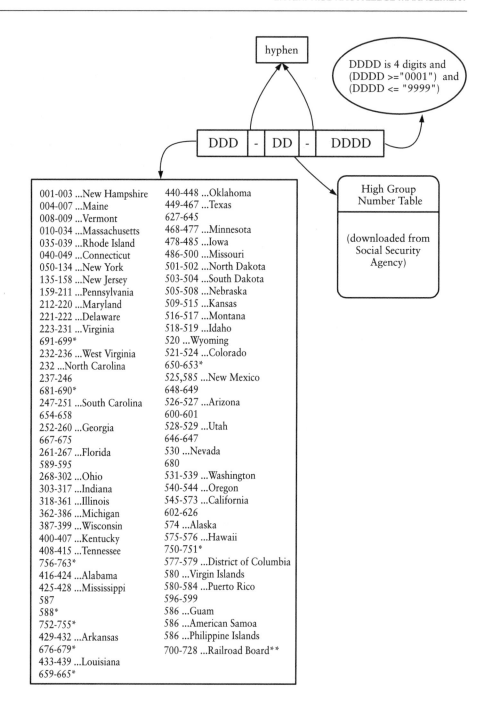

FIGURE 7.6   Social Security Number

7.6.2   Domains and Mappings as Metadata

Another way of looking at domains and mappings is that they belong to a metacollection of information: the class of data sets that have some meaning to at least one set of users. The fact that a data domain or a mapping between domains has been identified carries more information than the knowledge about the data set or sets alone. Rather, the knowledge of the existence of a new domain should be available to anyone in the enterprise (modulo any usage or privacy restrictions), as well as the ability to browse the domain or mapping.

This is an example of metadata that adds to the enterprise knowledge base. We can manage a repository of domain names and meanings that can be accessed from across the enterprise. In the next section, we will see how this metadata can be used.

7.7   THE PUBLISH/SUBSCRIBE MODEL OF REFERENCE DATA PROVISION

The natural conclusion of our discussion on the identification and isolation of domains and mappings is putting into place a framework that allows that information to be shared across the enterprise. Before this can be done successfully, these four pillars must be in place.

1. Senior management must support a centralized reference data system complete with assigned stewardship responsibilities.
2. There must be a usage agreement between the users and the centralized reference managers.
3. There must be a means for the efficient publication and distribution of reference data.
4. There must be a means for users to subscribe to published information.

7.7.1   Reference Data and Stewardship

If we know that the organization has overcome any political issues regarding data ownership (as discussed in Chapter 2), most likely senior management supports a knowledge-based enterprise. In this case, it is imperative that a data steward be selected and empowered to oversee the management of the domain set. These are the responsibilities of a data steward for domains and mappings.

1. *Authorization of Access and Validation of Security*　　This involves authorizing users of domains and mappings, validating security for access to the domains and mappings, authorizing modifications to the reference data, and providing access to the metadata for the purposes of browsing.

2. *Support the User Community*　　If there are any issues regarding the use or availability of reference data, the steward must resolve them.

3. *Maintenance of Data*　　This involves scheduling any periodic updates, making sure that the resources required for data provision are available and working, and acquiring any technology required to maintain the data. Any issues of data aging or retention are handled within the scope of maintenance.

4. *Responsibility for Data Quality*　　This includes defining the data quality rules associated with the domains and mappings and making use of any technology required to assess and maintain a high level of data quality within each domain or mapping.

5. *Distribution of Information*　　This involves enabling the capability to disseminate reference data in an efficient manner, which may include replication strategies or data delivery systems using message integration software.

6. *Management of Business Rules*　　This incorporates the documentation of all domain and mapping metadata, the documentation of all associated business rules, and identification and documentation of the way the reference data is being used and by which users.

7. *Management of Metadata*　　This involves developing and approving business naming standards, data definitions, aliases, and the documentation of the information about the data domains and mappings.

8. *Source Management*　　This involves managing the sources of reference information, whether it means internal data providers or external data providers. This integrates with the preceding data quality responsibility.

7.7.2   Agreement of Usage

The agreement of usage is essentially a contract between the users of a data domain (or mapping) and the responsible data stewards. It specifies what reference data sets are to be used, which users are authorized to use them, and a service and support arrangement. In addition, a level of service is negotiated based on the users requirements and priorities.

The agreement of usage is the method for the data stewards, as representatives of the knowledge-based enterprise, to measure and categorize the value of stored reference data. Usage agreements are also managed as metadata.

7.7.3   Publication of Reference Data

The pivotal point of the accumulation of reference data managed under the watchful eye of a data steward is when the information itself can be distributed to enterprise users. In order to benefit from the management of reference data, there must be a scalable mechanism for publication of reference data.

What do we mean by "publication"? In most cases, it represents the channel through which requested information is delivered. This can be via standard database queries, specialized database views that are materialized on demand, or network information agents that propagate replicated copies of information through the enterprise.

The requirements for a publication system are predicated on these conditions.

- The system must supply information to all subscribers within a prearranged level of service and timeliness.
- The system must guarantee that the information is consistent across the enterprise.
- The delivery mechanism must be scalable as the number of subscribers increases.
- The delivery mechanism must be robust in the presence of different kinds of system platforms and data architectures.

7.7.4   Subscription-Based Distribution

What do we mean by "subscribers"? In our system, a subscriber is any user (or group of users) that has contracted an agreement of usage for a particular set of reference information and has been authenticated to access that information. While a subscriber is allowed access to the information, the means for that access is defined in accordance with the data publication framework described in Section 7.7.3.

How can these ideas be actualized? Since many organizations migrate their information systems toward a multitiered architecture, the notion of a "broker" is gaining in popularity. A broker is an application agent that sits between the source of information and the destinations that have requested information (see Figure 7.7). Brokers are a useful paradigm because the existence of a mediator for data requests provides a means for providing support at all negotiated levels of service, for guaranteeing a level of consistency across the network, for providing scalability as the system grows, and for providing seamless connectivity in the presence of different hardware systems.

7.7.5   Privacy Using Anonymous Publish/Subscribe

Sometimes the knowledge of who is reading which information is also subject to a degree of privacy. Because the broker acts as intermediary, it is possible to configure an enterprise information distribution system using a more refined concept known as anonymous publish/subscribe that can provide a level of privacy. In this model, it is the broker that completely manages the relationship between requestor and data source. While the data stewards may know that a number of subscribers exist, it is only really important for them to know about the contracted levels of service for those subscribers. Alternatively, the subscribers only care about getting the information but they do not care where it comes from.

To this end, the data publisher can post information into a blind data channel that is managed by one or more brokers. In turn, the broker can feed that information into blind data channels that are directed at the subscribers. It is possible to configure this system so that the publishers are unaware of the subscribers and vice versa — thus, the name anonymous publish/subscribe.

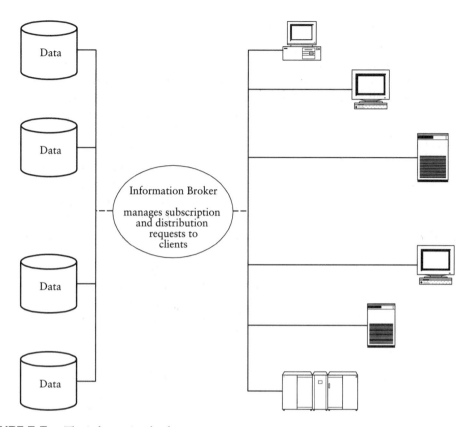

FIGURE 7.7   The information broker

7.8   SUMMARY: DOMAINS, MAPPINGS, AND REFERENCE DATA

In this chapter, we looked at a more refined notion of data typing called a domain, which represents restrictions on sets of data values within a data type. Relations between domains are expressed as mappings. Domains can either be represented as enumerations of values or rules. Together, domains and mappings are a source of reference information, and as more commonality in usage between domains and mappings is discovered across the enterprise, the more relevant the used domains become as enterprise reference data.

As domains and mappings are consolidated from different data sets, they can be captured and managed not only as knowledge content but also as metadata. Data stewards are assigned to manage the reference data and are responsible for service, support, maintenance, data quality, and source management, among other responsibilities.

When a catalog of domains and mappings is available for all users, they can use the reference data to contract an agreement with the information suppliers or data stewards. Information is disseminated using a publish/subscribe mechanism, which can be implemented using intermediary agents processes known as brokers. If there is any sensitivity in reference to the users themselves or the specific reference data, an anonymous publish/subscribe mechanism can be implemented.

8

DATA QUALITY ASSERTIONS AND BUSINESS RULES

In this chapter, we explore the formal way to describe what we expect to see in terms of data quality. Through the definition of data quality rules, we can derive a means to both assess the current state of and measure the progress in improvement of the data's quality.

Remember this basic principle: For any rule, given a set of data items and a data quality rule base, the data set can always be grouped into (1) items that conform to the rule and (2) items that do not conform to the rule. We will see more about this principle in Chapter 13 when we look at the automated discovery of data quality rules and in Chapter 17, where we explore the transformation of these rules into implementable objects.

8.1 DATA QUALITY ASSERTIONS

Our discussion of data quality rules focuses on four kinds of assertions.

- Definitions
- Proscriptive assertions
- Prescriptive assertions
- Conditional assertions

Each class in its own way defines some aspect of how information is extracted from data and how the business operations depend on the quality of the data.

8.1.1   Definitions

Definitions describe metainformation about the data that is under scrutiny. The set of definitions forms the basis for the remainder of the rules. Definitions include the domain and mapping definitions, described in Chapter 7, as well as null value definitions.

8.1.2   Proscriptive Assertions

Proscriptive assertions define what is *not* allowed to happen in a data set. For example, there may be a rule that an attribute may not have a null value. These are the kind of rules that can be used to determine what is wrong with data. We use these rules for specifying and quantifying the levels of data quality in a data set. In other words, we can use these rules to quantify a level of data quality. Proscriptive assertions may appear in either a positive or negative form — either describing a restriction on what is or is not allowed in a field.

8.1.3   Prescriptive Assertions

Prescriptive assertions define what is supposed to happen in a data set. An example is a rule that indicates that attribute A's values are composed of the sum of attribute B and attribute C. These are rules that can represent application logic for data population as well as data extraction, transformation, and migration. These rules can also be used for message passing and content-based data flow.

8.1.4   Conditional Assertions

Conditional assertions specify that an action must take place if a condition is true. These describe what should happen if conditions are met. An example is if the value of attribute A is greater than 10, then attribute B may be blank. Conditional assertions essentially add logic to the rules' definitions.

8.2 DATA QUALITY ASSERTIONS AS BUSINESS RULES

Today, businesses are increasingly distinguished by their ability to accumulate, process, and disseminate information. A goal for increasing competitiveness is increased automation and the use of straight-through processing, which depends on discrete data interchange definitions and high-quality data.

Successful businesses will gain greater scalability and higher operational margins by achieving a high level of automated information processing. The success factors can only be reached by building an enterprise whose business rules dictate the guidelines for the validation of information quality. Since high information throughput can be achieved if nothing "gums up the works," maintaining high levels of data quality affects the proper operation of the business. Therefore, any rule that decreases the number of exceptions in an operation stream is a business rule. In other words, in a knowledge-oriented business, business rules *are* data quality rules.

8.3 THE NINE CLASSES OF DATA QUALITY RULES

Data quality rules can be separated into nine classes.
1. Null value rules
2. Value rules
3. Domain membership rules
4. Domain Mappings
5. Relation rules
6. Table, cross-table, and cross-message assertions
7. In-process directives
8. Operational directives
9. Other rules

8.4 NULL VALUE RULES

Null value rules specify whether a data field may or may not contain null values. A null value is essentially the absence of a value, although there are different kinds of null values. Consequently, we will work with one method for defining and characterizing null values and two kinds of null value rules. The first asserts that null values are allowed to be present in a field, and the second asserts that null values are not allowed in a field.

8.4.1 Null Value Specification

Our goal for null value specifications is to isolate the difference between a legitimate null value and a missing value. Since a data record may at times allow certain fields to contain null values, we provide these deeper characterizations.

1. *No value*   There is no value for this field — a true null.
2. *Unavailable*   There is a value for this field, but for some reason it has been omitted. Using the unavailable characterization implies that at some point the value will be available and the field should be completed.
3. *Not applicable*   This indicates that in this instance, there is no applicable value.
4. *Not classified*   There is a value for this field, but it does not conform to a predefined set of domain values for that field.
5. *Unknown*   The fact that there is a value is established, but that value is not known.

Considering that we allow more than one kind of null value, we also need to allow different actual representations, since there is usually only one system-defined null value. Therefore, any null value specification must include both the kind of null along with an optional assigned representation. Here are some examples.

Use "U" for unknown
Use "X" for unavailable
Use "N/A" for not applicable

Of course, in building our rule set, it is worthwhile to assign a handle to any specific null value specifications. In this way other rules can refer to null values by their handle, which increases readability.

Define X for unknown as "X"
Define GETDATE for unavailable as "fill in date"
Define U for unknown as "?"

This way, we can have different representations for the different kinds of null values in a way that allows flexibility in defining the null value rules. Figure 8.1 gives examples of each null value specification.

Type of Null	Description	Example
No value	There is no value for this field.	In a field for "mobile phone," if there is no mobile phone number associated with the customer, this is left null, since there is no value for it.
Unavailable	There is a value for this field, but for some reason it has been omitted.	In a field for "mobile phone," there is a mobile phone number associated with the customer, but it has not been filled in.
Not applicable	In this instance, there is no applicable value.	In a product order, when the buyer is a not-for-profit agency, their tax field is not applicable and will be null.
Not classified	There is a value for this field, but it does not conform to a predefined set of domain values for that field.	In an order for a sweater, where the colors are limited to red, blue, or black, if the buyer requested a color that was not available, the field might be left blank.
Unknown	The fact that there is a value is established, but that value is not known.	In a field for "mobile phone," it is known that there is a mobile phone number associated with the customer, but the number has not yet been acquired.

FIGURE 8.1   Different kind of nulls

8.4.2   Null Value Rule

The null value rule is a proscriptive rule that specifies that null values may be present in the indicated field. A null value rule will specify the kinds of null values that may be present and a representation (if any) used for those null values.

A null value rule may allow traditional null values (such as system nulls, empty fields, or blanks), generic null values as defined in null value specifications, or a detailed list of specific null value representations. Note that if we only allow certain kinds of null values, this will most likely mean that we want to restrict the appearance of the traditional nulls!

Here are some examples.

Rule ANulls:
Attribute A allowed nulls {GETDATE, U, X}

In this example, we only allow certain kinds of null values, as described in Section 8.4.1.

Rule BNulls:
Attribute B allowed nulls

With the null value rules, the resulting validation depends on the types of null values allowed. If any nulls are allowed, then there is really nothing to do — whether or not a value is in the field, the field is conformant. But if only certain kinds of nulls are allowed, then the validation for that rule includes checking to make sure that if any other null values appear (such as the system null or blanks), the record is marked as violating that rule.

8.4.3 Non-Null value rules

A non-null value rule, as its name implies, is a proscriptive rule that specifies which kinds of null values are *not* allowed. If the rule indicates that no nulls are allowed, then the rule is violated if the system null or blanks appear in the field. The non-null value rule can also specify that certain predefined null representations are not allowed, in which case any appearance of those defined null values constitutes a violation. Here is an example.

Rule BnoNulls:
Attribute B nulls not allowed

8.5 VALUE MANIPULATION OPERATORS AND FUNCTIONS

In order to further define rules, we need a battery of functions that can express manipulations or conditions on values. Table 8.1 lists these functions and their purposes.

8.6 VALUE RULES

Rules covering particular values that may be assigned to a designated field are referred to as value rules. The classifying name for rules that constrain field values are called Attribute Value Restriction rules, which limit the set of valid values that can be assigned. Value rules are prescriptive, but are used in the proscriptive sense when looking for violations.

TABLE 8.1

Manipulation Operators and Functions

Function Name	Arguments	Result	Description
PLUS	X, Y: arithmetic values	X + Y	Addition
MINUS	X, Y: arithmetic values	X - Y	Subtraction
TIMES	X, Y: arithmetic values	X * Y	Multiplication
OVER	X, Y: arithmetic values	X / Y	Division
MODULO	X, Y: arithmetic values	Integer remainder after division	Modulo
SUBSTR	S: String, X, Y: integer	The substring of S starting at position X and continuing for Y characters	Takes a substring of specific start and length
INDEX	S1, S2: Strings	The position in S1 where S2 appears	Searches for location of S2 in S1
LENGTH	S1: String	The length of S1	
<	X, Y: comparable values	Returns TRUE if X is less than Y	Less than
<=	X, Y: comparable values	Returns TRUE if X is less than or equal to Y	Less than or equal to
>	X, Y: comparable values	Returns TRUE if X is greater than Y	Greater than
>=	X, Y: comparable values	Returns TRUE if X is greater than or equal to Y	Greater than or equal to
==	X, Y: comparable values	Returns TRUE if X is equal to Y	Equals
!=	X, Y: comparable values	Returns TRUE if X is not equal to Y	Not Equals
AND	L1, L2: two logical values	TRUE if both values are TRUE; FALSE otherwise	Logical AND
OR	L1, L2: two logical values	TRUE if either value (or both) is TRUE; FALSE if both are FALSE	Logical OR
NOT	L1: a logical value	TRUE if L1 is FALSE: False if L1 is TRUE	Logical NOT

8.6.1 Attribute Value Restriction Rules

All attributes are associated with some preassigned data type, such as string or integer. While the data type provides a level of data validation, it is limited in its extent, since there may be many values that are data type conformant, yet are inappropriate for a particular field.

One example would be an attribute GRADE associated with a student course database. The data type for the field would be CHAR(1) (a character string of length 1), but we can presume that the only valid values for GRADE are {A, B, C, D, F}. An entry for this field of the letter J would be completely valid for the data type. To further restrict the set of valid values, we can add an attribute value restriction rule for that field.

> **Rule GradeRestrict:**
> **Restrict GRADE: (value >= "A" AND value <= "F") AND (value != "E")**

This rule contains all the restrictions necessary for the field: The value is between A and F but cannot be E. All value restriction rules indicate a narrowing of the set of values valid for the attribute and are usually expressed using range operations combined with the logical connectors "AND," "OR," and so on.

These kinds of rules exist in many places, and they are the ones most frequently embedded in application code. Exposing these rules can be very useful, especially if there is a possibility that there are contradictions between the restrictions. If more than one rule is associated with an attribute, both rules must hold true, the equivalent of creating a new rule composed of both restrictions connected using the logical AND operator. A contradiction exists when two rules exist that are applied to the same field, yet it is not possible for both to always hold. Here is an example of two contradicting rules.

> **Rule StartRestrict1:**
> **Restrict STARTDATE: value > "June 21, 1987" AND value < "December 1, 1990"**
> **Rule StartRestrict2:**
> **Restrict STARTDATE: value < "February 1, 1986"**

In the first rule, the date must fall within a certain range, while the second rule says that the date must be earlier than a different date. Combining the rules yields a restriction that can't be true: The date is before February 1, 1986 but is also between June 21, 1987 and December 1, 1990.

These contradictions may not be discovered in standard use because application code is executed in a sequential manner, and the time dependence masks out what may be a harmful oversight. Once the rules are enumerated, an automated process can check for contradictions.

8.7 DOMAIN MEMBERSHIP RULES

We described domains and mappings in Chapter 7. Now we examine the rules affecting domains. As with the null rules, we have both definition specifications as well as conformance rules. There are two kinds of definition rules, one prescriptive rule, and two proscriptive membership rules.

8.7.1 Syntactic (Descriptive) Domain Definition

In Chapter 7, we discussed the difference between descriptive domains and enumerated domains. A descriptive domain uses a "formula" to determine whether the value is in the domain. Our examples included the U.S. Postal Service ZIP + 4 code, which can be described as having a base type of CHARACTER(10), where characters 0–4 must be numeric digits, the fifth character is a hyphen, and the last four digits must be numeric digits.

Here is that rule expressed more formally, using the variable val to represent the value.

Define ZIP4 as: substr(val, 0, 5) >= 00000 AND substr(val, 0, 5) <= 99999 AND substr(val, 5, 1) == "-" AND substr(val, 6, 4) >= 0000 AND substr(val, 6, 4) <= 9999

We refer to these definitions as syntactic because there is a distinct syntax that can be applied to each value to determine whether it belongs to the domain.

8.7.2 Enumerated Domain Definition

In contrast, some domains are defined as a list of valid values. Our examples in Chapter 7 included United States state names, national holiday dates, or catalog items. Here is a formal representation of one of these domains.

Define NationalHolidays as:
{"New Year's Day,"
"Martin Luther King Day,"
"President's Day,"
"Memorial Day,"

"Labor Day,"
"Veteran's Day,"
"Thanksgiving,"
"Christmas"}

8.7.3 Domain Assignment

In some data environments, data values that appear in one field always belong to the same domain, although it may not be clear a priori what the complete set of values will be. For example, we may define a domain of "Current Customers," but values are added to this domain dynamically as new customers are added to the database. But once a value appears in the field, it will always be considered as a domain member. This becomes especially useful when other data consumers rely on the values in that domain. Because of this, we have a rule that specifies that all field values define a domain.

Domain assignment is a prescriptive rule. A domain assignment rule, when applied to a data field, specifies that all values that appear in that field (or list of fields) are automatically assigned to be members of a named domain. This domain is added to the set of domains and can be used in other domain rules.

Our formal representation includes a domain name and a list of database table field names whose values are propagated into the domain. The domain is constructed from the union of all the values in each of the table columns. Here is an example.

Define Domain CurrencyCodes from {Countries.Currency, Orders.Currency}

In this example, the domain CurrencyCodes is created (and updated) from the values that appear in both the Currency column in the Countries table, and the Currency column in the Orders table. This rule may have been configured assuming that the right currency codes would be correctly set in the Countries table, but in reality, the currencies that are used in customer orders are those that are actually used, so we'll include the currencies listed in the Orders table.

8.7.4   Domain Membership

We now have three ways to define domains. We are therefore ready to restrict field values to named domains. A domain membership rule is a proscriptive rule that says all values that appear in a specified field must belong to a named domain.

As an example, the addresses of our U.S. customers in our sales database must have states that are drawn from the US_STATES domain. Our formal rule must include the field name that belongs to a domain and the domain to which it belongs:

Rule StatesMembership:
SALES.CUSTOMER_STATE Taken from Domain US_STATES

8.7.5   Domain Nonmembership

Conversely, there may be times that we want to make sure that no attribute's value is taken from a specific domain. We can specify this using the proscriptive domain nonmembership rule. For example, if we have divided our sales database into regional tables, we may want to make sure that no states in the customer addresses in our Eastern region table belong to WESTERN_STATES:

Rule StatesSelect:
EASTERN_SALES.CUSTOMER_STATE NOT Taken from
Domain WESTERN_STATES

Formally, a domain nonmembership rule must include a field name and a domain from which the field's values may *not* be taken (see Figure 8.2).

8.8   DOMAIN MAPPINGS AND RELATIONS ON FINITE DEFINED DOMAINS

As we discussed in Chapter 7, domain mappings relate the values in a source domain to values in a target domain. Like domains, we have five kinds of mapping rules — two are for definition, one is a prescriptive rule, and two proscriptive rules.

All domain mapping definitions must specify the source domain and the target domain. Base types are valid for domain names, although

Rule Type	Description	Rule Format
Syntactic Domain Definition	Definition of a rule specifying those values valid within the domain	*DEFINE <domain-name> AS <condition>*
Enumerated Domain Definition	Definition of a rule specifying those values that belong to the domain	*DEFINE <domain-name> AS {<value-list>}*
Domain Assignment	A rule that indicates that an attribute's values define the domain	*DEFINE Domain <domain-name>FROM {<attribute-list>}*
Domain Membership	A rule that indicates that an attribute's values must be taken from the domain	*<attribute-name> TAKEN FROM <domain-name>*
Domain Nonmembership	A rule that indicates that an attribute's values may not belong to the domain	*<attribute-name> NOT TAKEN FROM <domain-name>*

FIGURE 8.2   Domain rules

true domains are preferred. A mapping can be used both as a validation reference (do the two values belong to the mapping?) and as a functional reference (what is the mapped result of value X?).

8.8.1   Functional Domain Mapping

One way to define a domain mapping is through the use of a functional map between source values and target values. In this rule, a function is used to describe how to map from the source value to a target value. This functional mapping may incorporate some conditional logic, and the function must be able to provide a result for every value in the source domain.

An example from Chapter 7 is the mapping from numeric score to alphabet grade. The functional mapping can be described like this.

Define Mapping ALPHAGRADE(val):INTEGER TO CHAR(1):
```
{
"A" if val > 90 AND val <= 100;
"B" if val > 80 AND val <= 90;
"C" if val > 70 AND val <= 80;
"D" if val > 65 AND val <= 70;
"F" otherwise
}
```

What would happen if the value being mapped is an integer but is not less than or equal to 100? An invalid input to this functional spec would provide an answer, but most likely not one that we expect. Of course, we would probably have already defined two domains to help us in this rule, one domain for valid numeric scores, and one for the alphabetic grade:

Define Domain VALIDSCORE as: val >= 0 AND val <= 100
Define Domain GRADES from {"A", "B", "C", "D", "F"}

The functional mapping becomes:

Define Mapping ALPHAGRADE(val): VALIDSCORE TO
GRADES:
{
"A" if val > 90 AND val <= 100;
"B" if val > 80 AND val <= 90;
"C" if val > 70 AND val <= 80;
"D" if val > 65 AND val <= 70;
"F" otherwise
}

The benefit of basing the definition on predefined domains is that it adds a level of encapsulation in which business logic can be automatically embedded.

8.8.2   Domain Mapping Enumeration

A domain mapping can also be defined using an explicit enumeration of mapping pairs. In Chapter 7, we discussed USPS state abbreviations. Here we show the mapping between USPS state abbreviations to the actual full state names.

Define Mapping STATE_ABBREV_TO_NAMES:STATEABBREVS
TO STATENAMES:
{{"AL", "ALABAMA"},
{"AK", "ALASKA"},
{"AS", "AMERICAN SAMOA"},
{"AZ", "ARIZONA"},
{"AR", "ARKANSAS"},
{"CA", "CALIFORNIA"},

{"CO", "COLORADO"},
{"CT", "CONNECTICUT"},
{"DE", "DELAWARE"},
{"DC", "DISTRICT OF COLUMBIA"},
{"FM", "FEDERATED STATES OF MICRONESIA"},
{"FL", "FLORIDA"},
{"GA", "GEORGIA"},
{"GU", "GUAM"},
{"HI", "HAWAII"},
{"ID", "IDAHO"},
{"IL", "ILLINOIS"},
{"IN", "INDIANA"},
{"IA", "IOWA"},
{"KS", "KANSAS"},
{"KY", "KENTUCKY"},
{"LA", "LOUISIANA"},
{"ME", "MAINE"},
{"MH", "MARSHALL ISLANDS"},
{"MD", "MARYLAND"},
{"MA", "MASSACHUSETTS"},
{"MI", "MICHIGAN"},
{"MN", "MINNESOTA"},
{"MS", "MISSISSIPPI"},
{"MO", "MISSOURI"},
{"MT", "MONTANA"},
{"NE", "NEBRASKA"},
{"NV", "NEVADA"},
{"NH", "NEW HAMPSHIRE"},
{"NJ", "NEW JERSEY"},
{"NM", "NEW MEXICO"},
{"NY", "NEW YORK"},
{"NC", "NORTH CAROLINA"},
{"ND", "NORTH DAKOTA"},
{"MP", "NORTHERN MARIANA ISLANDS"},
{"OH", "OHIO"},
{"OK", "OKLAHOMA"},
{"OR", "OREGON"},
{"PW", "PALAU"},
{"PA", "PENNSYLVANIA"},
{"PR", "PUERTO RICO"},
{"RI", "RHODE ISLAND"},

{"SC", "SOUTH CAROLINA"},
{"SD", "SOUTH DAKOTA"},
{"TN", "TENNESSEE"},
{"TX", "TEXAS"},
{"UT", "UTAH"},
{"VT", "VERMONT"},
{"VA", "VIRGINIA"},
{"VI", "VIRGIN ISLANDS"},
{"WA", "WASHINGTON"},
{"WV", "WEST VIRGINIA"},
{"WI", "WISCONSIN"},
{"WY", "WYOMING"},
{"AE", "ARMED FORCES EUROPE, THE MIDDLE EAST, AND CANADA"},
{"AP", "ARMED FORCES PACIFIC"},
{"AA", "ARMED FORCES AMERICAS"}
}

8.8.3 Mapping Assignment

Again, similar to domains, we may have mapping relationships that exist within the data environment, but the existence of a pair in the system automatically adds it to the mapping. It is slightly more complex with mappings, since there must be some pivotal means for linking the source value to the target value. In our case, we will allow the mapping to be pivoted on a pair of data fields linking records then choosing the two fields holding the source and target domain values. Mapping assignment is a prescriptive rule, since it is through the data relations described in the rule that the mapping is defined.

As an example consider the mapping between country names and currency codes. In one table, each record with a country name is accompanied by a country code; in the second table, each record with a country code is accompanied by a currency code. We can use this definition.

Define Mapping COUNTRY_TO_CURRENCY:
    COUNTRY_NAMES TO CURRENCY_CODES:
{
With Pivot Geography.CountryCode with Orders.CountryCode,
Map Geography.CountryName to Orders.CurrencyCode
}

In this definition, we have established the relation between two tables based on a single pivot value (that is, the one that appears in both the CountryCode fields of tables Geography and Orders). Using this relation, we assert that an implicit mapping exists between the CountryName field of the Geography table and the CurrencyCode field of the Orders table. This mapping can now be embedded in the metadata repository and can be used in other rules.

8.8.4   Mapping Membership

Mapping membership is a proscriptive rule that asserts that the relation between two attributes or fields is restricted based on a named mapping. More formally, if one specifies that two fields, A and B, are members of domain mapping Z, where Z is a mapping between domain X and domain Y, it means that any value in field A must belong to domain X, any value in field B must belong to domain Y, and the pair of values from fields A and B, (a,b) must belong to the mapping Z.

Mapping membership is formally specified by indicating a mapping and two fields that belong to that mapping, making sure to indicate which is the source field and which is the target.

Rule OrdersCountries:
(Orders.CountryName, Orders.CountryCode) Belong to Mapping
    COUNTRIES_TO_CODES

8.8.5   Mapping Nonmembership

Conversely, mapping nonmembership asserts that a pair of values may never belong to a named mapping. This rule is a proscriptive rule that says that if one specifies that two fields, A and B, are not members of domain mapping Z, where Z is a mapping between domain X and domain Y, it means that any value in field A must belong to domain X, any value in field B must belong to domain Y, and the pair of values from fields A and B, (a,b) may not belong to the mapping Z.

Note that in this rule, we indicate that the fields must belong to the domains. Violation of the rule only occurs if the two values belong to their respective domains but the pair does not belong to the mapping. If one of the fields contains a value that is not a member of its specified domain, the rule is violated.

Mapping nonmembership is formally specified by indicating a mapping and two fields that do not belong to that mapping, making sure to indicate which is the source field and which is the target. Assume that we have a mapping called DISCONTINUED_ITEMS between product line names and model numbers, which represents all product name and model combinations that are no longer sold. An example of a rule forcing nonmembership could be used to make sure that a customer order does not refer to a discontinued item.

Rule Discontinued:
(Orders.ProductLine, Orders.ModelNumber) Does not Belong to
Mapping DISCONTINUED_ITEMS

Figure 8.3 details the types of rules.

8.8.6 Mappings as Functions

Mappings can also be used to provide the resulting mapped value belonging to the second domain from a submitted value belonging to the first domain. In other words, a mapping can be used as a relation. If the mapping is one-to-one, then it is a function. If the mapping is one-to-many, then the result of applying the mapping is a randomly selected value from the set of values mapped in the second domain.

Rule Type	Description	Rule Format
Functional Mapping Definition	A list of functions describing mapping	*DEFINE <mapping-name>:<source-domain> TO <target domain> AS <function-spec-list>*
Enumerated Mapping Definition	Definition of a rule specifying those value pairs that belong to the mapping	*DEFINE <mapping-name>:<source-domain> TO <target domain> AS {<value-pair-list>}*
Mapping Assignment	A rule that indicates that two attributes' values define the mapping via a "hooked" third pivot attribute	*Define Mapping <mapping-name>: <source-domain> TO <target domain> AS:* *{ Pivot <table1.column> with <table2.column>* *Map <source attribute> to target attribute}*
Mapping Membership	A rule that indicates that two attributes' values must conform to the mapping	*(<source-attribute-name>:<target-attribute-name>)* *BELONG TO <mapping-name>*
Mapping Nonmembership	A rule that indicates that two attributes' values may not conform to the mapping	*(<source-attribute-name>:<target-attribute-name>)* *DOES NOT BELONG TO <mapping-name>*

FIGURE 8.3   Mapping rules

8.9　RELATION RULES

The relation rules refer to data quality rules that apply to more than one data field. We have two versions of these rules: intra-record and inter-record. The intra-record version is limited to fields within a single record or message, and the inter-record version allows referral to fields in other records, messages, or tables.

There are four kinds of relation rules. Three kinds — completeness, exemption, and consistency rules — are proscriptive rules. One kind — derivation — is a prescriptive rule that describes how some fields are filled in. Completeness rules describe when a record is fully complete. Exemption rules describe times that a rule may be missing data. Consistency rules indicate the consistency relationship between fields.

8.9.1　Completeness Rule

Completeness is one of the dimensions of data quality discussed in Chapter 5, and, therefore, it is useful to have a rule overseeing it. Completeness governs the proper population of a record's fields, possibly depending on other fields' values. Completeness rules are conditional assertions.

A completeness rule specifies a condition followed by a list of attributes that must have values. For example, a sales order must have a billing address if the total of the bill is greater than $0.00.

```
Rule OrdersComplete:
IF (Orders.Total > 0.0), Complete With
{Orders.Billing_Street,
Orders.Billing_City,
Orders.Billing_State,
Orders.Billing_ZIP}
```

All completeness rules must have a condition and a list of attribute names. If the condition evaluates to true, then each attribute enumerated in the list must have a non-null value. Completeness conditions may refer to more than one attribute, and these conditional clauses are grouped together using the logical operators described in Table 8.1.

8.9.2   Exemption Rule

There are times when some attributes are not required to have values, depending on other values in the record. An exemption rule specifies a condition and a list of attributes, and if the condition evaluates to true, then those attributes in the list are allowed to have null values. Exemption rules, like completeness rules, are conditional assertions.

For example, a catalog order might require the customer to specify a color or size of an article of clothing, but neither is required if the customer orders a nonclothing product.

> **Rule NotClothing:**
> IF (Orders.Item_Class != "CLOTHING") Exempt
> {Orders.Color,
> Orders.Size
> }

If a null value rule has been specified for any of the attributes in the list, then the null value representations for those attributes may appear as well as traditional nulls.

8.9.3   Consistency Rule

Consistency is another of the dimensions of data quality described in Chapter 5. Consistency refers to maintaining a relationship between two (or more) attributes based on the actual values of the attributes. Consistency rules are conditional assertions, expressed as "if-then" statements that include both a condition and a consequent. Our consistency rule indicates that if a particular condition holds true, then a following consequent must also be true. For example, if a human resources data manager wants to make sure that the record for each employee has a salary that is within the range for that employee's title, we might have a set of consistency rules:

> **Rule Salary1:**
> IF (Employees.title == "Staff Member") Then (Employees.Salary >=
> 20000 AND Employees.Salary < 30000)
> **Rule Salary2:**
> IF (Employees.title == "Senior Staff Member") Then
> (Employees.Salary >= 30000 AND Employees.Salary < 40000)

Rule Salary3:
IF (Employees.title == "Manager") Then (Employees.Salary >=
    40000 AND Employees.Salary < 50000)
Rule Salary4:
IF (Employees.title == "Senior Manager") Then (Employees.Salary
    >= 50000 AND Employees.Salary < 60000)

For each consistency rule, there is a condition and a consequent. The condition may consist of clauses referring to more than one attribute, and the consequent may also refer to more than one attribute.

8.9.4   Derivation Rule

A derivation rule is the prescriptive form of the consistency rule. In a derivation rule, if a condition evaluates to true, then a consequent dictates how another attribute's value is defined. A derivation rule defines a data dependency between the attributes in the condition and the attribute in the consequent.

As an example, if we want to fill in the total amount charged for a catalog order, that total would be computed as the sum of the product of the number ordered and the price, plus the computed sales tax of 5 percent.

Rule DerivedTotal:
IF (Orders.NumberOrdered > 0) Then {
Orders.Total = (Orders.NumberOrdered * Orders.Price) * 1.05
}

Derivation rules can expose "virtual attributes." Such attributes don't really need to have their values filled in because the value can be derived as long as the dependent attributes have been filled.

8.10   Table, Cross-Table, and Cross-Message Assertions

So far we have mostly focused on rules that apply between the values of attributes within the same record. In fact, there are rules that apply between records within a table, between records in different tables, or between fields in different messages.

The rules in this section are important in terms of traditional relational database theory. The most powerful of these rules is the functional dependency rule, which indicates the relationship between the values of attributes across all records in a table. The other rules refer to what is called referential integrity.

8.10.1   Functional Dependency Rule

In database jargon, a functional dependency between two columns X and Y, means that for any two records R1 and R2 in the table, if field X of record R1 contains value x and field X of record R2 contains the same value x, then if field Y of record R1 contains the value y, then field Y of record R2 must contain the value y. In other words, attribute Y is said to be determined by attribute X.

In Section 8.9 we looked at consistency rules applied to records that defined restrictions on some attribute values based on the values of other specific attributes. These consistency rules are applied at the record level, which means that if the condition does not apply, there are no constraints on the target attributes' values. Functional dependency rules, on the other hand, describe the same inter-record constraints on all records in a table.

Essentially, a functional dependency rule is like a consistency rule that covers all records in the table. Based on this understanding, we can see that aside from the standard database use of functional dependence to ensure normalization, functional dependencies may actually represent a governing rule about what is represented in the data — in other words, a business rule!

Functional dependencies can hold between sets of attributes as well. A functional dependency is likely to represent either an implicit domain mapping or a business rule embedded in the data. We denote a functional dependency by specifying two sets of fields: the defining set and the determined set. For example, if we say that an employee's salary is determined by her title and her years of service, and this rule holds true for all employees, then this is a functional dependence that is expressed like this.

Rule SalaryDetermination:
{Employees.Title, Employees.Years} Determines {Employees.Salary}

Functional dependencies are particularly powerful because they can be manipulated using a series of inference rules.

1. *Reflexivity*   If the set of values in attribute X is a proper superset of the values in attribute Y, then X determines Y.
2. *Augmentation*   If X determines Y, then {X, Z} determines {Y, Z}.
3. *Decomposition*   If X determines {Y, Z}, then X determines Y.
4. *Transitivity*   If X determines Y, and Y determines Z, then X
   determines Z.
5. *Union*   If X determines Y, and X determines Z, then X determines {Y, Z}.
6. *Pseudotransitivity*   If X determines Y, and {W, Y} determines Z,
   then {W, X} determines Z.

These inference rules clarify the embedded business rules in a database table. We can also use them to assist in the discovery of domain
mappings.

8.10.2   Key Assertions

A table key is a set of attributes such that, for all records in a table, no
two records have the same set of values for all attributes in that key set.
A primary key is a key set that has been designated as a key that identifies records in the table. A key assertion is a proscriptive rule indicating
that a set of attributes is a key for a specific table.

Rule CustomersKey:
{Customers.FirstName, Customers.LastName, Customers.ID} Key
   for Customers

If a key assertion has been specified, no two records in the table
may have the same values for the indicated attributes. Therefore, a key
assertion basically describes the identifiability dimension of data quality
as described in Chapter 5.

8.10.3   Primary Key Assertions

A candidate key is a key set consisting of attributes such that the composition of the values in the key set uniquely identify a record in the
table and that none of the keys in the key set may be removed without
destroying the uniqueness property. A primary key is an arbitrarily
selected candidate key used as the only record-level addressing mecha-

nism for that table. We can qualify the key assertion by indicating that the key is primary, as in this example.

Rule CustomersPrimaryKey:
{Customers.FirstName, Customers.LastName, Customers.ID} Primary Key for Customers

A primary key defines an entity in a table, and, therefore, the enforcement of a primary key assertion is that no attribute belonging to the primary key may have null values. This demonstrates an interesting point: Some rule definitions may have an impact on other rule definitions. Our framework already has the facility for defining null value rules, but implicit in a primary key rule are other null value rules! Figure 8.4 explains both key assertions.

8.10.4   Foreign Key Assertions

A foreign key represents a relationship between two tables. When the values in field f in table T are chosen from the key values in field g in table S, field S.g is said to be a foreign key for field T.f. A foreign key assertion must indicate that a field in one table is a foreign key for a field in another table. For example, if the part_number field in the Orders table is taken from the part_number field in the Parts table, then we would have a rules like this.

Rule PartsForeignKey:
{Parts.part_number} Foreign Key for {Orders.part_number}

Specified first in the rule is the foreign key, followed by the key target. Since keys may be composed of multiple attributes, the rule may specify more than one field for both the foreign key and the key target.

Rule Type	Description	Rule Format
Key Assertion	The attribute list forms a key.	*{<attribute-list>} KEY FOR <table name>*
Primary Key Assertion	The attribute list forms the primary key.	*{<attribute-list>} PRIMARY KEY FOR <table name>*

FIGURE 8.4

The application of a foreign key assertion is in ensuring what is called *referential integrity*. Referential integrity means that if table T has a foreign key matching the primary key of another table S then every value of the foreign key in T must be equal to the value of some primary key in table S, or be completely null. Therefore, a foreign key assertion specifies a consistency relationship between tables — for all non-null foreign keys that appear in table T, there must exist a primary key with the same values in table S. For example, every part number referred to in the ordered parts field must be listed in the parts table (see Figure 8.5).

8.11   IN-PROCESS RULES

We must not forget that the quality of data also affects the way the data is used, and if there is a processing stream that uses information, there may be rules that govern automated processing. Therefore, we also define a class of rules that apply "in-process." In-process rules are those that make assertions about information as it passes between interfaces.

It is through the use of in-process rules that we can add "hooks" for measurement, validation, or the invocation of any external application. Before we can specify the rules themselves, we must also have a way to express the data flow for the process, and we do that using processing chains. Given a processing chain, we can insert into that chain in-process rules.

8.11.1   Processing (or Data-Flow) Chains

A processing chain (also referred to as a data-flow chain) is a high-level encapsulation of the processing steps that are applied to a flow of information. In order to assign in-process rules, there must be steps in that process

Rule Type	Description	Rule Format
Foreign Key Assertion	The attribute list forms a foreign key.	*{<table name and attribute>} FOREIGN KEY FOR <table name and attribute>*

FIGURE 8.5   Foreign keys

at which the rules are to be applied. Therefore, we have a formalism for defining steps in a processing chain. Each processing step is either a source for data, a target for data, or a processing stage for data. Each step is declared with a name along with a set of comment fields (which can indicate the actual operations that take place at that step). The flow of information is indicated as a directed connection between two processing steps.

As an example, consider a process that reads customer order data from a file, selects out a subset of orders for credit card processing, processes payments, forwards the successfully paid orders to a second data file and forwards the unsuccessfully paid orders to a reconciliation file. Each step is defined first, followed by the connective statements. For each connective statement, we also name the connector.

> **Source OrderFile;**
> **Stage SelectOrders;**
> **Stage ProcessPayments;**
> **Target PaidOrders;**
> **Target Reconciliation;**
> **Selector: OrderFile TO SelectOrders;**
> **OrderPay: SelectOrders TO ProcessPayments;**
> **GoodPayment: ProcessPayments TO PaidOrders;**
> **BadPayment: ProcessPayments TO Reconciliation;**

This description is reflected in Figure 8.6.

Given a way to describe both processing stages and the connections between them, we now have a "hook" on which we can hang in-process data quality and business rules.

8.11.2 Measurement Directives

A measurement directive associates a set of rules with a location in a data-flow chain and indicates that at that point in the processing, those rules are applied. For each rule, the determination is made as to whether the data is in accordance with the rule or not, and the results are logged.

Measurement directives are used for two stages of data quality: The first is the current state analysis and isolation of data quality problems, and the second is for continued data quality assurance. Measurement directives act as probes into the data flow, giving the analyst the chance to "look under the hood" to look for potential problems or to just make sure everything is running soundly.

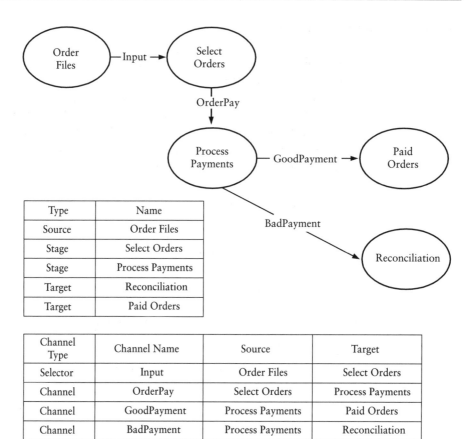

Type	Name
Source	Order Files
Stage	Select Orders
Stage	Process Payments
Target	Reconciliation
Target	Paid Orders

Channel Type	Channel Name	Source	Target
Selector	Input	Order Files	Select Orders
Channel	OrderPay	Select Orders	Process Payments
Channel	GoodPayment	Process Payments	Paid Orders
Channel	BadPayment	Process Payments	Reconciliation

FIGURE 8.6 Representation of an information chain

A measurement directive must specify either a processing stage, a connector, a source, or a target and a set of rules. For example, if we want to measure how frequently credit card fields have the wrong number of digits in the credit card number before the payment processing stage, we might use this directive.

Rule CCNumbers:
Restrict CreditCardNumber: LENGTH(value) == 16
Rule MeasureCCNumbers:
AT OrderPay Measure {CCNumbers}

8.11.3   Trigger Directives

A trigger directive indicates the invocation of a named operation at some point in the data-flow chain. We may include a condition to trigger the operation, or the operation may take place specifically when a record or a message hits a certain point in the data-flow chain.

We first must have a means for naming operations that can be invoked via triggers. All we really need is a declaration of the operation by its name. For example, consider an operation that sends an e-mail to your manager.

Operation EmailTheBoss;

When a message arrives at a particular point in the data-flow chain and an optional condition is fulfilled at that point, the operation is triggered. Therefore, a trigger directive includes either a processing stage, source, target, or connector, an optional condition, and the name of the operation to invoke. For example, if we want to e-mail the manager if an order's value exceeds $10,000, we might have a trigger directive like this.

Stage ProcessOrders;
Trigger at ProcessOrders if (Orders.Total > 10000): {E-mailThe-Boss};

We can include a list of operations that are invoked in sequential order instead of just a single operation.

8.12   OPERATIONAL RULES

There are other opportunities for inserting in-process rules that do not necessarily affect the data-flow chain but rather affect the data being transferred. In this section we discuss transformation rules, that describe how data is transformed from one form to another and update rules that define when information should be updated.

8.12.1   Transformation Rules

A transformation rule describes how data are mapped from a set of source locations to a destination location. These rules are used to define a portion of the extraction, transformation, and loading process for moving data between databases. Each transformation rule, which specifies how a single attribute is fulfilled, must indicate the sources of data needed for seeding the ultimate value and the operations that define how the attribute is ultimately defined.

For example, consider an international payment system that must accept payments in euros and disburse payments in dollars. The disbursement database field Disbursements.DollarsPaid is transformed from the Payments.Euros field in the payments database as a function of the currency exchange factor stored in the DollarsToForex mapping.

Transformation: Disbursements.Dollars =
{
Payments.Euros * DollarsToForex("Euro")
}

A transformation rule specifies the target attribute and a transformation expression.

8.12.2   Update Rules

Update rules indicate when a data set should be updated, whether it means the invocation of a new validation or the initiation of a new set of in-process rules. Update rules are basically trigger rules governed by timestamps. There are two directives that we need to allow update rules. The first is the initiation directive, which initiates an operation, and the second is the restart directive, which restarts an operation.

    At \<timestamp\> Initiate: DWPopulate
    At \<timestamp\> Restart: MeasureCCNumbers;

Both the initiate and restart directives can apply to operations or to in-process rules. An update rule, then, is indicated by a time/date-stamp and a list of initiate or restart directives. For example, if we want to restart the measurement directives after a certain time every day, we can use an update rule to indicate this.

    At 08:00:00 Restart MeasureCCNumbers;

This is shown in Figure 8.7.

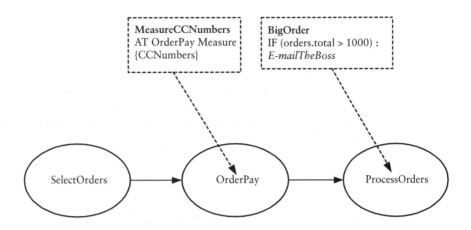

FIGURE 8.7   Inserting directives

8.13   OTHER RULES

There are other kinds of rules that are not discussed in this chapter. One class of rules is the approximate or fuzzy rules, which specify assertions allowing some degree of uncertainty. Another set is the navigation rules, which indicate appropriate navigation paths that can be executed by users at a Web site. Both of these classes will be treated at greater length in other chapters.

8.14   RULE MANAGEMENT, COMPILATION, AND VALIDATION

Once data quality and business rules have been defined, there are two more steps. The first is the accumulation and consolidation of all the rules into one working set, and the second step is confirming that the rules interact with each other correctly. These, together with the operation of storing, retrieving and editing rules, are part of the management of rules.

8.14.1   Rule Management

A benefit of defining rules is that we have described a formality that is simpler than a programming language and can express significant detail about the business and data quality rules that govern a data system. This simple formalism makes it possible for these rules to be defined, read, and understood by a nontechnician. The ultimate goal is a framework in which the data consumer can be integrated into the data quality process. In this way, data quality rules are integrated into the enterprise metadata and can be managed as content that can be published directly to all eligible data consumers.

8.14.2   Compilation

Rule compilation is more than just collecting rules. There is a possibility for interaction between rules, since more than one rule can reference the same set of data attributes. Another concern is the dimension across which the rules are applied — across a tuple, down a column, throughout a table, or across more than one table. Rule compilation is the process of collecting all the rules, ordering the rules, and preparing the rules for validation.

Rule compilation also identifies the tables, columns, and rows that are associated with rules. By collecting this information and allowing users to browse this data, both mapped from rule to data element and from data element to rule, users have a means for evaluating business rule dependencies between rows, columns, and tables. This gives users a valuable knowledge discovery tool.

In a more complex environment, rule compilation actually may involve translation from the rule format to an executable format. This may mean translating the set of rules into SQL calls or application code that can be used for data validation.

8.14.3   Rule Validation

Before rules can be compiled into an executable format, the rules themselves must conform to their own set of validity constraints. Specifically, the assertions about a data set cannot conflict with each other. For example, we can make these two assertions about our data.

> **Rule: IF (Customers.Cust_Class != "BUSINESS") Exempt**
> **{Customers.Business_Phone**
> **}**

Rule: RequiredBizPhone:
Customers.Business_Phone nulls not allowed

Each of these rules by itself is completely understandable. The first rule says that if the customer is not a business customer, the business phone attribute may be empty. The second rule indicates that the business phone field may not contain nulls. Put together, these two rules are contradictory: The first says that nulls are allowed under some conditions, while the second asserts that the same attribute may not be null. This is an example of violating a validity constraint on data quality rules.

Some other kinds of validity rules include the following.

- Restriction contradictions, where two restrictions create an assertion that cannot be true
- Uncovered consistency ranges, where consistency rules are defined for only a subset of data values but not all the possible values that can populate an attribute
- Key assertion violations, where an attribute set specified as a key is allowed to have nulls

8.15 RULE ORDERING

The last issue regarding rules is order. One of the nice things about the rule system is that if we want to declare that the data conform to the rules, all the rules and assertions hold true. But how do we test this? The answer is that we must apply each rule in its own context and validate that there are no violations.

8.15.1 Benefits of a Declarative System

This poses an interesting conundrum. A major benefit of having a rule set is that we have a declarative means for specifying expectations. But in order to actually test these rules, some of the rules must be transformed into an executable sequence of tests, which implies an assigned order of execution. It is because of the declarative nature of rules that in reality there are no constraints on the execution of the tests, although there are some exceptions.

The best way to order the rule execution, therefore, is dependent on the method by which the tests will be performed. If an automated method is used, then optimizing the runtime might be the overriding variable. If your junior data analysts are going to do the work, then the tests might be partitioned by table or by attribute. In other words, any suitable method is appropriate.

8.15.2   Dependencies

The only exceptions, as just noted, come into play when the rule itself includes a data dependence or a control dependence. A data dependence occurs when one piece of the rule depends on another part of the rule. Any of the rules with conditions and domain and mapping assignments have data dependences inherent in them. A control dependence occurs when an event must take place before the test is allowed. The trigger, update, and measurement directives imply control dependencies. Some rules may have both control and data dependence issues: Consider the transformation directives.

A dependence is said to be fulfilled if the no further modifications may take place to the dependent entity (attribute, table). A rule's dependence is violated if a test for that rule is performed before the associated dependencies have been fulfilled. The presence of dependences in the rule set forces some ordering on the execution of rule tests. The goal, then, is to determine the most efficient order that does not violate any dependence.

8.15.3   Benefits of Enforcing Dependence

Enforcing a valid order of execution in the presence of dependences provides a very nice side effect: it allows a user to pinpoint the location of a business rule or data quality violation at its earliest point in the information chain. When a violation occurs, there is an execution trail that can be used as a "debugging" device for the data steward. Not only does this provide the capacity to prevent unexpected data from passing through a quality gate, it also speeds up the problem determination and discovery process.

A second benefit is that the dependence constraints can help in the development of a user interface. Since the order of data acquisition can be determined by the data and control dependences embedded in the rules, a rule-directed sequence of query screens can be automatically generated. Because the rules guide the actual data acquisition, we can enforce our data quality and business rules on information as it enters the system — a significant step in building a high-quality knowledge enterprise.

8.16 SUMMARY

In this chapter, we looked at a formal way to define and describe our data quality expectations. Maintaining high-quality information levels allows a business to achieve a high level of automated information processing, which in turn allows for greater scalability. Because bad data can affect this operation, data quality rules are, in effect, business rules.

We then looked at the following nine different classes of data quality rules.

1. *Null value rules*   Including null specifications, null values, and non-null values
2. *Value rules*   Restrict the actual values that can populate an attribute
3. *Domain membership rules*   Covered restricted sets of values with business meanings from which attributes can draw their values
4. *Domain mappings*   Associate values from one domain with values from another domain, also with business meanings.
5. *Relation rules*   Including completeness, exemption, consistency, and derivation rules
6. *Table, cross-table, and cross-message assertions*   Including functional dependencies and key assertions
7. *In-process directives*   Including measurement directives and trigger directives
8. *Operational directives*   Including transformational rules and update rules
9. *Other rules*   Covered in other chapters

The use of a rule system has a number of benefits, especially when it comes to managing business and data quality rules as content. In particular, there are opportunities for automating a large part of the data acquisition and validation process, as well as the opportunity to pinpoint problem processes with respect to poor data quality.

9

MEASUREMENT AND CURRENT STATE ASSESSMENT

The first step in the mechanics of initiating a data quality improvement program is to perform an assessment of the current state of data quality. This approach provides a means to identify and document those areas with the greatest need of improvement as well as provide a baseline against which further improvements can be measured. This process, which we call current state assessment (CSA), is complementary to the economic analysis described in Chapter 4 and uses the rules framework described in Chapters 7 and 8.

The economic model described in Chapter 4 helps us determine the financial impact of poor data quality and identifies those locations in the information processing chain where there is a need for improvement. But the financial model does not give us any insight into what might be causing the poor data quality or any suggestions as to the kinds of improvements that are necessary. It is at this point in the analysis that the current state assessment adds value.

The CSA gives the analyst the opportunity to select and measure specific aspects of data quality that might be the source of economic discomfort. The results of this measurement are then used as the input to the next stage of the economic model, which is evaluating the costs associated with instituting improvements. This in turn helps in determining the return on investment associated with each improvement, which can help focus the management decisions when committing to particular improvement projects.

The result of the current state assessment is a document similar to the data quality scorecard, except that instead of measuring financial impact, we provide data quality levels associated with a set of data quality dimensions measured at each location in the information chain. We can then correlate the data quality measurements in the CSA to the high-impact areas in the scorecard. We then use those measurements to suggest target data quality measurements that will provide the needed improvement in quality to resolve any negative economic impact.

In this chapter, we detail the evolution of a current state assessment. This partially overlaps with the data quality scorecard, but we will see that at some point the development diverges. What is important for the CSA is that a choice is made about the kinds of data quality issues that are selected for analysis.

We start with identifying the data consumers, then working back to determine the information chain. At this point, we choose a subset of the dimensions of data quality we discussed in Chapter 5 to measure. The next step is to assert a set of what we call "sentinel rules" — those rules that can be most clearly articulated within the rules framework and constrained by what is known about the data at any particular point in the information flow.

These sentinel rules are then used for measurement. There are two kinds of measurement: static measurement, which measures the rules using a snapshot of the information under investigation, and dynamic measurement, which measure information in transit as it passes through any particular point in the information chain.

9.1   IDENTIFY EACH DATA CUSTOMER

A key to performing a successful current state assessment is identifying the data customers that consume the information produced. Because these customers are most likely to have experience with the quality of the information, and also because their investment is mostly in the value of the information produced instead of the information production process, they are more likely to provide anecdotal if not verifiable evidence of low data quality. The data customers are also more likely to report to the data quality analyst the effects low data quality.

We should note here that not all data consumers are real, live people — many are other processes or external automated customers. These are often more difficult to identify, but they are just as important within the "data ecosystem."

Building the information chain requires that we know the ultimate destination of the data. Whether the consumer is an automated system or not, we first tabulate the set of consumers as endpoints in the information chain. Starting with each endpoint, we can trace backward how the information reached that point.

9.2 MAPPING THE INFORMATION CHAIN

Let's review the steps in building the information chain that we discussed in Chapter 4.

9.2.1 Processing Stages

We define a set of processing stages through which data moves inside a system. Remember, these stages are not all-inclusive but rather a place to start building the information chain.

1. *Data supply*   Data suppliers forward information into the system.
2. *Data acquisition*   This is the processing stage that accepts data from external suppliers and injects it into the system.
3. *Data creation*   Internal to the system, data may be generated and then forwarded to another processing stage.
4. *Data processing*   Any stage that accepts input and generates output (as well as generating side effects) is called a data processing stage.
5. *Data packaging*   Any point that information is collated, aggregated, and summarized for reporting purposes is a packaging stage.
6. *Decision making*   The point where human interaction is required is called a decision-making stage.
7. *Decision implementation*   This is the stage where the decision made at a decision-making stage is executed, possibly affecting other processing stages or the data delivery stage.
8. *Data delivery*   This is the point where packaged information is delivered to a known data consumer.
9. *Data consumption*   As the data consumer is the ultimate user of processed information, the consumption stage is the exit stage of the system.

9.2.2   Directed Information Channels

Information channels are pipelines indicating the flow of information from one processing stage to another. A directed information channel is additionally attributed with the direction in which data flows. The delivery of supplier data to an acquisition stage is performed through an information channel directed from the supplier to the acquisition stage. We like to make our information channels directed because there may be bidirectional communication taking place between any two points, and this makes it possible to differentiate between data flowing in the different directions.

9.2.3   Information Chain Map

A map of an information chain is represented by the combination of the processing stages connected by directed information channels. Because we will need to analyze each location in the information chain where a data quality problem might arise, we need a naming scheme for the sites on the map. Each processing stage should be labeled with a name and attributed with its stage type. Information channels are named by composing the source and target processing stage names, separated by a hyphen.

9.2.4   Degree of Information Load

Each processing stage in the information chain can be characterized by the amount of information that passes into and out of that stage. We can count the number of directed channels that enter and leave the stage.

The number of directed information channels entering the stage is the degree of information input. A processing stage with a high degree of information input is called a collector. The number of directed information channels leaving the stage is the degree of information output. A processing stage with a high degree of information output is called a broadcaster. The sum of the information channels entering and leaving each processing stage is called the degree of information load. A processing stage with a high degree of information load is likely an important node in the information chain and is called a critical junction.

9.2.5 Creating the Information Chain

By starting with the endpoints and working backward, each critical processing point and information channel in the information chain can be identified and labeled. At each step, we ask the people responsible for the processing where they get their input and where the output goes. This way, the information chain is built incrementally and we know which employees or suppliers are responsible at each point in the data flow.

When the information chain is in reasonable shape (one can reasonably follow the flow of data from its supply or creation point to a set of consumers), the next stage of analysis can begin. Since the information chain is used as input to both the economic framework and the current state assessment, a completed information chain should be published and archived as enterprise metadata.

9.3 CHOOSE LOCATIONS IN THE INFORMATION CHAIN

When the information chain has been published, the next part of the current state assessment is to select locations in the information chain to use as the measurement points. The choice of location can be dependent on a number of aspects.

1. *Critical junction*   Any processing stage with a high degree of information load is likely to be a site where information from different data sources are merged or manipulated.
2. *Collector*   A collector is likely to be a place where information is aggregated and prepared for reporting or prepared for storage.
3. *Broadcaster*   A broadcaster is likely to be a processing stage that prepares information for many consumers and, therefore, may be a ripe target for measurement.
4. *Ease of access*   While some processing stages may be more attractive in terms of analytical power, they may not be easily accessed for information collection.
5. *High-profile stages*   A processing stage that consumes a large percentage of company resources might provide useful measurement information.

The important point is that a number of locations in the information chain be selected, preferably where the same data sets pass through more than one of the locations. This will add some depth to the measurement, since place-stamping the data along the way while registering data quality measurements will help determine if there are specific failure points in the information chain.

9.4   CHOOSE A SUBSET OF THE DQ DIMENSIONS

As we discussed in Chapter 5, there are many dimensions across which we can measure data quality. Because the number of dimensions is relatively large, the next stage of the current state assessment is to select a subset of the dimensions of data quality specifically for measurement.

Frequently, the kinds of problems that appear will suggest the dimensions of choice. If not, there are some logical choices to make with regard to generating a comprehensive CSA. It is a good idea to select at least one dimension from each of the five classes of data quality dimensions. The resulting CSA will then provide insight into the quality of the organization's data models, data values, data domains, presentation, and information policy.

9.5   IDENTIFY SENTINEL RULES

When we actually measure the levels of data quality, we will be looking at the degree to which what we examine meets our expectations, according to our definition of data quality from Chapter 3. We will define "sentinel rules" — rules that particularly capture the essence of the quality of data as per data consumer expectations. They are called sentinel rules because they act as a "red flag," or sentinel, in terms of a location in an information chain where there might be additional work associated with low data quality.

Sentinel rules can be associated with the data model, the data values, the data presentation, and so forth. They manifest themselves in the way that everyday operations staff members attack data quality problems, as well as in ways that increase levels of frustration from using the data.

As a simple example, consider a direct marketing company that sends out millions of addressed mailings. Some of the addresses on the mailing list are incorrect and thus undeliverable, and they are returned to the company. The operation would be to investigate each undelivered piece of mail to understand why it was returned. The goal would be to correct the incorrect addresses by looking up the names in a current address directory. The sentinel rule here is embedded in the reaction to the data quality incorrectness. The real assertion would be that no mail would have an incorrect address.

The more formal definition of a sentinel rule is an assertion that characterizes the minimum expectation of the most important aspect of data quality at a specific point in the information chain. Sentinel rules distinguish between assertions about data that are meaningful in the business environment from those that are irrelevant. Measurements of the data quality associated with a sentinel rule are an important part of the current state assessment, since the results of these measurements can give a sound characterization of the general quality of data overall.

How do we identify a sentinel rule? Since sentinel rules are the formal definition of vague notions of poor data quality, the best way to identify them is by asking employees to relate their most interesting anecdotes about data quality. Typically, these stories will revolve around situations that required the most cleanup work, and if any anecdotes reflect multiple occurrences or are related by several different employees, that's a good indication of an underlying sentinel rule. The rule itself is abstracted as the opposite of the problem in an anecdote.

For example, if a tale describes how an error in one attribute in a particular data record caused an overnight batch processing to halt, requiring a 2 A.M. paging of a support personnel team to determine the cause of the problem and fix it, the underlying sentinel rule describes the expectation that the one attribute must have its correct value. Further exploration should reveal which values are good and which are not, giving us a formal definition of the sentinel rule.

9.6 MEASURING DATA QUALITY

The next sections detail some ways to measure data quality in terms of the dimensions of data quality introduced in Chapter 5. In each section, we review a dimension of data quality and suggest ways to measure it. Of course, these are only starting points, and the ways to measure data quality may be dependent on the specific situation.

9.7   MEASURING DATA QUALITY OF DATA MODELS

First let's examine the dimensions of data quality affecting data models. In most cases, data quality associated with the data model is likely to be measured using static metrics. Each section will review the dimension of data quality and provide suggestions for measuring its level.

9.7.1   Clarity of Definition

Clarity of definition refers to the names and the naming conventions assigned to tables, fields, and relations within the system. The names assigned to tables and fields should clearly reflect the meaning contained in the sets of information they represent. Naming of different fields should be unambiguous, but similar attributes should share distinctive names.

There are a number of ways to measure clarity of definition:

- Measure the degree to which there is a defined organizational naming convention.
- Measure the degree to which the named objects conform to that convention. This quantifies how well the members of an organization participate in the naming convention.
- If there is no organizational convention, measure the number of different names used for attributes holding the same kind of data. This quantifies the levels of de facto naming standardization.
- Assign a score to each table and attribute name qualifying how well it describes the data it holds. This quantifies the relationship between name and meaningfulness.

9.7.2   Comprehensiveness

Comprehensiveness is a measure of how well the data model encompasses enough information to accommodate the current needs of all the users of the data set, as well as broad or extensible enough to provide for future user needs.

We measure comprehensiveness by looking at how easily the data model adapts to general use. We can measure the following:

- The number of requests over a period of time for adding new tables to the data model.

- The number of requests over a period of time for adding new attributes to data tables. These two items will quantify how well laid-out the original model was.
- The degree to which auxiliary database systems are being used in the organization. This quantifies whether the original model is being abandoned.

9.7.3 Flexibility

A data model's flexibility reflects the capacity to change in reaction to new user requirements. Flexibility is similar to comprehensiveness, the difference being that comprehensiveness addresses what is planned a priori, whereas flexibility addresses those situations that crop up but were not part of the original plan.

We measure flexibility in ways similar to measuring comprehensiveness:

- The number of requests over a period of time for adding new tables to the data model
- The number of requests over a period of time for adding new attributes to data tables
- The number of times an attribute is overloaded
- The amount of code needed to implement new functionality
- The amount of time it takes to implement new functionality

9.7.4 Robustness

Robustness represents the ability to reflect changes in the modeled world without excessive changes to the data model. Robustness also involves defining attributes in ways that adapt to changing values without having to constantly update the values.

Robustness can be measured as a function of the changes made to already existing tables and attributes. We can get a quantitative measure of robustness by counting the number of times within a specified period that there have been changes made to the data model aside from adding new tables or columns. Examples include changing the size or type of an attribute, changing relations between tables, modifying keys, and so forth.

9.7.5   Essentialness

Other than for specific needs such as planned redundancy or the facilitation of analytical applications, a data model should not include extra information. Extra information requires the expense of acquisition and storage and tends to decrease data quality levels. Also, there may be a lot of data attributes for which space has been allocated, yet these attributes are not filled. Statistics regarding the frequency at which data tables and attributes are referenced is a good source for measuring essentialness:

Here are some ideas for ways to measure essentialness.

- Count the number of data elements, tables, and attributes that are never read.
- Count the number of data elements, tables, and attributes that are never written.
- Count the number of redundant copies of the same data in the enterprise.

9.7.6   Attribute Granularity

Granularity refers to the number of objects used to represent one notion. It is defined on a scale from "fine," where a data field can take on more values, to "coarse," where it can take on fewer values. In a table, we can use more attributes to represent finer granularity. Fine granularity provides more detailed information, but there are added costs for storage and an increased possibility for introducing errors.

We can measure the granularity these ways:

- Count the number of attributes allocated for representing a specific component of a model (for example, are sales statistics measured by quarter or by month?).
- Determine if any attributes are used to represent more than one notion (attribute overloading).
- Determine if any data domains are limited in their ability to express the represented notion.

9.7.7 Precision of Domains

While the number of attributes in a set characterizes granularity, precision refers to the number of values that a single attribute may take. The precision is partially determined by the data type of the attribute, but it is also predicated on subtyping that is applied to the domain.

Domain precision can be measure these ways:

- Count the number of possible values that an attribute can take (if the attribute data type is a finite set).
- Determine the degree to which the data type has been subtyped. This can be seen as a characterization of the specialization assigned to specific domains (for example, two-letter strings vs U.S. state abbreviations vs Northeast U.S. state abbreviations).
- Determine the precision of attributes that can take on a representation of a continuous domain (such as floating point numbers or decimals).

9.7.8 Homogeneity

Homogeneity refers to the overloading of value classes within a used attribute. While a data model is intended to maintain a single class of entities, the use of the model may evolve to overload the data set to maintain multiple classes of entities within the same database.

Homogeneity can be measured in terms of the degree to which an entity is being used to exclusively represent the real-world object it is meant to model. This can be done these ways:

- Identify all attributes that have been overloaded to represent more than one object.
- Count the number of attributes that take values from more than one defined data domain.
- Examine the data domains used by all attributes and make sure that each describes a single aspect of the data model.

9.7.9   Naturalness

Naturalness is a qualification of the relationship between what is being modeled and the model's representation, meaning that each represented attribute should pair with a natural object in the world being modeled. Also, each attribute should represent a single fact about the object and pull its values from a meaningfully natural (not artificially restricted) domain.

Naturalness is a qualitative dimension, but it can be measured by grading the degree to which the data in the collection match the objects that are being modeled. This can be measured these ways:

- Does each data value pair with a real-world object?
- Does each attribute reflect a single aspect or fact about the object being modeled?

9.7.10   Identifiability

There is a presumption that when each entity in a particular set of entities (used in the generic sense, not the relational database sense) is expected to be unique, there must be some absolute means for distinguishing between any pair of entities. If not, there is a possibility that there are multiple records representing the same individual entity. Therefore, each entity type must allow for unique identification.

Identifiability is measured by determining which attributes (or sets of attributes) should represent unique entities, as well as a means for distinction, and then measuring how many duplicate records exists for the same entity. In Chapter 13 we explore ways to determine the identifiability attributes (commonly known as a primary key).

9.7.11   Obtainability

Obtainability qualifies whether the information to be modeled can be collected and stored. This obtainability may be characterized by a measure of the ease and feasibility of collection and storage, as well as more obtuse issues such as legality of information collection or storage. Building a model to represent values that are difficult (or impossible) to obtain will probably result in having attributes that will remain mostly empty.

There are two kinds of obtainability that can be measured. The first is whether data attributes represent values that are obtainable at all. The second measures the difficulty of obtaining data. These are measured these ways:

- Assign a grade that scores the difficulty in obtaining information, and score each table and attribute with an obtainability grade.
- Count the number of people required to participate in obtaining the data.
- Measure the amount of time required to obtain data.

9.7.12 Relevance

An irrelevant attribute is one that, if it were removed, would have no effect on either the application as it is being run today or on any of the planned features of the application. This is similar to essentialness, but it is more focused on data that is being collected or was already collected and no longer has any business relevance.

Relevance is measured by counting the number of attributes and tables, which if removed would have no business relevance. This implies some degree of reverse engineering to find out what the intended use is for each table and its attributes, but this exercise is particularly useful in that the reverse engineering is a good source of knowledge/content to be collected and managed.

9.7.13 Simplicity/Complexity

The simplicity dimension refers to the degree of complexity in the data model, whether it is due to extra attributes or a complicated relationship between attributes. Complexity in the data model manifests itself over time in terms of complications in the associated application code.

Simplicity (or more accurately, complexity) is very difficult to measure, and consequently, we must choose some aspect of the model to measure. Since it is commonly accepted that the more interconnections there are within a system, the greater the complexity, one place to start is by examining the number of tables in the system and the number of relationships that exists within each table and across tables.

A large number of anything in a data model may reflect a lack of simplicity. We can count (1) the number of attributes in each table, (2) the number of tables in a database, and (3) the number of foreign key relations in a database.

9.7.14 Semantic Consistency

Semantic consistency refers to consistency of definitions among attributes within a data model, as well as similarly named attributes in different data sets. Semantic consistency is a dimension that characterizes how the meanings and the names of objects within the data set are consistent.

Here are some ways to measure semantic consistency:

- Determine the degree to which similarly named attributes make use of the same data domain.
- Determine the degree to which data attributes using the same domain are similarly (or exactly) named.
- Grade data attribute definitions in terms of consistency across the enterprise data resource.

9.7.15 Structural Consistency

Structural consistency is a characterization of the care taken by the database modelers, administrators, and stewards in guaranteeing "strong-typing" of similar attributes. This dimension can be measured across two axes.

- The first regards how different attributes of the same virtual type are represented. For example, are customer names represented in all database tables using three fields such as first name, last name, middle initial? Or are some represented using just last name and first name without the middle initial? The measurement here counts the number of times the same kind of item is represented in more than one way.
- The second regards the degree to which there are different representations for the same value. In other words, this measures the different ways that the same data item appears in the data environment. For example, numeric data can be represented using integers, character strings, decimals, and so on. Another example is to ask if state names are spelled out or abbreviated.

There is a subtle difference between these two measures. The first is looking at how the same idea is spread out across the columnar structure of a database table; the second looks at whether different data domains are used to represent the same value.

9.8   MEASURING DATA QUALITY OF DATA VALUES

Next, we look at how to measure the data quality of data values. This is the kind of measurements most frequently associated with data quality and, consequently, is also the easiest for which to secure management support.

9.8.1   Accuracy

Data accuracy refers to the degree with which data values agree with an identified source of correct information. There are different sources of correct information: a database of record, a similar, corroborative set of data values from another table, dynamically computed values, the result of a manual workflow, or irate customers.

Accuracy is measured by comparing the given values with the identified correct source. The simplest metric is a ratio of correct values and incorrect values. A more interesting metric is the correctness ratio along with a qualification of how incorrect the values are using some kind of distance measurement.

It is possible that some of this measuring can be done automatically, as long as the database of record is also available in electronic format. Unfortunately, many values of record are maintained in a far less accessible format and require a large investment in human resources to get the actual measurements.

9.8.2   Null Values

A null value is a missing value. Yet, a value that is missing may provide more information than one might think because there may be different reasons for the missing value, such as:

- Unavailable values
- Not applicable for this entity

- There is no value in the attribute's domain that correctly classifies this entity
- The value may actually be missing.

The simplest way to measure null values is to count the number of empty or null attributes that are expected to have a value. More precise measurements can be collected after specifying the exact rules regarding the types of null values and measuring conformance to those rules. This involves specifying rules such as described in Chapter 8, and automatically checking conformance.

9.8.3   Completeness

Completeness refers to the expectation that certain attributes are expected to have assigned values in a data set. Completeness rules can be assigned to a data set in three levels of constraints and can therefore be measure using these constraints as well.

1. Mandatory attributes require a value — the measure counts the number of records conforming to some assertion but still missing the value. As an example, stock option records must have an expiration date field; any records without that attribute filled in are incomplete.
2. Optional attributes, which may have a value — again, this must be measured based on conformance to the specified data quality rule described in Chapter 8.
3. Inapplicable attributes (such as a maiden name for a single male), which may not have a value. The measurement, again, is based on conformance to a specified data quality rule.

9.8.4   Consistency

Consistency can be curiously simple or dangerously complex. In its most basic form, consistency refers to data values in one data set being consistent with values in another data set. Note that even though two data values drawn from separate data sets may be consistent with each other, both can be incorrect, so measuring consistency is not the same as measuring correctness.

How do we measure consistency? The simplest measure is to perform record linkage among the data sets under investigation and verify that the shared attributes in each set have the same values. The reported measure is the number of entities that do not have consistent representations across the enterprise.

9.8.5 Currency/Timeliness

Currency refers to the degree to which information is current with the world that it models. Currency can measure how "up-to-date" information is and whether it is correct despite possible time-related changes. The measure for currency can be similar to that of consistency — checking the data against a known up-to-date source. The measure counts the number of records that are not current.

The measurement for timeliness involves defining the time criteria and constraints that are expected for the arrival of the data and then measuring in the period how frequently the data are available when it is expected. A more interesting measurement details how late the data actually are. In other words, if the data acquirer expects that delivery will take place by a certain time each day, we would measure not only how often the data is delivered on time but exactly what time the data is delivered, how close to the expected time it was delivered, and the range of lateness over a period of time.

9.9 MEASURING DATA QUALITY OF DATA DOMAINS

Having made use of the concept of data domains and mappings between those domains, the next area of measurement is how well the different players in the enterprise are cooperating with the use of enterprise-wide data subtypes.

9.9.1 Enterprise Agreement of Usage

The notion of abstracting information into a data domain implies that there are enough users of the same set of data that it makes sense to manage that data set separately as a resource instead of having separate groups manage their own versions. The dimension of enterprise agreement of usage measures the degree to which different organizations conform to the usage of the enterprise data domain of record instead of relying on their own data set.

The first measurement involves counting the number of shared data domains that have been agreed to throughout the enterprise. We can further measure this dimension by the number of organizations within the enterprise that have agreed to use the shared data resource versus the number of holdouts.

9.9.2   Stewardship

A dimension of data quality is the degree to which responsibility has been assigned for the stewardship of information domains. Since a data domain represents a collection of data values that are recognized as a data source of record, it is advisable to appoint a steward to be responsible for the upkeep and maintenance of the data domains. Stewardship is measured by counting the number of groups that have appointed a steward to be responsible for a set of data.

9.9.3   Ubiquity

As a data quality–oriented organization matures, the agreement of usage will move from a small set of "early adopters" to gradually encompass more and more of the enterprise. Ubiquity measures the degree to which different departments in an organization use shared reference data and can be measured two ways. The first way looks at the number of distributed versions of the same reference data sets that exist in the enterprise. As more groups agree to the usage agreement or subscribe to a data ownership policy, they yield their control over their versions of the data sets and, therefore, the number of replicated sets will be reduced. The second way is counting the number of data users subscribed to the shared data resource. Even if a suborganization refuses to give up its copy of the reference data, there is nothing that prevents individual users from subscribing to the shared resource on their own. Therefore, we can measure individual usage as well.

9.10 MEASURING DATA QUALITY OF DATA PRESENTATION

Moving on to our next set of data quality dimensions, let's look at ways to measure the quality of data presentation. Many of these dimensions can only be measured through dialog with the users, since the presentation is an issue that affects the way information is absorbed by the user.

In each of these cases, though, the best way to get a feel for a score in each dimension is to ask the user directly! In the question, formulate each dimension definition as a positive statement — for example, "The format and presentation of data meets my needs" — and see how strongly each user agrees or disagrees with the statement.

9.10.1 Appropriateness

Appropriateness is the dimension that we use to categorize how well the format and presentation of the data matches the users' needs. To measure this dimension, we must explore the history of the interaction between the user group and the designers and implementers. If there are many occurrences of user requests that result in changes to the data model or to the data presentation layer, this may indicate a low level of appropriateness.

9.10.2 Correct Interpretation

A good presentation provides the user with everything required for the correct interpretation of information. Applications with online help facilities are fertile territory for measuring this dimension. The help facility can be augmented to count the number of times a user invokes help and log the questions the user asks.

Applications without online help can still be evaluated. This is done by assessing the amount of time the application developer spends explaining, interpreting, or fixing the application front end to enhance the user's ability to correctly interpret the data.

9.10.3   Flexibility

Flexibility in presentation describes the ability of the system to adapt to changes in both the represented information and in user requirements for presentation of information. Problems associated with flexibility are reflected in requests to change a user interface or to add a new component to a user interface. We can measure flexibility across two axes: (1) counting the number of times users make requests for changes in the presentation and (2) measuring the difficulty in implementing a change. That is measured either in the amount of time required, the number of parties involved, or the number of files, tables, or programs that need to be modified.

9.10.4   Format Precision

The presentation of an attribute's value should reflect the precision of the value based on both the internal representation and the needs of the users. Typical issues include the ability to display all possible values and to distinguish different values.

For example, floating point numbers may have a greater precision in storage than in presentation, or decimal data types may maintain six places to the left of the decimal point. In some cases, only two decimal places are displayed despite the greater precision, with the value presented having been rounded. In some cases, this may be tolerable (for example, when computing sales tax), but in others it may not be acceptable (displaying the concentration levels of arsenic in drinking water).

To measure this dimension, it is necessary to prioritize displayed values based on the importance placed on the users' ability to differentiate by degree of precision. In other words, we need to isolate those variables to which users focus and measure how well the precision conforms to the users' expectations.

9.10.5   Portability

In today's enterprise, it is likely that there will be a multitude of systems and software platforms. In this kind of environment, being able to take advantage of portability becomes critical in maintaining a high level of application availability. Aside from the ability to migrate an application from one platform to another, portability with respect to presentation will incorporate the use of standards and recognized symbolism and the ability to perform context-sensitive customization.

In an environment that uses different kinds of systems and applications, a portable interface is important so that as applications are migrated from one platform to another, the presentation of data is familiar to the users.

Alternatively, when we are "migrating users" (from one office to another office, for example) it is important to continue to provide a familiar interface (or not) dependent on user preferences. For example, consider an employee's transfer from a United States office to a London office. If the user has specified certain display preferences for daily reports, should the report's presentation be updated based on location when the user has moved? Would distance now be measured in kilometers instead of miles?

We measure portability based on the following:

- Subscription to data standards — do the systems make use of published recognized standards for representation of data?
- Ability to internationalize — how well do the systems reconfigure the presentation of information depending on reported location?
- Ability to allow personalized customization — how well do the systems reconfigure presentation of information based on user preferences?
- Use of known symbols and icons — are they well known and consistent throughout the enterprise?
- Platform transparency — does the presentation remain the same when seen from different hardware (or software) platforms?

We can grade the answers to these questions to provide a measurement of portability.

9.10.6   Representation Consistency

This dimension refers to whether instances of data are represented in a format that is consistent with the domain of values as well as consistent with other similar attribute values. In Chapter 5, we looked at the example of the display of time in a nonmilitary, 12-hour format as opposed to the 24-hour military format. If both formats are used in different parts of the same system, this could create confusion.

One of the first ways to measure this dimension is to see whether there is a style guide for data representation throughout the enterprise. This can range from printed guidelines that are to be followed by implementers to electronic style sheets and templates that are integrated into the development process.

A more granular investigation should be done to determine if there is a standard representation format associated with every base data type and domain. The next step would examine all presentations of values associated with every data type and domain and see if the representation is consistent with the standard representation.

9.10.7   Representation of Null Values

In Chapter 5, we first discussed null values, and in Chapter 8 we looked at the storage representation of nulls more carefully. Given that we know that there are what we might call "standard nulls," as well as our defined null types, when the null value (or absence of a value) is required for an attribute, there should be a recognizable form for presenting that null value that does not conflict with any valid values.

For example, a numeric null should not be displayed as a 0, which represents a specific numeric value. For character strings, the "missing" method of displaying the data should only be used if there are no distinguishing null type values.

If there are ways to distinguish the different kinds of null values, there should be different ways to present them to the user. These factors should be considered:

- Are there special ways of representing null values?
- If user-defined null types are used, can the user distinguish between null types in the presentation?
- Can the user distinguish between a null value and valid default or 0/blank values?

9.10.8   Use of Storage

We have established that despite the increasing availability of low-cost large data storage platforms, it is still important to measure how effectively the storage is being used. This includes the following considerations:

- If storage performance is meeting user requirements
- How well the use of storage will scale
- Whether there are embedded performance glitches inherent in the architecture
- Whether data replication is being used to good advantage
- Whether constraints on data normalization should be relaxed for performance reasons

9.11 MEASURING DATA QUALITY OF INFORMATION POLICY

In Chapter 3, we looked at the issue of defining a data ownership policy, and the topics of data policies (with respect to data sharing, usage, and management) are all themes that flow through the technical components of this book. An assessment of data quality in an enterprise cannot dismiss the importance of the existence of and the concurrence with general information policies.

In this section, we review those dimensions introduced in Chapter 5 associated with information policy, and we look at ways of characterizing the degree of conformance with information policy.

9.11.1 Accessibility

Accessibility refers to the degree of ease of access to information, as well as the breadth of access (whether all the information can be accessed). We can measure this dimension by answering these questions:

1. For each data set, how easy is it to automate access? In other words, we can measure the degree of ease of access by how easy it is to implement a system to access the data. Some systems may be set up such that special programs must be written to provide a hook into the data, while in others, the means for access for any data set is template and is easily configured.
2. Does the presentation allow for the display of all data? Sometimes the method of presentation does not adequately display all pertinent data items, either by fiat or through the constraints of "real estate." If an attempt is made to integrate a full display limited to a single screen, something is bound to be short-changed.
3. Is the presentation in a form that allows the user to absorb what is being presented? This question differs from the previous one in

that even if all the information has been presented, can the user get as much as possible out of the data.

4. How easy is it to get authorized to access information? This is not a question of automation but instead measures the steps that must be taken to authorize a user's access.

5. Are there filters in place to block unauthorized access? This questions whether there is a way to automate the access limits.

This dimension refers to that information that is allowed to be presented to any selected subset of users. Even though the last two questions border on the issue of security and authorization, there is a subtle difference. The dimension of accessibility characterizes the means for both providing and controlling access, but the dimension of security characterizes the policies that are defined and implemented for access control.

9.11.2   Metadata

As we will explore in greater detail in Chapter 11, metadata deals with the data in the system. When we attempt to measure the metadata policy, we investigate whether there is an enterprise-wide metadata framework and the support policies that go along with it.

To measure the metadata policy, we must score the following questions:

1. Is there a metadata policy defined? In some systems, there is no defined metadata policy, only small islands of managed metadata. This question focuses on whether the managers of the enterprise have deemed it important to have an organizational policy for managing metadata.

2. Is there a metadata repository? This next question focuses on the infrastructure provided for metadata management. Even with a metadata policy in place, there is a difference in usage if there is a well-defined infrastructure available.

3. Where is metadata stored and under whose authority? Is metadata stored in a location accessible to all users? Can users browse the metadata, especially if they are integrating a new information system component? The greater flexibility there is in reading metadata, the better chance there will be of reusing information that already exists instead of creating new tables and so forth.

9.11.3   Privacy and Security

Privacy is an issue of selective display of information based on internally managed permissions. Security is similar to privacy, except that privacy deals with protecting the entities being modeled by the system, whereas security protects the data itself.

We speak of privacy when asking about the kind of information that is being stored, the kind of control imposed over the storage and retrieval of that information, and who controls access to that information. In this chapter, we couple the measurement of privacy and security, since they are very closely intertwined. When we want to measure privacy policy, we need to ask these kinds of questions:

1. Is there a privacy policy? The lack of a privacy policy should be noted, but existing privacy policies can be confusing and should be examined to make sure that there is clarity in which levels of privacy are protected and which are not.
2. If there is a privacy policy in place, how well is privacy protected?
3. Are there safeguards in place to maintain privacy and confidentiality? How is data secured from unauthorized viewing?
4. Is private information encoded or encrypted in a way that prevents unauthorized reading, even if the data itself can be accessed?
5. Are there different storage procedures for confidential data versus nonconfidential data?
6. How does the policy enforce security constraints (such as loading secure information onto a portable data device like a laptop, personal digital assistant, or even pagers and mobile telephones)?

Privacy and security policies should cover more than just the transference and storage of information. The privacy policy should also cover the boundaries of any kind of information dissemination, including inadvertent as well as inferred disclosure. An example of inadvertent disclosure is the lack of care taken when using a mobile telephone in a public location. An example of inferred disclosure is when the accumulation and merging of information posted to, then subsequently gleaned from multiple Web sites can be used to draw conclusions that could not have been inferred from the individual Web sites.

9.11.4   Redundancy

Redundancy refers to the management of multiple copies of the same data sets. In some environments, redundancy is planned and desirable; in others, it is a by-product of poor management. Planned redundancy is desirable in that it provides fault-tolerance and may improve the accessibility of information. On the other hand, redundancy becomes unwieldy when there are many copies of the same data. In order to measure redundancy, we must look to these issues:

1. Is redundancy planned in the system or not?
2. If redundancy is planned, what is the hardware infrastructure for storage?
3. What is the policy for copy updates? Is updating performed in real time, or is synchronization performed across the enterprise at a specified time?
4. Who manages the source copy? Or are the multiple copies viewed as equals with a synchronization process coordinating all copies?
5. If redundancy is unplanned, is it undesired?
6. With unplanned redundancy, how well are the copies synchronized? Does the lack of synchronization create an environment for the creation of information errors?
7. If redundancy is unplanned, how do multiple copies affect the efficiency of operations?
8. How do multiple copies affect data synchronization across the enterprise?

9.11.5   Unit Cost

The cost of maintaining information contributes greatly to a company's ability to provide information-based services, information processing, as well as general overall efficiency. When the unit cost of information is low, greater volumes of information can be handled, which can open opportunities for increased margins.

To measure unit cost, we must measure (1) the cost to obtain values, (2) the cost of storage, (3) the cost of processing per unit, (4) the cost to maintain levels of data quality, and (5) the cost of building data quality into an information product, which must be weighed against the cost of not having data quality. These are issues that we dealt with in Chapter 4.

9.12 STATIC VS DYNAMIC MEASUREMENT

The different dimensions of data quality can be measured in two ways. The first way, static measurement, explores the aspects of data quality in a static set of data. The second method, dynamic measurement, assesses the levels of data quality as information flows through a working system.

9.12.1 Static Measurement

When we talk about static measurement, we refer to measuring what already exists within the system. Static measurement is a useful process, since it can expose many opportunities for measuring against our different data quality dimensions. A static assessment will essentially take a snapshot of the data environment that can then be copied to another location for separate analysis.

Static measurement is a tool that was used frequently in addressing the Y2K problem. Many organizations completely duplicated their processing systems in a separate, enclosed environment, grabbing copies of all data at a particular point in time. The assessments performed looked for instances of chronic problems that would be apparent in the system itself, as opposed to day-to-day data.

9.12.2 Dynamic Measurement

Alternatively, dynamic measurement inserts probes into the system in operation in order to assess and measure data quality on an ongoing basis. Dynamic measurement has many advantages over static measurement.

- Ability to see how well in-process data quality checks and transformations work
- Access to real-time measurements
- Ability to track poor data quality through a working system

Unfortunately, because dynamic measurement must be integrated into a working system, the coordination involved is much greater than the static measurement approach.

9.13 COMPILING RESULTS

In Chapter 4, we discussed the construction of a data quality scorecard that measures the cost associated with poor data quality. In this chapter, we actually drilled down into this process in greater detail, trying to characterize the specific issues regarding data quality and assessing exactly how well or poorly the actual data quality meets our expectations.

In Section 9.4, we specified that in order to perform a current state assessment, we would select a subset of the data quality dimensions for measurement. Having made that selection, we can use the guidelines laid out in this chapter to "insert probes" into the system and collect measurements.

We collect as much information as possible about the measure of data quality for each dimensions selected at each selected location. We hope to find the location of those sentinel rules that can "make or break" the data quality conformance in the system.

The last step in performing the current state assessment is to correlate the results with the data quality scorecard. For each location in the information chain and for each area of data quality, we will now be able to attach a set of dimensions of data quality and measurements of those dimensions. The result is a more detailed report that discusses the following:

- The cost of poor data quality throughout the system
- The locations associated with information errors
- The kinds of errors and/or nonconformance that exists in the system
- The measurement of the errors or nonconformance
- The distribution of cost of poor data quality

If we can attribute the costs associated with low data quality with specific dimensions of data quality, it presents the opportunity to use those results to define the data quality expectations inherent in a set of requirements. We discuss this process in Chapter 10.

9.14 SUMMARY

In this chapter, we discussed the process of actually measuring the levels of data quality with respect to the dimensions of data quality introduced in Chapter 5. Our goal is to perform current state assessment that we then use as input to the data quality requirements definition process.

We began the chapter by reviewing the process of mapping the information processing environment into an information chain. The information chain is the base map used to target the insertion of measurements of the different data quality dimensions. We then examined each of the dimensions of data quality from Chapter 5, deriving measurement procedures.

Finally, we looked at the consolidation of the measurements into a single report, correlating the occurrence of low data quality to the actual costs associated with it, giving us the input to the next step, the definition of requirements.

10

DATA QUALITY REQUIREMENTS

In Chapters 4, 6, and 9, we discussed creating a map of the information processing environment, determining the costs associated with low data quality, and measuring the levels of data quality. We looked at the hierarchy of associated roles within the organization, as well as the roles that are played by different system operators and components. Through the process of defining a data quality policy, hopefully we will have assigned the responsibility associated with those roles to individuals with the authority to manage data quality.

Now that we understand how low data quality can affect the economics of the information factory and we have explored ways to expressly define rules regarding assertions about our expectations about information, we have all the tools we need to express specific data quality requirements.

We have mapped the flow of information throughout the system and clearly identified each location within that chain. We have evaluated the actual costs and impacts associated with low data quality, and we have performed a current state assessment to determine the sentinel rules that gauge data quality. We are now at a point where we can evaluate the results of the assessment by identifying the critical locations in the information chain and attributing the costs of low data quality to those locations, as well as define our minimum standard expectations for data quality.

Our goal is to narrow the scope of each specific problem into a manageable unit of work. This is done by completely restricting the problem domain to specifics: the current measurement, the lowest measure of acceptance, and the optimal level of data quality. Additionally, we want to be able to rank each project in terms of its importance to the enterprise, and so we must attach some characterization of cost at each work granule. In order to achieve this, these are the areas of further analysis that we will perform:

1. Distribution of cost that combines the result of the data quality scorecard, which attributed the information chain with the costs associated with low data quality, and the current state assessment, which attributed the information chain with the measured levels of data quality.
2. Assignment of responsibility, which combines the result of the current state assessment with the enumeration of data quality actors within the environment, and assigns the responsibility for maintaining data quality with the appropriate actor.
3. Determination of internal requirements, which involves setting the required levels for data quality for the dimensions measured in the current state assessment, for places in the information chain where an individual internal to the organization is held responsible.
4. Determination of external requirements, which involves setting the required levels for data quality for the dimensions measured in the current state assessment, for places in the information chain where an individual external to the organization is held responsible.

In this chapter, we are going to look at the results of our assessment methods and see how to turn those assessments into actionable requirements. This process will incorporate the merging of collected data, along with the use of a requirements analysis tool called use-case analysis. This tool explores the way that the system is used in order to define how the system should interact with the users. Even though the operations of the system have already (most likely) been defined, we use this method to impose the requirements for the quality of content, which we can then use as input to the data quality and business rule definition process.

We also need to distinguish between "internal" requirements, which are requirements that are imposed on actors and system components within the control of the organization, and "external" requirements, which are imposed on data suppliers external to the organization. We deal with those requirements in Chapter 15.

In this chapter, we review some of the components that are used as input to the requirements definition process and ways to bound each requirement as a small task that can easily be implemented. Additionally, we look at how to define requirements and store them as metadata within a database table, yielding a flexible platform for modifying, searching, and reporting on the compliance with the requirements.

10.1   THE ASSESSMENT PROCESS, REVIEWED

It is worthwhile to review the components of the assessment that we have collected so far.

- A set of actors within the system
- A map of the information chain
- The impacts of low data quality
- The costs associated with those impacts
- A selection of dimensions of data quality that are measured

Basically, we have archived a record of the impact that bad data quality has with respect to the organization. When we are finished with the requirements phase, we will essentially have "finished the job" by translating the causes of those impacts into requirements.

10.1.1   ACTORS

Each stage in an information chain represents an action that can be performed by one of the actors in the system. Our use of the term *actor* will be apparent in Section 10.4, when we discuss use case analysis. Recall that we defined the following actors within the system.

1. *Suppliers*   Data suppliers provide information into the system.
2. *Acquirers*   Acquirers accept data from external suppliers for provision into the factory.
3. *Creators*   Internal to the factory, data may be generated and then forwarded to another processing stage.
4. *Processors*   A processor is any agent that accepts input and generates output, possibly generating some side effects.
5. *Packagers*   A packager collates, aggregates, and summarizes information for reporting purposes.
6. *Delivery agents*   A delivery agent delivers packaged information to a known data consumer.

7. *Consumer*   The data consumer is the ultimate user of processed information.
8. *Middle manager*   These people are responsible for making sure the actors are correctly performing their jobs.
9. *Senior manager*   The senior manager is responsible for the overall operation of the factory.
10. *Deciders*   These are senior-level managers associated with strategic and tactical decision making.

10.1.2   Information Chain

The information chain is a graphical representation of the way the data moves through the system. A node in the graph represents each processing stage, and a directed link from one node in the graph to another indicates a communication channel. Every node and every channel in the graph is allocated a unique name. This allows us to associate measurements, costs, and impacts with any specific point, or "location," in the graph.

10.1.3   Impacts

In Chapter 4, we discussed how the realm of impacts was divided into the *soft* impacts, which are clearly evident but hard to measure, and the *hard* impacts, whose effects can be estimated and measured. Hard impacts include the following:

- Customer attrition
- Costs attributed to error detection
- Costs attributed to error rework
- Costs attributed to prevention of errors
- Costs associated with customer service
- Costs associated with fixing customer problems
- Costs associated with enterprisewide-data inconsistency
- Costs attributable to delays in processing

Soft impacts include the following:

- Difficulty in decision making
- Time delays in operation

- Organizational mistrust
- Lowered ability to effectively compete
- Data ownership conflicts
- Lowered employee satisfaction

In Chapter 4, we described how to build the data quality scorecard by determining the locations in the information chain where these kinds of impacts are felt. In Chapter 9, we discussed how to measure the kinds of data quality problems that occur at each location by performing a current state assessment (CSA).

10.1.4   CSA

The process of performing a current state assessment includes the selection of some dimensions of data quality that apparently are related to the identified impacts, which are pinned down to selected locations within the information chain. During the CSA, we insert probes to measure the data quality levels of the selected dimensions, using defined metrics for each dimension. Ultimately, we measured the conformance of each dimension to either some level expected by users or some historical average as posited by the statistical control process.

10.2   REVIEWING THE ASSESSMENT

In reviewing the assessment, we are trying to achieve three goals. The first goal, distribution of impact, gives us the opportunity to more fully associate particular impacts we identified as part of the scorecard with the specific data quality dimension we measured. The second goal is to distribute the cost associated with each impact with the levels of data quality measured as part of the assessment. The third goal, which we will treat in its own section, is determining the expectations of data quality to be incorporated as requirements.

10.2.1   Distribution of Impact

At each location in the information chain, we indicated the impacts associated with low data quality and the measurements of specific dimensions of data quality. Now, for each dimension of data quality measured, we will assign some percentage of the overall impact at that location. For example, if we had projected that associated with this location was a hard impact due to error detection, at this point we should be able to specifically attribute the amount of error detection being performed for any of the data quality dimensions measured. Thus, if there are errors due to a problem with the data model, and there are errors due to timeliness, some percentage of the full impact will be allocated to the data model problem and the balance attributed to the timeliness problem.

Recall that our original impact decisions were estimates, and this can produce two possible outcomes. The first is that we have correctly estimated the impacts, and when we are finished, we will have fully assigned all assumed impacts to specific data quality problems.

The second, and more likely, possible outcome is that our original estimates were wrong, and we have discovered greater (or lesser) levels of impact at a specific information chain location. Another possibility is that there are impacts that we have not seen that suddenly become apparent. In this case, it is worthwhile to adjust our original scorecard to reflect this new insight, and then repeat the impact assignment step until we are satisfied with the assignment.

10.2.2   Distribution of Cost

The second goal, distribution of cost, can be achieved after the assignment of impact, as each impact is associated with a cost. This step is actually a refinement of the overall scorecard process, but it gives us a means for attributing a specific cost to a specific data quality problem, which then becomes input to the final step, determination of expectations. Figure 10.2 shows distribution of impact and cost.

10.3   DETERMINING EXPECTATIONS

This last goal of assessment review poses two generic questions for each data quality dimension measured with each associated set of impacts and costs.

1. What quantitative level of measured quality will remove the negative impact? This represents a base requirement of expected data quality.

Reference ID	Data Quality Problem	Information Chain Location	Activity	Impact	Overall Cost	Percentage	Cost
1	Malformed credit card Numbers	Node 5	Credit Card Processing	Detection	$60,000.00	40.00%	$24,000.00
			Contact customer	Correction		30.00%	$18,000.00
				Rework		30.00%	$18,000.00
2	Invalid addresses	Node 0	Direct marketing	Detection	$150,000.00	60.00%	$90,000.00
				Correction		40.00%	$60,000.00
			Reduced reach	Acquisition overhead	$600,000.00	33.00%	$198,000.00
				Lost opportunity		67.00%	$402,000.00
3	Incorrect pick lists	Node 7	Shipping processing	Detection	$24,000.00	20.00%	$4,800.00
				Correction		80.00%	$19,200.00
			Customer service	Warranty	$209,000.00	20.00%	$41,800.00
				Spin		10.00%	$20,900.00
				Attrition		70.00%	$146,300.00

FIGURE 10.1   Distribution of impact and distribution of cost

2. What quantitative level of measured quality will most efficiently improve the overall cost-benefit structure? This represents a target optimal level requirement for expected data quality.

This process assigns two threshold levels for our measurements and defines the parameters for any improvement project to be undertaken. The first threshold is the level at which the negative impact can be erased; the second is the threshold at which we have most efficiently achieved the most improved data quality. Note that we can always assign the second threshold to be 100 percent, but it may actually be more cost effective to achieve a lower threshold and take into account the Pareto Principle — that 80 percent of the work can be achieved with 20 percent of the effort.

Note that we must integrate the users' needs into the data quality requirement thresholds, since it is the users that can decree whether their expectations are being met. We therefore make use of a mechanism called use case analysis, which, although it is usually used in the system design process, is easily adapted to the data quality process.

10.4   USE CASE ANALYSIS

Use case analysis is a process that developed over a number of years and is described by Ivar Jacobson in his book *Object-Oriented Software Engineering* as a way to understand the nature of interaction between users of a system and the internal requirements of that system. According to Jacobson, a use case model specifies the functionality of a system as well as a description of what the system should offer from the user's perspective. A use case model is specified with three components.

- Actors, representing the roles that users play
- Use cases, representing what the users do with the system
- Triggers, representing events that initiate use cases

We will use of this model but altered slightly into what we could call the "data quality view." The data quality view focuses on the context and content of the communication interactions, so we can incorporate user expectations for the quality of information as a basis for defining the minimum threshold of acceptance.

10.4.1   Actors

We have already seen the term *actors* used in this book, and that choice of terminology was not arbitrary. In a use case analysis, an actor is a representation of one of the prospective users of the system, describing the different roles that a user can play.

Note that a single user may take on different roles, and each role is represented as a different actor. Actors model anything that needs to interact or exchange information with a system. Therefore, an actor can represent anything external to the system (either a human or another system) that interacts with our system. With respect to data quality, we want to look at those actors that can have some effect on the levels of data quality, so our list of actors, as reviewed in Section 10.1.1, is the appropriate set.

In Jacobson's model, actors correspond to object classes, and the appearance of a user taking on the role of an actor represents an instance of one of those objects. The collection of actor descriptions forms a model of what is external to the system. In our data quality view, we are less concerned with object instances and more concerned with expectations an actor will associate with information quality.

It is worthwhile to show a simple example that demonstrates a use case analysis. Let's consider a simple candy vending machine that makes use of a debit card. For the design of this candy machine, we expect there to be three different actors: the purchaser, the maintenance person, and the accounting system that keeps track of transactions that have taken place on the machine.

10.4.2   Use Cases

A use case is a description of a specific way of using the system by performing part of the functionality. It represents a course of events that takes place when an actor interacts with the system. The collection of use cases constitutes a specification of the system.

In our previous example, there are three actors. The purchaser inserts the debit card into the debit card slot, selects a candy bar by pushing a sequence of buttons, and then waits for the product to be dispensed. The cost of the candy bar is deducted from the debit card, and then it is released. The purchaser takes the candy bar, and the debit card is ejected from the card slot. We will call this the purchase use case.

The maintenance person checks that all the advertised products are available in the machine, that the passageways are clear, and that all trash is removed. He or she initiates this use case, called service machine, by opening the machine with a key. All material levels are checked and, if necessary, changed. A third use case, generate report, is initiated by the maintenance person to determine the activity that has taken place on the machine.

There may be many use cases in a system or only a few. Often, many of the use cases start out the same, and it may be difficult to identify the difference between two use cases until it the procedure is completed. For example, we might add another use case to the vending machine system — change parts. Here, the maintenance person initiates the use case by opening the vending machine with a key before replacing an inner part of the machine. Note that this new use case begins the same way as service machine.

10.4.3   Identifying Use Cases

In standard use case analysis, we identify use cases by first examining the set of actors and asking questions about the main tasks of each actor. These are the kinds of questions that are asked.

- Will the actor need to read or write to the system?
- Will the actor need to modify information in the system?
- Will the actor need to inform the system of changes in the external world?
- Does the system need to inform the actor about unexpected changes or events in the system?

In the data quality view, the systemic use cases are basically predefined. Instead, we want to identify the affiliated data quality components of the use cases, which address both the nature of communication within the use case and the content of those communications. We will want to ask these kinds of questions.

- What kind of information is communicated during this use case?
- What constraints are there (or should there be) for data entry?
- What data quality dimensions are involved in this communication?
- Is any data being communicated dependent on any other known data set?
- How is data quality guaranteed?
- What is the error resolution process?
- What are the minimum expected thresholds for data quality?

Figure 10.2 shows a use case analysis process.

10.4.4   Triggers

In the use case model, a trigger is an event that initiates a use case. A trigger event may occur as a result of an input data structure, an actor

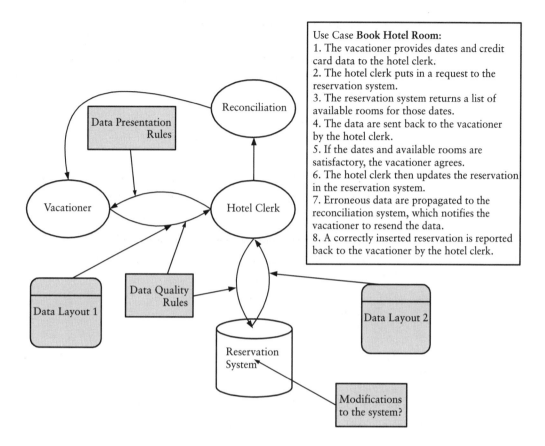

Use Case **Book Hotel Room:**
1. The vacationer provides dates and credit card data to the hotel clerk.
2. The hotel clerk puts in a request to the reservation system.
3. The reservation system returns a list of available rooms for those dates.
4. The data are sent back to the vacationer by the hotel clerk.
5. If the dates and available rooms are satisfactory, the vacationer agrees.
6. The hotel clerk then updates the reservation in the reservation system.
7. Erroneous data are propagated to the reconciliation system, which notifies the vacationer to resend the data.
8. A correctly inserted reservation is reported back to the vacationer by the hotel clerk.

FIGURE 10.2   Uses case analysis characterizes a component of the information chain

requesting an action (for example, a report) but providing no input data, time, or some internal database or system event. In the vending machine example, time may be used as a trigger to initiate the maintenance person's machine service routine.

The specification of the actors, the collection of use cases, and the collection of triggers will completely model the user requirements of a system. This model, which defines the user expectations, can be used to derive the user's quality requirements, the user's performance requirements, and perhaps the user interfaces. Because the model focuses on what the actors need from the system, there are no direct impositions on the system implementation. The use cases enumerate the design constraints of the system needed to provide the required service.

10.4.5   Identifying Triggers

We begin identifying triggers by examining the operations of the system that are not initiated by an actor. Any modification to the data set or generated report that is not initiated by an actor is probably associated with a trigger. For example, time-based events (for example, hard real-time constraints, end of trading day) or capacity issues (for example, limiting the number of transactions allowed per user) are likely related to triggers.

In the data quality view, executing a rules engine to test a data quality condition will also act as a trigger. The implication is that there are embedded data quality use cases that describe the process for testing data quality and business rules and performing some action based on the result of the test.

10.4.6   Variants

Often it isn't clear if certain functionality is to be placed in a new use case or if it is a variant of a previously described use case. Small differences would indicate that the new use case is a variant of the original, whereas large differences would lead to creating a new use case. When describing variants, the most important course of events is called the basic course, whereas the variants (such as different options of the same use case or errors that can occur) would be alternative courses. A use case will normally have one basic course, and zero or more alternative courses. In the data quality view, variants typically represent different courses dependent on different kinds of validation errors.

10.4.7   Extensions

Extensions describe how one use case can be inserted into (extend) another use case. In the vending machine example, the product may get stuck during product release. The result would be that the purchaser's debit card is debited, but the product is not properly dispensed. This implies a new use case, product stuck, to extend get product. In this use case, the maintenance person is alerted to fix the machine and provide a refund for the purchaser's debit card.

Here are some other reasons for extensions.

- Optional parts of use cases
- Complex alternatives that seldom occur
- Subcourses that are executed only in special cases
- When several different use cases can be inserted into a special (or general purpose) use case

In the data quality view, we might assign to each validation test and error reconciliation a specific use case. These use cases can then extend other system use cases that will make use of the validation and reconciliation components.

10.5 ASSIGNMENT OF RESPONSIBILITY

In Chapters 2 and 3, we talked about data ownership and the different roles that are played in the information factory. At this point in our analysis, we have determined the locations where low data quality affects the operation of the system, and we have allocated both the impacts and costs among the different sources of low data quality. We now have a dissection of the source of problems at level granular enough to be able to assign responsibility for managing the information up to the standard.

Our next step is to refer back to the data ownership policy and decide who has ultimate responsibility for each individual problem. That person will then be tasked with defining the project that brings the level of quality in line with the expectations. Because the tasks are well defined in terms of the metric against which success can be achieved and each task is a small, manageable unit, it is more likely that any political ownership issues can be overcome.

In other words, we have broken the amorphous "bad data" problem into individual regions of operation, management, and ownership. We can now make use of the data ownership policies we defined earlier to invoke the responsibilities of maintaining a high level of quality, but hopefully the fine granularity will ease the implementation process.

10.6 CREATING REQUIREMENTS

When defining data quality requirements, the system designer can derive requirements from the actors, the use cases, and the triggers. These requirements can be derived from these five areas.

1. Model generation/relational inputs
2. Invariants, boundary conditions, constraints
3. Explicit quality questions
4. Report generation and queries
5. Performance

In the general sense, all of these components are important, but in the data quality view, the most important are the middle three: invariants and constraints, explicit quality questions, and (to a lesser extent) report generation and queries.

10.6.1   Model Generation and Relational Inputs

In general system design, the systems designer begins with the use case model to determine the information model that will encompass the users' requirements. Typically, the process of figuring out the domain objects begins with isolating all the nouns used in the use cases. These nouns, along with their meanings, become a glossary for the system.

For the requirements stage, the degree of detail in describing each object's attributes and its interactions with other objects in the system is probably sufficient. Often, a set of objects with similar attributes can be isolated and abstracted using a higher description. For example, the vending machine may vend different sizes of candy bars. Each of these objects are different kinds of products, which might imply that product is a base class with the different sizes or flavors of candy being attributes of the product class.

10.6.2   Invariants, Boundary Conditions, Constraints

Invariants are assertions about a system that must always be true and are used to identify error conditions. In the case of a vending machine, an invariant may be that dispensing a product may only be performed if the inserted debit card has sufficient credit. Boundary conditions describe the extents of the usability of the system. In the vending machine, one boundary condition is that each row can only hold 15 candy bars, so there is a maximum number of products that may be sold between maintenance periods. Constraints deal with issues that impede the usability of the system. A constraint of the vending machine is that only one actor may be served at a time.

We have already seen these issues in Chapters 7 and 8. In the general sense, invariants and constraints focus on what we expect to be true about the system, and so we have encompassed this as our data quality rules. Invariants, boundary conditions, and constraints are used to identify usability, correctness, and perhaps performance requirements of a system. These force the designer to augment the use cases with error checking and handling and performance metrics.

10.6.3   Quality Issues

Quality issues also drive usability requirements. In our case, much of the quality requirements will focus on data quality, and so we drive this aspect the same way as discussed in Section 10.3.

Ultimately, for each important aspect of data quality, we will have defined the minimum expected level based on a specific measurement of a well-defined metric associated with some aspect of one of the dimensions of data quality. Since we will have measurement methods in place, we will be able to provide a running update using control charts, graphing each day's progress toward meeting the specified goals.

10.6.4   Report Generation and Queries

Both of these issues focus on the retrieval and presentation of accessed information, and, therefore, this also drives the data quality requirements. This aspect concentrates on both what information is to be reported and what information is to be requested from the system. Based on the information that is to be published out, we must incorporate measurement of the aspects of presentation, accessibility, as well as the dimensions of data quality related to data models.

10.6.5   Performance

Despite the importance of system performance, we have not addressed this issue to any great extent with respect to the data quality requirements. In fact, performance is a critical concern because we do not want to put strain on the system by inserting data quality measurement and validation.

Therefore, we must consider the means for implementing the data quality projects. In all cases, we must impose some performance constraints on both measurement and validation, such that there is no significant decrease in system performance. This may imply that additional resources will be needed, and those resources will need to be integrated with a production system.

10.7   THE DATA QUALITY REQUIREMENTS

We employ a use case analysis to impose our data quality requirements on top of each interaction within the system where a decrease in data quality can cause a relevant impact. Our data quality requirements become those threshold measurement levels associated with our selected data quality dimensions.

The details of each of the requirements are then compiled into a requirements catalog that can be stored, reviewed, and queried. Each individual requirement can be retrieved and measured to ascertain how well the requirement is being met, which provides a single measure of data quality within the system. The overall level of data quality of the system can be defined as a function of the levels of each individual requirement. Some scaling factors may be introduced based on the costs and impacts. For example, if we have defined 10 requirements, but one of them is tied to a problem that accounts for 60 percent of the costs of poor data quality, we might weight it by a larger factor in accounting for the overall system data quality score.

In terms of requirements management, it is useful to have a platform from which we can both accumulate and query the details of the definition of the requirements as well as the implementation thereof. We can actually implement this catalog as a database table and then incorporate our data quality requirements as part of our system metadata.

10.7.1   A Data Quality Requirement

The format for the statement of a requirement specifies that at a specific location in the information chain, a specific measurement must be equal to or greater than a specified threshold. The measurement may be based on any of the criteria for measurement described in Chapter 9, or it may be defined by the users of the system. All measurements should be translated into a value between 0 and 1.0 to provide a percentage score for conformance.

10.7.2   Data Quality Requirements Database

Each specification of a data quality requirement must include the following.

- A unique identifier for the requirement
- A name for the requirement
- The name of the responsible party
- The location in the information chain where the requirement is applied
- A reference to the dimension of data quality that is being measured
- A description of the measurement method
- The measurement rule, if possible
- The minimum threshold for acceptance
- The optimal high threshold
- The scaling factor as a percentage of the overall system data quality

We can create a database table to hold this metadata.

```
create table requirements (
    reqID                   integer,
    reqName                 varchar(100),
    responsible             varchar(100),
    locID                   integer,
    dimensionID             integer,
    description             varchar(1000),
    reqRule                 varchar(1000),
    minThresh               float,
    optThresh               float,
    scaling                 float
);
```

As we will see in Chapters 12 and 17, if the data quality rule system is implemented using a rules engine, we can automate the measurement and thresholding process by retrieving the rule for each requirement, executing the measurement in the location in the information chain, reporting whether the threshold(s) have been met, and integrating the overall score based on the scaling factor.

10.7.3 The Data Quality Requirements Document

By managing our requirements in a metadata database, we provide the means to automatically generate a requirements document that can be reviewed by the end users for correctness and compliance. The requirements document will display all the pertinent information described in the previous section, but the benefits of maintaining the requirements as content include the following.

- The statement of the requirements is easy to augment or modify, since it can be managed via a simple user interface.
- Since the requirements are in a table form, subselection of the requirements based on specific attributes of the requirements table (such as data quality dimension, or responsible party) yield specific data about the requirements.
- Integrating the requirements table with a history table indicating daily measurements provides a platform to measure improvement over time.
- As opposed to a static definition in a print document, the requirements specification can be kept up to date in a more manageable way, and a new print version can be regenerated any time the requirements change.

10.8 SUMMARY

In this chapter, we looked at how to use the analytical information collected via the map of the information chain, the construction of the data quality scorecard, and the current state assessment to provide input to the data quality requirements specification. Our goals in defining requirements include the distribution of the weight of the impacts and costs associated with low data quality and the definition of a pair of threshold values for each measurement we take.

The first threshold is the minimum acceptance threshold, below which we cannot decree the information to meet our criteria for fitness for use. The second threshold represents an optimal level of data quality, defined as the point at which the most efficient expenditure of resources achieves the greatest improvement. Together we can use these thresholds to determine data quality scores for individual requirements, as well as customize an overall system data quality score.

We looked at how a system design technique called use case analysis can be used for the assignation of requirements based on the application services provided to the user. We can build on top of the use case analysis to see at which points the more significant issues with respect to data quality emerge.

We examined the definition of the requirements and the management of those requirements in a well-defined database. By using a database table, we can manage the requirements themselves as content, as well as provide a platform for automatically generating requirements documents and reports of requirements conformance, indexed by data quality dimension, by responsible party, by location in the information chain, or any other stored attribute.

11

METADATA, GUIDELINES, AND POLICY

In Chapters 7, 8, and 10, we discussed maintaining a repository of information about the data within the system. We used the term *metadata* to refer to this repository. In this chapter, we explore metadata in more detail, since a major component of a knowledge management program is the maintenance of as much information as possible about an organization's data resource.

The simplest definition of metadata is "data about data." In practice, metadata is a repository of information that enables a user to independently learn and understand what information is available and extractable from a given data resource. Because of the many different ways that information is used, this reflects the many different ways metadata can be represented and used. In general, metadata represents all structural and definition aspects of any set of data, whether from a technical or a business perspective.

On the technical side, metadata is used for the design, implementation, development, maintenance, and ongoing management of data. On the business side, metadata encompasses all contextual meaning associated with a data set, covering definition of all objects within the system, the relations between the objects, the derivation of the data, the change history, data quality rules, and business rules associated with the use and exploitation of the data.

In today's world, where the number and magnitude of data sets grow exponentially with the ability to manage them, without a framework for encompassing information about the data, we would get lost in a sea of fragments. Different kinds of information platforms depend on different kinds of metadata. Clearly, the metadata needs of an online transaction processing system are different from those of analytical systems or a Web environment. Yet, industry players have recognized the need for a common ground for defining and communicating metadata. The Meta Data Coalition (MDC) is a consortium of vendors and end-users that has agreed to cooperate on the definition of a standard form for defining, sharing, and managing metadata.

In this chapter, we summarize some of the best practices from the data industry to provide the baseline version of a metadata framework. We will rely on some of the ideas present in the MDC's Open Information Model (OIM), an evolving standard for the definition, communication, and management of metadata, and we will incorporate other ideas found in the literature. Our goal is to provide a baseline guide for building a metadata repository, and this list should by no means be considered complete.

We will explore how metadata relates to data quality and how metadata can be used as a management tool for driving enterprise information policy. Since the kinds of data domains, mappings, and rules discussed in Chapters 7 and 8 can be viewed as enterprise reference data that doubles as metadata, we will discuss how to manage domains, mappings, and rules. We will also look at how a well-defined metadata repository can become a useful enterprise information publication and subscription tool when used as the basis for information browsing.

11.1　GENERIC ELEMENTS

In any metadata framework, there are some generic elements that can tag most data or metadata elements in the system. This section enumerates some of the generic metadata elements that would be incorporated into the repository.

11.1.1　Contact Information

This is all the information needed to contact a particular party, including the following.

- Name
- Title

- Location (see Section 11.1.5)
- E-mail address
- Telephone numbers, including the type of telephone number (office, mobile, home, pager, FAX, home office, etc.)

11.1.2 Description

This is a text description of any entity. This might also incorporate references to more advanced descriptive objects, such as text documents, graphical pictures, spreadsheets, or URLs.

11.1.3 Iconic Representation

Is there any kind of iconic representation for an entity? If so, is there more than one? This kind of metadata describes any types of icons, as well as the visual representation of the icon based on the state of the represented object. This incorporates the graphical representation and specific picture files, colors, conditions, and rules for display.

For example, an icon can be associated with the access attribute of a data field. If the specified user has read-only access, the color of the icon might be red to indicate that the user may not write to the field. If the specified user has write access, the same icon might be green.

11.1.4 Keywords

Keywords are used for classification of objects. Associated with any entity is a set of keywords that can be used for indexing purposes when building a browsable metadata catalog.

11.1.5 Location

A location represents a physical location, such as a street address, an office building, a room number, as well as any attribution such as whether the location is home or office. A location attributes contact information as previously described.

11.1.6   Author/Owner/Responsible

These are all contact information references to parties. The author is the original major creator of the entity being described. The owner is the person that manages the described entity. Sometimes, there is an additional party who is responsible for the described entity but is not the owner.

11.1.7   Help Source

This represents a resource that provides help for the described entity, such as a URL, a README file, or the phone number of a support person.

11.1.8   Version

This is a way to keep track of user-defined version information, such as major version, minor version, and revision numbers associated with a particular entity.

11.1.9   Handler

This describes some kind of object that serves as a handler for the entity, such as an application component that handles the user interface for directing operations on the entity.

11.1.10   Menus

These are the menus associated with the user interface for a described entity.

11.2   DATA TYPES AND DOMAINS

In all types of computer systems, data objects are defined as belonging to a preassigned data type. When information is passed from one system to another, it is good to use some base standard representation of the types that are available among all platforms. In our metadata repository, we keep track of all the types that are available within the environment, as well as the ways that types are defined and used.

11.2.1   Alias

An alias is a name used to describe a type that is known by another name. In C/C++, the *typedef* denotes a type alias. We associate as metadata all type aliases in the enterprise essentially as a mapping (as described in Chapter 8).

11.2.2   Enumeration

Any enumerated list of data values that is used as a type is kept as metadata. Enumerated types, such as our domains from Chapter 8, are represented using a base type and a list of values.

11.2.3   Intrinsic

Any defined type that is intrinsic to the data model should be denoted as such, and the information about both the size of objects and the physical layout of values of that type should be maintained as metadata. For example, decimal values may be maintained in a number of different ways on different platforms, although the presentation of values of type decimal may be identical across all those platforms. In this case, the exact representation should be denoted in case the data need to be migrated to other platforms.

11.2.4   Namespace

This is the namespace associated with the object types or origination context in which an entity exists, such as an application name and version number in which the entity was created. This is used to guard against incompatibilities that crop up between objects created in different contexts. We have already talked about namespaces in reference to rule sets. A single collection of rules accompanying a data set must be accumulated under a single "rule set," the name of which defines a rules namespace.

11.2.5 Object Type Mapping

This represents a mapping from object types in one namespace to object types in another. This gives the user the opportunity to see the best matches between object types that belong to different namespaces, so that any kind of comparison or migration between objects of the different types can be planned accordingly.

11.2.6 Scalars

Atomic data types used in a system as base types are scalar types. Examples include integers, floating point numbers, and strings. We enumerate a set of base intrinsic scalar types in Section 11.2.11.

11.2.7 Structure

A structure is the definition of a structured data type used within the system.

11.2.8 Union

Similarly, a union is the representation of the union data type definition, such as in C or C++.

11.2.9 Array

An array is a linear collection of objects of the same type.

11.2.10 Collections

With objects that can be bundled using collections, the collection metadata maintains all information about the maximum size of a collection, the way that collection members are accessed, whether there is any inherent ordering to members in the collection, and the operations that are permissible on the collection, such as insert, delete, sort, and so forth. If there is some inherent ordering, there must also be descriptions of equality of objects and an ordering rule (that is, a "less-than" operation).

11.2.11   Base Types

Here is a list of base types that are typically used. Any metadata repository should keep track of which of these types are valid within each enterprise system.

- *Binary*   A large unbounded binary object, such as a graphic image, or a large text memo
- *Boolean*   TRUE or FALSE
- *Character*   The metadata repository should log which representation is used for characters, such as ASCII or UNICODE
- *Date*   A date that does not include a time stamp
- *Datetime*   A datestamp that does include a timestamp
- *Decimal*   The exact decimal value representation, as opposed to float, which is approximate
- *Double*   Double precision floating point
- *Float*   Single precision floating point
- *Integer*   Standard integer type
- *Small integer*   Small integer type
- *Long integer*   Extended size integer type
- *Long long integer*   Larger-sized extended integer type
- *Numeric*   Fixed-size decimal representation. This should be attributed by the number of numeric digits that can be stored and the number of digits to the left of the decimal point.
- *Pointer*   A reference to another data object
- *String*   A sequence of characters that must be attributed with the length as well as the character type
- *Time*   A timestamp data type
- *TimePrecision*   The precision of the counting period associated with a timestamp type
- *Void*   The standard intrinsic void data type (as in C/C++)

11.3   SCHEMA METADATA

In our data environment, the actual layout of information is critical metadata as well as any relation, access, and usage data. We characterize all of
this metadata as *schema metadata* — metadata about the data schema. In
each of these sections, we use the metadata elements described in the previous sections.

11.3.1   Catalog

A catalog is a collection of schemas, and combined, a catalog of
schemas can be used for browsing through the enterprise information
metadata resource.

11.3.2   Connections

In an operational system, there must be a means to describe the ways
that users can interact with the database system. Client references to
databases are called connections, and for each connection we must
maintain the following as metadata.

- Names used to establish the connection
- Connection string (may include user name and password,
  although typically this may include other information)
- The name of the database used in the connection
- The name of the data source used by the connection (DSN)
- Indication of read-only status
- Whether the connection can be shared
- Connection timeout (the time in which initialization takes place; if
  this time is exceeded, a timeout may have occurred)

11.3.3   Tables

For each table in the system, we want to maintain the following.

- Table name
- Description of what the table models
- Physical location of the table (which server does it live on?)

- Size of the table and growth statistics (and upper size limit, if necessary)
- Source of the data that is input into the table
- Table update history, including date of last refresh and results of last updates
- Primary key
- Foreign keys
- Referential integrity constraints
- Cross-columnar data quality assertions
- Functional dependences
- Other intratable and cross-tabular data quality rules
- Data quality requirements for the table

11.3.4 Attributes/Columns

For each table, we will also maintain a dictionary of the attributes or columns of the table. For each column, we want to maintain the following.

- Column name
- Description of what is in the columns
- Business definitions associated with the column
- Data type
- Column size
- Whether the column is searchable
- Domain membership
- Source of the data values that populate the column
- Is this an auto-generated unique key?
- Null value rules
- Value restriction rules
- Data transformation rules
- Consistency rules
- Data quality requirements for the attribute

11.3.5 Load Programs

This is a list of the programs used to load data into the tables or that feed data into the tables. We maintain this information as metadata.

- The name of the program
- The version of the program

- Description of what the program does
- The source code
- Revision history
- Dependency information, such as what other programs must precede this program in execution
- The author of the program
- The current owner of the program

11.3.6   Views

Views are table-like representations of data joins that are not stored as tables. For each view, we want to maintain the following.

- The name of the view
- The owner of the view
- The source tables used in the view
- The attributes used in the view
- Whether updates may be made through the view

11.3.7   Queries

Queries represent sets of records extracted from database tables. We can maintain this metadata for queries.

- A name for the query
- The columns involved in the query
- The text of the SQL for the query

11.3.8   Joins

We can represent joins as metadata as well. We must maintain the following.

- The name for the join
- The join key used for comparison from each table
- The tables that participate in the join
- The columns that participate in the join from each table

11.3.9   Transformations

In any data extraction, transformation, and loading scheme, we can maintain metadata about the transformations that are performed. We already have a format for defining transformations using our rules from Chapter 8, but for clarification, each transformation can be represented like this.

- The collection of source data items (including table/column references)
- The destination value
- The transformation that is applied
- The person responsible for this transformation
- The description of the transformation
- The business aspect of the transformation

11.3.10   Data Sources

In all data sets, data come from different original sources. While some originates from user applications, other originates from alternate sources. For supplied data, we want to maintain the following.

- The name of the data package
- The name of the data supplier
- The name of the person responsible for supplying the data (from the supplier side)
- The name of the person responsible for accepting the data (on the organization side)
- The expected size of the data
- The time the data is supposed to be delivered
- Which tables and attributes are populated with this data
- The name of any data transformation programs for this data
- The name of the load programs for this data
- External data quality requirements associated with provision agreement

11.3.11   Triggers

Triggers are rules that are fired when a particular event occurs. These events may be table update, insert, or deletes, and in the metadata we want to maintain the following.

- Name of the trigger
- The author of the trigger
- The owner of the trigger
- Whether the trigger fires on an update, insert, or delete
- Whether the trigger fires before or after the event
- The trigger frequency (once per row or once per table)
- The statements associated with the trigger
- Which columns are associated with the trigger

11.3.12   Stored Procedures

Stored procedures are collections of SQL statements that may be executed (as a program) by database users. We want to maintain metadata for the following.

- The name of the stored procedure
- The author of the stored procedure
- The version history
- The description of what the stored procedure does
- The SQL statement sequence (or at least a pointer to the sequence)

11.3.13   Indexes

We can manage the collection of indexes as metadata. We will keep track of the following.

- The table or view on which the index is made
- The columns associated with the index
- Whether nulls are allowed
- Whether the index needs to be rebuilt or is updated automatically
- Whether the index is sorted

11.4   USE AND SUMMARIZATION

Usage statistics for a data set are useful for system resource management, system optimization, and for business reasons (answering questions such as "Which data set generates the most interest among our customers?").

11.4.1   Time Constraints

If there are any time constraints, such as in processing or delivery of data, these should be documented as metadata.

11.4.2   Users

We want to maintain this metadata associated with users in the community.

- Name of user
- Location
- Telephone numbers
- E-mail address
- List of data objects to which this user has access rights

11.4.3   Access Rights

For each touchable entity in the system, we want to keep track of which users in the community have which levels of access.

- User name
- Data object name
- Access rights

This metadata is used both for enumerating the access rights a user has for a particular data set, as well as enumerating which users have rights for a given data set.

11.4.4   Aggregations

In a data warehouse, aggregations are used for precalculating information for performance reasons. Aggregation metadata keeps track of what dimensions make up the aggregation.

11.4.5   Reports

End users that expect summarization of information stored in a database, as well as usage or behavior characteristics, may request reports. A report is a formatted view of summarized data. For each report, we will want to maintain the following.

- The name of the report
- The creator of the report
- The consumers of the report
- The time the report is available
- The tables and columns that are source data for the report
- The data transformations or calculations used in making the report
- The format of the report
- The means by which the report is distributed

11.5   HISTORICAL

11.5.1   History

We will want to keep track of different kinds of history. The first kind is versioning associated with the data schema itself, and the second kind is usage history.

11.5.2   Enumeration of Readers

For all data objects, we want to keep track of who is reading the data.

- The user name
- The program name
- The data object being read
- The frequency of object reads

11.5.3   Enumeration of Writers

For all data objects, we want to keep track of who is writing the data.

- The user name
- The program name
- The data object being written
- The frequency of object writing

11.5.4   Last Update

It is also useful to keep track of which user or program last updated a data object.

11.5.5   Change in Representation, Precision, Derivation

Any time a change is made to the data environment that involves a change to the data model (representation), a change to the precision of the information (such as changing from a float type to a double type), or a change is derivation (such as modifying the inputs that populate a data field), that change should be logged in a change history. The information that is logged may include:

- Modification name
- Date of change
- The object that was modified
- The reason for the modification
- Was this a change in representation, precision, or derivation?
- If this was a change in representation, what was the old representation and the new representation?
- If this is a change in precision, what is the old precision and what is the new precision?
- If this is a change in derivation, what is the replaced source and derivation process and what is the new source and derivation process?
- The person responsible for effecting the change
- Transformations associated with the change

This last item is quite important. It provides a way to bridge historical aggregation and summarization across time from the point before the change to after the change.

11.6   MANAGING DATA DOMAINS

In Chapter 7 we discussed the definition of data domains. Since it is probable that the same domains are being used in different parts of the enterprise, maintaining a single source directory of those domains is beneficial when it comes to being able to browse a domain catalog. If we want to manage our data domains as reference metadata, we can do this using three data tables.

The initial component of our domain metadata catalogs the names of all defined domains used within the system as well as the domain types. Therefore, the first table is a domain reference table, which contains the name of the data domain, the class of the domain (base data type, enumerated or rule-based), a reference to the base domain or data type on which it is based, a text description of the domain, and the source of the data that populates this domain, along with an assigned identifier for the domain. We will include in this table a reference to the base data types, and the `dType` component refers to another domain reference within the table. Here is one way to define the table.

```
create table domainref (
name               varchar(30),
dClass             char(1),
dType              integer,
description        varchar(1024),
source             varchar(512),
domainid           integer
);
```

The values can all be stored in a single table, referenced by a domain identifier. The component `domainID` refers to one of the named domains in the `domainref` table. In this case, we arbitrarily limit the size of the values to 128 characters or fewer.

```
create table domainvals (
   domainID    integer,
   value       varchar(128)
);
```

Finally, we represent our rules-based domains using records that consist of rule statements.

```
create table domainrules (
   domainid    integer,
   rule        varchar(1024)
);
```

One other table is useful in the metadata repository, although it is not used for representing the domain. Rather, just as we maintain usage data about our data tables, we will also maintain usage data about our domains, basically keeping track of which data table attributes use defined domains (see Figure 11.1). We will look at the representation of rules in Section 11.8.

11.7 MANAGING DOMAIN MAPPINGS

Similar to representing data domains as metadata, we will also like to accumulate domain mappings as enterprise reference metadata. Even more so for mappings, since they can represent embedded functionality that may have ubiquitous use within the enterprise, it is desirable to make use of database tables to represent mappings between data domains.

Just as with domains, we can represent mappings using three data tables, where the first table is used as a catalog. The mapping reference table contains the name of the domain mapping, the domain id of the source domain, the domain id of the target domain, a text description of the mapping, and the source of the data that populates this mapping, along with an assigned identifier for the mapping.

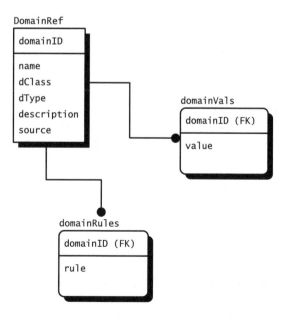

FIGURE 11.1   Domains database

```
create table mappingref (
name            varchar(30),
sourcedomain    integer,
targetdomain    integer,
description     varchar(1024),
source          varchar(512),
mappingid       integer
);
```

The value pairs can all be stored in a single table, referenced by mapping identifier. In this case, we arbitrarily limit the size of the values to 128 characters or fewer.

```
create table mappingpairs (
   mappingid   integer,
   sourcevalue varchar(128),
   targetvalue varchar(128)
);
```

Finally, we represent our rules-based mappings using records that consist of rule statements.

```
create table mappingrules (
   mappingid       integer,
   rule            varchar(1024)
);
```

By absorbing all the mappings into a centralized repository, we can provide users with a source for browsing the mappings that are used within the system, as well as allowing users the chance to explore the meanings of these mappings based on their use. Therefore, we will also maintain usage metadata on which attribute pairs conform to the relationship defined by known mappings (see Figure 11.2).

11.8   MANAGING RULES

Managing rules is slightly different from managing the domains and mappings. With the latter, most frequently we are managing enumerated data sets, and these are straightforward to represent using data tables. The rules we describe, though, are flexible enough that they defy standard data representation. The reason for this is in the nested nature of rule expressions. Many of our rules contain conditions or actions, which may be composed of smaller pieces, each of which is a valid con-

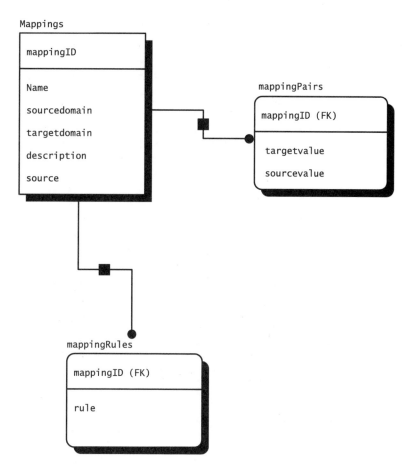

FIGURE 11.2 Mappings database

dition or action. Nested structures are not completely suited to storage in a database, mostly because the complete structure cannot be extracted with a single query. For example, consider this rule.

```
If (employees.salary < 20000) AND (employee.status <>
   "fulltime") then exempt (healthcarrier);
```

The condition in this rule is a conjunction between two simpler conditions, joined with the AND operator. In this case, the condition has two parts, each of which has its own operands. Naively, to represent this condition, we would need to keep track of four operands and three operators. The problem with representing this in a database table is that once a table is defined, we do not add additional columns to the table to account for each rule's essentially unlimited number of components. If we were to add more columns, most of them would be empty, which is a tremendous waste of space. We simply cannot represent all the pieces of this rule's condition in a single row of a database.

11.8.1 Approaches to Managing Rules

In fact, all operations can be represented using a tree structure, where the root of the tree represents the operator (in this case, "AND") and the leaves of the tree represent the operands (in this case (employees.salary < 20000) and (employee.status <> "fulltime")). We can apply this recursively, so that each of those two operands is also represented using a tree. This is shown in Figure 11.3.

There are two alternatives for maintaining the rules as metadata, both of which rely on programmatic means for implementation. The first alternative is to use a data table for embedding nested structures. We can create a single table to represent expressions, where each expression contains an operator (like "AND" or "<>") and a finite maximum number of operands. For argument's sake, let's constrain it to two operands.

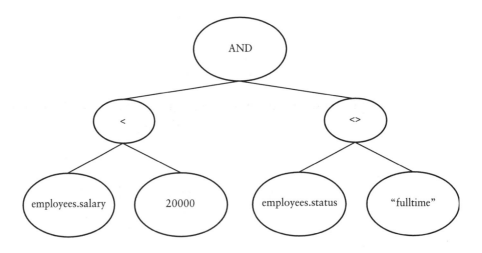

FIGURE 11.3   Metadata operations

```
create table expressions (
    expressionID         integer,
    isRule               logical,
    operator             integer,
    operand1             integer,
    operand2             integer,
    attrName             varchar(100)
);
```

The isRule attribute is set to true if this record represents the root of a rule tree. We will enumerate operators in a separate table, and the operator attribute refers to that table. Operands may take different forms; they may be attribute names, or references to other expressions. Therefore, we will have our expressions refer back into the expression table and allow for one attribute to be a character string representing attribute names. Here is how we could represent our previous example condition, although for clarity we will make the operator names explicit.

Expression ID	Operator	Operand 1	Operand 2	attr Name
0	NAME			Employees.salary
1	CONSTANT			20000
2	LESSTHAN	0	1	
3	NAME			Employees.status
4	CONSTANT			Fulltime
5	NOTEQUAL	3	4	
6	AND	2	5	

By careful inspection, we will see that all of our rule components can be represented in this format. Even lists of attribute names can be implemented in this binary format by using a LIST operator and making the second operand of a LIST operator be either an attribute name or another LIST node.

There are three issues with this representation, however. The first is that a program is needed to transform rules from a linear format (such as the syntax we used in Chapter 8) into the nested tree format for the database. The second is the difficulty in extraction; a stored procedure or a dedicated application is needed to cursor through the table, recreating the rule. The third issue centers on modifying the rules. When a user wants to change a rule, this requires a lot of maneuvering within the table.

The rule must be recreated from the representation in the table, but if the rule is truly modified, then those tuples that compose the rule within the table must be removed from the table, and the new version of the rule must be inserted into the table as if it were a new rule. This means that there is little opportunity for reuse, and rule editing is a very read/write-intensive operation.

11.8.2 Alternate Rule Management

A different approach to rule management is to maintain the text representation of the original rule within the database table. In this approach, the responsibility for managing the form of each rule is removed from the database and placed in application code.

A formal definition of the syntax of all rules must be defined, and a rule parser can be written to validate that each rule conforms to the correct syntax. The application would also incorporate semantic analysis to make sure that rules make sense contextually. This way, we can maintain each rule as text within a single field of a database table.

```
create table rules (
    ruleID      integer,
    ruleText    varchar(1000)
);
```

Using this approach, we have lost the ability to directly query the rule table to search for expression associated with a specific table attribute (except through substring searches). On the other hand, this approach greatly simplifies rule insertion, rule editing, and rule extraction. In addition, the benefit of using a rule parser for validation of the format is that the same parser can be used for transforming the rule specification back into a format suitable for in-process execution or for incorporation into a rules engine.

11.8.3 Rule Sets

One more table is needed to keep track of which rules are associated with specific rule sets, since different users may have different sets of rules, even for the same data. Managing rule sets requires defining a rule set name, associating it with a unique identifier, and having a separate table linking the rule set id with the identifiers associated with each defined rule.

```
Create table rulesets (
    RuleSetID   integer,
    RuleSetName varchar(100)
);

create table rulesetCollections (
    RuleSetID   integer,
    RuleID      integer
);
```

If we are using the first approach, the `ruleID` is the identifier associated with the root of the expression tree for that rule. If we are using the second approach, we use `ruleID`.

11.9 METADATA BROWSING

If we have competently integrated all metadata into a centralized repository, we now have a platform from which information about the enterprise can be communicated with all appropriate users within the organization. Users can query the domain tables and be provided with a list of domains, the description of each domain, and the other tables that use that domain. The same is true for mappings.

Data quality and business rules can be queried and reviewed, and domains, mappings, and rules can be reused. All of this can be easily accomplished with a metadata browser — a front-end tool that enables the dissemination of reference data and metadata to systems designers. Through the noncontrolled sharing of this information, the organization will organically become more intelligent and consistent, since de facto standards of usage will emerge through "natural selection." Valuable data domains, mappings, and rules will be accepted by growing groups of users, while ineffective metadata objects will wither and die from lack of use.

This also means that information usage policies can be effectively established through the definition of the accepted reference data components and controlled browsing. By selectively allowing users to subscribe to a data domain or a mapping, or by limiting the kinds of schema metadata available for review, senior information managers can influence many aspects of information system design, including the way that database tables are defined and the ways that information is extracted and presented to users. By controlling the flow of metadata, the managers of a data resource can control the way that knowledge is integrated throughout the enterprise. Figure 11.4 shows metadata browsing.

11.10   METADATA AS A DRIVER OF POLICY

The use of a metadata repository does not guarantee that the systems in use in the enterprise will subscribe to the philosophy of centralized knowledge management and control. Unfortunately, the existence of useful tools does not necessarily induce people to use them.

As a more practical matter, the instituting of metadata use can enhance an organization's overall ability to collect knowledge and reuse data. But without an enforceable policy behind the decision to incorporate a metadata framework, the benefits will not be achieved. In tandem, information policy drives the use of metadata, but the use of metadata will also drive information policy.

Creating a central core of reference data and metadata requires an organizational commitment to cooperation. As with the data ownership policy, the information management policy must specify the ways that data and metadata are shared within the company.

One more aspect of information policy embedded in the metadata question is that of enterprise-wide accessibility. Between issues of privacy and security and knowledge sharing, there is some middle ground that must indicate how metadata is shared and when accessibility constraints are invoked. This is a significant area of policy that must be effectively legislated within the organization.

11.11   SUMMARY

In this chapter, we explored the notion of metadata, starting with the basics about generic elements and moving through data types and domains, schema, and use and summarization. We then looked at the management of the sort of reference data and metadata that we have introduced in earlier chapters, namely data domains, mappings between domains, and data quality rules. Last, we looked at how the publication of metadata throughout the organization can improve knowledge management and data quality overall and that information policies are integrated closely with metadata.

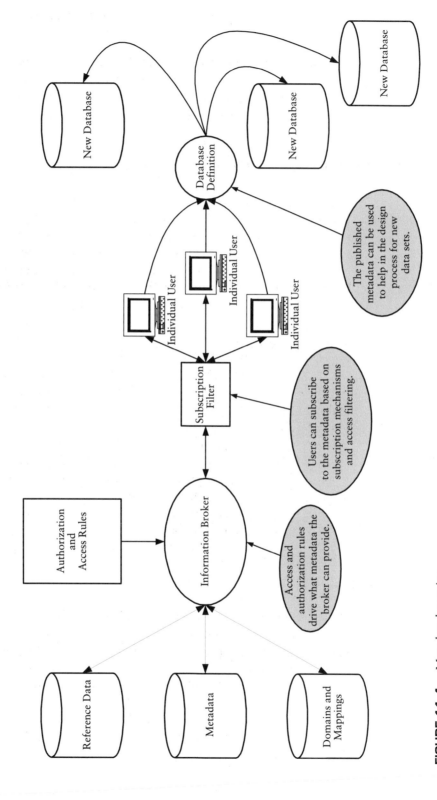

FIGURE 11.4 Metadata browsing

12

RULE-BASED DATA QUALITY

In Chapter 8, we discussed the definition of a formal system for describing data quality and business rules. For an organization, there is a significant advantage to consolidating its business and data quality rules and using an automated rules system to implement those rules.

Consolidating business and data quality rules is a way to capture and control strategic knowledge. In executable systems, this knowledge is most frequently incorporated into program logic, which is both hard to access and to control. Capturing and controlling the embedded knowledge requires that it be moved from the opaque representation of the computer program to a form that business users can manage and control.

Over the past 20 years, rule-based system technology has evolved from an assortment of niche products and languages into a set of integrated approaches and tools. Many of today's products are capable of supporting the knowledge consolidation process. Because a collection of rules is easier to browse and understand than a complex piece of C++ code, rule-based systems provide a reasonable approach to software flexibility and componentization.

In this chapter, we investigate the ideas behind rule-based systems, providing an introduction to business and data quality rules and the ways that rule-based systems make use of these rules. We also look at some of the "insides" of a rules engine, as well as some criteria for evaluating rule-based systems.

12.1   RULE BASICS

What is a rule? Back in Chapter 8, we defined a way to describe data quality rules, but we did not focus on the specifics of rule semantics. In reality, the formalism described in Chapter 8 carries to a large extent what is called "syntactic sugar" — an increase in the kinds of words used to describe rules to make them easier to read and understand.

In general, though, if rules are going to be used as a descriptive means for encapsulating operational business flows, it is important to be familiar with the lingo used in the definitions. In business systems, rules form the programmed representation of business policies and practices.

Here are some examples of rules.

- If the request is for more than $5,000, then a senior manager must sign the request form.
- If the customer's daily withdrawal limit is not exceeded, dispense the requested cash amount.
- If a reservation cannot be found for this ticket, escort the ticket holder to Customer Service.
- No customer may request a purchase that is greater than an assigned credit limit.

For all intents and purposes, a rule contains a condition and an action. More precisely, a rule is a statement that asserts some truth about the system, along with an optional action to be performed if the assertion is not true. Alternately, a rule is a condition followed by an action to be performed if the condition is true. Note that the previous four examples meet these definitions, and all the rules described in Chapter 8 can be restated in these simple forms. Rules stated in either way can be transformed into the other form. For convenience we will use the condition followed by action form.

Actions may consist of modifying the environment (which in turn may turn on other conditions or assertion violations) or restricting some modification to the environment, such as disallowing a transaction. Conditions are evaluated when some trigger event occurs. When a condition is evaluated to be true, the action is taken, and that rule is said to have been fired.

12.2   WHAT IS A BUSINESS RULE?

A business rule is a statement that describes some structural aspect of a business, defines some relationship between entities in a business, or controls or influences the behavior of the business. As Barbara von Halle explains in an article by Ellen Gottesdiener in the March 1997 *Application Development Trends,* business rules take the following forms.

1. Declarative and not procedural — rules stated as assertions, not as program logic.
2. Atomic — when each rule refers to one and only one issue.
3. Expressed in a well-formed language — there is a formalism for expressing rules.
4. Distinct independent constructs — each rule refers to a specific business notion.
5. Business oriented — the rule refers to the way business is done and is not bogged down as the technical implementation of business logic.
6. Business owned — ownership of the rules lies with the business stakeholders, not with the implementers of that business logic.

Even though these attributes are desirable in a business rules system, separating the management of business rules from business rule implementation does not necessarily remove the element of programming from the instantiation of a business rule system. Rather, the statement of and the execution of business policies as just described need not be tightly coupled with the implementation of those policies.

As an added benefit, the separation of business rules from both the data on which the rules operate allows for easier implementation of multitiered client/server applications. In other words, business operations can be divorced from the client side by implementing the execution of business rules at an application service level. Modifications to the environment, typically represented as an enterprise database, are abstracted from the business operation as well, since the rules transcend the data values themselves.

Business rules are a manifestation of a rule-based system that is bounded specifically by descriptions of business policies and relationships. The GUIDE Business Rules Project attempted to identify and articulate the rules that define the operation of a business. As described in the final report of November 1995, a business rule must be one of the following.

- *Structural assertion*   A fact that describes some aspect of the enterprise
- *Action assertion*   A constraint or condition that limits or controls the actions of the enterprise
- *Derivation*   A statement of knowledge derived from other knowledge in the enterprise

The GUIDE project drives the expression of rules in a formal way that can be superimposed on both a rules programming system and an entity-relationship form while maintaining a business focus. By doing this, the project members abstract the essence of business-oriented rules but allow for flexibility in the implementation of those rules while suggesting ways to archive those rules as content.

Since the specification of business rules can be transformed into a specification for any reasonably established rule-based system, we will concentrate on the ideas of a rule-based system and return to business rules later.

12.3   DATA QUALITY RULES ARE BUSINESS RULES (AND VICE VERSA)

We already saw data quality rules in Chapter 8. We can see that the rules described there fall into the definitions described in Section 12.2. Our data quality rules are structural assertions (such as domain and mapping definitions), action assertions (such as our transformation rules and domain assignment rules), or knowledge derivation rules (such as our domain mapping and assignment rules or our derivation rules). In any of these cases, our data quality rules match the specifications listed in Section 12.2.

1. Our data quality rules are declarative. The fact that we attempt to move data quality rules from the executable program to the world of content proves that our data quality rules are declarative and not procedural.
2. Each specific data quality rule applies to one specific operational or declarative assertion, demonstrating atomicity.
3. We have defined a well-formed semantic for specifying data quality rules, yielding a well-formed specification language.
4. Each rule in a system exists in its own context and can be viewed, modified, or deleted without affecting any other rule in the set.

5. Since we can view data quality as the "oil" in the machinery of operations, the data quality rule is business oriented.
6. In a perfect world, the ownership of the data quality rule lies with the data owner, who typically will be the major business stakeholder in the data.

Thus, in a not too roundabout way, data quality rules *are* business rules. An even more daring comment would be that a majority of business rules could actually be characterized as data quality rules. Data quality rules are specifications on the activity associated with allowing information to pass from one platform to another, whether that means from data suppliers to the enterprise, between clients inside the enterprise, or between the enterprise to their clients or customers.

12.4 WHAT IS A RULE-BASED SYSTEM?

A rule-based system is a set of rules that describes business policies to be executed in process. A rule-based system provides a mechanism for creating and editing a rule base, along with an engine that tests conditions or triggers and fires off actions.

12.4.1 Rules Languages

A rules language is a framework for describing sets of rules. Because our description of a rule includes both a condition and an action, any standard programming language that contains IF-THEN-ELSE constructs like C and C++ can be used as a rules language. However, because the standard procedural programming languages impose a sequential order of execution, their use as rules languages is limited.

These languages are limited because there is nondeterminism associated with events and assertions in the modeled world. A procedural language will impose an artificial dependence on the sequence of events and can lead to unexpected results if those events take place in different orders. Instead, rules languages, by virtue of their declarative syntax, provide a way to express a set of rules without imparting any order or execution.

12.4.2   Rules Engines

A rules engine is an application that takes as input a set of rules, creates a framework for executing those rules, and acts as a monitor to a system that must behave in conjunction with those rules. Rules engines work together with a rules language. A rules engine always acts abstractly. In other words, the operation of a rules engine is the same no matter what the rule base specifies. It is through this mechanism that the rules are separated from the implementation.

Complex rules engines allow for multiple concurrent evaluations of rules as well as parallel triggered execution. Other kinds of rules engines perform complex mathematical reductions to verify the continued truth values of the system. Simpler rules engines will (perhaps in a nondeterministic way) select a rule for evaluation and possibly execute an action if the condition evaluates to true (see Figure 12.1).

12.5   ADVANTAGES OF THE RULE-BASED APPROACH

12.5.1   Augmented Capabilities

A major difference between procedural programming languages (such as C and C++) and rules languages is the constraints on order of execution. Rules engines operate in stages: evaluate the environment, check for triggered conditions, and execute corresponding actions. Only those rules that are affected by inputs or triggers at each execution stage are going to be executed. In procedural languages, execution of a sequence of rules is predetermined by the programmer. This not only forces many "rules" (as embedded in "if-then" statements) to be unnecessarily executed, it opens up the possibility for incorrect execution if the nesting of rules is not appropriate.

12.5.2   Efficiency in Policy Automation

Rule-based programming provides a more efficient manner for automating business policies. One reason is that the formality of description encourages a more precise thought process that in turn is more thorough. This provides better "up front" definition of the business process.

Here are some more reasons.

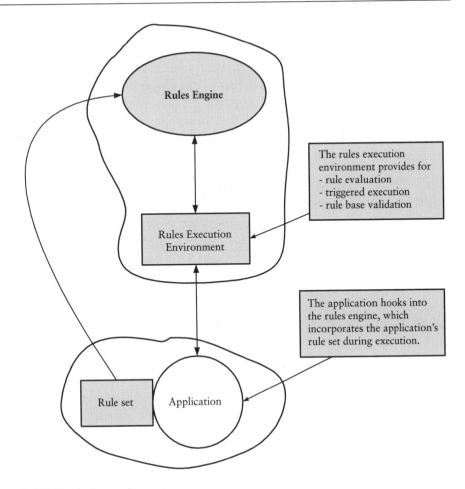

FIGURE 12.1   Rules engine

- Separating the implementation of complex business logic from nonexperts will help narrow the time needed to complete an application.
- The time needed to test will be reduced.
- The rules engine manages the mechanics of the application, so the amount of coding is decreased.

12.5.3   Opportunities for Reuse

Data quality and business rules reflect the ongoing operations of a business. In any large environment, there are many situations where the same business rules may affect more than one area of operations. This permits us to collapse enterprise-wide usage of predefined domains and mappings into a coordinated centralized repository. We can see that not only data-driven defining rules represent enterprise knowledge, but executable declarations can also represent operational knowledge that can be centralized. Once the repository of rules is centralized, the actual processing and execution of these rules can be replicated and distributed across multiple servers located across an enterprise network.

12.5.4   Rapid Response to Changes in the Business Environment

Because the rules are not embedded in source code in unmanageable (and indeterminate) locations, when the business operation changes, it is more efficient to update the rule base to speed up the implementation of modified policies. Changes to the rule base, as long as they do not cause inconsistencies within the rule base, can be integrated quickly into execution.

12.5.5   Ease of Reengineering

Managing business rules as content enables easier business process reengineering. Having all the policies situated in one location enables analysts to understand what the application under investigation was meant to do.

12.6   INTEGRATING A RULE-BASED SYSTEM

12.6.1   The Rule Base and the Knowledge Base

There is a subtle difference between a rule base and a knowledge base (though for our purposes we can use the terms interchangeably). A rule base is the collection of rules that have been predefined in the system. It is a statically defined set and is not modified during the execution of an application. A knowledge base contains all true statements in a system, whether those statements are predefined rules or truths derived during the execution of the system.

A pure rule base has no state, and any external event triggers one (or more) of certain rules that may apply. A knowledge base incorporates both state ("memory") and inference ("knowledge") into the system. As the execution progresses, the choices of rules change as information about the external events is integrated into the knowledge base. As an example, consider these two rules.

1. If the oil consumption exceeds 21 gallons, then fax an order to the oil delivery company.
2. If the oil consumption exceeds 21 gallons for 10 days in a row, then fax an order to the oil delivery company.

Rule 1 implies no state, and if the external event occurs, the rule should be fired. Rule 2 requires that some knowledge be maintained — days in a row — so these facts are integrated into a knowledge base.

12.6.2   Scalability

Naturally, resource requirements increase as the number of rules increases. A knowledge base may require even more storage because all facts that may be relevant to the triggering of rules will need to be maintained.

12.6.3   Integration Granularity

How tightly coupled is a rules engine to other components of an application? The integration granularity measures how closely the rules engine must be affiliated with any other application code. Depending on the application, either a tightly coupled or loosely coupled integration may be desired.

When the rules engine is completely integrated with the application at compile and link time, the granularity of integration is very tight. When a separate engine is executing as an intact server at one or more distributed locations, the granularity of integration is very loose.

12.7   RULE EXECUTION

12.7.1   Firing a Rule

Rules can be restated in action form, if not already worded that way. All assertional form rules are changed so the assertion becomes the condition, and if the assertion is not true, then an alert action takes place. A rule is then said to be *fired* when its condition is evaluated to true. This is also referred to as *triggering* a rule.

For interactive systems, a set of inputs signals the evaluation stage of the rules engine. An input value that allows one or more conditions to evaluate to true is called a *triggering event*.

12.7.2   The Rules Engine

A rules engine is an application that manages the rule base, interacts with the outside world for the triggering events, and fires associated rules when conditions are satisfied. The rules engine acts as the controller of the rule execution; it operates in a loop.

1. Evaluate the current state.
2. Identify the rules whose conditions are fulfilled.
3. Select one of those rules for firing.
4. Execute that rule's action.
5. Start again at Step 1.

While some rules engines allow for multiple rule firings (based on firing all the rules whose conditions are fulfilled), because the actions may actually create a contradictory state, most rules engines will arbitrarily select one of those rules to fire. Another option is to put all fired rules on a worklist, and as each action is taken, the items on the worklist are reexamined to make sure there are no inconsistencies.

A rules engine monitors interaction, and as rules are fired and new facts are established, the rules engine will integrate the new facts into the knowledge base. New facts (and new rules) are established as rules are fired and actions are taken. Frequently, an action may be to assert a new rule. For example, consider these rules.

1. If the customer's credit limit has been reached, then increment the occurrence count of invalid credit charging attempts.
2. If three invalid charging attempts have occurred, then invalidate the purchase.

Each time rule 1 is fired, there is a change in the knowledge base. At some point, the effect of having fired rule 1 some number of times will trigger the firing of rule 2.

As a more complex example, consider these two policies.

1. All successful customer purchase requests must be reported back to the customer within 90 seconds of execution.
2. If the product is not in stock, the failure to accommodate the customer request must be reported back to the customer within 60 seconds.

The first policy can be encapsulated as a rule.

A. If a customer's request is satisfied at time t1, then the customer must be notified no later than time t1 + 90 seconds.

The second policy can be encapsulated as these rules:

B. If the product is not in stock, then replace rule A with rule C.
C. If a customer's request cannot be fulfilled, then the customer must be notified no later than time t1 + 60 seconds.

Therefore, the second policy not only has an effect on the order of events, it actually changes the set of rules. This shows the difference between a static rule set and a dynamic knowledge base.

12.8   DEDUCTION VS GOAL-ORIENTATION

In dynamic rules systems, the knowledge base is increased as new facts are established. There are two ways that facts are derived in a knowledge-based system The first way, forward chaining, is a generative mechanism that uses the knowledge base incorporated with all trigger events to deduce new information. The second way, backward chaining, starts with a specific goal and attempts to establish the truth of the goal by establishing the truth of the conditions that lead to that goal.

The suitability of these two methods depends on the actual application. In applications where the intention is to identify as much information as possible to be presented to the application owners, forward chaining is appropriate. If the intention of the application is to alert the users when a certain fact can be determined, backward chaining may be the ticket. In some cases, a combination strategy may be in order — when some facts need to be established before there are enough facts to establish the truth of the goal.

12.8.1 Forward Chaining

In a forward chaining system, the knowledge base starts with a default collection of facts and rules. From the set of facts and any inputs to the system, the rule conditions are iteratively checked, and new facts are generated. A forward chaining system derives conclusions from the data.

An example of forward chaining uses this rule:

1. If a customer is purchasing automobile insurance, and that customer's car is red, then the customer's insurance premium is $1,000 a year.

If the following facts are introduced

- Mary has a red corvette, and
- Mary is purchasing automobile insurance, then the conditions on rule 1 are satisfied, leading us to the conclusion
- Mary's insurance premium is $1,000 a year.

Forward chaining works through a process of pattern matching. All the rules initially are represented by holding spots for the components of each condition. Then, as facts are introduced, the rules engine attempts to fill in the holding spots with each fact. If all the holding spots can be filled, then the conditions associated with the rule have been established, and the associated conclusion is now added to the knowledge base.

12.8.2 Backward Chaining

In a backward chaining system, the system begins with a conclusion and iteratively works backward to find justification for having made that conclusion. For each rule conclusion, the system looks in the knowledge base to satisfy that rule's conditions.

An example of backward chaining uses these rules.

1. If a customer has any energy accounts, that customer's monthly expenditure is the sum of the expenditures on all of that customer's energy accounts.
2. If a customer spends more than $100 a month on natural gas, she is considered to be a high-volume customer.
3. If a customer is a high-volume customer, she is eligible for a 10 percent discount on all charges over $100 a month.

For example, look at these account records.

Customer	Meter ID	May Natural Gas Charges
Smith, John A.	71804940951	$25.00
Johnson, Steven	71808751965	$76.64
Johnson, Steven	71808751966	$25.98
Corlino, Ralph	71803871094	$140.02
Radzov, Vanessa	71803875823	$18.88

If we ask if Steven Johnson is eligible for the discount, a backward chaining system would attempt to establish the truth of the conclusion "Steven Johnson is eligible for a discount of 10 percent on all charges over $100." Since there is a rule with that conclusion (3), the system then tries to establish the condition to that rule: "Steven Johnson is a high-volume customer." As rule (2) addresses the conclusion of high-volume customers, the next backward step is to establish that "Steven Johnson spends more than $100 a month on natural gas." The next step is applying rule (1) backward, implying that the total charges are composed of the sum of all accounts. Since Steven Johnson has two accounts, the total monthly charge is $102.62. Rolling back, this establishes the truth of the conditions of all of the rules, establishing that the answer to the query is "yes" — Steven Johnson is eligible for the discount.

12.8.3 The Execution Sequence

In a rule-based system, execution is not sequentially specified but scheduled. Execution is based on stepped iterations. This means that at each step all the rules with conditions set to be true by any inputs are collected and placed on a queue (the "agenda") for evaluation (that is, the rules are "activated"). The rule engine determines the sequence of evaluation, and the actions are executed.

12.9 EVALUATION OF A RULES SYSTEM

In the article "Business Rules — Automating Business Policies and Practices," Mitchell Kramer describes four basic requirements of a rule-based approach: isolation, abstraction, integration, and responsiveness to change. We will use these requirements as the dimensions across which vendor products will be evaluated.

12.9.1 Isolation

Throughout the book, we have seen that a major driver for defining and using a rules system is the disengagement of the statement of the business operations and policies from the technical implementation of those rules and policies. Therefore, the ability to isolate the rules from the application that uses those rules is a requirement.

A strategic benefit of isolation is the encapsulation of the rules as content, which can then be managed separately from any application that uses those rules. The rule definitions in Chapter 8 are designed to provide this isolation, especially when managed through a separate interface.

12.9.2 Abstraction

Abstraction refers to the way that rules are defined in the system. This can encompass a GUI that queries the user for rules or a rules language for describing rules. This requirement dimension covers the question of how rules are defined and not necessarily how the rules actually interact within an executing system. The rules in Chapter 8 are meant to be edited, modified, and tested from within a separate GUI.

12.9.3 Integration

Integration refers to the way that a rule-based system is integrated with existing applications. Refer back to Section 12.6.3 for more information on integration.

12.9.4 Responsiveness to Change

As a business changes, so do its policies and rules. A robust rules system will allow significant responsiveness to changes in policies, rules, operations, and so on, allowing an easy means to browse, edit, modify, validate, and test changes to rules as well as controlling the integration of new rules into a running system.

12.9.5   Evaluating a Rules Engine

When looking at potential rules engine platforms, these questions should be asked.

1. Can the rules engine execute as a server? If so, then the rules engine is likely to be loosely coupled and can be implemented as a distributed component or even replicated across the enterprise.
2. Are the rules read at runtime or compile time? The rules being read at compile time would indicate that the rules are read once when the application is built, as opposed to the application having access to a rule base during execution. The implication is that at execution/runtime, there is a more dynamic system that allows for rules to evolve as time moves forward.
3. Does the rules engine require access to a database? On the one hand, requiring a database forces an additional cost constraint, but on the other hand, the engine may store rules in a proprietary format.
4. How is a rule system created? How are rules defined, and how are they stored? How are rules moved from the definition stage to the execution stage?
5. Is the rule system integrated as a library in an application, or is it a standalone application? This question asks whether you can integrate a rules engine and a set of rules as part of another application.
6. When updating a rule base, does the entire application need to be rebuilt, or are builds limited to a subset of the application? To what degree is the system dependent on the definition of rules?
7. How is the knowledge base maintained during execution? Is there a database that holds the newly defined assertions?
8. How is the knowledge base maintained during application update? This question asks how a knowledge base is stored and restored when the application is halted. If there is a state that exists in the system, then when the system is brought down, there should be some format for state persistence.
9. If the rules are integrated directly into a compiled application, is there a facility for management of the distribution of the application? This question asks how rules are distributed to server or broker applications that execute in a distributed fashion.

10. How are rules validated when updated? It is possible that a new rule can invalidate or be inconsistent with other rules that are already in the rule base. Is there a way to check the validity of a rule set?

11. Is there a debugging facility? Is there a separate means for testing out a rule set before putting it into production? If there is a problem with a production rule base, and is there a tracing facility that can be turned on so that the execution can be monitored?

12.10   LIMITATIONS OF THE RULE-BASED APPROACH

12.10.1   Detail Management

Associated with any set of rules is the specter of a rule base gone wild, filled with meaningless trivialities and stale rules that only clog up the system. When using a rules system, one must be detail oriented to the extent that the rules engineer is willing to commit to understanding the rule definition system and the rule management system.

The rules approach requires a dedication to detail, since all objects operating in the business process as well since all attributes of each object must be specified. This requires a dedication to detail as well as an understanding of business process analysis.

In Chapter 10, we looked at use-case analysis and how it affects requirements. It is at this level of granularity that these skills come in handy. Ultimately the rule specification operates on a set of objects representing entities in the real world, and whether the implementation of rules is data-oriented or object-oriented, the application must be aware of all potential actors.

12.10.2   Inflated Expectations

Enthusiastic adopters of rule-based technology may have expectations that a converted set of complex business policies into a rule-based system will always be faster to implement, easier to maintain, and more efficient to execute. While this may be true for some applications, the fact is that frequently business policies themselves are poorly specified, and the business process of converting a policy statement into a rule base can be very complicated.

The reality is that implementing an application based on rules requires a senior management-level commitment to seeing the project all the way through the analysis and definition process. Also, as discussed in Section 12.10, there must be a dedication to details. The reason for this is that the rule definition process bridges a gap between consumer and technical producer. The analysis required involves both domain expertise and technical savvy and forces a close partnership between the technology provider and the application consumer. The reward is that the implementation of the technology is not "hoarded" by a technician and managing the application after it has been completed can be done in a more cost-effective manner.

12.10.3 Programmers Are Not Eliminated

Because of the "natural language" qualities of rule descriptions, there is a general impression that a business process application can be built by non-programmers and that the IT resources and association can be eliminated. This is a naive assumption because rule specification itself is dominated by strict syntactical structure, and even if it is not called "programming," the skill and experience required match that of a programmer.

With the right tools, though, the learning curve for a nonprogrammer should not be a steep one. A visual tool that encourages the user to define more effective rules but lets the user retain the capability for testing and debugging rules without affecting a production system would help bring a nonprogrammer up to speed.

12.11 RULE-BASED DATA QUALITY

So now that we know more about rules and rules engines, how do we use the data quality rules described in Chapter 8? This requires a few steps.

12.11.1 Rules System Selection

The first step involves the selection of a rules system that will execute our data quality rules. We can use the guidelines and questions discussed in Section 12.9. In the case of data quality rules, depending on whether the rules system is being used for real-time purposes or for offline purposes, there may be different answers to each of the questions in Section 12.9.5.

For example, if we are using the data quality rules for validating a data mart, we might want our rules engine to be slightly decoupled but still integrated with the data loading process. If we are using a rules engine to generate GUIs, the system can be completely decoupled. If we want to use rules to ensure the correct operation of our systems, we might want a tightly coupled rule engine (see Figure 12.2).

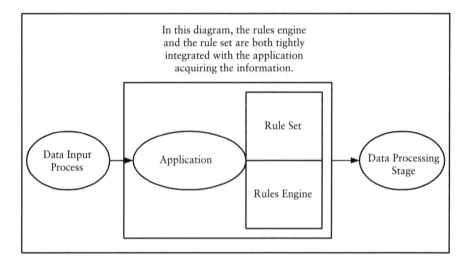

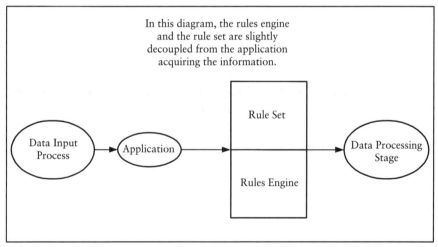

FIGURE 12.2   Rules systems

12.11.2   Rule Translation

To use the rules in Chapter 8, we must translate them from their syntactic definitions into a form suitable for an off-the-shelf rules engine. To demonstrate, let's turn some of our rules from Chapter 8 into a form that either is a direct assertion or an if-then statement.

Non-null value rule

Attribute B nulls not allowed

is changed into

Assert !isNull(B);

Attribute value restriction

Restrict GRADE: value >= 'A' AND value <= 'F' AND value != 'E'

is changed into

Assert (GRADE >= 'A') AND (GRADE <= 'F') AND (GRADE != 'E')

For the most part, this translation is relatively straightforward. In order to represent domains and mappings, any chosen rules engine must support set definitions with a syntax that allows for inserting strings into sets and checking for set membership. Domains are then represented as sets of string values, and mappings can be represented as sets of strings composed of the source domain value, a separator string, and the target domain value.

One more example would be the completeness rule.

IF (Orders.Total > 0.0), Complete With
{Orders.Billing_Street,
Orders.Billing_City,
Orders.Billing_State,
Orders.Billing_ZIP}

this would change into the following.

IF (Orders.Total > 0.0) THEN !isNull(Orders.Billing_street) AND !isNull(Orders.Billing_City) AND !isNull(Orders.Billing_State) AND !isNull(Orders.Billing_ZIP);

A thorough walkthrough of the rules will clarify a mapping into the assertion/if-then format. Then the rules are ready for the next step (see Figure 12.3).

12.11.3   Rule Validation

We briefly discussed rule validation in Chapter 8, but rule validation is outside the scope of this book. No matter what, any rule set must be

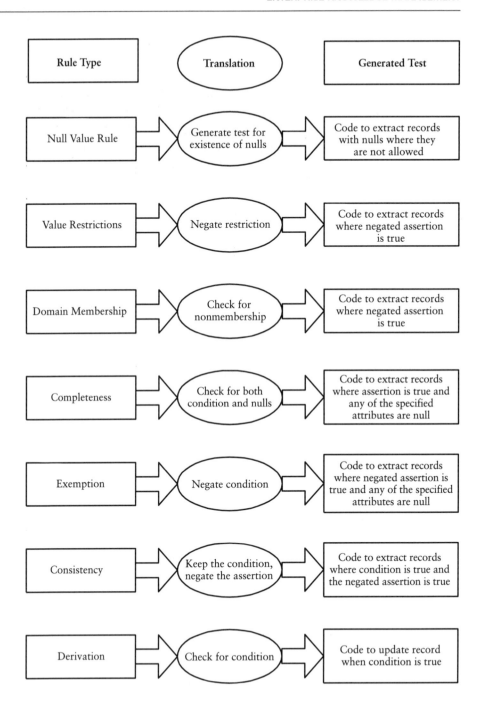

FIGURE 12.3   Rule translation

validated, and that entails guaranteeing that no set of two or more rules are contradictory.

Actually, the brevity of this section belies many issues, the most important one being that validation of rule-based systems is extremely difficult and is a current topic of research in the world of databases, artificial intelligence, and knowledge-based systems. In essence, it is easy to say, "Validate the rules" but much harder to actually do it. Hopefully, if we constrain our system somewhat and don't allow dynamic inclusion of new rules, the process may be easier (see Figure 12.4).

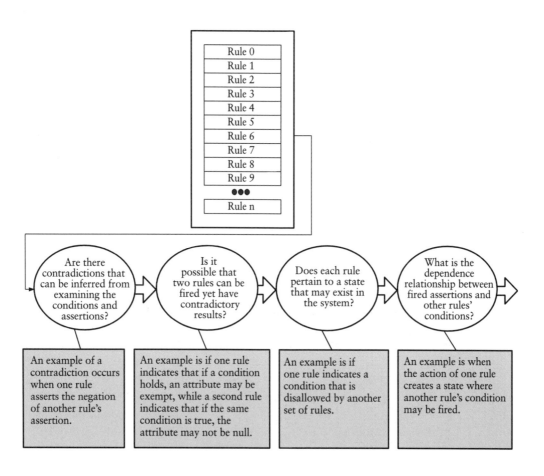

Figure 12.4 Rule validation

12.11.4 Rule Importing

The last step is importing the rules into the rules system. Depending on the system, this process may involve something as simple as inserting rules into a database or as difficult as converting rules from a natural-language-based format to instances of embedded C++ or Java class objects.

An interesting goal is to use automatic means to translate rules defined with the natural language format into a format that can be loaded into a rules system. The process of translation from one format to another is called "compilation."

12.12 SUMMARY

In this chapter, we looked more closely "under the hood" of a rules system. First we further refined our understanding of what a rule is, and then we discussed the specifics of business rules. In reference to our rules formalism defined in Chapter 8, we again posited that data quality rules and business rules are really the same thing.

We then looked a little more closely at rules systems. A rules engine drives the execution of rules by identifying which rule conditions have become true and selecting one of those rules to execute its action. This process can be repeated on all rules whose conditions have been fulfilled.

We discussed the advantages and disadvantages of the rules approach, including the augmented capabilities, the ability to implement business policies relatively quickly, and opportunities for reuse. A discussion of how rules engines worked followed. We also looked at how to evaluate a rules system and different philosophies embedded in rule systems.

We focused a bit on some of the drawbacks of using a rule-based system, including the work required to focus on details, as well as the fact that many users have inflated expectations when moving from an exclusively programmed system to one that is rule based. We also saw that using a rules system does not eliminate programming from the environment, although rules "programming" may be simpler than using complex programming languages.

Finally, we looked at the steps in transforming the data quality rules that were discussed in Chapter 8 into a format that can be imported into a real rules system. This involves selecting a rules system, translating the rules into the appropriate form, validating the rules to make sure that there are no contradictions, and importing those rules into the rules system.

13

METADATA AND RULE DISCOVERY

Up until now, our discussion has centered on using data quality and business rules as tools for leveraging value from enterprise knowledge. We have shown that we can use data domains and the mappings between those domains to consolidate distributed information as a single metadata resource that can be shared by the entire organization. Thus far, however, we have concentrated on the *a priori* definition of data domains, mappings, data quality and business rules, and general metadata.

In this chapter, we focus on analyzing existing data to distinguish the different kinds of metadata. The processes and algorithms presented help us find metadata that can be absorbed into a centrally managed core resource and show us how to manage the metadata and its uses.

Domain discovery is the process of recognizing the existence and use of either enumerated or descriptive domains. The existence of the domain is interesting metadata; the domain itself can be absorbed as enterprise reference data. Having identified a domain, it is also interesting to explore whether there are any further derived subdomains based on the recognized domain. Along with domain discovery and analysis is the analysis of domains to detect any multiple domains embedded in the discovered domain. We can also analyze columns that use data domains to see whether attributes are being overloaded (used for more than a single purpose) and attempt to perform mapping discovery.

Another significant area of investigation is the discovery of keys in collected data, merged data, and legacy databases. Older, nonrelational database management systems did not have primary key requirements, so when migrating a legacy database into a modern RDBMS, it may be necessary to find primary and foreign keys and to validate the referential integrity constraints.

A third area of investigation involves the discovery of data quality/business rules that already exist in the data. There are two steps to formulating these rules: identifying the relationships between attributes and assigning meaning to those relationships. We will look at a technique for discovering association rules and the methodology of figuring out what those associations mean.

13.1   DOMAIN DISCOVERY

You will recall that data domains, based on a base data type, consist of either enumerated lists of values or a set of rules that specify restrictions on the values within that data type, using operations that are allowed on values within that data type. In Chapter 7, we covered the definition of data domains through enumeration and description. In many data sets, common data domains are already used, whether by design or not. We can presume that if data domains are used by design, they will already have been documented. But if not, we can make use of heuristic algorithms to find used data domains.

Domain discovery is the recognition that a set of values is classified as a set and that one or more attributes draw their values from that set. Once a domain has been discovered, there is a manual validation phase to verify the discovered domain. Subsequent analysis can be performed to understand the business meaning of the discovered domain. This stage applies a semantic meaning to a domain and can then be used as the basis for the validation of data domain membership (see Figure 13.1).

13.1.1   Benefits of Domain Discovery

These are some of the benefits of the domain discovery process.

- Determining that an attribute belongs to a domain makes it possible to document the domain and create a means for validating domain membership rules.
- Determining that attributes from different tables use the same domain provides a means for consolidating shared reference data from across the enterprise, thereby lowering risk of inconsistency

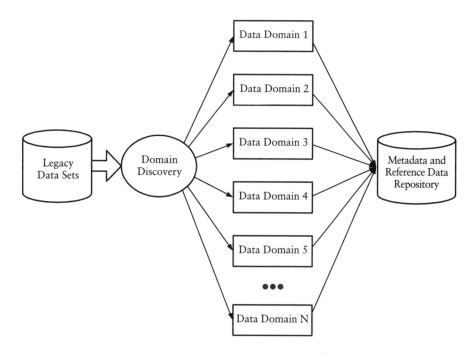

FIGURE 13.1   Domain Discovery

in enterprise data. It also establishes the existence of a relationship between those attributes that is inadvertent, or simply had been forgotten, but may prove to be valuable.

- Managing domains under explicit stewardship is a key component of the management and maintenance of information as an enterprise resource.
- If the data stewards choose, the domain values may be stored once and referenced via a numeric encoding, thereby saving space when referring to domain values.
- Extracting the rules into a formal definition transforms an execution-oriented object into one that can be treated as content, increasing the value of the enterprise information resource.
- Relational metadata is embedded in domain information. For example, if all customer account numbers referred to by ACCOUNT in one table are the same accounts referred to by ACCT_NUM in another table, we infer that the two attributes refer to the same set of objects.

- Information about descriptive domains may be embedded in application code; extracting these domain descriptions from program code helps uncover hidden historical business rules.

13.1.2   Representing Data Domains

As we discussed in Chapter 11, we will have a means for storing, cataloging, browsing, and managing data domains. As a review, we will need three metadata database tables to represent our data domains.

The first table is the domain reference table, which contains the name of the data domain, the class of the domain (base data type, enumerated or rule based), a reference to the base domain or data type on which it is based, a text description of the domain, and the source of the data that populates this domain, along with an assigned identifier for the domain.

```
create table domainref (
name                  varchar(30),
dClass          char(1),
dType                 integer,
description           varchar(1024),
source          varchar(512),
domainid              integer
);
```

The values can all be stored in a single table, referenced by domain identifier. In this case, we arbitrarily limit the size of the values to 128 characters or fewer.

```
create table domainvals (
   domainid      integer,
   value         varchar(128)
);
```

Last, we represent our rules based domains using records that consist of rule statements.

```
create table domainrules (
   domainid             integer,
   rule                 varchar(1024)
);
```

13.1.3   Domain Identification Through Expertise

While our predilection may be to rely on automatic knowledge discovery methods to find our domains, before we focus on automated ways to identify potential data domains, there is another often overlooked, yet valuable method. This is the process of interviewing the experts familiar with the data to benefit from their domain expertise.

Our first step should be to avoid using automatic means to extract knowledge that can be gleaned from conversations with those who know the most about the data. Assuming that we have already taken some of the steps described earlier in this book, we will have mapped out the information chain as well as determined the actors and their roles within the information factory. We can use the results of this exercise to pinpoint the best individuals to explain known data domains. An afternoon of conversations may prove to be more productive than weeks of computer processing time.

13.1.4   Domain Identification Through Exhaustive Set Analysis

Our first focus is in identifying enumerated domains. Despite the fact that these domains are not explicitly enumerated in any place, we can propose sets of data values that might possibly be enumerated domains by finding sets of values that exhibit the behavior of enumerated domains. This includes but is not limited to the following:

- The number of values is relatively small when compared to the context in which it is used (that is, the number of possible values that an attribute might take is limited to a small set).
- The values are "intuitively distributed." This means that the distribution, while not always even, will take on characteristics specific to the context. In some cases, there is a relatively even distribution, and in other cases, there may be more weight given to a small subset of those values.
- Other domains exist that may be derived from this domain.
- The domain is used in more than one table.
- The attribute that uses the value from the domain is rarely null.

Unfortunately, these are more guidelines than rules, since exceptions can be found for each characteristic. The brute force method for identifying enumerated domains is to look at all possible value sets. We begin by presuming that each column in each table potentially draws its values from a defined domain. For each table, we go through each column and extract the distinct values. This set is now a candidate domain, and we apply heuristics to make a decision about whether to call this set a domain. It turns out that sometimes we can make some kind of determination early in the analysis, and sometimes we have to wait until we know more.

Here are some of the heuristics applied:

1. Are there columns in different tables with the same column name? If so, this may be a good indication that the base data set is shared among multiple tables, and if some other of these heuristics apply, this is likely to house a data domain.
2. If the number of distinct values is similar to the number of records from which the values were extracted, there is a smaller likelihood of that set being a domain than if the number of distinct values is much smaller than the record count.
3. Conversely, if the distribution of the values over the column is relatively equal, then there is a greater likelihood of that set being a domain.
4. The number of null occurrences is counted. If it is relatively small, then the values are likely to belong to a domain. If it is not, it does not eliminate the data set from domainhood, since there may be other rules that apply within the data set that indicate that the value is null under some circumstances and takes its value from a domain under others. In the case of many nulls, hold the data set for further analysis.
5. Is this data set similar or the same as another data set already identified as a domain? If so, then it is likely to be the same domain or perhaps a super- or subset of the other domain.

The automated process can only propose candidate domains. The set of data values only becomes a domain once a user assigns a context and meaning to those values. When a user decides that a candidate data set is a true domain, the following steps should be taken:

1. A name is assigned to the domain.
2. A semantic meaning is assigned to that domain.
3. The domain values, the domain name, and the semantic meaning are inserted into the reference data tables.
4. For each attribute that takes its value from that domain, a domain membership rule is documented.

Repeating this process builds the domain inventory. Because some domains are easier to recognize than others, the method of documenting domains, as well as their intended meanings, eases the way for further domain analysis. Being able to build on a known base will provide insight into some of the less identifiable domains (see Figure 13.2).

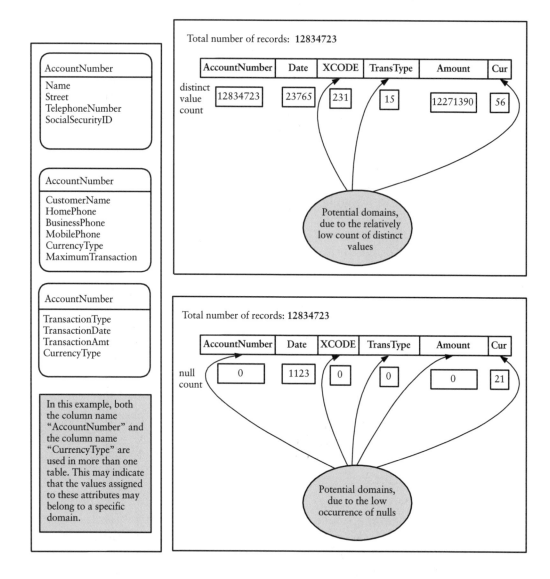

FIGURE 13.2   Heuristics for Domain discovery

13.1.5 Domain Membership Analysis Through Value Matching

Presuming that we have already started to build the domain inventory, the next step is to see whether other data attributes make use of the same domain. We do this by a process called value matching, in which we analyze how well the set of values used to populate one attribute match the values of a known domain. This process is useful in determining if any table attributes use a subdomain of a known defined data value set.

In this process, we can be a little more exacting when it comes to deciding domain membership. The value matching process for a specific attribute can be described using these steps.

1. The attribute's distinct values are collected and counted.
2. The set of unique values is matched against each domain. Fast matching techniques are used for scalability.
3. For each domain, we compute three ratio values. The *agreement* is calculated as the ratio of distinct attribute values that are present in a domain to the total number of distinct values in the attribute. The *overlap* is calculated as the number of domain member values that do not appear in the attribute divided by the number of domain values. Finally, we compute the *disagreement* as the number of values that appear in the attribute but are not members of the domain.
4. The domains are sorted by their agreement percentages. The highest agreement percentages are presented as likely identified domains.

When we compare an attributes value set to a known domain, there are four cases.

1. All of the values used in the attribute are members of the known domain, and the all of the values in the domain are used in the attribute (*agreement* = 100%, *overlap* = 0%, *disagreement* = 0%). In this case, it is safe to say that the attribute takes its values from the known data domain.
2. All of the values in the attribute are members of the known domain, but there are domain members that are not used in the attribute (*agreement* = 100%, *overlap* > 0%, *disagreement* = 0%). In this case, it is also likely that the attribute takes its values from the domain, but this may also indicate the attribute's use of a subdomain, which should be explored.

3. Some of the attribute values are members of the known domain, but some of the values used in the attribute are not members of the known domain (*agreement* < 100%, *disagreement* > 0%). In this case, there are two possibilities. The first is that the there is no real agreement between the attribute's values and the domain, in which case the search for a match should continue. The second case is an indication that the known domain may actually be a subdomain of a much larger set of values, which should be explored. The decision will probably depend on the percentages computed.

4. None of the values used in the attribute are taken from the known domain (*agreement* = 0%, *overlap* = 100%, *disagreement* = 100%). In this case, it is probably safe to say that the attribute does not take its values from the domain. Figure 13.3 shows the domain membership analysis process.

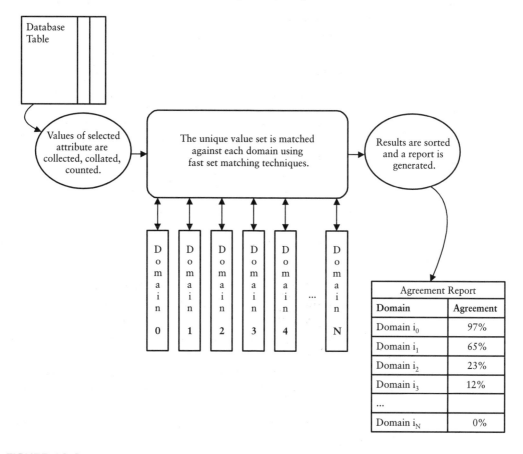

FIGURE 13.3   Domain membership analysis

13.1.6 Domain Identification Through Pattern Analysis

Aside from looking at enumerated value sets, which are easily analyzed when presented with already extant data value collections, it is also useful to look for patterns that might signal membership in a rule-based data domain. For string-based attributes, our goal is to derive a rule-oriented domain by analyzing attribute value patterns.

For example, if we determine that each value has 10 characters, the first character is always A, and the rest of the characters are digits, we have a syntax rule that can be posited as a domain definition. We can use discovered definition as a validation rule, which we would then add to a metadata database of domain patterns. Simple examples of rule-based data domains include telephone numbers, ZIP codes, and Social Security numbers. What is interesting is that frequently the pattern rules that define domains have deeper business significance, such as the geographical aspect of Social Security numbers, as we discussed in Chapter 7, or the hierarchical location focus associated with ZIP codes.

As a more detailed example, consider a customer accounts database containing a data field called ACCOUNT_NUMBER, which turned out to always be composed of a two-character prefix followed by a nine-digit number. There was existing code that automatically generated a new account number when a new customer was added. It turned out that embedded in the data as well as the code were rules indicating how an account number was generated. Evidently, the two-character code represented a sales region, determined by the customer's address, while the numeric value was assigned as an increasing number per customer in each sales region. Because this attribute's value carried multiple pieces of information, it was a classical example of an overloaded attribute. The discovery of a pattern pointed to a more complicated business rule, which also paved the way for the cleaving of the overloaded information into two separate data attributes.

Our first method for pattern analysis is through the superimposition of small, discrete "meaning" properties to each symbol in a string, slowly building up more interesting patterns as meanings are assigned to more symbol components. Initially, we make use of these basic symbol classifications:

- Letter
- Digit
- Punctuation
- White space

Symbol pattern assignment is the first pass at pattern analysis. In each string, we assign one of these classifications to each character appearing in a data value. When all the characters in a string have been classified, the string will have an associated pattern string as well. For each value string, we prepare and record its pattern string. When all value strings have been analyzed, there is a column of associated pattern strings ready to be collated and counted.

At this point, there are two tasks to be done. The first is to look for recurring patterns within the set of generated pattern strings; the second is checking the generated pattern strings against the known sets of patterns. Either way, the goal is to present candidate patterns representing rule-based domains to the user.

If no candidates reveal themselves through simple symbol pattern assignment, then there may be additional embedded information in the patterns themselves that should be investigated. Our next method for pattern analysis takes a more macro view of the data by categorizing strings instead of symbols. At this point, all strings can be classified in one of the following ways.

- Alphabetic
- Alphanumeric
- Numeric
- First name
- Last name
- Business word
- Address words
- One of any other categorized word class

In each attribute value, we now assign to each white space-separated string one of the word categories, forming a new pattern string. After all the strings have had patterns assigned, these patterns can be collated and counted and examined for recurring patterns and matches to previous patterns (see Figure 13.4).

If during the symbol or whole word analysis we discover common patterns that have not yet been registered, they may be a new pattern, which should be documented. At this point, it is a good idea to do a little detective work and see if there is some implicit business rule embedded in this pattern. It may turn out that there is some historical reason for the pattern, which may reflect some business condition that currently exists and must be maintained or that existed at some point but is no longer valid, thereby allowing the rule to be changed.

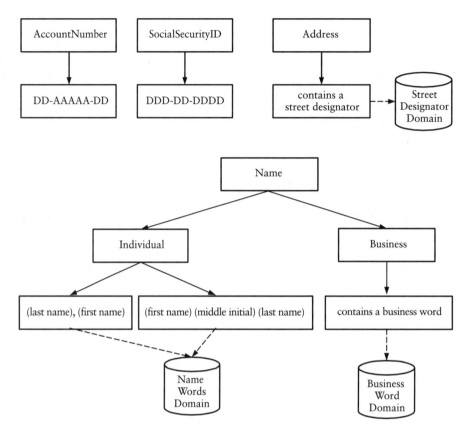

FIGURE 13.4   Pattern analysis

The existence of a reason for a rule is one of the subtle differences between a data quality rule and a business rule. Declaring that all values assigned to a field in a database record must conform to a pattern supplies a means to validate data within a record, but it gives no insight into why the value must be in that form. When we associate meaning with the data quality rule, we suddenly have a context that allows us to understand why values must conform to that format as well as a context to explain what deviations from that format mean.

13.1.7   Superdomains and Subdomains

The domain discovery process is adaptable to parallelization, since many attributes may be analyzed simultaneously. In addition, we may also find that as our domain inventory grows, it is possible that similar, but not exact, data value sets may appear in our set of domains. When this occurs, there are two possibilities. The first is that one domain may be completely contained within another domain, and the other is that two (or more) similar domains may actually be subsets of a larger data domain.

We refer to the first case as a *subdomain,* which is a set of values that is a subset of another domain. The second case is a *superdomain,* in which the true domain that the attributes rely on is the composition (or union) of the smaller domains.

Note that unless an occasional "self-test" of each domain against the rest of the set of domains is performed, the only way to recognize these kinds of overlapping domain value issues is when comparing an attribute's values against many different known domains. If an analyzed attribute appears to belong to more than one domain, it may signal the existence of a subdomain lurking among the known domains. This subdomain may represent another business rule, or we might infer that two similar domains represent the same set of values, in which case the domains might be merged.

13.1.8   Keeping Domains Current

Recalling the currency/timeliness dimension of data quality, it is important that we keep our discovered domains current as well. Since our sources for data domains are either through expert input, discovered enumerated domains, and discovered rule-based domains, we must address the upkeep associated with each of these sources.

For expert-oriented data domains, typically if there is a domain expert consulting on the analysis of used domains, that expert is likely to know when there are any changes to the value set. Whether the domain values are sourced from an external party or the values are based on business rules, the expert user will be aware of any modifications, although a proactive knowledge manager will contact the expert on a periodic basis to make sure any changes can be documented and updated.

For example, consider a data domain consisting of International Standard Organization (ISO) country codes. This data may be sourced directly from the ISO, but since the enumeration of world nations changes relatively infrequently, this is not the kind of data set that is refreshed on a consistent basis. Yet, any geopolitical event that causes an addition or subtraction to the set of nations should trigger a refresh of the domain. This is the kind of event where an expert's opinion would properly keep the information current.

For discovered domains, there is a more serious issue, which has to do with the degree of uncertainty that exists when we rely on discovered knowledge that cannot be vetted through a corroborative source. If we claim that a set of data values extracted from a column is a domain, we basically state that any values that are not in that data set are incorrect for that attribute. Yet, it is possible that the data values that were extracted are a subset of the data values that, over time, could be used for that attribute. This means that we may have documented an incomplete domain, and if we use a domain membership rule to validate the data values in that column, we will have spurious violations due to the incomplete domain.

This implies that in order to maintain currency with discovered domains, some amount of continuing investment must be made by the organization. If we see that certain attribute domain membership rules are being violated with an increasing frequency, this may be a sign that the associated domain(s) are not current. We can incorporate the duties of domain maintenance into the role of data steward.

13.1.9   Overloaded and Split Attributes

When checking an attribute's data values against known domains, what is indicated by medium-to-high agreement with relatively low overlap between an attribute and more than one data domain? This can happen when there is two attributes' worth of information in one column! This could also indicate an overloaded attribute, where the same column is used to represent more than one actual attribute (see Figure 13.5).

Alternatively, when a single attribute uses more than one domain, it might be an indication that more complex business rules are in effect, such as the existence of a *split attribute*, which is characterized by the use of different domains based on other data quality or business rules. As a simple example, consider a banking application that registers customer account activity. When a customer makes a deposit, a credit is made to the customer's account in the form of a positive amount of money. When the customer withdraws money, a debit is made to the account in the form of a negative amount of money. In this case, the same column is used, but in fact there are two domains used for this attribute — positive decimal values (when the action is a credit) and negative decimal values (when the action is a debit).

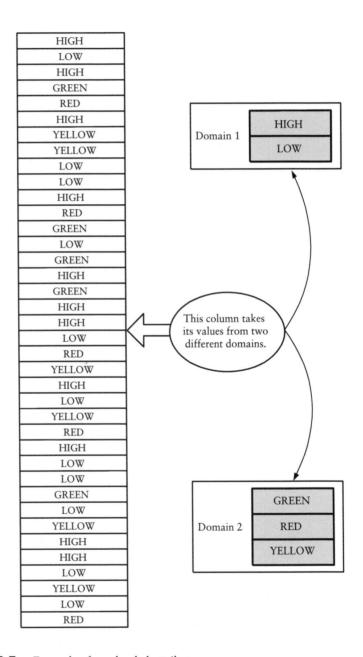

FIGURE 13.5 Example of overloaded attributes

The affinity of the values in a single data field to multiple domains may also mean that the domain as recorded is incomplete and an adjustment must be made in the reference data set. One plan of action would be to merge the domains, as long as the constraints associated with those domains are consistent (both are character strings).

This would result in a superdomain. In this case, any attributes that use either of the original subdomains may need to be "reregistered." Either the previously analyzed attributes use the newly created superdomain with a set of constraints (making it a true subdomain) or, in fact, the attribute may use any of the values in the newly formed superdomain.

One other possibility is that there are real inaccuracies in the column. The records with nonconforming data values should be flagged and made available for correction.

13.2   MAPPING DISCOVERY

Recall that a mapping between domain A and domain B is a set of pairs of values $\{a, b\}$ such that a is a member of domain A and b is a member of domain B, and that there is an intuitive understanding of the relationship between the values a and b. In Chapters 7 and 8, we looked at the definition of mappings between domains that we could later integrate as data validation rules. In this section, we look at the discovery of inherent data mappings embedded within preexisting data sets.

13.2.1   Mapping Discovery

A mapping membership rule applies between two attributes if each attribute's values are taken from a known domain and each pair of values in each record exists in a domain mapping. Mapping memberships represent consistency relationships between the values within each record and can be used for validation of data records on entry to the data warehouse. Unfortunately, identifying mappings between domains is not as simple as identifying domains because domain mappings represent relationships between sets of data values. Since in each data set there are many possible mapping relationships (between any pair of attributes and, in fact, between any pair of sets of composed attribute values), the algorithm must explore all sets of pairs, which results in a quadratic number of comparisons of attribute pairs.

The simplest method for identifying a mapping is to iterate over all pairs of attributes and test to see if the value pairs within each attribute pair constitute a mapping. For each attribute pair, extract all value pairs as they appear in the data set. This set can be subjected to some heuristics to see if the value pairs within the set form a mapping. Since there are different kinds of mappings, we will want to examine this data set to see if the potential mapping is one-to-one, one-to-many, many-to-one, and so on. In any mapping, we refer to the first attribute as belonging to the source domain and the second attribute belonging to the target domain.

13.2.2   Benefits of Mapping Discovery

Mapping discovery is the recognition that two distinct sets of attributes X and Y each belong to a specific domain and that the relation between those two sets is embodied in a mapping between those domains.

These are the benefits of mapping discovery.

- Managing mappings between domains under explicit stewardship provides a framework for the maintenance of that enterprise resource.
- Discovering that two sets of attributes are related via a domain mapping establishes a business rule going forward with respect to those sets of attributes.
- Normalization metadata, such as identifying relations between attributes within the same table when there is pairwise correlation (for example, there is a one-to-one relationship between street address and telephone number), can be used to transform an unnormalized table into normal form.

13.2.3   Representing Data Domain Mappings

As we discussed in Chapter 11, we have a means for storing, cataloging, browsing, and managing mappings between data domains. As a review, we need three metadata database tables to represent our data domain mappings.

The first table is the mapping reference table, which contains the name of the domain mapping, the domain id of the source domain, the domain id of the target domain, a text description of the mapping, and the source of the data that populates this mapping, along with an assigned identifier for the mapping.

```
create table mappingref (
name                 varchar(30),
sourcedomain   integer,
targetdomai     integer,
description         varchar(1024),
source               varchar(512),
mappingid           integer
);
```

The value pairs can all be stored in a single table, referenced by mapping identifier. In this case, we arbitrarily limit the size of the values to 128 characters or fewer.

```
create table mappingpairs (
   mappingid   integer,
   sourcevalue varchar(128),
   targetvalue varchar(128)
);
```

Finally, we represent our rules-based mappings using records that consist of rule statements.

```
create table mappingrules (
   mappingid         integer,
   rule               varchar(1024)
);
```

13.2.4   Mapping Discovery Through Expertise

Just as with data domains, the best way to identify mappings between domains is through conversations with experts in the area. Since mapping discovery is more complex than domain discovery, any way to avoid relying on an automated process can only be beneficial.

13.2.5   One-to-One Mappings

A one-to-one mapping represents an interesting value determination rule within the data set that probably represents an embedded business rule. It implies that for each unique occurrence of a value of the first attribute, the second attribute must match what is described in the mapping. Therefore, given the value of the first attribute, the second attribute's value is predetermined, so this rule can be used for both validation and automated completion. These kinds of mapping memberships may exist between composed sets of attributes as well and are also referred to as functional dependencies.

A one-to-one mapping has certain characteristics that are useful for integration into the discovery process:

1. All values from the first attribute must belong to one domain.
2. All values from the second attribute must belong to one domain.
3. When all distinct pairs have been extracted, there may not be any duplicate entries of the source attribute value.

Note that because different source values can map to the same target value, the third characteristic does not hold for the target attribute value.

These are some of the heuristics used to determine a one-to-one mapping:

- The number of distinct values in the source attribute is greater than or equal to the number of distinct values in the target attribute. This reflects the one-to-one aspect. Since each source must map to one target and multiple sources may map to the same target, we cannot have more values in the target than in the source.
- The attribute names appear together in more than one table or relation. The existence of a tightly bound relationship between data sets will be evident if it appears more than once, such as a mapping of ZIP codes to cities.
- The attribute values appear in more than one table. In this case, we are not looking for the names of the attributes occurring frequently but the actual usage of the same domains.

In reality, one-to-one mappings are essentially equivalent to functional dependencies, and we can use the association rule discovery algorithms (in Section 13.5) to find mappings.

13.3   CLUSTERING FOR RULE DISCOVERY

In a number of the rule classes discussed in Chapter 8, there is a significant difference between the definition of the rules from the automated discovery of embedded rules. When users describe their expectations of the data, they already have some ideas as to the set of validation rules that should be applied. But in the discovery process, we don't always know what to look for, which makes that process particularly hard. In addition, we need to be able to distinguish between rules that make sense or have some business value and spurious or tautological rules, which do not have any business value. Automated rule discovery is not a simple task, but we do have some tools that can be uses for rule discovery. The first tool we will look at is clustering.

13.3.1 What Is Clustering?

In general, clustering refers to a set of algorithms used to segment items in a set into separate partitions, where each value is assigned to a specific partition. One of the major purposes of clustering is for classification, in which we group items by some set of properties and assign a meaning to each cluster. Clustering hinges on the notion of "distance" between items in a set, using a distance function to determine how close any two items are to each other.

There are two kinds of clustering: *hierarchical* and *nonhierarchical*. Hierarchical clustering is used when the set is subject to nested classification, such as the taxonomies applied to biological species. Nonhierarchical clustering is used to group items together in situations where there is no subclassing.

Clustering can be performed either as a *divisive* or an *agglomerative* process. In the divisive method, the process begins with all data items in a single cluster, and iterative steps break down clusters into smaller pieces. In the agglomerative approach, each data item starts out in its own cluster, and each iterative step attempts to join clusters (see Figure 13.6).

While the many uses of clustering are applied to very high-tech applications, such as focused direct marketing or advanced data mining techniques, remember that the concept behind clustering is identifying subsets of items within a larger set where all the values within the subset share some properties. Chapter 8 briefly discussed that given a data set and a rule base, for each rule the data set can be divided into two groups: those that conform to the rule and those that do not.

In general, this means that we are classifying data records *a priori* by defining a rule (which is equivalent to a set of properties) that can be imposed on all those records. If we are trying to discover rules instead

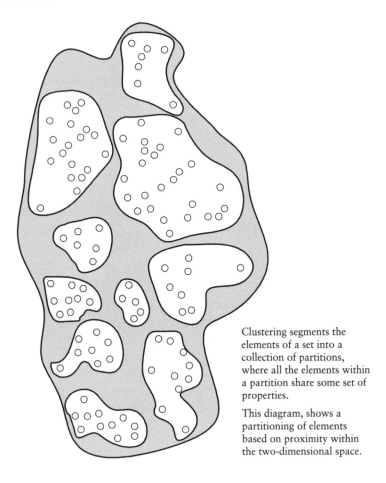

Clustering segments the elements of a set into a collection of partitions, where all the elements within a partition share some set of properties.

This diagram, shows a partitioning of elements based on proximity within the two-dimensional space.

FIGURE 13.6   Clustering

of defining them from the start, our goal is the same: classifying records based on a rule. We can use the clustering process to help perform this classification. In the next sections, we will look at ways of using clustering to discover certain kinds of rules.

13.3.2   Distance and Similarity

Whenever clustering is performed, there must be some measure of distance between two data items being compared. In order to cluster data items, we need to create some kind of quantization of the value and then project each data item (for example, record) into a point in an n-dimensional space (where n is the number of attributes being observed).

Distance is used in calculating nearness for data items during the clustering process. There are a number of measures used in clustering.

- *Euclidean distance* This uses the distance measure derived from the Pythagorean theorem, namely that the distance between any two points is the sum of the squares of the difference between the corresponding data points.
- *City block distance* Similar to the way that a pedestrian must traverse a street grid, this measures the distance in terms of walking along the line segments in a grid. The measure is the sum of the differences between each pair of points.
- *Exact-match distance* For variables whose values are not allocated along continuous dimensions, the values assigned are either 1 for an exact match or 0 for not a match.

Figure 13.7 shows these more clustering methods. We will look more at similarity and distance in Chapter 16.

13.3.3 Divisive Clustering

This is the basic approach for divisive clustering.

1. Assign all values into a single cluster.
2. Determine a division of each cluster that will maximize the similarity between all the elements within one side of the division and maximizes the difference between any pair of items across the division.
3. Repeat Step 2 until either some predefined limit of clusters has been found or some predefined limit of cluster size (minimum, of course, is one) has been reached.

What is glossed over in the simple statement of Step 2 is that the determination of this division requires examining a huge amount of information and processing. For example, for each proposed division, each pair of clusters must be examined to measure the difference between them, and all the values within each proposed new cluster must be examined for similarities between values. This is particularly computationally intensive, and divisive methods are typically not as popular as agglomerative methods.

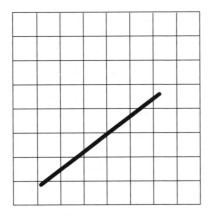

Euclidean Distance

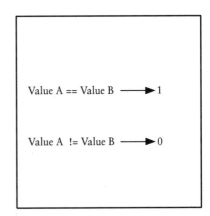

Value A == Value B $\longrightarrow$ 1

Value A != Value B $\longrightarrow$ 0

Exact Match Distance

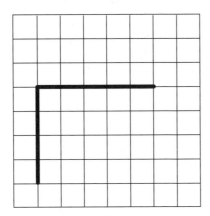

City Block Distance

FIGURE 13.7   Distance measures

13.3.4   Agglomerative Clustering

The approach for agglomerative clustering is as follows.

1. Assign each data element to its own cluster.
2. Find the two closest clusters and combine them into a single cluster.
3. Repeat Step 2 until there is only one cluster left.

Again, the essence of the algorithm is embedded in the second step, where the two closest clusters are combined. It turns out that the determination of the two nearest neighbors is the tricky part, and there are a number of methods used for this determination.

- *Single link method*   The distance between any two clusters is determined by the distance between the nearest neighbors in the two clusters.
- *Complete link*   The distance between any two clusters is determined by the greatest distance between any two data items in the two different clusters.
- *Unweighted pair-group average*   The distance between any two clusters is calculated as the average distance between all pairs of data items in the two different clusters.
- *Weighted pair-group average*   This method is similar to the unweighted pair-group average, except that the size of the cluster is used as a weight.
- *Unweighted pair-group centroid*   A centroid is a point calculated as the average point in a space formed by a cluster. For any multi-dimensional space, the centroid effectively represents the center of gravity for all the points in a cluster. In this method, the distance between any two clusters is measured as the distance between centroids of the two clusters.
- *Weighted pair-group centroid*   This is similar to the unweighted pair-group centroid method, except that the size of the cluster is used as a weight.
- *Ward's method*   This method measures the distance between two clusters based on the total distance between all members of the two clusters.

13.3.5   Value Ranges Using Clustering

In Chapter 8, we discussed value restrictions, which can be applied to both numeric and character string typed values. In the analysis process, it would be useful to be able to identify occurrences of the use of value restriction rules, which we could then incorporate into the rule base.

For any numeric value set, we will initially assume that there are no restrictions on the values. Then, the simplest value restriction rule for numeric values bounds the set by a maximum and a minimum value, which we respectively call the upper and lower bounds. Numeric restrictions can be composed of either a single contiguous range or a collection of noncontiguous regions. A contiguous region is any numeric range that incorporates at least an upper or a lower bound, or both. Two regions are noncontiguous if the upper bound of one is less than the lower bound of the other.

The best way to remedy this problem is to reverse it from being a divisive clustering problem to being an agglomerative problem. We begin by assuming that each value is its own cluster, and then we begin to aggregate clusters based on the distance between the different points. Since these points are all along a single dimension, this clustering is relatively simple. Each cluster represents a value range.

If we believe that there are noncontiguous regions incorporated into the set of value ranges, we can propose a minimum distance between clusters that we expect will exist within the data set. This becomes a parameter to the clustering algorithm that signals to stop trying to merge clusters when the distance between clusters is greater than the minimum. For example, if we think there might be more than one value range with a distance of at least 15 points between them, we will stop clustering unless there are two clusters whose distance is less than 15.

13.3.6 Clustering and Generalized Rule Discovery

Clustering is useful for more than just value range detection. When we can characterize each data record as a combination of measurable properties, we can use clustering as a classification method that depends on those properties. Since all members of a cluster are related because they are near to each other based on some set of metrics, we can aim toward translating the clustering characteristics into a description that explains why those records belong together. If the distinction is clear, it is a strong argument to represent those characteristics as one of our data quality rules.

For example, let's assume that we have a database of customers that includes a significant amount of demographic information as well as sales histories. If we wanted to determine whether there were different classes of customers based on both their sales histories and their demographics, we can apply a clustering algorithm to break down the set of customers into different classes. If our goal is to determine the characteristics of different classes of customers, we can direct the clustering based on fixing the "type of customer" property by assigning one of a set of values based on sales volume. Once the clustering has been done, those characteristics that are the drivers in determining similarity can be used as the basis for defining new business rules.

13.3.7   K Means Clustering

The example from the previous section is a good opportunity to use a K means clustering algorithm. In the K means algorithm, the K stands for the number of clusters we would like to find. These are the steps we take next.

1. Arbitrarily select K seeds that are to be the first guess at determining the centroids of the clusters.
2. For each record, assign the record to a cluster based on the cluster centroid to which it is nearest.
3. After all records have been assigned to a cluster, recompute the centroids of the clusters.
4. If the centroids changed from the previous iteration, then repeat the process starting at Step 2.
5. If the centroids did not change from the previous step, then the process is finished.

We use our distance measurement in Step 2, where we assign each record to a cluster based on nearness to the presumed centroid.

13.4 KEY DISCOVERY

In legacy data from systems that do not have key requirements, we might like to be able to discover candidate keys within the data. Recall that a table key is a set of attributes such that for all records in a table no two records have the same set of values for all attributes in that key set.

In the key discovery process, our goal is to find sets of attributes within a table that we expect to have a key such that the set of attributes uniquely identifies a record in the data set. Initially, we can presume that the combination of all the attributes must uniquely define an entity in the table; otherwise, there would be duplicates, which violates our assumption.

The process for determining keys is an exhaustive one. We can use a recursive process.

1. Initialize key list K to null.
2. Call the tester function with the complete set of attributes.

The tester function looks like this, using pseudocode and the use of the SQL select statement. The input is a set of attributes, the original table, and the count of records in the original table. The second statement selects out the count of records based on the distinct appearances of the attributes in the attribute set S. If the count of records is the same as the complete table count, the attribute set forms a key. For each attribute in the set, remove it and call Tester recursively until the set is of size 0.

```
Tester(S: attribute set, Tab: database table, count:
  integer) {
  If size(S) == 0, return;
  Integer i = select count (distinct S) from Tab;
  If (count == i) then add S to key list K;
  For each attribute a in S {
        Set S' = S – attribute a;
        Call Tester(S', Tab, count);
  }
}
```

When this process completes, the key list K will contain all attribute sets that are unique across the table. We can sort this list in ascending order by attribute set size, which will tell us which attribute sets are the smallest candidate keys.

13.5 DECISION AND CLASSIFICATION TREES

A different way to look at the classification of data is based on a tool called a decision tree. In a completed decision tree, each node in the tree represents a question, and the decision as to which path to take from that node depends on the answer to the question. For example, we can have a binary decision tree where one internal node asks whether the employee's salary is greater than $50,000. If the answer is "yes," the left path is taken, but if the answer is "no," the right path is taken.

At each step along the path from the root of the tree to the leaves, the set of records that conforms to the answers along the way continues to grow smaller. At each node in the tree, we have a representative set of records that conforms to the answers to the questions along that path.

Each node in the tree represents a segmenting question, which subdivides the current representative set into two smaller segments. Every path from the root node to any other node is unique. Each node in the tree also represents the expression of a rule, and at each point in the tree we can evaluate the set of records that conform to that rule as well as the size of that record set (see Figure 13.8).

13.5.1   Building Decision Trees: The CART Algorithm

Obviously, decision trees are useful for harvesting business rules from a data set. But how do we build a decision tree? Here we discuss the CART algorithm. CART is an acronym for Classification and Regression Tree, and a CART tree is built by iteratively splitting the record set at each step based on a function of some selected attribute.

The first step in building a CART tree is to select a set of data records on which the process is to be performed. We might want to sub-

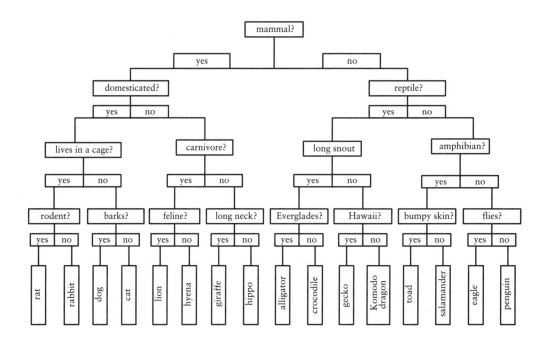

FIGURE 13.8   Decision trees

select some records that we know already have properties in common such that we can use the result of the decision tree to perhaps enhance new records based on these dependent variables. All other data attributes become independent variables. This selected data set is used as a training set, and the results of the decision tree process are to be applied to the entire data set at a later date.

The next step in the process is deciding which of the independent variables is the best for splitting the records. The choice for the next split is based on choosing the criteria that divide the records into sets where, in each set, a single characteristic predominates. The standard method is to evaluate the possible ways to split based on each independent variable, measuring how good that split will be. The measure for evaluating a decision to split is based on a heuristic. Here are some examples:

- *Gini*   This splitting rule looks at ways to maximize the set differentiated by a split, with the goal of isolating records with that class from other records.
- *Twoing*   This is a method that tries to evenly distribute the records at each split opportunity.

When using the Gini method, we basically want to create a split such that the difference in the amount of diversity from the original data set to that within each set (after a split) is increased. Diversity is measured based on the probabilities of records falling into the classes as defined by the split.

The complete tree is built by recursively splitting the data at each decision point in the tree. At each step, if we find that for a certain attribute all values are the same, we eliminate that attribute from future consideration. When we reach a point where no appropriate split can be found, we determine that node to be a leaf node.

When the tree is complete, the splitting properties at each internal node can be evaluated and assigned some meaning. There are some advanced issues regarding error rates and probability (especially at the leaves, where the lack of a decision may not necessarily define a class), as well as pruning algorithms to reduce the size of the tree.

13.5.2   Turning Decision Trees into Rules

Each path of the tree represents a set of selection criteria for classification. If we decide that the leaf represents a valid set of records (that is, there is some valuable business relevance), we walk the tree from the root to the leaf, collecting conditional terms, to accumulate search criteria in the data set. By the end of the traversal, we basically have the condition under which the records in that set are classified. If that classification should enforce some assertion, we can use the condition as the condition in a data quality consistency rule. Other rules can be constructed similarly.

13.6   ASSOCIATION RULES AND DATA QUALITY RULES

Association rules, as applied to databases, are rules that specify a relation between attributes that appears more frequently than expected if the attributes were independent. Basically, an association rule states that the values of a set of attributes determine the values of another set of attributes, with some degree of *confidence* and some measure of *support*.

Note that this definition strongly resembles our functional dependence rule from Chapter 8, except that in the association rule sense, we are looking for distinct occurrences of values within the attributes as opposed to all values within the attributes. Actually, if there are association rules that cover all possible values of the attributes, we can declare the existence of a functional dependence. Otherwise, association rules define potential consistency rules.

An association rule is specified as {source attribute value set} fi {target attribute value set}. The source attribute set is referred to as the "left-hand side" (for obvious reasons), and the target attribute set is the "right-hand side." The confidence of the association rule is the percentage of the time that the rule applies. For example, if 85 percent of the time that a customer buys a network hub he also buys a network interface card (NIC), the confidence of the rule {item1: Buys network hub} fi {item2: Buys NIC} is 85 percent. The support of a rule is the percentage of all the records where the left-hand side and right-hand side attributes have the assigned values. In this case, if 6 percent of all the records have the values set {item1: Buys network hub} and {item2: Buys NIC}, then the support for the rule is 6 percent.

An association rule with a high confidence may represent a data quality rule, where the occurrences that do not conform to the rule are actually errors that could be corrected. What is nice about the association rule is that it can be used for both validation as well as correction!

Algorithms for association rule mining are relatively complex and are outside the scope of this book. On the other hand, many vendors provide tools that can discover association rules, as well as tools for building decision trees, along with other data mining applications that can be used for data quality rule discovery.

13.7   SUMMARY

Finally, what do we do with the results of our discovery? By accumulating the discovered domains, mappings, and rules as managed content, integrated with an access control system and a metadata browsing system, we can build an environment for user subscription to the centralized metadata resource. This is consistent with our discussion in Chapter 11, where we saw how to manage and present enterprise metadata.

The bulk of this chapter has been spent looking at ways to discover data quality and business rules. Part of any data quality program should be a knowledge discovery component, where the goal is to discover the domains, mappings, and rules that have not been disclosed by the experts or have been lost due to employee turnover. This enterprise reference and metadata, embedded in the data sets themselves, can be set free through the use of relatively straightforward heuristic algorithms and data mining techniques.

14

DATA CLEANSING

It may be surprising that a book on data quality doesn't talk about "cleansing" until nearly the end of the text. Yet, while data cleansing may be the first thing on one's mind when thinking about data quality, cleansing actually encompasses only a small part of the data quality universe. The reason for this is that if we have treated data quality properly, planned from the beginning, then we should not really *have* to worry about ever cleaning data, since it should already be fit for use by the time the user sees it.

In actuality, though, since we have been largely operating for 40 years without considering data quality *a priori,* we live in a world where data have been subject to significant entropy and there is a significant data cleansing problem. But first, what is data cleansing?

For our purposes, we define data cleansing as transforming data perceived to be incorrect into a form that is perceived to be correct. In some environments, we rely on a data standard to define what is and is not correct. In other realms, the notion of correct or incorrect is almost inherent in the application.

Most data quality tool vendors concentrate on name and address cleansing. This typically consists of the following areas.

- **Customer record parsing**, which takes semistructured customer/entity data and breaks it up into component pieces such as title, first name, last name, suffix, and so forth. This also looks for connectives (DBA, AKA, &, "IN TRUST FOR") that indicate multiple parties in the data field.
- **Address parsing**, which is a similar activity for addresses.

- **Address standardization,** which makes sure that addresses conform to a published postal standard, such as the USPS Postal Standard. This includes changing street designations to the standard form (ST for street, AVE for avenue, W for west).
- **Address cleansing,** which fills in missing fields in addresses (such as ZIP or ZIP + 4 codes) and corrects mistakes in addresses, such as fixing street names or reassigning post office locality data, such as changing the city field in an address from a vanity address ("ROLLING HILLS HEIGHTS" to "SMALL VALLEY").

A primary example is in the world of direct mail marketing. Marketing material is addressed and mailed, but if the mailing address is incorrect, the mail cannot be delivered and is returned to the sender. But there is a well-designed standard for names and addresses defined by the U.S. Postal Service, and a process called address standardization relies on the standard plus data published by the Postal Service to automatically correct addresses that are thought to be undeliverable.

While there is a well-defined standard for addressing, the address does not *have* to be perfect to reach its destination. It only has to be addressed "well enough." This is a fine distinction, since in the case of U.S. addresses, there is a standard, and it is easy enough (for the most part) to correctly modify an incorrect address. But in those cases where there is no defined standard, there may still be issues of data cleansing that will bring data into a form that is, as per our definition of data quality, fit for use.

In this chapter, we explore data cleansing. We start with a discussion of data standards and the process of bringing data into conformance with a standard (standardization). We also look at common error paradigms that create the need for cleansing. We then discuss what we call metadata cleansing — making sure that the enterprise metadata reflects the defined metadata guidelines, as well as making sure that the data resource conforms to the metadata.

We then look at some of the more routine forms of data cleansing. The first is merge/purge and duplicate elimination, which looks at the combination of multiple data sets and the determination (and subsequent elimination) of duplicate entries. This is followed by a section on updating missing fields — how to determine what a missing field means and how it can be automatically filled. A specialized treatment of updating missing fields is the addition of salutations, titles, and other kinds of expansions.

We also focus a significant section on U.S. Postal address standardization, since it is a good working example of a well-defined standard for which there is a well-developed application solution for data cleansing. Finally, we talk about data cleansing in terms of migration of data from legacy systems to new application systems.

14.1   STANDARDIZATION

According to the *Webster's New Collegiate Dictionary*, a standard is "something set up and established by authority, custom, or general consent as a model or example." In the data world, we can say that a standard is a model to which all objects of the same class must conform.

When we talk about standardization, it means confirming that a data record or a message conforms to a predefined expected format. That format may be defined by an organization with some official authority (such as the government), through some recognized authoritative board (such as a standards committee), through a negotiated agreement (such as electronic data interchange (EDI) agreements), or just through de facto convention (such as the use of hyphens to separate the pieces of a U.S. telephone number, as opposed to other national formats that might use commas or periods).

We examine the definition of a standard and the benefits of using one. More important, we talk about two critical ideas with respect to a good standard. The first is the ability to automatically test for standard conformance, and the second is the provision of a means for automated transformation into standard form. A well-designed standard form will allow for both of these concepts to be realized.

14.1.1   What Is a Standard?

A data standard is a format representation for data values that can be described using a series of rules. In addition, in order for a format representation to be a standard, there must be an agreement among all interacting parties that their data values will conform to that standard.

A standard may enforce some cosmetic string formatting. An example is the format of a U.S. telephone number. As per our definition, the format of a U.S. phone number is discussed by a committee called the Industry Numbering Committee, and the standards are agreed to by the members of that committee, comprising all major telecommunications companies.

The simplest standard governs the grouping of symbols

1-XXX-XXX-XXXX

where each **X** is a character symbol. We can further refine this standard by imposing the rule that each **X** represents a digit between 0 and 9.

A standard may also enforce the use of a specific set of data domains and domain mappings. To continue our U.S. telephone number example, we can insist that the standard format is

1-AAA-XXX-XXXX

where, as before, each **X** represents a digit between 0 and 9 but where the **AAA** component must be drawn from the list of valid Numbering Plan Area (NPA) codes for the United States. To take our standard even further, we can also impose a rule that says that the standard format is

1-AAA-BBB-XXXX

which adds the rule that the second triplet of numbers, **BBB**, must refer to a valid NXX sequence (NXX represents the central office code) associated within an NPA area (see Figure 14.1).

There are many further constraints that can be added, depending on the application. If you are working for a phone company and you need to validate billing data, you may have more constraints than if you are collecting telephone numbers for a customer database.

One quick note: Telephone numbers in North America use a different format standard than telephone numbers in other parts of the world! So, even if you have all the rules down for the United States, there is still a *world* of rules (literally) that might need examination.

14.1.2 Benefits of Standardization

If we try to compare two items that are not of the same class, we are told that we cannot compare apples with oranges. When we talk about standardization, we are really trying to make sure that we compare apples with apples and oranges with oranges. Standardization is a process by which all elements in a data field (or a set of related data fields) are forced to conform to a standard.

There are many benefits to this process, the first of which we have already mentioned: conformity for comparison. When aggregating data down a column (or set of columns), we will be in much better shape when we know that all the values in those columns are in standard

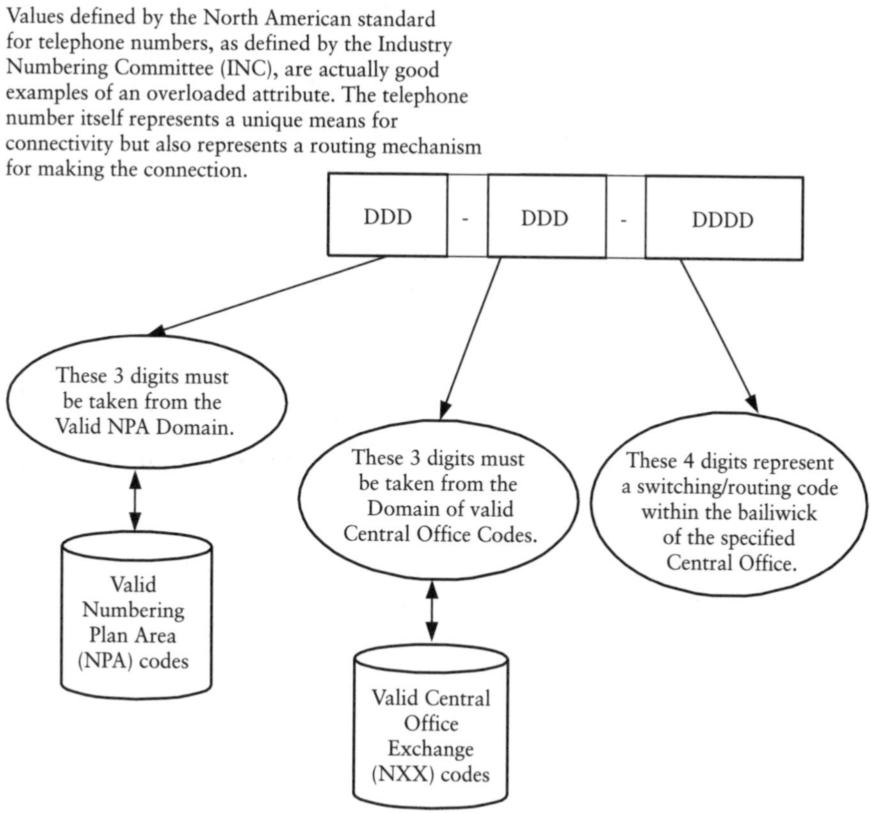
Values defined by the North American standard for telephone numbers, as defined by the Industry Numbering Committee (INC), are actually good examples of an overloaded attribute. The telephone number itself represents a unique means for connectivity but also represents a routing mechanism for making the connection.
DDD
-
DDD
-
DDDD
These 3 digits must be taken from the Valid NPA Domain.
Valid Numbering Plan Area (NPA) codes
These 3 digits must be taken from the Domain of valid Central Office Codes.
Valid Central Office Exchange (NXX) codes
These 4 digits represent a switching/routing code within the bailiwick of the specified Central Office.

FIGURE 14.1 Telephone number standards

form. That way, our sums will not be skewed by erroneous data values. The same goes for using standard values as foreign keys into other tables — we can feel comfortable that referential integrity is more likely to be enforced if we stay within the standard.

Another interesting benefit of standardization is the ability to insert an audit trail for data error accountability. The process of standardization will point out records that do not conform to the standard, and these records can be tagged as incorrect or forwarded to a reconciliation process. Either way, by augmenting a table with audit trail fields and recording at which point in the data processing chain the tables are standardized, we can trace back any significant source of errors. This gives us a head start in analyzing the root cause of nonstandard data.

Probably the most important benefit of standardization is that through the standards definition process, organizations create a streamlined means for the transference and sharing of information. As companies agree on how to exchange information, they also create a means for increasing the volume of exchanged information. With formal standards, more organizations can subscribe to the standard and participate. Examples include the use of data standards for financial transaction exchange (such as SWIFT or FIX), standards for the health industry, standards for geospatial mapping, and so on.

14.1.3   Defining a Standard

The first step in defining a standard should be obvious: Invite all data consumers together to participate in defining the standard because a standard is not a standard until it is recognized as such through the concurrence of the users. In practice, a representative body is the best vehicle for defining a data standard.

The second step is to identify a simple set of rules that completely specify the valid structure and meaning of a correct data value. The rules in this set may include syntactic rules that define the symbols and format that a data value may take as well as data domain and inclusion rules that specify the base data domains from which valid value component may be taken. The most important part of this step is making sure that there is a clear process for determining if a value is or is not in standard form.

The third step in standard definition is presenting the standard to the committee (or even the community as a whole) for comments. Sometimes small items may be overlooked, which might be caught by a more general reading. And, remember, a standard only becomes a standard when it is accepted by all the data consumers. After a brief time period for review and comments, an agreement is reached, and the standard is put in place.

14.1.4   Testing for Standard Form

One critical idea with respect to data value standards is that if a value is dictated to conform to a standard, there must be a way to test to see if a data value conforms to the standard form. This means that the definition of a standard must by association imply the test.

This test can usually be embodied using application code and reference data sets. Going back to our U.S. telephone number example, it is easy to write a program that will check if the telephone number string itself matches the defined format. In addition, two reference tables are needed. The first is a domain table listing all valid NPA prefix codes that are valid for the covered geographical area. The second is a domain mapping between NXX codes (the second digit triplet) and the valid NPA codes associated with each NXX. The first table is used to test our first rule — that the NPA code is a valid one. The second tables allows us to test if the local exchange code is used within that NPA.

Another very good example is the U.S. Postal Standard. The Postal Service has a well-defined standard for mail addressing. This standard includes a definition of each component of an address (first name, last name, street, street suffix, city, etc.), as well as standard and nonstandard forms for the wording of particular components. For example, there is a set of standard abbreviations for street types — the address suffix "AVENUE" has a set of commonly used abbreviations: {"AV," "AVE," "AVEN," "AVENU," "AVENUE," "AVN," "AVNUE"}, but only one ("AVE") is accepted as the Postal Service standard. The Postal Service also has a predefined domain of valid ZIP codes, as well as a mapping between valid street name and city combinations and an assigned ZIP code. In each case, though, an address can be tested to see whether it is in valid form. We look at this in greater detail in Section 14.9.

14.1.5 Transforming in Standard Form

The other important feature involving data standards is the ability to transform data in nonstandard form to standard form. While this may sound simple, it can be quite complex because there are many ways that a data value can violate a standard form. Using our Postal Service example, an address may not be standard because the ZIP code has six digits, the ZIP code is not valid for the named city, or the city named does not exist.

Transformation into standard form can range from straightforward, in cases where the standard form is defined based on values of other fields (such as figuring out the right ZIP code), to impossible, from which nonstandard data is completely unrecoverable (especially when the data values are incorrect).

14.2   COMMON ERROR PARADIGMS

Many types of what appear to be random errors actually are due to relatively common problem paradigms, as we see in the next sections. They are outlined in Figure 14.2.

Error Type	Description	Example
Attribute Granularity	Data model is not configured for proper granularity of values.	Using one data attribute holding street, city, state, and ZIP code
Strict Format Conformance	Format for data entry is too restrictive.	Insisting on a first name, middle initial
Semistructured Format	Format for data entry is too permissive.	Freeform text used in a description field
Finger Flubs	Errors come from mistakes in data entry.	Typing INTERANTIONLA instead of INTERNATIONAL
Transcription Error	The data entry person makes a mistake when transcribing data.	Spelling the name LOSHIN as LOTION
Transformation Flubs	An automated process makes a mistake in data extraction and loading.	Some defined function merging data from two tables is incorrect
Misfielded Data	Data from one attribute appears in a different attribute.	The street address appears in an ADDRESS2 field, instead of ADDRESS1
Floating Data	Small-sized attributes cannot support longer values, so data flows from one field into the next.	Company name data spills out of the name field and into the street address field
Overloaded Attributes	The same attribute contains data associated with more than one value, or the attribute respresents more than one property of the entity.	Inserting both names of a couple in the name field of a customer database when both members of the couple should be listed

FIGURE 14.2   Common error paradigms

14.2.1   Attribute Granularity

In this paradigm, the data model is not configured to correctly incorporate the granularity of information required. A good example is a customer name field, which incorporates first, middle, and last names all in one field. If the user wants to have each name separated, it would be better to use three fields: last name, first name, middle name.

14.2.2   Strict Format Conformance

When the format of the data attributes is too restrictive, the data entry user may not be able to correctly put the right information into the database. Using the same example of customer name, let's assume that we broke up one data field for name into three fields: last name, first name, and middle initial. But the are many people who prefer to be called by their middle names instead of their first names, in which case the correct data should be last name, first initial, middle name. But since there is only room for a middle initial, either both first initial and middle name are crammed into the first name field, or the middle name is placed in the first name field and the first initial is placed in the middle initial field, thereby reversing the customer's first two names!

14.2.3   Semistructured Formats

Semistructured data are data that map to a heuristically determinable format. In other words, the user knows what to expect in general, although not all the data conforms to the expected form all the time. Therefore, there is some intuition about how to get the information. As an example, given an account name field in a bank database, the name field might be semistructured, in that different data entry personnel may have transcribed the name into one of these formats.

- First name, middle name, last name
- Last name, comma, fist name, middle name
- Last name, comma, title, first name

The result is a localized, though potentially widespread inconsistency of format in the context of an imposed structure.

14.2.4   Finger Flubs

Typists are not infallible, and typing errors creep into data. Common mistakes are transcribed letters inside words, misspelled words, and miskeyed letters. In one environment that maintained information on businesses, many of the company names in the database had the ampersand (&) character as part of the name (Johnson & Smith). A frequent error that occurred was the appearance of a 7 instead of the ampersand (Johnson 7 Smith). This makes sense, however, when you see that on one key the & character is shift 7. (So, the 7 might be due to a sticky shift key!)

14.2.5   Transcription Errors

When information is being transcribed, variations in spellings or abbreviations or phonetic similarities may be introduced.

14.2.6   Transformation Flubs

Sometimes errors are introduced when applications extract from one source and transform it before depositing it into the target database. If the transformation rules are not completely correct or if there is a flaw in the transformation application, errors will be created where none originally existed.

For example, in an interesting case, a database of names was found to have an inordinately large number of high-frequency word fragments, such as "INCORP," "ATIONAL," "COMPA." It turned out that the field had been reconstructed from data extracted from a legacy database, which had a limit on the size of an attribute, forcing the data modeler to use more than one actual field to make up one virtual field. When the data was merged, the merging application inserted a space between each of the original fields when they were concatenated. Since some of the original data spanned two of the actual data fields, the insertion of the space created a collection of fragments that did not appear in the original data.

14.2.7 Misfielded Data

Another common error is data placed in the wrong field. In a similar example, the street address field was insufficiently sized, so the entry person just continued entering street address data into the city field.

14.2.8 Floating Data

When a data model is not specified well or the metadata is unclear about what kind of data goes into which fields, we can get errors associated with floating data — where information that belongs in one field is contained in different fields in different records in the database.

14.2.9 Overloaded Attributes

Either a reflection of poor data modeling or as a result of changing business concerns, there is information stored in one data field that actually contains more than one data value.

Examples of this are prevalent in the financial industries, where companies are moving from an account-oriented to a customer-oriented view. Typically, account names are the official names associated with a financial account and may include many combination forms with many associated "context terms." The context terms represent business relationships that might need to be exposed in a customer or parties database. Here are some examples.

1. John Smith and Mary Smith
2. John and Mary Smith
3. John Smith in Trust for Charles Smith
4. John and Mary Smith UGMA Charles Smith
5. John and Mary Smith Foundation, John and Mary Smith Trustees

In the first example, there are clearly two parties, John Smith and Mary Smith, and the two names are separated by the connector "and." In the second example, we also have two parties, although the semantics of the connective are a little more complicated because it relies on a business rule that says that married women take their husband's last name.

In the third example, we also have two parties, but in this case there is a different kind of relationship represented by the business phrase "in Trust for." The two parties here are John Smith and Charles Smith.

In the fourth example, we now have three parties: John Smith, Mary Smith, and Charles Smith, linked together via a different business term ("UGMA," an acronym for Uniform Gift to Minors Act).

In the fifth example, we have three parties but more relations between the parties. To start off, we have John Smith and Mary Smith, and now we also have the John and Mary Smith Foundation, which is an entity in its own right. The relationship here is that John Smith and Mary Smith act as trustees for the foundation that bears their names.

14.3   RECORD PARSING

In all of these cases, the first step in data cleansing is the identification of distinct data elements embedded in data records. In the most common situations, where the data set under investigation consists of name, address, and perhaps other important information, the data elements may be as follows.

- First names
- Last names
- Middle names or middle initials
- Title (MR, MRS, DR)
- Name Suffix (JR, SR, MD)
- Position (SALES MANAGER, PROJECT LEADER)
- Company name
- Building
- Street address
- Unit address (Apt, Floor, Suite)
- City
- State
- ZIP code
- Business terms

The goal of data parsing is to absorb the data embedded in an attribute and produce the data components that exist in the field. In order to do this, we need four pieces.

1. The names and types of the data components expected to be found in the field
2. The set of valid values for each data component type
3. The acceptable forms that the data may take
4. A means for tagging records that have unidentified data components

If this sounds familiar, it should! The names and types of the data components are the metadata for this parse model; the sets of valid values for each data component type are the same domains that we discussed in Chapters 7 and 8. The acceptable forms that the data may take can be expressed using our data quality rules as well.

Most tools that are on the market that provide a data parsing activity are either experience based or pattern based. Experience-based tools take into account the vendor's experience working with large customer name and address databases, letting the tool rely on predetermined data parsing rules and inferred data domains. The pattern based tools are more flexible in that they provide some analysis of the user's data set to look for common patterns in the data. The resulting patterns are presented back to the user for analysis, whereupon the selected patterns may be integrated back into the parsing and cleansing stages. The next sections describe the algorithmic components needed to build a data cleansing system (see Figure 14.3).

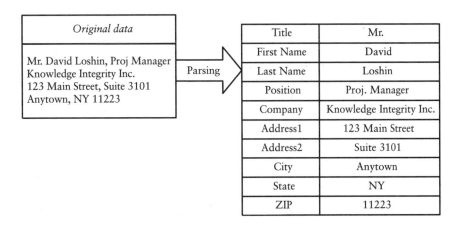

FIGURE 14.3   Example of record parsing

14.3.1   Parsing Metadata

We will need some metadata intended specifically for parsing rules. The first metadata items we need are the data element types. In other words, we want to know what kinds of data elements we are looking for, such as names, street names, city names, telephone numbers, and so forth.

For each data element type, we need to define a data domain for the valid values. This allows us to test to see if any particular data element is recognized as belonging to a specific domain.

14.3.2   Token Parser

The next component we need for data parsing is the parser itself: a program that, given a data value (such as a string from a data field), will output a sequence of individual strings, or tokens. These tokens are then analyzed to determine their element types. The token is at the same time fed into a pattern analyzer as well as a value lookup analyzer.

14.3.3   Pattern Matching

A different kind of parsing is based on the format of the data as opposed to the content per se. We can go back to the example described in Section 7.5 of the Social Security number. We can specify that Social Security numbers take the **XXX-XX-XXXX** format and use this structure format as a pattern for matching strings that we want to identify as Social Security numbers.

In general, we want a format specification for pattern matching for the purpose of parsing. When we evaluate strings, we can characterize their similarity to known data element structure based on how well they conform to defined structure patterns. This can be used for comparing data fields that we expect to have a pattern, such as telephone numbers, addresses, and identification numbers (see Figure 14.4).

We use structure to infer meaning once we have imposed a first cut of attribution to our strings. Typically, we would run the data element parser initially and assign data types to data elements before a pattern comparison stage. We then can specify structural similarity through the definition of patterns. Patterns can range from single character strings

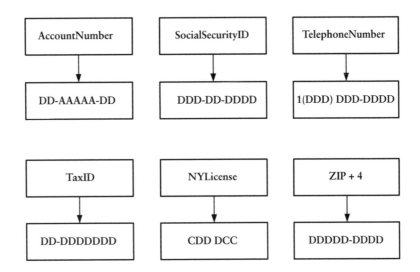

FIGURE 14.4 Examples of pattern matching

to sequences of strings. Our Social Security number example is one kind of single-string pattern, as are telephone numbers.

If we are parsing data items for element type membership by structural pattern, we need a program that will match a token to a defined pattern. We can use our structural domain rules from Chapters 7 and 8 to describe structural patterns.

We should also note that while a data value may structurally resemble a known format, the actual data within may be incorrect for that form. For example, we may have a string "(513) 409-F5H5" that is similar in format to a telephone number, but the value of the string is not a telephone number.

A very popular way for performing pattern matching is using applications known as parser generators. A parser generator takes as input a description of a set of patterns and generates a program that will recognize those patterns and report back which pattern was matched. Parser generators are usually used in building programming language compilers, but they can be used in any situation where a well-defined language can be defined.

Consider the problem of freeform names appearing in a name data field. Presuming that we can assign a data element type to each of the strings, the next step would be to determine whether the entire string matches a specific pattern. For example, if we were able to differentiate between last names and first names, along with initials, we might define the following patterns for recognizing individual names.

- (first name) (first name) (last name)
- (first name) (initial) (last name)
- (initial) (first name) (last name)
- (last name) (comma) (first name)
- (last name) (comma) (first name) (first name)
- (last name) (comma) (first name) (initial)

While not all names will conform to these patterns, a large number will. If we can distinguish male first names from female first names, we can use the pattern system to infer gender assignment as well.

14.3.4   Value Lookup

If the token does not match a particular pattern, then we will see if that value exists in one of the predefined data domains associated with the parsing metadata. Note that a token may appear in more than one data domain, which necessitates the next component, probability assignation.

14.3.5   Probability Assignation

Whenever a token value is recognized as belonging to more than one data domain, we must also assign some probability that the token belongs to each recognized domain. We can do this based on some heuristic rules, which may depend on the context from which the data value was originally taken. For example, if the token was taken from the name field, it is more likely that the token "HOWARD" is a first name than a city name.

14.4   METADATA CLEANSING

We need to be careful when making use of metadata for data cleansing, since if the metadata is not clean, the cleansing operation will effectively fail. Metadata cleansing is a process of validating that the metadata that we are using is correct.

Our cleansing metadata is essentially composed of data domain definitions. A way to cleanse the metadata is to perform some analysis on the conformance of data sets to the metadata. This process includes the following.

- Looking at how frequently the metadata is used to correctly parse tokens
- Determining if there are values included in the metadata domains that never appear in the actual data
- Determining if there are more than one overlapping data domains (that is, do two or more domains share a large percentage of values?)
- Determining if there are overloaded domains (that is, are a small number of domain values accounting for most of the token matches?)
- Checking if new data values emerging in the data belong to known data domains but have not yet been assigned
- Checking if new patterns emerging in the data require changes to the metadata patterns

The cleansing metadata repository requires an occasional review by a domain expert to make sure that the metadata is correct.

14.5   DATA CORRECTION AND ENHANCEMENT

The parsing stage identifies those data elements that are recognized as belonging to a specific element type and those that are not recognized. The next stage of the process attempts to correct those data values that are not recognized and to tag corrected records with both the original and the corrected information.

14.5.1   Automation vs Human Interaction

It is a noble goal to attempt to completely automate the data correction process. Many data cleansing tools try to correct data based on long-time experience and records of the types of corrections that analysts perform while cleaning data. This accounts for large knowledge bases of rules that are incorporated into these products and a proliferation of obscure rules that reflect special cases.

Unfortunately, there are a few flaws in this approach. First of all, the effect of accumulating correction rules based on analyzing certain kinds of data will bias the corrective process to that kind of information. Thus, if a company's set of correcting rules is based on direct marketing databases, there may be an abundance of rules for correcting individual names but a dearth of rules for correcting business names.

The second flaw is that every organization's data is somehow different from any other organization's data, as are the business rules that govern the use of that data. Relying on the business rules from other organizations will still add value, especially if the data content is similar, but there will always be some area where humans will need to interact with the system to make decisions about data corrections.

The third flaw is that data can only be perceived to be incorrect when there are rules indicating correctness. Again, if we rely on other sets of correctness rules, we may miss errors in the data that may pass through provided correctness tests. An example of this in address correction is the famous East-West Highway in suburban Washington, D.C. Because the expectation with addresses with the word "East" at the beginning is that the word is being used as a direction prefix and not as part of the street name itself, some applications inappropriately "correct" this to "E. West Highway," which is not the correct name.

14.5.2   Correction

Obviously, if we can recognize that data is in error, we want to be able to fix that data. There are a few different ways to correct data, and these all rely on some sort of intelligent knowledge base of rules and transformations or some heuristic algorithms for recognizing and linking variations of known data values. One form of correction involves finding string values that are similar to correct values but are slightly varied. In context, an assumption can be made that the intent is to use the correct form.

Another form of correction is the transformation from vanity names and aliases to real names. A vanity name is a euphemized or alternative name that is applied to an item with an already existing name. Place names are frequent holders of vanity names, which are a way to project an image different from the image associated with the surrounding area. Aliases are similar and are also associated with locations that have more official names, such as buildings or office parks.

In general, the correction process is based on maintaining a set of incorrect values as well as their corrected forms. As an example, if the word "International" is frequently misspelled as "Intrnational," there would be a rule mapping the incorrect form to the correct form.

Again, this should sound familiar. We can use the domain mappings we discussed in Chapters 7 and 8 to create the correction rules. In these cases, our mappings are many-to-one mappings, where the source domain is a set of incorrect forms and the target set is of correct forms of value strings.

14.5.3   Standardizing

As we discussed in Section 14.1, standardization is the process of transforming data into a standard form. In the cleansing environment, we use standard forms as a preparation for consolidation, where we try to link different records together. This is different from using standard forms for data normalization. Instead, we use standardization as a means of reducing the search space when looking to link entities together.

For example, consider these two customer records.

1. Elizabeth R. Johnson, 123 Main Street
2. Beth R. Johnson, 123 Main Street

In the absence of any information to the contrary, our intuition says that these two records represent the same person, since Beth is a nickname for Elizabeth. This is an example of the use of a standard form: Elizabeth is the standard for Beth, so we can augment the second record with the standard form.

There are many different data element areas that carry with them some intuitive set of content-related standardization rules. Each culture's set of first names comes along with variation forms, nicknames, and so on that all can relate any name to at least one standard form. For example, Bob, Rob, Bobby, and Robbie are all different forms of Robert. Liz, Lizzie, and Beth, may all be nicknames for Elizabeth. We can create a mapping from known names to some standard form that can then be used as a linking value for later cleansing phases. This holds true for other kinds of data as well: last names, business words, addresses, industry jargon, and transaction types are just a few element types where this technique can be used.

It doesn't even matter if the standard form is applied in a manner that is not consistent with real life. For example, Beth Smith's name might not be Elizabeth, but we can assign Elizabeth to the records anyway just in case. In this context, standardization is being used purely as a means to a different end: enhancement and linkage.

As we have seen in other sections, we can implement standardization using the same kind of data domain and domain mapping methodologies from Chapters 7 and 8. As an example, we can create a data domain for what we will consider to be the standard male first names and a separate domain called "alternate names" consisting of diminutive, shortened, and nicknames. This allows us to have a mapping from the alternate names to the standard names, which we will use to attribute each name record.

14.5.4   Abbreviation Expansion

Similar to standardization, abbreviation expansion is a rule-oriented process that maps shortened forms to expanded forms. Again, the purpose of expanding abbreviations is so that different records can be merged or linked together.

Abbreviations come in different flavors. One type of abbreviation shortens each word in a set to a smaller form, where the abbreviation consists of a prefix of the original data value. Examples include "INC" for incorporated, "CORP" for corporation, "ST" for street. Other abbreviations shorten the word by eliminating vowels or by contracting the letters to phonetics, such as "INTL" or "INTRNTL" for international, "PRGRM" for program, or "MGR" for manager. We call these kinds of abbreviations contractions.

A third form of abbreviation is the acronym, where multiple words typically seen together are characterized with a single string, such as "IBM" for International Business Machines, or "RFP" for request for proposal.

Abbreviation expansion makes use of either predefined mappings from the abbreviated form to the full form or is oftentimes ignored until record linkage and data matching takes place. In the first case, abbreviation is similar to standardization, but in the second case, more free-form abbreviations (those that are not performed in a standard way, such as contractions) can still be linked based on approximate matching techniques.

14.5.5   Application of Business Rules

After the standard corrections, standardizations, and abbreviations have been addressed, there is one more stage at which business rules particular to the application domain may be applied. In our example from Section 14.2.9 where we looked at the overloading of data values within attributes, there were certain business rules within the domain.

There are a number of cases where business rules can be applied. In the case we have discussed, the application is both to determine if there is content overloading and if so to split the overload values out of the single attribute. Another case for using business rules is filling in missing data fields. A third area is knowledge inferences, which we will explore in Chapter 16. In any case, these business rules should be expressible using the rules formats we have discussed in this book.

14.5.6   Enhancement

Data enhancement is the process of appending additional data to a record that increases the value of the data. We talk about data enrichment in Chapter 16 as a greater process of intelligently merging data from different data sources, but in this section, we look at enhancing the information embedded in a record by appending all the knowledge inferred from the associated parsing and cleansing.

The data parsing process attributes a data element type to each string appearing in a record's field. That information is communicated to the analyst by reformulating the data in a presentation indicating the data element type associated with each string. So if, for example, we have determined that there is a business name embedded in an attribute called name, then we will associate the recognized business name with a tag indicating the "business-ness" of the name. As another example, if we determine that the value of the city field is actually a vanity name, we would append the official name of the address's city to the record as well. Ultimately, our record is presented back as a set of element type, value pairs.

By appending standardization information, we provide multiple pivot points which help streamline the later data matching and record linkage process. This lends an advantage, which we will see especially in the duplicate elimination and merge-purge processes.

In more general terms, we are creating an associative representation of the data that imposes a metacontext on the data. By indicating detail about the content of the data, we are promoting bits and bytes to more concise information, which then allows us to exploit business rule relationships that exists in the data. This allows more interesting inferences to be made about the data, as we will see in Chapter 16.

If we have found an error in some value's form, or if we standardize data values, we should not just append the corrected form but we should also log the error occurrence and the rule used in correction or standardization. We gain insight both by having the information represented in its parsed and standardized form but also through the analysis of the process itself. Aside from having the data corrected, for example, we can also measure how many different ways errors existed in the original data set and how frequently each kind of error occurred. This yields significant value, as we can analyze the root cause of the errors and try to prevent them from occurring in the first place.

14.6   APPROXIMATE MATCHING AND SIMILARITY

In all of our discussion so far, we have been gravitating toward a more abstract concept that is inherent in the application of data cleansing. If all the data were clean, the processes that depend on clean data would be extremely straightforward. For example, eliminating duplicate entries is simple if we are sure that all entries are 100 percent correct — the duplicates will be trivially found after sorting the data, for example. The need for data cleansing is purely based on the fact that errors creep into the data set and prevent the straightforward algorithms from working.

This implies that we must use a more complex means for finding *similar* data values, not just identical values. We refer to this as "approximate matching." Approximate matching functions take as arguments two data values and return a score of how similar the two submitted values are. We can characterize an approximate match based on the function used for similarity scoring and the score returned.

14.6.1   Similarity Measures

In order to provide a scoring function for any approximate matching, we need to define what similarity means. Similarity measures are based on a distance function — the closer the distance between two data values, the more similar those two values are to each other. The simplest form of a distance function is a Euclidean distance on a Cartesian coordinate system.

For example, across a single integral dimension, we can compute a distance between two integers as the absolute value of the difference between the two values. In a plane, the distance between two points, $(x1, y1)$ and $(x2, y2)$ is the square root of $(x1 - x2)^2 + (y1 - y2)^2$.

Even with nonnumeric data, we still have to formulate some kind of quantitative similarity measure. Because a similarity measure yields a score that measures the closeness of two data values, there must be some way to characterize closeness, even if the values are character strings. In general, we will want to be able to compute the similarity between two multiattribute records, and that means that we must have distance functions associated with all kinds of data types, as well as our constrained data domains.

14.6.2 Difference and Similarity

We will use a definition of a difference function $d(x, y)$ that maps a pair of values of the same data type to a real value between 0 and 1.0, where a difference of 1.0 indicates no similarity, and a difference of 0 indicates an exact match. A difference function is symmetric, which means that $d(x, y) = d(y, x)$. Difference functions and similarity functions are essentially inverses of each other. The measure of how similar two objects are is the same as the inverse of how different they are.

The literature also imposes a property on difference functions known as the triangular inequality, which states that $d(x, y) + d(y, z) >= d(x, z)$. This basically says that given three objects, x, y, and z, the difference between x and z is less than or equal to the sum of the differences between each of those two objects and some third object. This becomes very useful when clustering points within the dimensional space, since any previously measured differences can be used to look for matches within a certain area.

When comparing any two objects, we must compare their individual components. We can represent any data record or message as a set of (attribute, value) pairs. Each attribute represents some dimension, and each associated value is a specific point along that dimension. Similarity comparison is then basically comparing the distance in some multidimensional space (see Figure 14.5).

	Source Record	Search Record		Weight
Name	H D Loshin	David Loshin	Similarity is based on approximate string match.	5
Address	123 Main St	123 Main	Similarity is based on value parsing and component matching.	3
City	Anytown	Anytown	Similarity is based on equivalence (including vanity names).	2
State	NY	NY	Similarity = 1if both are equal; 0 otherwise.	1
ZIP	11223-6523	11223	ZIP + 4 exact match = 1; ZIP match ZIP + 4 = .85; ZIP = ZIP = .75.	2
Telephone	509-652-9822	509-652-9822	Similarity = 1if both are equal; 0 otherwise.	9
INC	Y	N	Similarity = 1if both are equal; 0 otherwise.	1

FIGURE 14.5 Distance and similarity

For each data type or data domain, we assign a similarity function, and for each set of data attributes, we also provide some weight to be factored in when computing an overall similarity or difference. So, given a set of data records with name, address, telephone number, and Social Security number, we can configure a similarity function that is the composition of the weighted similarity functions associated with each of the components. When we use weighting, though, we must be careful to provide a scaling factor as well so that the overall similarity value falls between 0 and 1.0.

Simply, given a set of properties, $p_0, \ldots, p_n$, a set of difference functions $d_0, \ldots, d_n$ associated with each of the properties, and a set of weights, $w_0, \ldots, w_n$, the difference between any two vectors of values $x_0, \ldots, x_n$ and $y_0, \ldots, y_n$ is

$$\frac{\sum_{i=0}^{n} w_i \bullet d(x_i, y_i)}{\sum_{i=0}^{n} w_i}$$

This gives us a basis for defining similarity measures. The next step is in defining the difference function for each particular data type. We have already seen the use of Euclidean distance for numeric domains. Next we explore similarity measures for different data domains.

14.6.3   Thresholding

When performing approximate matching, how do we determine what is and is not a match? With exact matching, the answer is easy — either two values are the same or they are not. With approximate matching, though, we are not given a definitive answer but rather some point along a continuum indicating the degree to which two values match.

With approximate matching, it is up to the user to define the point at which two values are considered to be a match. We would specify a threshold score, above which the two compared values are considered a match and below which the two values are not considered a match. We can be more precise and actually define three score ranges: match, not a match, and questionable. The threshold above which two values are considered a match to 1.0 is the match range. The not match range would be between 0 and a second threshold value, below which the two strings are definitely not a match. The range between the lower threshold and the higher threshold is the questionable range. Two values whose similarity falls within the questionable range would be candidates for human intervention — a user might need to specify that the two values under investigation are matches or not (see Figure 14.6).

This process of incorporating people into the matching process can have its benefits, especially in a learning environment. The user may begin the matching process by specifying specific thresholds. Because the process integrates user decisions about which similarity values indicate matches and which do not, a learning heuristic may both automatically adjust the thresholds and the similarity scoring, yielding a better similarity measurement.

14.6.4   Edit Distance

The first nonnumeric data type we will look at is the character strings. Clearly, comparing character strings for an exact match is straightforward. It is the determination of closeness for character strings that becomes hazy. For example, we know intuitively that the last names Smith, Smyth, and Smythe are similar. Or do we? If we are not native English speakers, or if we had never heard all three names pronounced, how would we know that these names all sound the same?

One way to measure similarity between two character strings is to measure what is called the *edit distance* between those strings. The edit

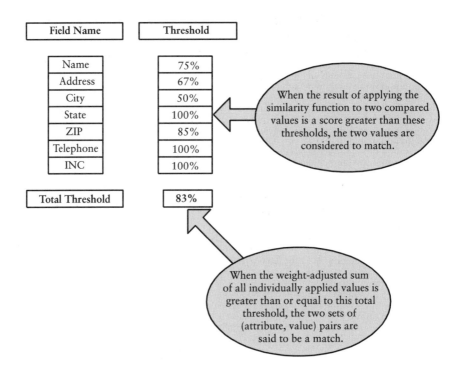

Field Name	Threshold
Name	75%
Address	67%
City	50%
State	100%
ZIP	85%
Telephone	100%
INC	100%

When the result of applying the similarity function to two compared values is a score greater than these thresholds, the two values are considered to match.

Total Threshold	83%

When the weight-adjusted sum of all individually applied values is greater than or equal to this total threshold, the two sets of (attribute, value) pairs are said to be a match.

FIGURE 14.6   Using thresholds for the decision process

distance between two strings is the minimum number of basic edit operations required to transform one string to the other. There are three basic edit operations.

1. Insertion, where an extra character is inserted into the string.
2. Deletion, where a character has been removed from the string.
3. Transposition, in which two characters are reversed in their sequence.

So, for example, the edit distance between the strings "INTERMURAL" and "INTRAMURAL" is 3, since to change the first string to the second, we would transpose the "ER" into "RE" and delete the "E" followed by an insertion of an "A."

Some people include substitution as an automatic edit operation, which is basically a deletion followed by an insertion. Strings that compare with small edit distances are likely to be similar, whereas those that compare with large edit distances are likely to be dissimilar.

Edit distance is computed using an iterative dynamic programming method. Given two strings, $x = x_1 x_2 \ldots x_n$ and $y = y_1 y_2 \ldots y_m$, the edit distance $f(i, j)$ is computed as the best match of two substrings $x_1 x_2 \ldots x_i$ and $y_1 y_2 \ldots y_j$ where

$$f(0,0) = 0$$
$$f(i, j) = min[f(i-1, j) + 1), f(i, j-1) + 1, f(i-1, j-1) + d(x_i, y_j)]$$

where $d(x_i, y_j)$ is 0 if x_i is the same as y_j and is 1 otherwise. This recurrence relation defines the format for the dynamic programming framework, where the function f is computed at each point while traversing through both strings, looking for the minimal value of the function to determine the next step to take. The result is the computation of the minimum edit distance between the two strings (see Figure 14.7).

14.6.5 Phonetic Similarity

Another measure of similarity between two character strings is the phonetic similarity, or how much the two strings sound alike. In the early

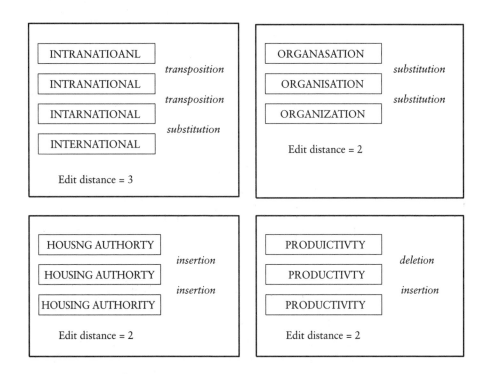

FIGURE 14.7 Example edit distances

twentieth century, a system called Soundex was developed to help in the indexing of U.S. census data. The system involves encoding a name string as a four-character code. The goal is that similarly sounding names would be encoded as the same or similar Soundex codes.

The Soundex method works like this: The first character of the name string is retained, and then numbers are assigned to following characters. The numbers are assigned using this breakdown.

1 = B P F V
2 = C S K G J Q X Z
3 = D T
4 = L
5 = M N
6 = R

All other vowels and consonants are ignored. If the same character appears more than once in a row, the run is reduced to a single number value. In traditional Soundex, the code is truncated after one character, followed by three digits. If there are not enough digits, zeros are appended. For example, the Soundex code for "Smith" is S530, and the Soundex code for "Smythe" is also S530, which indicates that these two names are similar.

Soundex is flawed as an approximate matching tool for the following reasons:

- The constraint of using the first letter followed by a phonetic code means that names that sound alike but do not share the same first letter would not necessarily match. Consider "Dixon" (D250) and "Nixon" (N250), which can sound similar over a poor telephone connection.
- Because Soundex uses consonants in the name string, as opposed to phonetic units, names that have "silent" letters or letter combinations with different sounds will skew a match. Consider the name "Loshin" (L250) and the word "lotion" (L350).
- Because Soundex only uses the first letter and next three consonants, longer names will be encoded in a truncated form.
- Soundex is geared toward English names and is not effective when used with non-English names.

There are other phonetic systems, such as the one developed for the New York State Identification and Intelligence System (NYSIIS) coding. NYSIIS is similar to Soundex, except that while Soundex removes all vowels, NYSIIS retains at least the placement of vowels by replacing them all with the symbol "A." Unfortunately, the NYSIIS encoding is also faulty in that it is biased toward English names. Figure 14.8 shows some Soundex and NYSIIS encodings.

A system called Metaphone, developed in 1990, claims to better represent English pronunciation. The Metaphone system reduces strings to a one- to four-letter code, with some more complex transformation rules than Soundex or NYSIIS. Specifically, Metaphone reduces the alphabet to 16 consonant sound: {B X S K J T F H L M N P R 0 W Y}, where the zero represents the *th* sound. Transformations associated with character sequences are defined based on the different phonetic constructs. For example, a T can reduce to an X (representing a *sh* sound) if it appears in the –TIA– or –TIO– context or to a 0 if it appears in the –TH– context. Otherwise, it remains a T.

There are some ways to improve on the efficacy of these phonetic representations, especially when addressing the issues described here. In terms of similar sounding words that do not share the same initial sound, the phonetic encoding algorithm can be applied to strings in both the forward (in English, left to right) and the backward (right to left) directions.

Word	Soundex	NYSIIS
LOSHIN	L250	LASAN
JACKSON	J222	JACSAN
LINCOLN	L524	LANCALN
FINGERHUT	F526	FANGARAT
DIXON	D250	DAXAN
PETROFSKY	P361	PATRAFSCY
BARTLETT	B634	BARTLAT

FIGURE 14.8 Sample phonetic encodings

In this way, words that are similar, like "DIXON" and "NIXON," may have a chance of matching on the reversed phonetic encodings.

The problem with Soundex's inability to deal with silent letters or alternate phonemes is to use a more complex algorithm such as Metaphone. The issue of the truncated encoding is easy to address: Encode the entire string without truncation.

Unfortunately, it is difficult to overcome the fact that these phonetic schemes are biased toward English names.

14.6.6   N-Gramming

Another way to measure similarity between strings in the presence of errors is using a technique called *n-gramming*. We can look at any string as a composition of its substrings, grouped consecutively in discretely sized chunks moving from left to right. We break a word into its n-grams by sliding a window of size *n* across the word and grabbing the *n*-sized string chunk at each step. The chunk size is determined by the "n" in the n-gram; in other words, if we look at substrings of size 3, we are 3-gramming. If we select chunks of size 4, we are 4-gramming.

As an example, consider di-gramming ($n = 2$) the word "INTERNATIONAL." We end up with the following digrams:

- IN
- NT
- TE
- ER
- RN
- NA
- AT
- TI
- IO
- ON
- NA
- AL

For a string of length 13, we would generate 12 digrams. If we were 3-gramming, we would have these chunks:

- INT
- NTE

- TER
- ERN
- RNA
- NAT
- ATI
- TIO
- ION
- ONA
- NAL

We can use the n-gramming technique as part of another similarity measure. If two strings match exactly, they will share all the same n-grams as well. But if two strings are only slightly different, they will still share a large number of the same n-grams! So, a new measure of similarity between two strings is a comparison of the number of n-grams the two strings share. If we wanted to compare "INTERNATIONAL" with "INTRENATIONAL" (a common finger flub, considering that "E" and "R" are right next to each other on the keyboard), we would generate the n-grams for both strings, then compare the overlap. Using $n = 2$, we have already generated the digrams for the first string; the digrams for "INTRENATIONAL" are:

- IN
- NT
- TR
- RE
- EN
- NA
- AT
- TI
- IO
- ON
- NA
- AL

The two strings share 9 out of 12 digrams — 75 percent. For a two-string comparison, this is a high percentage of overlap, and we might say that any two strings that compare with a score of 70 percent or higher are likely to be a match. Given two strings, X and Y, where *ngram*(X) is the set of n-grams for string X and *ngram*(Y) is the set of n-grams for string (Y), we can actually define three different measures.

1. *Absolute overlap*   This is the absolute ratio of matching n-grams to the total number of n-grams. This is equal to $(2 \cdot (|ngram(X) \cap ngram(Y)|)) \div (|ngram(X)| + |ngram(Y)|)$

2. *Source overlap*   This is the number of matching n-grams divided by the number of n-grams in the source string X.
$(|ngram(X) \cap ngram(Y)|) \div |ngram(X)|$

3. *Search overlap*   This is the number of matching n-grams divided by the number of n-grams in the search string Y.
$(|ngram(X) \cap ngram(Y)|) \div |ngram(Y)|$

When comparing longer strings or data fields that contain many string tokens, we can try different percentage thresholds and the different overlap measures, depending on the data set and the application.

14.6.7   Other Similarity Functions

Considering that we are able to define more constrained data domains, we should also be able to define similarity methods specific to the data domain. For example, if we have a data domain for U.S. states, we could define a new similarity measure between values from that domain that is based on geographical distance instead of lexicographic distance. As another example, values within a color attribute might be scored for similarity based on closeness within their composite red/blue/green values.

For similarity functions within enumerated domains, we can define a mapping between a composed pair of domain values mapped to a similarity score. For generated domains, functions can be defined for the comparison of any two generated values. These similarity measures will define a similarity score between any two domain values and can be used in combination with the similarity or difference measurement of two data multiattribute records, as described in Section 14.6.2.

14.7   CONSOLIDATION

Consolidation is a catch-all phrase for those processes that make use of collected metadata and knowledge to eliminate duplicate entities, merge data from multiple sources, and other data enhancement operations.

14.7.1   Scoring Precision and Application Context

One of the most significant insights into similarity and difference measurements is the issue of application context and its impact on both measurement precision and on the matching criteria. Depending on the kind of application that makes use of approximate searching and matching, the thresholds will most likely change.

As our first example, let's consider a simple direct mail sales program. While our goal would be to find duplicate entries, if a pair of duplicates is not caught, the worst that can happen is that some household might get some extra unwanted mail. In this case, we might prefer that any borderline matches be assumed to be mismatches so our coverage is greater.

For our second example, let's consider an antiterrorist application used to screen incoming visitors. If the visitor's name matches one of the names on the list of known terrorists, the visitor is detained, and a full investigation is performed to determine if the visitor should be allowed into the country. In this instance, where safety and security are concerned, the worst that can happen if there is a missed match is that a dangerous person is allowed to enter the country. In this case, we might prefer that the match threshold be lowered and any borderline matches be brought to the attention of the examiners so as to avoid missing potential matches (see Figure 14.9).

The basic application in both of these cases is the same (matching names against other names), but the precision depends on our expected results. We can group our applications into those that are *exclusive* searches, which are intended to distinguish as many individuals as possible, and *inclusive* searches, which want to include as many potential matches into a cluster as possible. The direct marketing duplicate elimination would be an exclusive application, while the terrorist application is an inclusive application.

14.7.2   Duplicate Elimination

Duplicate elimination is a process of finding multiple representations of the same entity within the data set and eliminating all but one of those representations from the set. In some instances, such as with a primary key in a relational database table, duplicates are not allowed, and so it is imperative that duplicate records be found and reduced to a single entity.

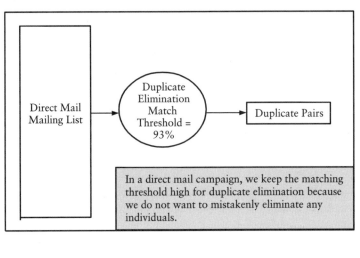

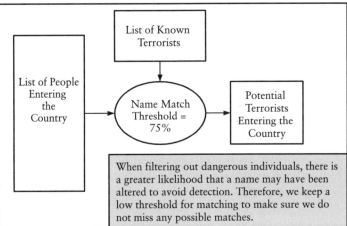

FIGURE 14.9   Different degrees of search precision

When duplicates are exact matches, they can be discovered through the simple process of sorting the records based on the data attributes under investigation. When duplicates exist because or erroneous values, we have to use a more advanced technique such as approximate searching and matching for finding and eliminating duplicates.

Duplicate elimination is essentially a process of clustering similar records together, then using the three-threshold ranges described in Section 14.6.3. Depending on the application, as we discuss in Section

14.7.1, the decisions about which records are duplicates and which are not may either be made automatically or with human review.

14.7.3   Merge/Purge

Merge/purge is a similar operation to duplicate elimination, except that while duplicate elimination is associated with removing doubles from a single data set, merge/purge involves the aggregation of multiple data sets followed by eliminating duplicates. Data from different sources will tend to have inconsistencies and inaccuracies when consolidated, and therefore simple matching is insufficient during an aggregation phase. Again, using approximate matching can be used to cluster similar records, which again, depending on the application, can either have a reduction phase automated or passed through human review (see Figure 14.10).

14.7.4   Householding

Householding is a process of joining a number of records into a single set associated with a single household. A household could be defined as a single residence, and the householding process is used to determine which individuals live within the same residence.

Householding is more than just finding all individuals with the same last name living at the same address. Associated with householding is a more advanced set of knowledge, such as marital status, family structure, and residence type (single versus multifamily home versus apartment). As in other areas that we have discussed, the goal of the application determines the result of the householding process.

For example, a mail-order catalog company might want to ensure that only one catalog was being sent to each residence. In that case, the householding process is meant to aggregate records around a particular delivery address, attempting to recognize those names that all belong to the same address, whether or not they belong to the same family. Alternatively, an application that is targeting only the teenagers in a household would want to identify all members of the same family as well as each family member's role. A third application might be to find unmarried couples living together. In each of these applications, the process is similar, but the details of which attributes are used in the process may differ. Figure 14.11 shows an example of householding.

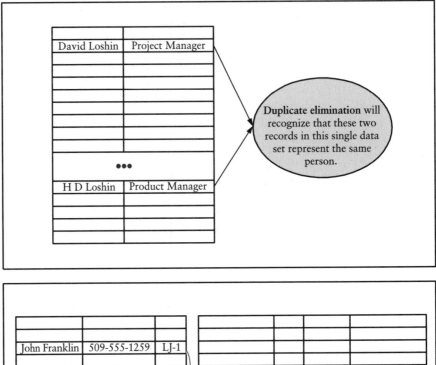

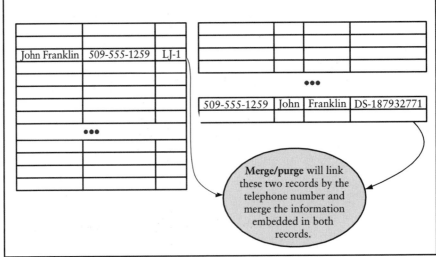

Figure 14.10 Duplicate elimination and Merge/Purge

The general algorithm for householding naturally revolves around the address.

1. All addresses are cleansed and standardized (more about this in Section 14.9).

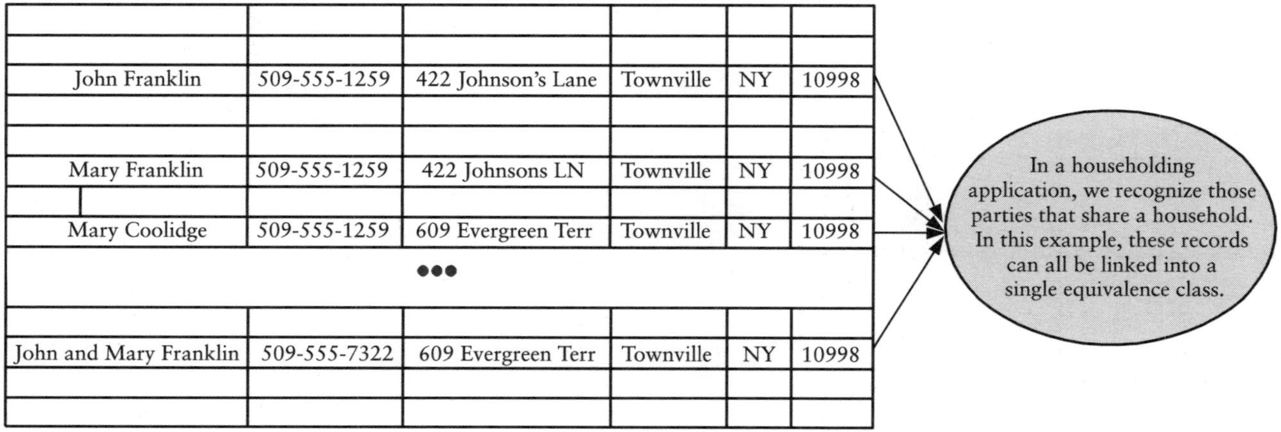

John Franklin	509-555-1259	422 Johnson's Lane	Townville	NY	10998	
Mary Franklin	509-555-1259	422 Johnsons LN	Townville	NY	10998	
Mary Coolidge	509-555-1259	609 Evergreen Terr	Townville	NY	10998	
		• • •				
John and Mary Franklin	509-555-7322	609 Evergreen Terr	Townville	NY	10998	

In a householding application, we recognize those parties that share a household. In this example, these records can all be linked into a single equivalence class.

FIGURE 14.11 Householding

2. Groups are clustered based on the same address.

3. The address is enhanced based on its location status. Some location statuses include single-family home, two-family home, multi-family dwelling, small apartment, large apartment, storefront, business address, and so forth. This information is available for enhancement from third-party sources.

4. The clusters now represent sets of entities residing at the same location. If any distinction must be made based on individual occupancy unit (apartment number, floor, suite, etc.), it is done at this time.

5. Within each cluster, each entity is considered as to its relationship to other entities within the cluster. Two entities are related if some connection can be established between them using corroborating data. This might include sharing a last name, having the same telephone number, or a third record that contains both names. When two entity records are determine to be related, that relation is documented as a virtual link between them.

6. As entities are linked via relationships, a set of mini-networks of interrelated entities is formed. Within each set, the application may attempt to assign one of a list of roles to each entity, depending on the application.

14.7.5 Consolidation and Currency

There are other applications that use a consolidation phase during data cleansing. One application is currency and correctness analysis. Given a set of data records collected from multiple sources, the information embedded within each of the records may be either slightly incorrect or out of date. In the consolidation phase, when multiple records associated with a single entity are combined, the information in all the records can be used to infer the best overall set of data attributes.

Timestamps, placestamps, and quality of data source are all properties of a record that can be used to condition the value of data's currency and correctness. Presuming that we can apply the data quality techniques prescribed in this book, we can quantify a data source's data quality level and use that quantification to consolidate information.

14.7.6   Consolidation and Aggregation

Another application is aggregation based on standard reduction functions across the data set. This includes counts, summations of individual columns, averages, maximums, and minimums, among others.

14.7.7   Network Analysis

A third consolidation activity is a more advanced form of the network analysis described in Section 14.7.4. In general, in any transactional environment, entities acting within the system must communicate with each other. As a component of the consolidation process, one application is the determination of which entities are related to other entities within the system (see Figure 14.12).

This process can have one of a number of goals, including a search for strongly related entities, inference of community, or determination of a communication chain. A simple example is the analysis of inferred "minicommunities" within a newsgroup environment. Within a single newsgroup, there may be many threads to which the users may post messages. Over time, an analyst may find that certain newsgroup regulars may tend to cluster together in smaller groups — the same people always participate together within threads, and other groups participate in other threads.

The general method for this kind of analysis involves some straightforward steps and some more complex ones. Our network will consist of a set of individual entities connected with weighted edges. The simple part is attaching an edge between any two entities when evidence of a relationship exists. If an edge already exists between a pair of entities, the edge's weight is increased. The more complex part of the process involves the clustering of entities grouped via highly weighted connections. Groups where all entities are fully connected (each entity is connected to all others within the group) with highly weighted edges are obvious clusters, but there may be groups where the connection weights between different entities is higher or lower, which requires heuristics to determine cluster membership.

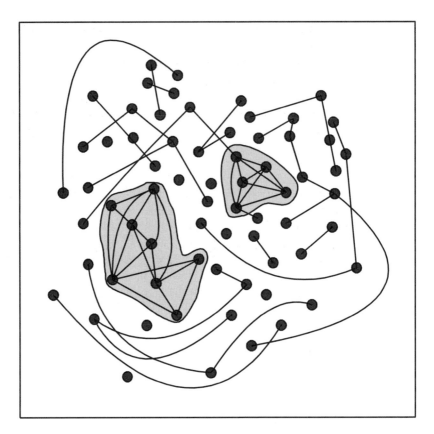

In this example, each node represents a party, and a link between two nodes indicates an established connection between those two nodes. The shaded areas cover networks that indicate a "minicommunity," where (for the most part) each member has an established link with all (or almost all) other members.

FIGURE 14.12   Network analysis

14.8 UPDATING MISSING FIELDS

One aspect of data cleansing is being able to fill fields that are missing information. Recall from Chapter 8 that there are five types of empty attributes:

1. *No value*   There is no value for this field — a true null.
2. *Unavailable*   There is a value for this field, but for some reason it has been omitted. Using the unavailable characterization implies

that at some point the value will be available and the field should be completed.

3. *Not applicable* This indicates that in this instance, there is no applicable value.

4. *Not classified* There is a value for this field, but it does not conform to a predefined set of domain values for that field.

5. *Unknown* The fact that there is a value is established, but that value is not known.

The data cleansing process will not address categories 1 or 3, since by definition there is no way to attack those missing fields. But with the other categories, the reason for the missing value may be due to errors in the original data, and after a cleansing process, there may be enough information to properly fill out the missing field.

For unavailable fields, if the reason for the omissions has to do with the dearth of data at the time of record instantiation, then the consolidation process may provide enough information leverage to supply previously unavailable data. For unclassified fields, it may not be possible to classify the value due to erroneous data in other attributes that may have prevented the classification. Given the corrected data, the proper value may be filled in. For unknown attributes, the process of cleansing and consolidation may provide the missing value.

14.9   ADDRESS STANDARDIZATION

One last area of data cleansing is address standardization. Because address data quality is a critical business operation in many businesses, the ability to use address data as a data merging and consolidation point is very important. While many countries have postal standards, very few of these standards are actually enforced. In some countries, the allocation of addresses is not well defined, but in the United States, both the way that addresses are assigned to new buildings and streets and the way that addresses are formed for mailing purposes are well defined.

In fact, the U.S. Postal Service addressing standards are extremely well defined, and they give us a good example of a template for a data standardization process. The standard is documented in the USPS Publication 28 and is very comprehensive. In this section, we will give a flavor of the degree of detail expressed in this standard by reviewing some aspects of the USPS addressing standards. In many cases, there are acceptable forms and preferred forms, the use of which is suggested to enable better automated address standardization. Figure 14.13 shows these addressing standards.

14.9.1   Recipient Line

The recipient line indicates the person or entity to which the mail is to be delivered. The recipient line is usually the first line of a standard address block, which contains a recipient line, a delivery address line, and the last line. If there is an "attention" line, the standard specifies that it should be placed above the recipient line.

| ALPHA INCORPORATED 123 N ELM ST SPRINGFIELD, OH 31338-0228 | Recipient Line Delivery Address Line Last Line | Secondary address designators may be placed on the delivery address line. The last line contains the city, state (using the standard abbreviation), and a ZIP + 4 code. |

| ATTN Jason Smith ALPHA INCORPORATED 123 N ELM ST SPRINGFIELD, OH 31338-0228 | Attention Line Recipient Line Delivery Address Line Last Line | An attention line is placed above the recipient line. |

| ALPHA INCORPORATED SUITE 3100 123 N ELM ST SPRINGFIELD, OH 31338-0228 | Recipient Line Alternate Location Delivery Address Line Last Line | If all the information for the delivery address cannot be continued in the delivery address line, the secondary address information can be placed in an alternate location line above the delivery address. |

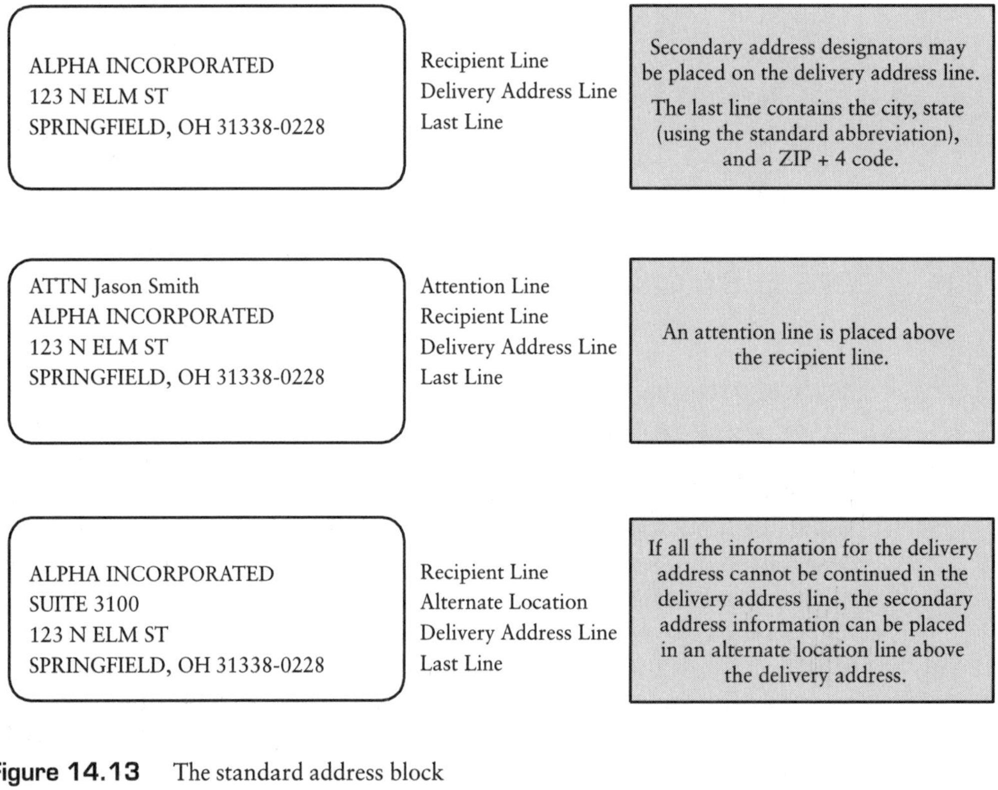

Figure 14.13   The standard address block

14.9.2   Delivery Address Line

The delivery address line is the line that contains the specific location associated with the recipient. Typically, this line contains the street address, and should contain at least some of these components:

Primary Address Number   This is the number associated with the street address.

Predirectional and Postdirectional   A directional is the term the Postal Service uses to refer to the address component indicating directional information. Examples of directionals include "NORTH," "NW," "W." The predirectional is the directional that appears before the street name; the postdirectional is the directional that appears after the street name. While spelled-out directionals are accepted within the standard, the preferred form is the abbreviated one. When two directionals appear consecutively as one or two words before or after the street name or suffix, the two words become the directional, the exception being when the directional is part of the street's primary name. When the directional is part of the street name, the preferred form is not to abbreviate the directional.

Street Name   This is the name of the street, which precedes the suffix. The Postal Service provides a data file that contains all the valid street names for any ZIP code area.

Suffix   The suffix is the address component indicating the type of street, such as AVENUE, STREET, or CAUSEWAY, for example. When the suffix is a real suffix and not part of a street name, the preferred form is the abbreviated form. The standard provides a table enumerating a large list of suffix names, common abbreviations, and the preferred standard abbreviation.

Secondary Address Designator   The secondary address unit designator is essentially a more precise form of the address, narrowing the delivery point to an apartment, a suite, or a floor. Examples of secondary unit designators include "APARTMENT," "FLOOR," "SUITE." The preferred form is to use the approved abbreviations, which are also enumerated in Publication 28.

Additionally, there are other rules associated with the delivery address line. Numeric street names should appear the way they are specified in the Postal Service's ZIP + 4 file and should be spelled out only when there are other streets with the same name in the same delivery area and spelling the numeric is the only way to distinguish between the two streets. Corner addresses are acceptable, but it is preferred to use the physical numeric street address. There are also rules associated with rural route delivery addresses, military addresses, post office boxes, Puerto Rican addresses, and highway contract route addresses.

14.9.3   Last Line

The last line of the address includes the city name, state, and ZIP code. Besides the dash in the ZIP + 4 code, punctuation is acceptable, but it is preferred that punctuation be removed. The standard recommends that only city names that are provided by the Postal Service in its city state file be used (this addresses the issue of vanity city names).

The format of the last line is a city name, followed by a state abbreviation, followed by a ZIP + 4 code. Each of these components should be separated using at least one space. The standard also prefers that full city names be spelled out, but if there are labeling constraints due to space, the city name can be abbreviated using the approved 13-character abbreviations provided in the city state file.

14.9.4   Standard Abbreviations

The Postal Service provides in the appendixes to Publication 28 a set of enumerations of standard abbreviations, including U.S. State and Possession abbreviations, street abbreviations, and common business word abbreviations. Each of these tables can be embodied as enumerated data domains, and we can establish the standard abbreviations as a mapping from the common word domain to the corresponding standard abbreviation table. Other standard abbreviations, such as for city names, are included in the city state file, which can be purchased from the Postal Service.

14.9.5   ZIP + 4

ZIP codes are postal codes assigned to delivery areas to improve the precision of sorting and delivering mail. ZIP codes are five-digit numbers unique to each state, based on a geographical assignment. ZIP + 4 codes are a further refinement, narrowing down a delivery location within a subsection of a building or a street.

ZIP + 4 codes are essentially represented as a mapping from a domain consisting of a composed street address and city name to a domain of ZIP + 4 codes. These data are available for purchase from the Postal Service.

14.9.6   Business-to-Business Data Elements

Business-to-business addressing is more complicated than individual addressing, since more information is embedded in a business address. Consequently, the postal standard explores the complexity of business addressing by defining a set of data element types that can be included in a business address, many of which are irrelevant when it comes to mail delivery! These data element types are essentially a superset of the components of an address described earlier in this section. Here is a full listing, although we only elaborate on those that we have not yet discussed.

- Name prefix (such as MR, MRS, DR)
- First name
- Middle name or initial
- Surname
- Suffix title (such as maturity (JR, SR) and professional (PHD, DDS))
- Professional title (this includes job titles, such as PROJECT MANAGER)
- Division/department name (such as ACCOUNTS PAYABLE)
- Mailstop code (this is usually associated with large office environments)
- Street number
- Predirectional
- Street name
- Street suffix
- Secondary unit indicator
- Secondary number
- Company name
- PO box number
- City
- State
- ZIP/ZIP + 4

- Carrier route code. The carrier route is the list of addresses to which a carrier delivers mail. A code is assigned to each individual route. Addresses with a carrier route code may qualify for discounts on postage.
- Operational endorsement. An endorsement is a marking within the address indicating handling instructions, a special service, or a request for service. An example of an endorsement might indicate that delivery of the piece must take place within a certain time period.
- Key line code. The key line code is optional information printed in the address and may contain information about a piece's presort level or just include other information about the piece.
- POSTNET barcode. POSTNET is an encoding system that encodes delivery point and ZIP + 4 data as a barcode.
- POSTNET address block barcode.

Business addresses will usually contain business words, whose presence can tip off the data cleansing application as to whether the address is associated with a business or not. The standard suggests that business words not be abbreviated, but when label size restrictions indicate that space is needed, the preferred method is to abbreviate the last business word, using those approved abbreviations enumerated in the appendix of Publication 28.

14.9.7 Address Standardization

The Postal Service gives this very straightforward definition of a standardized address, which is taken directly from USPS Publication 28: "A standardized address is one that is fully spelled out, abbreviated by using the Postal Service standard abbreviations shown in Publication 28 or as shown in the ZIP + 4 files." The implication, though, for the process of data cleansing is that there must be a method to convert a nonstandard address into one that meets the USPS definition.

What this really means is that any address standardization process must include these components:

- A method to verify that an address is in standard form
- An address data element parser and tokenizer
- A method to disambiguate data elements that might cause a conflict (such as the use of directionals as part of a street name or the

difference between the use of the abbreviation ST for street or saint)

- A method to perform the necessary lookups in the Postal Service data files (ZIP + 4 and the city state file)
- A method to reformulate the data address elements in a standard form

14.9.8 NCOA

It is said that 20 percent of the United States population changes addresses each year, making it very difficult to maintain up-to-date address lists. Fortunately, the Postal Service provides National Change of Address (NCOA) data to a number of licensees who then incorporate that data into either application services or packages. This allows an aspect of data cleansing in terms of currency to be done on name/address records.

14.10 SUMMARY

This chapter, one of the most comprehensive in this book, focused on many aspects of data cleansing — the process of evaluating, validating, and correcting incorrect data. We began the discussion with a discussion of standardization — benefits of using a data standard and the process of defining a data standard and conforming to it.

We then explored some common error paradigms — the sources of different kinds of errors, including attribute granularity, format conformance, and a discussion of semistructured form. Other common errors include finger flubs, transcription errors, transformation errors, and the problems associated with information appearing in the wrong context.

We then began to explore the process of data cleansing, including record parsing, pattern matching, and probability assignation. We also looked at the automation of data cleansing applications, including data correction, data standardization, expansion of abbreviations, and the application of business rules.

It became clear that a large part of the data cleansing operation involves approximate matching. The ability to find errors in data may be contingent on distinguishing between good and bad data, and that means being able to match up incorrect data with its correct equivalent. Approximate matching requires some kind of similarity and difference metrics, which provides a framework for measuring the similarity between any two values. The simplest form of similarity measurements involve numeric distance. For string data, we looked at a number of different ways of measuring similarity, including edit distance, phonetic similarity, n-gramming, as well as similarity functions defined on user-defined domains.

The consolidation phase of data cleansing looks at the precision used for assigning thresholds for matching based on similarity scores. If the application requires that all matches be found, the threshold for a potential match may be set relatively low. On the other hand, if the application's penalty for missing a match is low, then the threshold should be set high. Approximate matching can be used during the consolidation phase for eliminating duplicate records, merging data from multiple sources, and other applications such as householding and role assignment.

Finally, we considered the process of address standardization, using the United States Postal Standard as the basis for standardization. We looked at some important points from the standard and discussed the application components that must be available for automated address standardization.

Obviously, data cleansing is an important part of information management, although we would hope that a good data quality program could finesse the need for ongoing data cleansing.

15

ROOT CAUSE ANALYSIS AND SUPPLIER MANAGEMENT

Being able to identify the location and magnitude of a problem is one thing, but being able to figure out what is going wrong is another. Up to this point, we have focused on discovering the locations of problems. In this chapter, we concentrate on figuring out the source of the problem. We will do this with root cause analysis, an iterative process of asking questions that exposes the actual cause of a problem.

For data quality issues, root cause analysis is performed as a sequence of stepping backward through the information chain to look for the source of a problem. During this process, we may find multiple variations on the same problem that all stem from the same root cause. If we can trace the problem to its actual source, we can address all the variants associated with that problem at once by fixing the problem, not the symptoms. The next step is to understand what is causing the problem by looking at how the processing stage or communications channel affects the data and proposing a correction.

Not all problems originate within the organization. In many companies, a significant amount of data is provided by external suppliers. These suppliers may not always address the issue of data quality as carefully as is done within the company, but the data quality problems must still be addressed. When the root cause of the problem can be tracked to data that are being supplied by an external vendor, we apply a technique called supplier management. While it might appear that in this situation, the quality of the data appears to be beyond your control, it is possible to take a direct approach of managing the relationship with the data supplier based on concrete measurements and statistics, leading to the establishment of Service Level Agreements.

This technique is a useful way of addressing the problem of low-quality supplied data.

15.1 WHAT IS ROOT CAUSE ANALYSIS?

When we build a database or write a program, it is possible for small implementation errors to creep into the system. When the implementer is made aware of the problem, he or she must find and fix the error; this process is called debugging. Root cause analysis is like application debugging, but in our case it is applied to a bug in the data.

More formally, root cause analysis is an iterative process of analyzing a problem to determine the actual cause. The most effective question that can be asked in this process is "Why?" At each iteration, we ask how and why the problem appears, and the answers to these questions usually can be subject to the same questions, until the source of the problem is finally revealed.

15.1.1 Symptoms vs Cause

Most of the time, when a problem is detected based on some set of symptoms, the symptoms are treated, but the root cause of the problem is ignored. Obviously, when this happens, there is an appearance of having "fixed" the problem, but the problem usually resurfaces later. In some cases, the problem will resurface elsewhere in the system under someone else's jurisdiction. In addition, treating the symptoms sometimes creates other system failures.

Certainly, treating the symptoms is not a scalable solution. As the system grows, the percentage of errors associated with root causes will grow as well, sometimes linearly and sometimes even exponentially. Root cause analysis is a process to iteratively track back the problem to its earliest appearance and determine the root cause at that point. To demonstrate the usefulness of this process, let's look at a simple example dealing with data quality.

15.1.2 Example

Consider a product pricing system in a department store. Each week, new prices are advertised in a shopping circular that is distributed with the newspaper. Supposedly, the correct price for each product is posted within the store at each product display. But when a shopper brings the products to the checkout counter, it turns out that many products do not ring up at the advertised sale price.

If the shopper is keeping track of the prices as they are being rung up, it is possible to catch these errors at checkout time. When the shopper alerts the cashier that an incorrect price has come up, the cashier must call for an attendant to go to the product display or the weekly circular and confirm the price. This usually takes time, but when the correct price is found, the incorrect price is voided, and the correct price is keyed into the register. This may happen two or three times per purchase. The result of this process is that the amount of time it takes for the shopper to check out and pay for the purchase increases, resulting in longer lines. When the store manager sees this, he instructs another cashier to open up a new register.

If the shopper does not catch the error until after the payment has been made, the procedure is a bit different. The shopper must go to the customer service line and wait until a cashier can evaluate the price difference. At that point, an attendant is sent to do the same price check, and if there is a price discrepancy, the shopper is reimbursed the overcharge. Typically, this line is very long because aside from the multitude of incorrect charges, there are other customer services being provided at this location also.

The cashier's process of crediting the incorrect price and then directly typing in the correct price is one example of treating the symptom. The problem, to the cashier's eyes, is an incorrect charge that must be fixed. Unfortunately, the cashiers are usually not in a position to correct the product price in the store database. Also, since they are paid based on the number of hours they work and not as a function of the number of customers they service, there is no compelling business reason to care how long it takes to process each customer.

The fact that longer lines precipitate the manager's opening of more registers is another example of treating the symptom. In the manager's eyes, the problem, which we could call a throughput problem (slow-moving lines), can be fixed by creating additional bandwidth (additional registers), but it does not occur to the manager to examine the root cause of the low throughput. If he did, though, he might notice that approximately 15 percent of the purchased articles ring up at an incorrect price.

We can see a number of important impacts from these incorrect prices.

- Customers are getting irritated that they have to wait so long in line. This may lead to customer attrition and blockading.
- There are likely to be as many undercharges as overcharges, but the customers are more likely to speak up about the overcharges and ignore the undercharges. This is a direct cost to the department store in the form of a loss in revenues.
- More employees are needed to support the cashiering process and, therefore, cannot be employed in more productive pursuits. This includes the additional cashiers needed to cover the registers, and the attendants to scout out the actual prices.

The next step would be to ask why the prices in the computer are not correct. According to some of the cashiers, sometimes the prices are not updated until after the circular has been released. Sometimes the cashiers have no excuse. It is now up to the manager to figure out when the correct prices are supposed to be entered into the system and make sure that the data entry is performed on time and correctly. This is probably the root cause of the problem, and addressing the root cause will eventually solve the overall problem of low throughput.

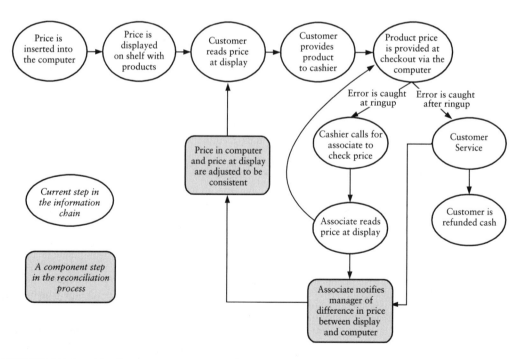

FIGURE 15.1   The department store example

15.2   DEBUGGING THE PROCESS

We can think of root cause analysis as a process of detective work. Essentially, our catalog of data quality problems represents a set of clues, only a subset of which actually contributes to the ultimate problem. In general, we follow these steps in determining a root cause.

1. Gather data. This is discussed in this section.
2. Identify the key causal factors. We will look at this in Section 15.2.1.
3. Chart the causal factors. We look at this in Section 15.2.2.
4. Determine the root cause of the causal factors. This is covered in Section 15.3.
5. Develop corrective actions. This is discussed in Section 15.4.

We have actually put into place all the factors needed to gather data, ranging from the definition of expectations (Chapters 8, 9, and 10) and the insertion of measurement of key data quality assertions. In addition, we can construct a reconciliation system into which nonconforming data is shunted, enhanced with the name of the assertion that was violated.

We can break the analysis into two parts. The first part is tracing the problem backward in the system until the problem occurrence point is found. The second part is determining what caused the problem in the first place and devising a solution. In this section we will explore the first part. We start with the information collected through our assessment and measurement process and then trace the problem back through the information chain until we find its first appearance.

15.2.1   Our Starting Point: Reconciliation Records

In a large system with many problems, the first question to ask is "Where to begin?" A multitude of problems poses a daunting task for determining root causes. In Chapter 6, we introduced the Pareto Principle in which the claim is made that 80 percent of the effect is caused by 20 percent of the causes. Our plan is to build a Pareto chart, which highlights those areas that are responsible for the greatest percentage of a problem and which variables are involved in those areas.

We can implement this by making use of our rules engines coupled with our data quality rules to create a reconciliation system. The goal of the reconciliation system is to automatically collect information about nonconformance in the system. The resulting information collected can be fed into a histogram, sorted by violated assumption, which will act as the Pareto chart.

The system is composed of three parts (see Figure 15.2).

1. A reconciliation database table
2. A set of data quality rules
3. An executable rules engine

The reconciliation database is a repository for records denoting the failure of tested records to conform to the specified rules. Each rule has a unique identifier and can be referenced through that identifier. The reconciliation table maintains a reference to the data being tested and the rule that failed.

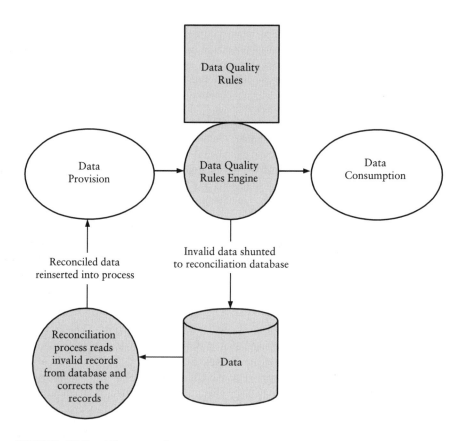

FIGURE 15.2 The reconciliation system

```
create table recon(
reconciliationID      integer,
tableName             varchar(100),
recordID        integer,
violatedRule    integer
);
```

We can use the data quality rules defined in Chapters 7 and 8, or we can rely on the kinds of measurements performed for the current state assessment as described in Chapter 9. The rules can be incorporated into a rules engine as described in Chapter 12.

Every time a data record is passed through the rules engine, the pertinent rules are fired. If the data in the record violates one of the rules, this record is said to be nonconforming, and a reconciliation record is created, incorporating the name of the table, the record being tested, and the rule that failed.

When we have completed some amount of validation, our reconciliation database will have a collection of references to records that do not conform to our assertions. The reconciliation database provides two benefits. The first is that analysts wishing to correct database records have an enumeration of the incorrect records and the reason that each failed (that is, tagged back to the violated rule). The process of correction is simplified because the reason for the nonconformance is highlighted.

The second benefit is that the reconciliation records can be sorted according to the rules that were violated, and this can be used as input to our Pareto chart. We can group nonconformities by count by violated rule, which we can also weigh based on business factors to provide the histogram representing the problems that call out for attention.

The fact that we have attached to each nonconformance the name of the rule that was violated means that we have a head start on identifying the causal factors. The dependent data values described in the violated rules are the targets for analysis, and aggregating nonconformance by rule violation not only provides a place to start in the analysis but also points us in the right direction for tracing back the nonconforming data.

15.2.2 The Problem Trace-Back

The next step is charting the causal factors. In our case, the causal factors are likely to be manifested as incorrect data values, and to chart these factors we must trace the provenance of the incorrect data back to its origin. Luckily, we already have a road map for this trace — the information chain.

The Pareto chart will direct the selection of a particular problem to address. Once this selection has been made, the way to proceed is to start tracing the problem backward through the information chain. At each point in the information chain where the offending value can be modified, we can insert a new probe to check the right values' conformance with what was expected.

There are two important points to note. The first is that since the value may be subject to modification along the information chain, the determination of what is a correct versus incorrect value is needed at each connecting location (such as the exit from a communication channel and entrance to a processing stage) in the information chain. The second is that at each location in the information chain, any specific data value may be dependent on other values sourced from other locations in the chain. If one of those source values causes the nonconformity, it is that value that is picked up as the one to continue with the trace-back.

15.2.3   Identifying the Problem Point

Eventually, this kind of value tracing will result in finding a point where the value was correct on entry to the location but incorrect on exit from that location. We can call this location the problem point because that is the source of the problem.

Finding the problem point is also interesting if we were to recalibrate some of our other analysis processes. As we traced back the value, we may have encountered the source of other problems along the information chain. For example, the appearance of an incorrect product price might affect the customer checkout process but also the daily bookkeeping process. This means that what we originally considered to be two problems is actually only one problem, and the impacts and costs associated with the two problems can be aggregated.

As we trace backward through the information chain (see Figure 15.3), we can decide whether we want to move forward along other paths and check the effect of the traced nonconformity. This allows us to subsume both the impacts and the costs associated with low data quality (as we analyzed using our tools from Chapters 4, 6, and 9) at earlier

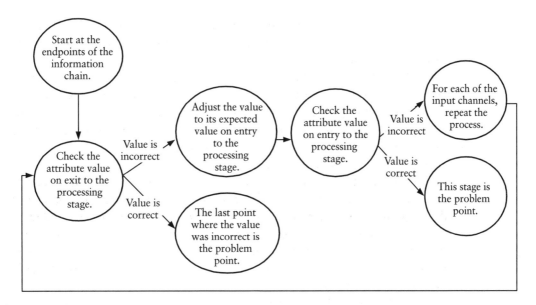

FIGURE 15.3 Tracing the problem back through the information chain

points in the information chain. This "cost accumulation" determines the recalibration and may also point out that many significant problems associated with low data quality can be attributed to a few root causes.

15.3 DEBUGGING THE PROBLEM

Having narrowed the analysis to the problem point, the next step is to determine the cause of the problem. We can segregate problems into chronic problems (those that have been around for a long time and ignored) and acute problems (those that have cropped up recently and are putting new pressures on the system). Depending on the type of problem, there are different approaches to debugging.

Often, organizations choose to address chronic problems only when the cost of the solution is disproportionate to the growth of the system. On the other hand, organizations address acute problems because their appearance disrupts normal operations. Debugging the problem may be as simple as determining that incorrect data are being input, but this may be difficult when faced with legacy application code that is not actively being supported.

Most likely, the root cause falls somewhere in between. To track down the source of a chronic problem, it is beneficial to ask some of these questions.

- How long has this been a problem? This will provide some insight into the history of the problem, who was working on the application or data when it first appeared, or whether anyone really knows when the problem first appeared.
- How long has the code at this processing stage been in production? The answer might help in determining whether this problem has always been there or is not related to the implementation.
- What has prevented any previous root cause analysis? If there has never been a good reason to track down this problem before, what has changed in the environment to increase this problem's priority?

If the problem is an acute problem, it may be due to some recent change in the system environment. These questions may be helpful.

- How recently has the application code been modified? If the change in the application code correlates to the appearance of the problem, that is a good place to start looking.
- What areas of the code have been changed? Again, this focuses on the source of the problem.
- Has the input to this processing stage changed? Perhaps it is not the processing that is flawed but the source data. If so, that may be the focal point.
- Has the delivery of data to this processing stage been disrupted? It might be that neither the code nor the data have changed but the process by which the data is provided to the code.
- Are other data sets upon which this processing stage depends made available? For example, if the data input is sourced from a database that was traditionally updated before a certain time and the scheduling of the updates changed, the processing stage may be using out-of-date input data.
- Has the supplier of information into this processing stage changed recently? Perhaps the new supplier's data is not of as high quality as the previous supplier's data.
- Has the business process changed recently? In this case, it is the fact that what was expected out of the application changed, but

perhaps the application and/or the data have not been brought into synchronization with the business change.

The answers to these questions will lead to other questions. The debugging process is one of narrowing down the set of possible causes by the process of elimination. Eventually, the precise point of the non-conformity will be isolated, and that leads to the next question: How do we fix the problem?

15.4 CORRECTIVE MEASURES — RESOLVE OR NOT?

Now that the problem location has been isolated, it is the job of the analyst to work with the system engineers to determine what needs to be done to correct the problem. If we go back to our department store example, we see that the location of the root cause was at the product price update process. If the product price database were updated at a consistent time with the correct prices, the effect would be seen at the cash registers.

We have two goals at this point: further analyze to propose a correction to the problem and register what we have learned, and then decide whether to implement the correction. Knowledge about the trace of the problem backward through the system and the accumulated knowledge about the specifics of the problem and suggestions for correction both fall into the area of enterprise knowledge that should be absorbed under enterprise management. This information should be registered within a centralized repository, so if the decision is made not to correct the problem at this time, the history of that decision can be reviewed at a later date.

15.4.1 THE CORRECTION REPORT

The collected root cause analysis information should be represented in a format that enables the problem's correction. The most efficient method to effect a correction to a problem is to provide a correction report that completely specifies these elements (see Figure 15.4).

- A concise description of the problem. This can be used as a summary for high-level review. The bulk of the other components of the report will supply a detailed description.

High-Level Description	
Characterization	
Local Information Chain	
Suggested Correction	
Date	
Analyst	

Impact Table	Impact	Cost

FIGURE 15.4   The correction report template

- A characterization of the problem. Is it an error associated with incorrect input data, or is there an incorrect computation embedded in the code?
- The location of the problem. We have just pinpointed the location of where the errors or nonconformities first occur, both within the information chain as well as inside a particular data set or code module.
- The suggested correction. This captures the knowledge learned from the root cause analysis process and provides insight to the next set of interested parties in how to proceed.
- The date of the analysis
- The name of the person providing the report
- A description of the impacts and costs associated with this problem. This is a summary of the results of the trace-back process, where information is collected about the overall impact of specific nonconformities.

This information can be embedded in its own set of database tables, which provides a way to archive the analyses.

```
create table problemReports (
    reportId        integer,
    reportDate      date,
    shortDesc       varchar(1000),
    problemType     integer,
    location        integer,
    correction      text,
    analyst         varchar(100)
);
```

The `problemType` attribute refers to a domain of defined problem types. An auxiliary table logs the impacts.

```
create table problemImpacts (
    reportID        integer,
    impactType      integer,
    cost            float
);
```

The `impactType` attribute refers to a domain of defined impacts, similar to those described in Chapter 4. The cost attribute can be used to tally the individual associated costs by correction report or by impact type.

15.4.2   Resolve to Resolve

In our department store example, the corrective measure was described relatively easily, but the description of the correction does not necessarily justify its implementation. There is actually a decision point when we reach this stage for a number of reasons, including the following.

- The cost of fixing the problem is greater than the continued treatment of the symptoms.
- The resources required are not available.
- It is not always clear how to solve the problem or whether it is worthwhile.
- Taking a system offline to correct it may result in significant losses.

As before, the ultimate decision to make the correction is based on a return on investment justification. The projected cost for making the correction needs to be offset against the continued cost of living with the problems, and a decision can be made based on whether and when a breakeven point occurs.

To extend our management of the correction reports, we should also keep track of the decision of whether or not to implement the correction, and if so, the party responsible for that correction.

15.5   SUPPLIER MANAGEMENT

It is possible that the trace-back determined that the problem originated outside the organization. This means that the problem actually originates with a supplier to the organization, either as an external data provider or as an external application provider. At this point, we can address the problem through the process of supplier management.

Supplier management is a term that covers the range of interactions between a product or service vendor and a purchaser. Vendor-purchaser relationships are forged before the sale is made, but afterward there is likely to be less oversight applied to the supply process. The result is that the level and quality of the provided service may suffer in the long run. As with all manufactured goods, information products and information services are subject to quality controls. It is just that few organizations implement these controls. This is due to the same reasons that internal information quality is not measured, as discussed in Chapters 3 and 4.

The key to supplier management is being able to specify a set of requirements that must be met by the supplier in order to satisfy the purchaser. The same way that an automobile manufacturer can set specifications on the products that are produced by OEMs for inclusion in a finished automobile, information-based businesses can set specifications for supplied information. For simplicity, our discussion will focus on the data supplier, but the process can be applied to service providers in a similar fashion (see Figure 15.5).

A company can set those specifications the same way internal requirements are defined: through the use of defined metrics based on the dimensions of data quality. We can use our data quality rules to specify assertions and expectations about the data as it enters the enterprise. The only difference is where the data is being tested: after it has

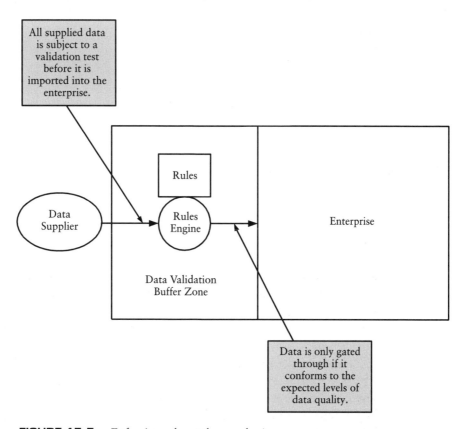

FIGURE 15.5   Enforcing rules at the supply site

been injected into the information chain or before it enters the system. Obviously, it is better to prevent bad data from entering the system than having to deal with it once it is in the system.

Supplier management is best implemented as a "compliance codicil," which is included as a component of the original agreement between the supplier and purchaser. The agreement should include a provision for a periodic review of the levels of data quality, a minimum threshold for acceptance, and a definition of how the threshold is computed. The compliance codicil should also specify the penalty when the data provided by a supplier do not meet the purchaser expectations, as well as a set of actions to be taken whenever a serious violation of the requirements has occurred.

The threshold can be expressed as a function of the measured conformance to the set of requirements. In Chapter 10, we looked at the definition of data quality requirements, as well as a way to collect and manage requirements in a set of metadata tables. Each requirement is specified as a rule, along with a description of that rule's implementation. It is the responsibility of the purchaser to provide a copy of these rules to the supplier so that the desired levels of data quality are understood equally well by both supplier and purchaser.

One interesting way to make sure that both sides are complying with the agreement is for each side to develop the testing application for requirements testing, agree that each implementation correctly validates the information, and then exchange those applications. This means that when the supplier is running its validation engine, it is using the application written by the purchaser, and vice versa.

15.6   SUMMARY

In this chapter, we looked at completing the data quality improvement cycle. We have looked at analyzing the economic impact of low data quality and the costs associated with those impacts. We are able to define sets of data quality rules and perform a current state assessment based on measuring conformance to our expectations with respect to the dimensions of data quality. We can use the results of these measurements to create a requirements document. We can analyze our data sets, looking for reference data and metadata, and we now can analyze the system to find the root cause of data quality problems.

We can now provide a full analysis of the data quality of our system and create a framework for selecting and implementing improvements in implementable units of work. In the next chapters, we look at improving the value of our data through enrichment, and then we discuss the actual means to implement our data quality improvement program.

16

DATA ENRICHMENT/ENHANCEMENT

Data enrichment (also known as data enhancement) is a process of increasing the value of a pool of information by combining data from multiple sources. The goal of enrichment is to provide a platform deriving more knowledge from collections of data. We can use enrichment as a means for learning more about entities in a set of databases to create a "value-added" information product, to investigate fraudulent behavior, or even to increase the quality of a given data set.

A simple enrichment example is in targeted marketing. Let's assume that a preferred customer is one who spends more than $100 a month on a set of products and whose credit history indicates strong predilection toward prompt payment of bills. We can use data enrichment to combine customer sales data with customer credit data to build a data mart that can be used to make special offers to these preferred customers.

Another example involves investigating fraud. Suppose that when more than a certain amount of money is paid to members of a professional organization, then there is a suspicion of fraud. In this case, we would merge health insurance claim information with professional billing information to search for this kind of behavior.

A third example involves enabling efficient financial transaction interchange. In the financial world, different companies have different representations for securities trades, but there are unique identifiers for each stock, option, bond, and so forth. Through combining incoming transaction messages with internal data tables, we can enrich financial electronic data interchange messages to enable automated straight-through processing.

In any case, data quality is critical to successful enrichment. In this chapter, we discuss how data standardization, clustering techniques, and the use of data quality rules can be used to express enrichment directives. We will also look at some enhancement examples and how they can be affected by poor data quality.

16.1   WHAT IS DATA ENHANCEMENT?

Let's imagine this brief scenario. You are a sales manager, and your entire compensation is based on commissions on the sales that you and your team make. Imagine that the director of sales handed each member of your sales staff a list of sales leads that contained names, addresses, and telephone numbers. Each sales representative might have some chance of closing a sale with any one of those leads, but it would be anybody's guess as to which lead is more likely to convert to being a customer than any other. Without any additional information, each call is a crapshoot.

Now imagine if the list contained each sales lead's annual salary, the amount of money they've spent on similar products over the last five years, a list of the last five purchases the lead has made, and the propensity of that lead's neighbors to purchase your product. Which of these lists would you rather have?

That second list contains enhanced data. The value of the original list has been improved by adding the extra personal and demographic information. By having the extra data added to the original set, the sales team can increase its effectiveness by prioritizing the sales leads in the order of propensity to buy.

The value of an organization's data can be greatly increased when that information is enhanced. Data enhancement is a method to add value to information by accumulating additional information about a base set of entities and then merging all the sets of information to provide a focused view of the data.

16.2   EXAMPLES OF DATA ENHANCEMENT

In any situation where there is an opportunity for enhancement, the goal in to produce a data set whose added value can help optimize a business process. In the customer relationship world, the goal is to produce a set of customer profiles that can provide both a framework for more efficient sales efficiency and a streamlined mechanism for customer service. In the sales analysis world, this may imply enhancing point-of-sale data to understand purchase patterns across the organization's sales sites. In the health/pharmaceuticals industry, a goal could be to understand the interactions between different drugs and to suggest the best possible treatments for different diseases.

There are different ways to enhance data. Some of these enhancements are derived enhancements, while others are based on incorporation of different data sets. Here are some examples of data enhancement, which are shown in Figure 16.1.

16.2.1   Temporal Information

A relatively simple way to improve data is to add a timestamp. Understanding aspects of the "ebb and flow" of transactions over a specific time period adds significant value. Also, being able to track historical data is useful in understanding trends.

16.2.2   Auditing Information

One frequent data enhancement is the addition of auditing data to a record in a database. For example, in a customer support database, each time a customer has a discussion with a customer support representative, not only is the conversation noted but also the name of the representative with whom the customer spoke, along with a timestamp.

16.2.3   Contextual Information

The context in which a piece of information is manipulated may yield an opportunity for enhancement. Location, environment, path of access are all examples of context that can augment data. For example, an e-commerce company may monitor Web accesses to determine if the users are visiting Web pages from a computer at work or at home. Contextual enhancement also includes tagging data records in a way to be correlated with other, external pieces of data during later analysis.

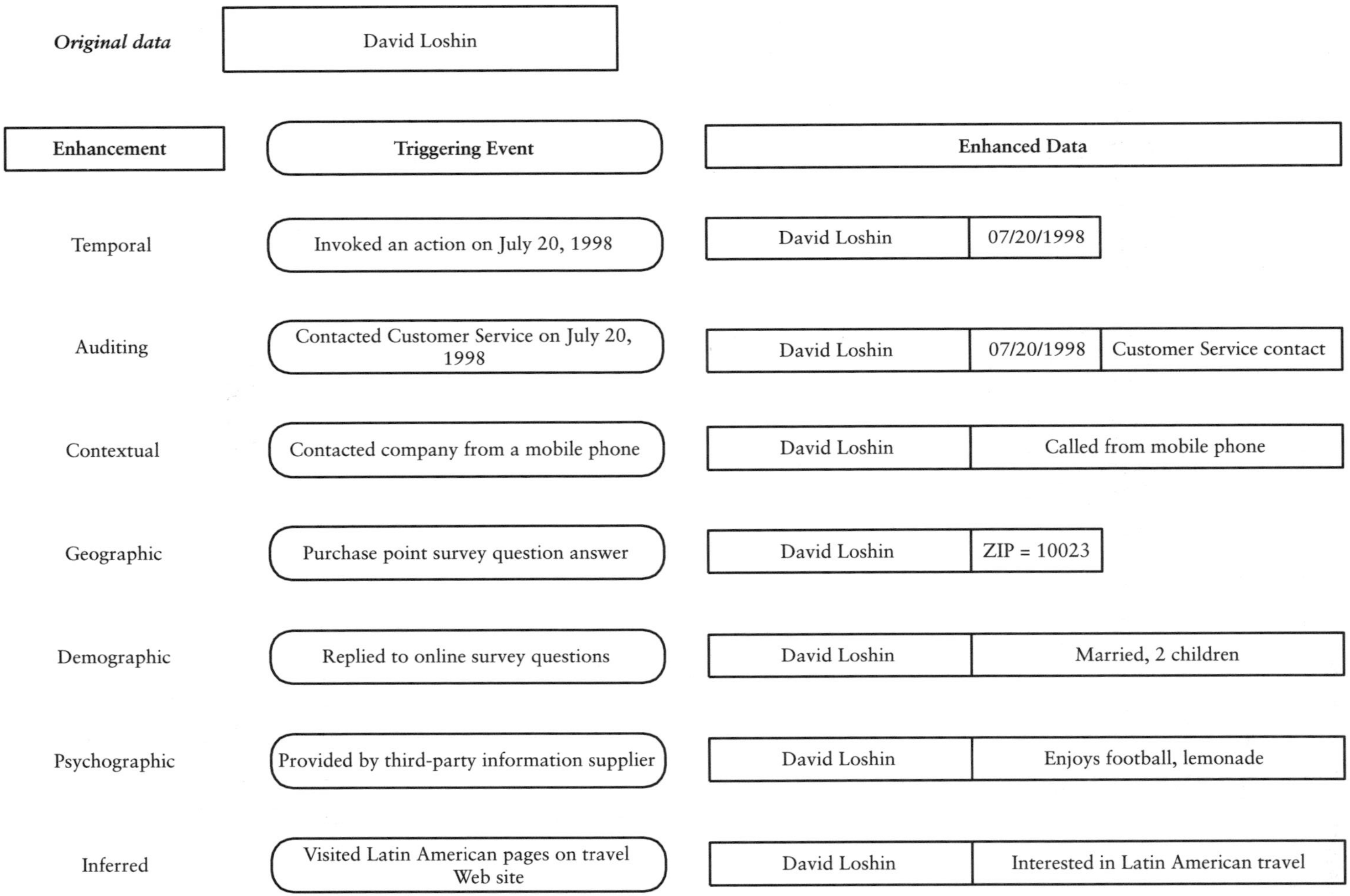

Original data		
David Loshin		

Enhancement	Triggering Event	Enhanced Data		
Temporal	Invoked an action on July 20, 1998	David Loshin	07/20/1998	
Auditing	Contacted Customer Service on July 20, 1998	David Loshin	07/20/1998	Customer Service contact
Contextual	Contacted company from a mobile phone	David Loshin	Called from mobile phone	
Geographic	Purchase point survey question answer	David Loshin	ZIP = 10023	
Demographic	Replied to online survey questions	David Loshin	Married, 2 children	
Psychographic	Provided by third-party information supplier	David Loshin	Enjoys football, lemonade	
Inferred	Visited Latin American pages on travel Web site	David Loshin	Interested in Latin American travel	

FIGURE 16.1 Some examples of enrichment

16.2.4   Geographic Information

There are a number of geographic enhancements. Data records containing addresses are initially enhanced through address standardization. Addresses are cleansed and then modified to fit a predefined postal standard, such as the United States Postal Standard. Once the addresses have been standardized, other geographic information can be added. This includes regional coding, neighborhood mapping, latitude/longitude pairs, or other kinds of regional codes.

16.2.5   Demographic Information

For customer data, there are many ways to add demographic enhancements. Demographic information includes customer age, marital status, gender, income, ethnic coding, to name a few. For business entities, demographics can include annual revenues, number of employees, size of occupied space, and so on.

16.2.6   Psychographic Information

Psychographic information is used to break the target population down into its component lifestyles defined by how each individual behaves. This includes product and brand use, product and brand preferences, organization memberships, leisure activities, vacation preferences, commuting transportation style, shopping time preferences, and so on.

16.2.7   Inferred Information

Having a base set of data whose quality we can trust gives us the opportunity to aggregate, drill, slice, and dice that data. When we can infer knowledge based on that data, we can augment the data to reflect what we have learned.

16.3   ENHANCEMENT THROUGH STANDARDIZATION

When we talk about standardization, we refer to making sure that a data record or a message conform to a predefined expected format. That format may be defined by an organization with some official authority (such as the government), through some recognized authoritative board (such as a standards committee), through a negotiated agreement (such as electronic data interchange (EDI) agreements), or just through de facto convention (such as the use of hyphens to separate the pieces of a U.S. telephone number — as opposed to other national formats, which might use commas or periods).

Converting data to a standardized format is an extremely powerful enhancement. Because a standard is a distinct model to which all items in a set must conform, there is usually a well-defined rule set describing both how to determine if an item conforms to the standard and what actions need to be taken in order to bring the offending item into conformance.

Aside from the data quality benefits that we discussed in Chapter 14, the value of data standardization lies in the notion that given the right base of reference information and a well-defined rule set, additional data can be added to a record in a purely automated way (with some exceptions). A very good example is ensuring that a U.S. street address has been assigned the correct ZIP code and inserting the correct ZIP code when it is missing.

This is not to say that automated standardization is simple. As we discussed in Chapter 14, sometimes transforming into standard form can be relatively complex. There is significant benefit when a standard can be translated into a set of rules from which a standardization process can be formed. Using our example from the previous paragraph, we can standardize the ZIP code portion of a U.S. street address through a process that is determined based on the specification of the assignment of ZIP codes.

The entire country is divided into geographical regions designated by a five-digit ZIP code. Each region includes a number of the streets within a political geography, and the Postal Service maintains a database of which ZIP code regions contain which streets in each city (along with address ranges). So, given a street address within a named city and state, the determination of the correctness of the ZIP code is the same as the process for standardizing the address by adding a ZIP code.

1. Determine if the city is a valid city name within the state. This corresponds to a query in a city-state mapping table.
2. If so, determine if the street name is a valid street name within that city. Again, this corresponds to a query in a database mapping between streets and cities.
3. If the street is valid, check to see if the address (the street number) is in a range that is valid for that street. Do another mapping lookup, and this mapping should also reflect the ZIP code mapping as well. A test will compare the found ZIP code, and an assignment will just use that found ZIP code.

Note, by the way, how this process uses the data domain mappings we discussed in Chapter 7! But what happens if one of these lookups fails? The default would be to resolve the ZIP code to the closest level in the geographical hierarchy. For example, if the street is valid but the number is not, then assign the ZIP code for the street. If the street does not exist within the city, assign a default ZIP code for that city. While the result is not always correct, it may still be in standard form.

16.4   ENHANCEMENT THROUGH PROVENANCE

This enhancement is a generalization of the temporal and auditing enhancements just described. A provenance of an item is its source. An interesting enhancement is the operation of associating a provenance with a data record, which would consist of a source code and a time stamp (marking the time at which the data was updated).

16.4.1   SIMPLE PROVENANCE

A provenance can be as simple as a single string data field describing the source or as complex as a separate table containing a time stamp and a source code each time the record is updated, related through a foreign key. Because there is a complete audit trail for all tagged data records, this second approach allows for a more complete itinerary to be compiled.

One interesting benefit is that later analysis can show the value of different sources of data, as well as different pathways or traces of modifications to data. For example, if it can be shown that one particular original data source consistently provides information that is never updated, it can be inferred that that provider's information is more reliable than that of a provider whose records are consistently made current. Another example might allow for measures of volatility with respect to information acquired through different tracks.

16.4.2   Audit Trails

The more advanced form of this enhancement supplies not only a source for creation or an update of a record but also additional activity fields. When we combine source, time, and activity information into a record, we can trace back all occasions at which a piece of information was touched, giving us the opportunity to truly understand how activities cause data to flow through a system.

16.5   ENHANCEMENT THROUGH CONTEXT

In today's Web-based environment, there are ways to not only track when a user is touching a data set but also where the user is sitting when the activity occurs. In these cases, we can enhance data with what we call context information. This kind of information includes the virtual location from which the activity takes place (visiting a particular Web domain name), a physical location (from a home computer versus an office computer), as well as other data that can be collected directly from the user through direct interaction.

In this kind of environment, substantial marketing benefit can be derived, since this context information can be fed into a statistical framework for reporting on the behavior of users based on their locations or times of activity. For an e-commerce concern, this information can be quite revealing and can be used for strategic benefit. As an example, a Web-based business can determine that many of its customers browse through catalog entries during the daytime while at work but peruse the content for a subselection of entries at home in the evening. The business can retool the Web site to provide different kinds of presentations during work hours or leisure hours, which will encourage users to purchase products.

16.6   ENHANCEMENT THROUGH DATA MERGING

An effective method for data enhancement is combining the information that is stored in more than one database into an enhanced database. These kinds of operations are performed all the time, mostly represented as database joins. Frequently, these joins exist for some operational purpose, and the enrichment of the data is purely done for an operational reason. For example, straight-through processing systems may require record data enrichment as data are passed from a source organization to the target so that the next step in the process can be determined and executed (see Figure 16.2).

How is data merging done? It is basically a matching operation: select a number of attributes that most likely characterize the entity, (we'll call them the characterizing attributes) and then search for all records that have the same attributes. Those records form a candidate set for enhancement — all of those records may contribute data to a new enhanced piece of information. This process works well when merging new records into an already existing data set but may be less effective when applied directly to different data sets. But hold on to that thought — we will explore this issue more in Section 16.7.

Strategic value can be attained through combining data sets. In this case, the talent in creating a data enhancement environment is less in the SQL skill and more in the qualitative analysis of what information needs to be merged and what other techniques can build a more effective data merge. Several scenarios exist in which data merging may be necessary.

16.6.1   Corporate Mergers

When two companies merge, eventually they will have to merge their customer databases, employee databases, and base reference data. Consolidating customer records prevents potentially embarrassing marketing snafus (such as having more than one sales representative contacting the same customer on the same day). More interesting, additional business intelligence can be collected on those customers that existed in both original data sets.

Hotel Database

Last name	First name	Nights	Arrival	CreditCard#	RoomType
Jefferson	William	2	12/08/1999	3977-6725-9877-0295	Double
Jefferson	William	1	12/18/1999	3977-6725-9877-0295	Double

Airline Database

Last name	First name	CreditCard#	From	To	Dep	Ret
Jefferson	William	3977-6725-9877-0295	LGA	LAX	12/08/1999	12/19/1999

Car Rental Database

Last name	First name	Days	Arrival	CreditCard#	CarType
Jefferson	William	12	12/08/1999	3977-6725-9877-0295	Midsize

By merging the data embedded in these collected records, we can infer more details about William Jefferson's trip than if we looked at any of the tables alone. For example, we might infer that William is traveling outside the Los Angeles area between the dates of December 8 and December 18. We guess this because the car rental covers the entire time of the trip, but the hotel is booked for three nights on arrival and the night before the departure.

FIGURE 16.2 Enhancement through merging

16.6.2   Affinity Programs

An affinity program attempts to sell a product customized to a particular group of customers, based on a preexisting characteristic shared by all of them. One example is a university alumnus credit card with a picture of a university's main library on the card and a program through which some small percentage of a customer's annual charges are donated to that university. Once the affinity product has been created, an affinity program can be effected by merging a customer lead list, such as a bank's current account holders with average balances greater than $5,000, with an affiliation database, such as the alumni directories from the Ivy League schools.

Other affinity programs include health and life insurance tie-ins, product discounts, and service discounts. In each of these cases, there is some aspect of data merging.

16.6.3   Cooperative Marketing

Many companies take advantage of synergies when partnering with other organizations in cooperative marketing campaigns. Frequently, the originators of these campaigns attempt to influence the decision to purchase one product, based on a customer's previous experience with another product. A good example of a cooperative marketing campaign is when a long-distance telephone provider teams with an airline to give the customer a bonus of frequent flyer miles if that customer opts for the offered long-distance service.

Typically, organizations that try to build cooperative marketing programs will do so in a "brute force" manner by combining data sets and blasting out offer letters. While this may a workable means of acquiring new business, a more refined method exists that can create a more effective marketing campaign. This method combines data enhancement techniques with database merging to provide a narrowed focus for marketing.

16.6.4   Data Cleansing

Because customers move, get married or divorced, change their name, and so forth, very often, large customer databases tend toward entropy in turns of accuracy. Not only that, when people are involved in the data entry process, mistakes can be made. This leads to the existence of duplicate records for many individuals or corporate entities. As seen in Figure 16.3, which contains real data extracted from the U.S. Securities and Exchange Commission's EDGAR database, many of these duplicates are not always simple to recognize. Linking the duplicate records together is a way to cleanse the database and eliminate these duplicates.

16.6.5   Householding

Another process, called householding, attempts to consolidate a set of individuals to a single grouping unit based on the database record attribution. A household consists of all people living as an entity within the same residence. The simplest example is that of consolidating husband and wife records to a single household.

Households can be differentiated by demographics as well as geographics, and in one household there may be different subsidiary roles, such as primary earner and primary decision maker (these two may be different individuals). More complex examples include the identification of dependents, categorizing dependents by class, as well as separating out boarders or transient residents. Householding can be used to improve demographic analysis, marketing optimization, as well as targeting particular defined roles in the household.

16.6.6   Medical Diagnosis and Treatment

In the health industry, data merging is performed both for diagnosis and for determination of treatment. A collection of medical professionals may pool their individual patient information (most likely having been anonymized first) as a cooperative means for building up a knowledge base particular to a set of illnesses. The information, which consists of a patient's history, diagnosis, and treatment, must be enhanced to fit into the collaborative data model.

For diagnostic purposes, a new patient's history and profile are matched against other patients' histories in the hope of finding a close match that can help determine the cause of a health problem. Once a number of matches have been found, the matched patients' treatment protocols are examined to suggest a way to treat the new patient's problem.

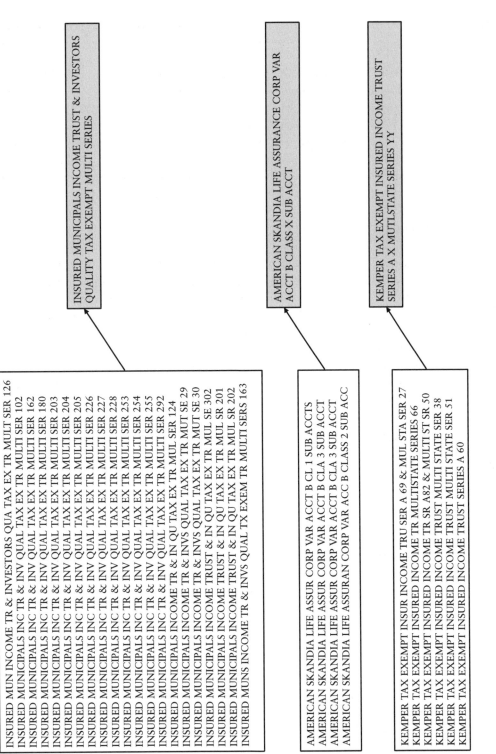

INSURED MUNICIPALS INCOME TRUST & INVESTORS QUALITY TAX EXEMPT MULTI SERIES

INSURED MUN INCOME TR & INVESTORS QUA TAX EX TR MULT SER 126
INSURED MUNICIPALS INC TR & INV QUAL TAX EX TR MULTI SER 102
INSURED MUNICIPALS INC TR & INV QUAL TAX EX TR MULTI SER 162
INSURED MUNICIPALS INC TR & INV QUAL TAX EX TR MULTI SER 180
INSURED MUNICIPALS INC TR & INV QUAL TAX EX TR MULTI SER 203
INSURED MUNICIPALS INC TR & INV QUAL TAX EX TR MULTI SER 204
INSURED MUNICIPALS INC TR & INV QUAL TAX EX TR MULTI SER 205
INSURED MUNICIPALS INC TR & INV QUAL TAX EX TR MULTI SER 226
INSURED MUNICIPALS INC TR & INV QUAL TAX EX TR MULTI SER 227
INSURED MUNICIPALS INC TR & INV QUAL TAX EX TR MULTI SER 228
INSURED MUNICIPALS INC TR & INV QUAL TAX EX TR MULTI SER 253
INSURED MUNICIPALS INC TR & INV QUAL TAX EX TR MULTI SER 254
INSURED MUNICIPALS INC TR & INV QUAL TAX EX TR MULTI SER 255
INSURED MUNICIPALS INC TR & INV QUAL TAX EX TR MULTI SER 292
INSURED MUNICIPALS INCOME TR & IN QU TAX EX TR MUL SER 124
INSURED MUNICIPALS INCOME TR & INVS QUAL TAX EX TR MUT SE 29
INSURED MUNICIPALS INCOME TR & INVS QUAL TAX EX TR MUT SE 30
INSURED MUNICIPALS INCOME TRUST & IN QU TAX EX TR MUL SE 302
INSURED MUNICIPALS INCOME TRUST & IN QU TAX EX TR MUL SR 201
INSURED MUNICIPALS INCOME TRUST & IN QU TAX EX TR MUL SR 202
INSURED MUNS INCOME TR & INVS QUAL TX EXEM TR MULTI SERS 163

AMERICAN SKANDIA LIFE ASSURANCE CORP VAR ACCT B CLASS X SUB ACCT

AMERICAN SKANDIA LIFE ASSUR CORP VAR ACCT B CL 1 SUB ACCTS
AMERICAN SKANDIA LIFE ASSUR CORP VAR ACCT B CLA 3 SUB ACCT
AMERICAN SKANDIA LIFE ASSUR CORP VAR ACCT B CLA 3 SUB ACCT
AMERICAN SKANDIA LIFE ASSURAN CORP VAR ACC B CLASS 2 SUB ACC

KEMPER TAX EXEMPT INSURED INCOME TRUST SERIES A X MUTLSTATE SERIES YY

KEMPER TAX EXEMPT INSUR INCOME TRU SER A 69 & MUL STA SER 27
KEMPER TAX EXEMPT INSURED INCOME TR MULTISTATE SERIES 66
KEMPER TAX EXEMPT INSURED INCOME TR SR A82 & MULTI ST SR 50
KEMPER TAX EXEMPT INSURED INCOME TRUST MULTI STATE SER 38
KEMPER TAX EXEMPT INSURED INCOME TRUST MULTI STATE SER 51
KEMPER TAX EXEMPT INSURED INCOME TRUST SERIES A 60

FIGURE 16.3 Sometimes there are many ways to represent the same concept

16.6.7   Fraud Detection

In many areas where there is a potential for fraud, data merging is used as a way to both identify fraudulent behavior patterns and use those patterns to look for fraud. Opportunities exist for fraud in all kinds of businesses, such as transaction based (telephone and mobile-phone service), claim based (all kinds of insurance), or monetary transaction-based (where there are opportunities for embezzlement, for example). In fact, there are many areas of crime that call out for data matching and merging: money laundering, illegal asset transfer, drug enforcement, and "deadbeat dads," to name a few.

16.7   DATA MATCHING, MERGING, AND RECORD LINKAGE

Simple data merging between records is a process of choosing a set of attributes for characterization, using a base reference record and searching through a set of records for those records whose attributes match the reference record. Thos records are candidates for linkage, and the other attributes are examined to determine the closeness of a match.

When any two records can be associated based on a set of chosen attributes, we say that those two records are linked. Usually, record linkage is performed only when the chosen attributes match exactly. But simple record linkage is limited for the following reasons.

Information sources are in different formats. It is easy to say that two records match when they come from the same table with the same attributes (with the same column names, etc.). But when the records come from different data sets, it may not be clear which are the right attributes to match. For example, in one data set, there may be a column called **ACCT_NUM**, and in a second data set the column representing the same information is called **ACCOUNT_NUMBER**.

Information is missing. As we have discussed many times in this book, there is significant importance in properly identifying the kind of information that is *not* there — in other words, the different kinds of null values. When a characterization attribute's value is missing, all other attributes may match and still prevent two records from linking.

Record Linkage is imprecise. While two records might actually represent the same entity, a slight difference in one (or more!) attribute's value will prevent those records from being linked.

Information sources are out of synchronization. Customer information in a database can stay relatively static, even if the customer herself is not. People move, get married, divorced. The data that may be sitting in one database may be completely out of synch with information in another database, making positive matching difficult. For example, recently I moved from Washington, D.C. to New York City. It took a year before any of the online telephone directories had my listing changed from the D.C. address and telephone to the New York one. (Incidentally, by the time those listings had changed, I had already moved to a new address!)

Information is lost. The actual database joins may be constructed in a way that important information that is originally contained in one of the data sets is lost during the merge. For example, when my baby daughter receives a letter asking her to switch her long distance service in return for an extra 5,000 frequent flyer miles, the information that my wife and I just purchased a child's seat for her is apparently lost.

When the limitations of standard linkage are combined, it eventually causes inefficiencies and increased costs. Here are some real examples:

- A large frequent traveler program had fielded many complaints because patrons who had visited member hotels were not credited with the points corresponding to their purchases. It turns out that the company providing the frequent traveler program had recently merged with a few other hotel chains, and the number of different data formats had ballooned to more than 70, all out of synchronization with each other.
- A bid/ask product pricing system inherited its prices from multiple market data providers, the information of which was collected and filtered through a mainframe system. When the mainframe did not forward new daily prices for a particular product, the last received price was used instead. There was significant embarrassment when customers determined that the provided prices were out of synchronization with other markets!
- Very frequently with direct mail campaigns, multiple mailings are sent to the same household or to the same person, and a large number of items are sent to the wrong address.
- Current customers are pitched items that they have already purchased.

Some silly data merging mishaps can be embarrassing to the organization and cause customer distrust. For example, if a service company can't keep track of who its customers are, how can they be trusted to supply the right level of service as well as provide a correct bill every month?

16.8 LARGE-SCALE DATA AGGREGATION AND LINKAGE

Databases and data warehouses are not the only place where data merging is an important operation. In our ever-growing World Wide Web, anyone can publish anything, and that information can be aggregated as well. Closer to the fact, many Web sites act as front ends to different underlying databases, and clicking on a Web page is effectively the invocation of a query into a database, and the presentation of information posted back to the client Web browser is a way of displaying the result of the query.

If we configure an application to act as a client front-end replacing the standard browser but still making use of the HTTP protocols to request and accept replies, we can create a relatively powerful data aggregation agent to query multiple Web sites, collect data, and provide it back to the user. Effectively, the World Wide Web can be seen as the world's largest data warehouse. Unfortunately, the problems that plague standard record linkage as described in Section 16.7 are magnified by at least an order of magnitude. The reason for this lies in the relative free-form style of presenting information via the World Wide Web.

16.8.1 Semistructured Data

For a large part, Web data are "semistructured data." While database records and electronic data interchange messages are highly structured, information presented on Web pages conforms to the barest of standards, some of which are bent based on the selection of Web browser targeted. On the other hand, there are some Internet "motifs" that appear regularly. For example, business home pages most often contain links to other sections of a Web site, with a contact page, an information page, a products page, a services page, a privacy policy page, and a "terms of service" page. Information on each of these pages also tends to follow a certain style.

For example, a corporate data page will often have a list of the top managers in a company, followed by a short biography. We can even drive down to finer detail in our expectations — in the corporate biographies, we can expect to see some reference to college and graduate school degrees, an account of prior work experiences (with durations), and professional affiliations. Yet while the format of these biographies is not standardized at all, in general we learn the same kind of stuff about each manager in each company.

Personal Web pages will also conform to some semistructure. These pages will include names, contact information, perhaps some work history, interests, and so on. But there is not standard format for a personal Web page. Perhaps we can take a cue from some of the more popular Web page editing tools and, understanding their templates and motifs, use that as a guide for identifying particular pieces of data that are relevant or interesting.

16.8.2   Web Sites That Are Really Databases

To borrow an idea from Phillip Greenspun's book *Philip and Alex's Guide to Web Publishing*, some Web sites are really front ends to databases, and the pages that are published reflect queries into the database. For example, searching an online book store for a particular author "Smith" is really asking (in pseudo-SQL), "Select all records where author's name is 'Smith.'"

Because different providers configure their replies to requested data in different formats, we have the same set of issues as we have seen before. What differentiates this situation is that the amount of information that can be collected from each site and the multitude of sites that can be visited. The result is a very large-scale data aggregation framework.

16.8.3   Web Sites That Are Broadcasters

In contrast to database-oriented Web sites, some content providers are broadcasters of information that can be valuable for enrichment. There are two clear examples of this kind of Web site — news providers and financial information providers. In both cases, data that are broadcast may have different value to different visitors, and any aggregation application must ultimately be able to allow the end user to identify what data items are important and which are less important.

16.8.4   The Breakdown in the Data Warehouse Analogy

The data warehouse analogy partially breaks down when it comes to the actual aggregation and presentation of information at the presentation site. A critical value that can be derived from the aggregation of information is its coagulation, enrichment, and presentation in terms of critical business intelligence that is meaningful to the user.

One reason for this is simple — similar types of information available across the Web are represented in different ways. Whether using different storage formats, different names, different visual representations, the data that are presented at different Web sites and that can be collected and delivered to the client location can be made much more valuable when that data is massaged into business intelligence guided through client-defined requirements.

Another reason for the breakdown in the analogy has to do with governance (or more clearly, the lack thereof). Anyone can publish anything on the Internet, yet there is no governing body that oversees the quality of any information published. Therefore, it is up to the user to characterize his or her data quality requirements to which the information should conform before the information is presented.

16.8.5 Aggregation and Linkage

The key to making the best use of aggregated Web data is that the presentation and packaging of the information is effectively an exercise in data enhancement. Before the information is presented to the client, any data quality rules, business rules, validation filters, or trigger rules should be applied. This can only be done when there is a method for linking data items from different sources coupled with the definition and usage of business and data quality rules, as we have explored in other sections of this book.

16.9 IMPROVING LINKAGE WITH APPROXIMATE MATCHING

One way to counter the limitations of standard record linkage is the use of a technique called approximate, or approximate matching. Standard linkage requires that the sets of values in the characterizing attributes all must match exactly. But in databases, just as in real life, sometimes things are not always as they seem. Approximate matching relaxes the exact matching requirement, giving us the chance to find those elusive near (and sometimes not-so-near) matches.

16.9.1   Approximate Matching

What constitutes an approximate match? There are two aspects to approximate matching. The first is the distance, or similarity measure, and the second is the threshold.

In Chapter 14, we learned that "approximate" can be measured in terms of what is called a *distance measure*. In review, this term is inherited from mathematics from geometry problems that identify how close two points are in a given multidimensional system by measuring the distance between them. There are many kinds of distance measures, ranging from integer comparisons to traditional geometric measures (pull out those high school math texts!) to measures based on the number of alphabetic symbols that are shared between two character strings. In most cases, then, a distance measure provides a measure of closeness between any two data items of a particular type or domain.

To further level the field, we like to scale all distance measurements so that they are between 0 and 1. In essence, we are using a percentage to indicate a measure of closeness. This leads to the second element of approximate matching: the threshold. Because the matches are not exact, depending on the degree of the problem, we must have some point at which we determine two values to be a match or not. This point is defined by a threshold value — the value above which a similarity measure is deemed a match.

Even for the same set of data values, thresholds may change based on the application. For example, if we are trying to prevent terrorists from entering the country, our criteria for an approximate match might be looser than if we are trying to eliminate duplicates from a direct marketing mailing.

16.9.2   An Example of Approximate Matching

We can best illustrate approximate matching by looking at an example. Once I received invitations to an upcoming data warehouse seminar. One was addressed this way.

David Loshin
Prod Manager
Jones Smith Co
750 X Ave
New York, NY 10019

And the second one was addressed this way.

H D Loshin
Product Manager
Jones Smith & Co
750 X Ave Fl 12
New York, NY 10019

By examining these two records, one can easily see that they would not have been linked using exact matching. In a approximate matching scheme, a similarity score would be assigned to each field in these name and address records. Let's say these are the scores.

Record 1	Record 2	Score
David Loshin	H D Loshin	70% (D matches David, Loshin matches Loshin)
Prod Manager	Product Manager	90%
Jones Smith Co	Jones Smith & Co	95%
750 X Ave	750 X Ave Fl 12	80% (due to the floor designation)
New York, NY 10019	New York, NY 10019	100%

Since all the scores are relatively high, even outside of the context of the material being sent, our intuition would say that these are likely to be the same person. Now adding in one more piece of information, which is the psychographic item of "interest in data warehousing," this might tip the balance to an automated process to automatically link the two records. One more interesting note: I received the same invitation at my home address!

16.9.3 Approximate Matching Rules

For any attribute where we want to use approximate matching, we must provide both a similarity measure and a threshold value. When performing approximate matching over a set of characterizing attributes, there must be a similarity measure and threshold for each pair, as well as an overall aggregation function (one that collects the individual similarity measures) and threshold value.

We discussed in Chapter 8 that there were other data quality rules. Here we formally add approximate matching rules to that rule set. A similarity measure can be defined in two ways — either within the system (using code definitions for calculating similarity) or as a reference to an external processing phase. We can assume that there are some built-in similarity measures, such as linear (how close two numbers are), the geometric similarity (for multidimensional systems), and edit distance for character strings. A approximate matching rule for a specific attribute is then defined using a domain (or base data type), a similarity measure, and a threshold. Here is an example that defines similarity in terms of the relative closeness of two values, indicating a match when the score is greater than 75 percent.

ScoreMatch: APPROXIMATE   MATCH{1 − (ABS(Value1 − Value2)/MAX(Value1, Value2))}:threshold=0.75

In this example, we specify an approximate matching rule we call **ScoreMatch**, with an embedded similarity score computed by scaling the difference between the two values to a percentage and subtracting that from 1. We also specify a threshold of .75, which means that for any compared values, if the result of applying the similarity measure yields a result greater than 0.75, the two values are deemed to be a match.

A set of characterizing attributes can be combined using an aggregation function over all those attributes under an approximate aggregation rule.

APPROXIMATE   AGGREGATE   CustomerAgg   :{(((ScoreMatch (Customers.Loyalty, Leads.Loyalty)*3) + (NameMatch(Customers.Last-Name, Leads.LastName)) + AddressMatch(concat(Customers.Address, Customers.City,Customers.State),concat(Leads.Address,Leads.City, Leads.State))/5}:0.81

In this aggregation, we are scaling the score match to have a weight that is three times greater than the other two match rules that complete the set. Included in an aggregation rule must be an expression designating the approximate rules to be included, the weighting of each of the scores, a function describing the aggregation, and the threshold above which two records match. Also, within each approximate match rule we indicate the data values that are to be matched.

16.9.4   Where Approximate Matching Changes the Outcome

Approximate matching gives businesses the opportunity to be more effective in its data merging operation because it weakens the requirements for determining a match of two entities by allowing some degree of heuristic capability. Approximate matching allows for a wider net to be cast when merging data from different data sets, accounting for differences in the way that the information was collected, entered, and so forth.

Being able to identify different representations of the same entity (customer, address, business, etc.) in the same large data set is beneficial for many reasons:

- You can gain greater insight into your customers when more records can be linked together.
- For direct marketing campaigns, costs can be reduced by eliminating double and triple mailings.
- The same fraudulent behaviors may manifest themselves in different patterns, which can be detected only through approximate matching.
- Data sets can be updated with more recent information.
- Important customer information can be derived from the results of approximate linkage (for example, lifestyle changes such as marriages, new home purchases, the birth of children).
- A single data set of record can be used to validate other data sets.

16.10   ENHANCEMENT THROUGH INFERENCE

Having discussed any number of mechanical enhancements such as the ones described in this chapter, it is time to discuss one set of enhancements that is less mechanical and more intuitive — enhancement through inference. An inference is an application of a heuristic rule that essentially creates a piece of information where it didn't exist before. Even though inferencing represents the application of intuition, it is done so in a way that can be automated.

An example of an inference for credit card databases might be if there are two names associated with the account number, if more than 70 percent of the dollar amount of purchases is made by one of the two account holders, and if that account holder is the primary decision maker for that account. Using this rule, we can populate an attribute for the primary decision maker with either a definitive value or an "indeterminate" null value.

Inference rules usually reflect some understood business analysis that can be boiled down to a set of business rules. We have explored a way to define these kinds of inferences — we called them derivation rules in Chapter 8. These are rules that specify how certain attribute values are determined by operations applied to other attributes.

Combining inference rules with data merging yields a powerful process for enhancement. For example, in a householding operation, determining those parties that share an address is one thing; isolating a role for each party within the household is more difficult. But imagine a rule called the "power of purchase" rule: When any purchase incorporating products that are bought directly for named individuals is paid for by a single person, we can infer that the nonbuying individuals are dependent on the purchaser. Travel tickets, school tuition, personalized gifts, health insurance, trust accounts, address labels, personalized mementos (like bronzed baby shoes), and automobile insurance are all examples of this kind of purchase. This rule suggests two roles: the dependent and the spending authority.

We already have a structure for the definition of enhancement rules based on the rule definitions from Chapter 8. An enhancement can be characterized using new attributes, and these attributes can have derived values.

16.11 DATA QUALITY RULES FOR ENHANCEMENT

Another step in intelligent enhancement is adding data quality rules. As we have seen in Chapter 8, we can define rules that both validate assertions as well as modify or transform data values. We can use these rules for enriching data in one of two ways. If the data record (or message) completely conforms to the data quality rule set, then we can tag the record with a new field indicating the location in the information chain where the record was validated and a "stamp of approval." If the record does not conform to the rule set, the record can be enriched with a new field including the rule (or rules) violated and the location in the information chain where the validation failed.

When the information is evaluated at a later time, it is then possible to identify those locations in the information chain that are good "data quality performers" and those weak links in the chain for data quality.

One interesting aspect of enhancement is the possibility of inferring information based on patterns of poor data quality. Patterns of certain data quality problems may appear chronically, which may hint toward particular root causes. In addition, the fact that these patterns may be taggable to particular sources enables a certain degree of inference possibilities.

For example, we can log the types of data quality errors that appear and then measure their frequencies. When there are frequently occuring errors, we can evaluate the sources of those errors to see if there are any interesting patterns. If so, we can enhance incoming data by identifying its potential for certain errors, thereby characterizing its quality level and its improvement history.

16.12   BUSINESS RULES FOR ENHANCEMENT

The next step in intelligent enhancement is the addition of business rules. In our previous data merging example, we snuck in a business rule to help our matching process. That rule was the addition of the property "Interested in Data Warehousing" to our data records for the purposes of linkage. While it is unlikely that two people with the last name of Loshin work with the same company in the same building, it is entirely possible that two people with the last name Smith and the first name John may work in the same 50 floor New York City skyscraper. That is why adding additional business rules to the merging process can improve its usability. Another benefit of adding business rules is that you can impose more advanced logic on where and when not to link records.

16.12.1   What Kinds of Rules Are Used?

We can use rules when the result of the merging/linkage operation depends on content embedded in the merged record. For example, if the long-distance company that sent the offer to my baby daughter had a rule that states, "Do not send this offer if the frequent flyer has had a child seat purchased within the past six months," they would have known that a child is most likely not going to have spending authority. A baby is the kind of direct marketing "mismatch" that one would want to eliminate from a targeted campaign. By eliminating these mismatches, a company can increase its return on investment for marketing strategies.

Business rules will typically take the form of an "if-then" statement, with a condition that must first be fulfilled before the guarded operation can take place. Once two or more records have been linked in the merging process, the content of those records is examined to see if the condition is true. So, to be more formal with our long-distance/frequent flyer rule, we might want to add these rules:

1. For each frequent flyer record, enhance the record by determining whether the flyer is "head-of-household," "second-in-command," or "non-decision-maker." This can be arbitrarily done by assigning "head-of-household" to the flyer whose credit card was used to purchase tickets.
2. If the flyer is a non-decision-maker, do not send a long-distance offer to that flyer.

Another option is to modify the campaign based on rules. When more than one flyer resides at the same household, the offer can be changed to distribute the bonus miles among all flyers within the household if the decision maker opts for the new long-distance service.

16.12.2   Where Rules Change the Outcome

In all these occasions for data merging, business rules can improve the outcome. When merging customer databases, derived analytical data enhancements such as "decision maker" can be inferred. Cooperative marketing programs can be made more efficient, thereby increasing response rate. Affinity programs can be improved if rules characterizing the target's tendency to respond can be inferred. And, of course, data cleansing operations such as de-duplication and householding are improved when rules are added.

16.13   SUMMARY

In this chapter, we looked at data enrichment as well as some examples of kinds of enrichment that can be applied to data messages and records. This includes temporal information, auditing information, contextual information, geographical information, demographic information, psychographic information, as well as different kinds of inferred information. We also revisited the notions of standardization as a means for enrichment.

We devoted a large part of the chapter to data merging, since it is through the merging process that we can derive more knowledge from our data sets. Sometimes regular joins are insufficient, and we must rely on more sophisticated means of linking together records. This includes approximate matching, for which we "enriched" our own set of data quality and business rules defined in Chapter 8. Finally, we looked at ways that business rules can be used for enhancement.

Combining information from multiple databases is not a new idea, but the advances in technology and system speed open up new vistas for applying intelligent techniques. Using a focused methodology for adding value through the data enhancement and enrichment process, companies can greatly improve the effectiveness of their customer relationship, marketing, customer service and sales programs.

17

DATA QUALITY AND BUSINESS RULES IN PRACTICE

In Chapters 7 and 8, we discussed the definition of data domains, mappings between those domains, and data quality assertions and directives guiding the specification of data quality requirements. In Chapter 13, we looked at the discovery of data quality rules out of legacy data, and in Chapters 14 and 16, we looked at some of the more complex issues revolving around data quality. In this chapter, we look at some of the more pragmatic issues associated with our data quality rules: the actual implementation of those rules for specific data quality purposes.

We begin this chapter by reviewing our data quality rules in a context that demonstrates ways to actually use these rules. Specifically, we have talked about the way that these rules partition the data into two sets: conforming records and nonconforming records. There is already a means for specifying set partitions in databases — the query language SQL, which is used not only for performing operations on databases but to turn rules into executable queries.

The rest of this chapter is designed to show how the implementation of a data quality rules process can add significant value to different operating environments. We will examine the following areas.

- Data quality and the transaction factory
- Data quality and the data warehouse
- Data quality and electronic data interchange (EDI)
- Data quality rules used to drive content-dependent user interfaces

Hopefully, this chapter will bring together a lot of the technical details and tie up loose ends while bridging the mechanics of assessment, user requirements analysis, and rules specification into a viable operational context. Figure 17.1 shows the complete rule system.

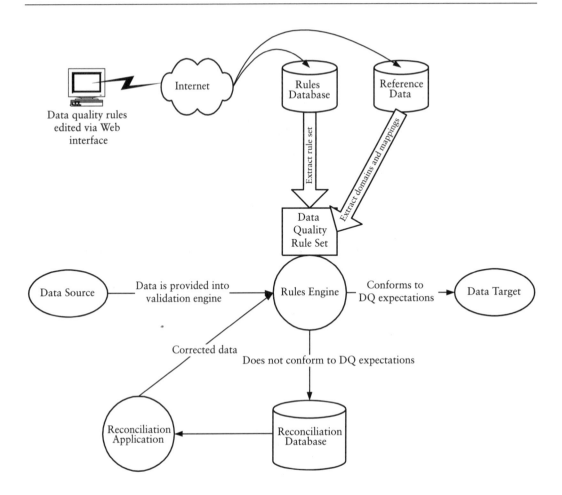

FIGURE 17.1 The complete rule system

17.1 TURNING RULES INTO IMPLEMENTATION

In relational databases, a query language called the Structured Query Language (SQL) is used to extract data from the database based on a set of criteria. Those criteria are represented as constraints in the query, and the SQL statement represents the set of records that conform to those constraints. For most of the rules that we have discussed, we can describe the set of data records that do not conform to the rule using SQL.

In this section, we begin with a brief review of the SQL select statement; if you are already familiar with SQL, you can skip that section. The rest of the section reviews the data quality rules, then shows how the set representing the nonconforming rule can be specified in SQL.

17.1.1 Review of SQL `select` Statement

Here is a quick refresher on the syntax of the SQL `select` statement.

```
select [all | distinct] <select_list>
   from [<table_name> | <view_name> ]
     [,[<table_name> | <view_name> ] . . .]
    [where <search_condition>]
    [group by <column_name> [, <column_name>]. . .]
     [having <search_conditions>]
    [order by {<column_name> | <select_list_number>}
     [asc | desc]
     [,{<column_name> | <select_list_number>}
        [asc | desc]] . . .]
```

When a query is executed, the list of data items returned is called the result set. If there are no records that match the query, the result set is of size 0. For our purposes, we will focus on the tables and columns selected and the where conditions. The `group by,` `having,` and `order by` components are not used in this chapter.

For the `<select_list>`, you can either use `*` to ask for all the columns, a list of column names, or operations applied to column names (such as `3*salary`). The `<table_name>` list can consist of multiple table names (or view names), and in many SQL dialects, an alias can be assigned to the table name and the selected columns can refer back to that alias. For example, this query

```
select e.empname, e.salary from employees e;
```

assigns the alias name e to the table named employees, and the selected columns refer to the aliased `employees` table.

When using the qualifier `distinct`, this limits the query to eliminate duplicate entries from the result set. The `where` clause is used to specify search conditions. SQL provides these operations to be used for constructing where conditions.

- Comparison operators, such as <, <=, >, >=, =, <>. Example:
  `Where e.salary >= 20000`
- Boolean combiners or negation (AND, OR, NOT)
  `Where e.salary >= 20000 AND e.salary < 50000`

- Ranges (BETWEEN, NOT BETWEEN)
  ```
  Where e.salary between 20000 AND 50000
  ```
- Lists (IN, NOT IN)
  ```
  Where e.title in ('STAFF MEMBER', 'MANAGER', 'PRESIDENT')
  ```
- Null values (IS NULL, NOT NULL)
  ```
  Where e.salary is null
  ```
- Character matches (LIKE, NOT LIKE)
  ```
  Where e.telephone not like (212)%
  ```

We can use the result of a `select` statement to generate a list that can be used as a subquery for the `in` component of a `where` clause.

```
Select e.empname, e.salary from employees e
    Where e.title in
        (select title from managerpositions);
```

In this example, there is a separate view that contains the records describing those positions held by managers. We select the titles associated with manager positions, and then we select out of the employees table those employee names and salaries for employees who are managers.

17.1.2 Naming of Rules

In each of the following sections, we focus on the context of specific rule types as discussed in Chapters 7 and 8. When we defined a rule set, we also will want to assign a unique name to each defined rule.

In general, our rule specification will incorporate an assigned rule name, followed by a colon and then the specification of the rule.

```
<rule name>: <rule text>
```

This way, we can integrate multiple rules into a single rule set that is to be applied to a data set. In the following sections, for clarity, we ignore the rule names.

17.1.3 Null Value Representations

In Chapter 8, we discussed the fact that there are different kinds of null values, including this list:

1. *No value*   There is no value for this field — a true null.
2. *Unavailable*   There is a value for this field, but for some reason it has been omitted. Using the unavailable characterization

implies that at some point the value will be available and the field should be completed.

3. *Not applicable*   This indicates that in this instance, there is no applicable value.
4. *Not classified*   There is a value for this field, but it does not conform to a predefined set of domain values for that field.
5. *Unknown*   The fact that there is a value is established, but that value is not known.

We allow the user to define named aliased representations for the different null types. This is the syntax for this definition.

```
Define <nullname> for <nulltype> as <string
    representation>
```

In this definition, <nullname> is the alias name, <nulltype> is one of the varieties of nulls described here, and <string representation> is the character string used for the null. For example, this definition specifies the null representation for an unavailable telephone number.

```
Define NOPHONE for UNAVAILABLE as "Phone Number Not
    Provided"
```

To implement the management of null value representations, we will need some metadata tables. The first is the null value type table, where we consolidate the different kinds of null value types exists in the system, what their names are, and their description.

```
Create table nulltypes (
   Name         varchar(100),
   Nullid       integer primary key,
   Description varchar(1000)
);
```

Next, we will need a table to manage the defined aliases. In this table definition, the nullrepid is a uniquely assigned id, nulltype is a foreign key to the nulltypes table, and nullrep is the actual representation of the null value.

```
Create table nullreps (
   Name         varchar(100),
   Nullrepid    integer primary key,
   Nulltype     integer,
   Nullrep      varchar(100)
);
```

17.1.4 Null Value Rules

There are two kinds of null value rules: those that allow nulls and those that disallow nulls. Let's look at those that allow nulls first.

If the rule indicated that system null values are allowed, with no qualification, there is really no validation, since the assertion states that the absence of a value is allowed. Alternatively, if the rule specified that only a particular kind of defined null value was allowed, then the validation is a little more complicated.

Our earlier definition of the null value rule allowed the restriction of use to defined null values, such as the following.

```
Attribute employees.phone_number allowed nulls
  {GETPHONE, NOPHONE}
```

More formally, our rule syntax will specify the name of the attribute, the keywords `allows nulls`, and a list of null representation types allowed.

```
Attribute <table>.<attribute> allows nulls
  {<nullreptype> [, <nullreptype> . . .]}
```

The restriction on the type of nulls allowed is meant to disallow the use of any other type. Therefore, the validation test of this rule is the test for violators, and we are really testing that no real nulls are used. This is the SQL statement for this test.

```
Select * from <table> where <attribute> is null;
```

Note that in older database systems with no system null, or in text (delimiter-separated file) data sets, blanks may appear is place of an "official" null, so we may add this validation test, which grabs the first character from the attribute and tests for a blank.

```
Select * from <table> where substring(<attribute>, 1, 1)
  = ' ';
```

If the rule is being obeyed, the size of the result set should be 0. If not, the result set represents those records that violate the rule.

Selecting records with null values or counting the number of records with null values is now a bit more complicated, since the null values allowed are those drawn from the null representation list. Since we have accumulated those null representations in our null representation table, the query can be specified either in the general sense (grabbing all records with nulls) or in the specific sense (getting all records with a "not available" null type) by using the null representation in the nullreps table. To locate all records with nulls, we use this SQL statement.

```
Select * from <table> where <attribute> in
    (select nullrep from nullreps where nullreps.name in
        (<nullreptype> [, <nullreptype> . . .]));
```

To specify the selection of those records associated with a specific null representation, we restrict the null representation list to the specific representation we care about.

```
Select * from <table> where <attribute> in
    (select nullrep from nullreps where
        nullreps.name = <nullreptype>);
```

17.1.5   Non-Null Rules

Similarly, when we specify that an attribute may not be null, the validation is the same as for the defined null case. This is the syntax of our original rule.

```
Attribute employees.empid nulls not allowed
```

The validation test is as follows.

```
Select * from employees where phone_number is null;
```

Along with the corresponding test for spaces.

```
Select * from employees where substring(phone_number, 1,
    1) = ' ';
```

If the rule is being obeyed, the size of the result set should be 0. If not, the result set represents those records that violate the rule.

17.1.6   Value Restrictions

Value restriction rules limit the set of valid values that can be used within a context. In our definition of a value restriction, we assigned an alias to the restriction and specified the expression that defines the restriction. Here is an example.

```
Restrict GRADE: value >= 'A' AND value <= 'F' AND value
    != 'E'
```

In general, the form for the value restriction rule includes the keyword `restrict`, a name assigned for the restriction, and a conjunction of conditions, where the operators associated with the conditions may be any drawn from predefined set (+, -, *, /, etc.) or from a user-defined set of functions (which must be provided for execution, of course).

```
Restrict <restriction name>: <condition> [(AND | OR)
    <condition> . . .]
```

We actually use this restriction for defining value ranges that could be associated with functional domains, as well as the restriction as a representation of the restriction of values for a specific attribute. This is the format for the latter specification.

```
Attribute <table>.<attribute> restrict by <restriction
    name>
```

This indicates that no values that show up in the named attribute may violate the named restriction. The validation test for this restriction is a test for violators of the restriction, and the query is composed by searching for the negation of the restriction. We apply DeMorgan's laws to generate the negation.

NOT (A AND B) => (NOT A OR NOT B)
NOT (A OR B) => (NOT A AND NOT B)

The where clause of the validation test is generated from the negation. This would be where clause from our previous example.

```
NOT (value >= 'A' AND value <= 'F' AND value != 'E')
```

After the application of DeMorgan's law, it becomes this.

```
(VALUE < 'A' OR VALUE > 'F' OR VALUE = 'E')
```

In general the validation test becomes this.

```
Select * from <table> where NOT <condition list>;
```

Again, if the rule is being obeyed, the size of the result set should be 0. If not, the result set represents those records that violate the rule.

17.1.7   Domain Membership

Recall that we maintain our defined enumerated domains in a set of database tables. The first table is the domain reference table, which is a metadata table for all named domains.

```
create table domainref (
    name                varchar(30),
    dtype               char(1),
    description         varchar(1024),
    source              varchar(512),
domainid        integer);
```

The actual values are stored in a single data table, referenced via a foreign key back to the domain reference table.

```
create table domainvals (
domainid                integer,
value                   varchar(128));
```

A domain membership rule specifies that the data values that populate an attribute be taken from a named data domain. This is the format for this rule.

```
<table>.<attribute> taken from <domain name>
```

The validation test for domain membership tests for violations of the rule. In other words, we select out all the statements whose attribute has a value that does not belong to the domain. We can do this using a subselect statement in SQL.

```
SELECT * from <table> where <attribute> not in
    (SELECT value from domainvals where domainid =
        (SELECT domainid from domainref
            where domainref.name = <domain name>));
```

If the rule is being obeyed, the size of the result set should be 0. If not, the result set contains those records that violate the rule. With a nonempty result set, we can also grab the actual data values that do not belong to the named domain.

```
SELECT <attribute> from <table> where <attribute> not in
    (SELECT value from domainvals where domainid =
        (SELECT domainid from domainref
            where domainref.name = <domain name>));
```

17.1.8 Domain Nonmembership

In a domain nonmembership rule, we indicate via a defined rule that no values from a specified domain are allowed within an attribute. More formally, the domain nonmembership rule includes the attribute name, the keywords not taken from, and the name of the domain.

```
<table>.<attribute> not taken from <domain name>
```

The validation test checks for any occurrences of records whose named attribute contains a value taken from the named domain.

```
SELECT * from <table> where <attribute> in
    (SELECT value from domainvals where domainid =
        (SELECT domainid from domainref
            where domainref.name = <domain name>));
```

If the rule is being obeyed, the size of the result set should be 0. If not, the result set contains those records that violate the rule. With a nonempty result set, we can also grab the actual data values taken from the domain that should not be in the attribute.

```
SELECT <attribute> from <table> where <attribute> in
    (SELECT value from domainvals where domainid =
        (SELECT domainid from domainref
            where domainref.name = <domain name>));
```

17.1.9   Domain Assignment

The domain assignment rule specifies that all the values from the attribute are implicitly to be included in the named domain. This rule, which is useful in propagating domain values to the metadata repository, must include the keywords define domain, the name of the domain, the keyword from, and a list of attributes from which the domain values are gleaned.

```
Define Domain <domain name> from
(<table>.<attribute> [, <table>.<attribute> . . .])
```

For each of the named attributes, we must have a select statement to extract those values that are not already in the domain.

```
SELECT <attribute> from <table> where <attribute> not in
    (SELECT value from domainvals where domainid =
        (SELECT domainid from domainref
            where domainref.name = <domain name>));
```

We then must merge all these values into a single set and for each of the values in this set, create a new record to be inserted into domainvals table. Each new record will include the identifier of the domain and the new value, and a SQL insert statement is generated. Here is the pseudocode for the entire process.

```
Dom_id = select domainid from domainref;
Nonmember set S = null;
For each table t, attribute a in attribute list AL do:
    S = S union
            SELECT a from t where a not in
                (SELECT value from domainvals where
                    domainid =
                        (SELECT domainid from domainref
                            where domainref.name =
                                dom_id));
For each value v in nonmember set S do:
    Insert into domainvals (domainid, value)
            Values (dom_id, v);
```

17.1.10   Mapping Membership

Mappings are maintained as metadata using two data tables. The first is the mapping reference table, into which we store the name of the mapping, the source domain identifier, the target domain identifier, a description, the source of the data, and an assigned mapping identifier.

```
create table mappingref (
name                    varchar(30),
sourcedomain    integer,
targetdomain    integer,
description             varchar(1024),
source             varchar(512),
mappingid               integer
);
```

The second table actually holds all pairs of values associated with a particular domain mapping.

```
create table mappingpairs (
    mappingid               integer,
    sourcevalue             varchar(128),
    targetvalue             varchar(128)
);
```

Mapping membership is similar to domain membership, although for mapping membership we need to make sure that both elements in a pair of values exist in the mapping. The format for a mapping membership rule includes a pair of attributes and the name of the mapping to which it belongs.

```
(<table1>.<attribute1>, <table2>.<attribute2>) Belong to
Mapping <mappingname> (Propagate | No Propagate)
```

The validation test is to find those records whose named attributes have pairs of values that do not belong to the named mapping. This involves selecting out those records whose composed attributes are not in the named mapping. This select statement shows how this is done when both attributes are in the same table, using the string composition operator "||".

```
Select * from <table> where
<table1>.<attribute1> || <table1>.attribute2> not in
    (select sourcevalue || targetvalue from mappingvals
        where mappingid =
            (select mappingid from mappingref where
                name = <mappingname>));
```

This select statement extracts those records that violate the mapping membership rule. We can also form a SQL statement to extract those value pairs that violate the mapping relationship.

```
Select <table1>.<attribute1>, ",", <table1>.<attribute2>
from <table1> where
<table1>.<attribute1> || <table2>.attribute2> not in
    (select sourcevalue || targetvalue from mappingvals
        where mappingid =
            (select mappingid from mappingref where
                name = <mappingname>));
```

17.1.11   Mapping Assignment

The mapping assignment rule specifies that all the value pairs from two specified attribute are implicitly to be included in the named mapping. This rule, which is useful in propagating mapping values to the metadata repository, must include the keywords define mapping, the name of the mapping, the keyword from, and a list of attributes from which the mapping values are gleaned.

```
Define mapping <mapping name> from
(<table1>.<attribute1>, <table2>.<attribute2>)
```

First, we extract the value pairs from those records that have attribute pairs not already in the mapping. Here is the single table SQL statement.

```
Select * from <table1> where
<table1>.<attribute1> || <table1>.attribute2> not in
    (select sourcevalue || targetvalue from mappingvals
        where mappingid =
            (select mappingid from mappingref where
                        name = <mappingname>));
```

For each of the value pairs in this set, create a new record to be inserted into the mappingvals table. First, though, we must make sure that the values actually belong to their corresponding domains. If we allow the mapping assignment rule to propagate domains, then domain values that are not already in their respective domains are propagated. If we do not allow domain propagation, we must validate domain membership for each of the values

Each new record will include the identifier of the mapping and the new value, and a SQL insert statement is generated. Here is the pseudocode for the propagation process, again, using the single table example.

```
map_id = select mappingid from mappingref where
name = <mappingname>;
Nonmember set S =
Select <table1>.<attribute1>, ",", <table1>.<attribute2>
  from <table1> where
  <table1>.<attribute1> || <table2>.attribute2> not in
    (select sourcevalue || targetvalue from mappingvals
        where mappingid =
            (select mappingid from mappingref where
                                name = <mappingname>));
```

For each value pair (a,b) in nonmember set S do:
```
    If (a not in select values from domainvals
        Where domainid = sourcedomain) then
        Insert into domainvals
            Columns (domainid, value)
                Values (sourcedomain, a);
    If (b not in select values from domainvals
```

```
          Where domainid = targetdomain) then
          Insert into domainvals
               Columns (domainid, value)
                    Values (targetdomain, b);
     Insert into mappingvals
          columns (mappingid, sourcevalue, targetvalue)
               Values (map_id, a, b);
```

For the no-propagation process, instead we must test for violation of the domain membership for the source and target domains and issue an error message when the attempt at inserting a new mapping value cannot proceed.

17.1.12   Mapping Nonmembership

Mapping nonmembership specifies that a record's value pair must not belong to a defined mapping. The format for specifying this rule must include the attribute names, the key words it does not belong to, and the name of the mapping.

```
(<table1>.<attribute1>, <table2>.<attribute2>)
does not belong to Mapping <mapping name>
```

The validation test for this rule selects out those records where the attribute pair does belong to the named mapping. Here is the SQL when both attributes are taken from the same table.

```
Select * from <table1> where
<table1>.<attribute1> || <table1>.attribute2> in
     (select sourcevalue || targetvalue from mappingvals
          where mappingid =
          (select mappingid from mappingref where
                    name = <mappingname>));
```

We can also grab all the pairs so that we can investigate the violations.

```
Select <table1>.<attribute1>, <table1>.attribute2> from
     <table1> where
<table1>.<attribute1> || <table1>.attribute2> not in
     (select sourcevalue || targetvalue from mappingvals
          where mappingid =
          (select mappingid from mappingref where
                    name = <mappingname>));
```

17.1.13   Completeness

Completeness governs the proper population of a record's fields, possibly depending on other fields' values. A completeness rule is a conditional assertion that specifies a condition followed by a list of attributes that must have values. Formally, a completeness rule includes the keyword `if`, a condition, and a list of attributes that must be non-null if the condition is true.

```
If (<condition>) then complete with (<table>.<attribute>
      [, <table>.<attribute> . . .])
```

The rule is observed if, for all records, the condition is true. Then the attributes in the attribute list are non-null. The validation test checks for nulls if the condition is true. Here is the test in SQL.

```
Select * from <table> where <condition>
and (<attribute> is null
      [, or <attribute> is null . . .];
```

This selects out the set of violating records. If the record set size if 0, there are no violations.

17.1.14   Exemption

An exemption rule specifies a condition and a list of attributes, and if the condition evaluates to true, then those attributes in the list are allowed to have null values. Exemption rules, like completeness rules, are conditional assertions.

Formally, an exemption rule indicates a condition, the keyword exempt, and a list of attributes, possibly qualified by the kinds of nulls allowed.

```
If (<condition>) then exempt
   (<attribute>[:<nullreptype>] [, <attribute>
      [:<nullreptype>] . . .])
```

In this rule, the attributes in the attribute list may only be null (or take on specific null representations) if the condition is true. Therefore, we can infer that the rule is violated if the condition is false and the attributes contain null values. Therefore, we apply DeMorgan's laws to the condition and extract those records with nulls in the specified fields.

Here is the SQL to extract nonconformers when there are no null representations specified.

```
Select * from <table> where not <condition> and
  (<attribute> is null
      [, or <attribute> is null . . .];
```

If we have qualified the attributes in the attribute list using a null representation, then the where condition is slightly modified to incorporate the null representation. Here is the same SQL statement with the null test replaced.

```
Select * from <table> where not <condition> and
<attribute> in
        (select nullrep from nullreps where
            nullreps.name = <nullreptype>);
```

17.1.15   Consistency

Consistency rules define a relationship between attributes based on field content. For example, we can specify a consistency relationship between the value assigned to an employee's position and that employee's salary.

```
IF (Employees.title == "Staff Member") Then
  (Employees.Salary >= 20000 AND Employees.Salary <
  30000)
```

A consistency rule must specify a condition, followed by an assertion.

```
If <condition> then <assertion>
```

The condition may refer to a number of attributes and the assertion may refer to a number of attributes. Records are valid if the condition is true and the assertion is true. It says nothing about the attributes referenced in the assertion is the condition is not true. The test for validation finds those records where the condition is true, but the assertion is violated. This involves creating a where clause with the condition ANDed with the negation of the assertion.

```
Select * from <table> where <condition> AND NOT
  <assertion>;
```

The records set selected are those that violate the rule.

17.1.16   Derivation

A derivation rule is the prescriptive form of the consistency rule. In a derivation rule, if a condition evaluates to true, then a consequent dictates how another attribute's value is defined. A derivation rule defines a data dependency between the attributes in the condition and the attribute in the consequent.

A derivation rule specifies a transformation and can be used in extraction, transformation, and loading processes. The formal specification for a derivation rule specifies a condition followed by an attribute assignment.

```
If <condition> then
<table>.<attribute> = <expression>
```

The expression is some operational combination of data pulled from other attributes, which may be scalar (refers to a single value) or a scalar result of an operation on a vector (a SUM or a maximum value pulled from a column).

The execution representation of a derivation rule tests for the condition and, if the condition is true, generates an update statement changing the value of the named assigned attribute as a function of the expression.

```
Update <table>
Set <attribute> = <expression>
Where <condition>;
```

If the rule specifies different tables and attributes, the execution is more likely to be transformed into intermediate code that extracts the data from the sources, performs the operations, and creates an update (or insert) into the target table.

17.1.17   Functional Dependencies

A functional dependency between two columns X and Y means that for any two records R1 and R2 in the table, if field X of record R1 contains value x and field X of record R2 contains the same value x, then if field Y of record R1 contains the value y, then field Y of record R2 must contain the value y. In other words, attribute Y is said to be *determined* by attribute X. Functional dependencies may exist between multiple source columns. In other words, we can indicate that a set of attributes determine a target attribute.

Essentially, a functional dependency rule is like a consistency rule that covers all records in the table. Based on this understanding, we can see that aside from the standard database use of functional dependence to ensure normalization, functional dependencies may actually represent a governing rule about what is represented in the data — in other words, a business rule!

A functional dependency must specify the defining attributes and the defined attribute, separated by the keyword `determines`.

```
(<table>.<S_attribute> [, <table>.<S_attribute>])
Determines (<table>.<T_attribute>)
```

We will refer to the attributes on the left-hand side of the keyword *determines* as the determining attributes and the attribute on the right-hand side the determined attribute. The validation test for this rule makes sure that the functional dependence criterion is met. This means that if we extract the determining values from the set of all distinct value set pairs, then that set should have no duplicates. First, we extract the composed pairs of determining, determined attributes from the table. Then we extract the determining attributes from the table. The count of the distinct determining attributes must be the same as the count of the combined attributes or there will be duplicate determining attributes, which constitutes a violation.

This process provides those determining attributes that are nonconforming. The next step is to extract those records where the nonconformance occurs. We can take the attribute combinations that were duplicated and extract those records where the determining attributes match those duplicates.

17.1.18 Primary Key

We can actually ratchet down the constraint from defining a specific primary key to just defining a key on a table. A key is a set of one or more attributes such that for all records in a table, no two records have the same set of values for all attributes in that key set. We specify the key assertion by listing the attributes that compose the key, along with the keyword key, and the table for which those attributes are a key.

```
<table>,<attribute [, <table>.<attribute> . . .] key for
  <table>
```

The test to validate that this attribute set is a key is to count the number of records in the table, then count the number of unique occurrences of those combined attributes.

```
Select count(*) from <table>;
Select count (distinct <attribute> [,<attribute> . . .])
  from <table>;
```

The two numbers returned from these two statements should be equal. If we actually want to extract those multiple record occurrences with the same set of values that should have been unique, we can use SQL such as this SQL statement (which can be used for a single attribute key).

```
SELECT *
FROM <table> AS t1, <table> AS t2
WHERE t1.<attribute> = t2.<attribute>;
```

This statement looks for instances in the table where a pair of values taken from a pair of records in the table are the same. If the key really is unique, the result set will still contain one entry for each record in the original set, since the selected record will match its value against itself in both instances of the table. On the other hand, if the value is not unique, there will be an additional pair of records that share a key.

17.1.19   Uniqueness

The uniqueness rule is a cousin to the primary key rule. The difference is that we may indicate that a column's values be unique without using that column as a primary key. We indicate that an attribute's value is to be unique with a simple assertion.

```
<table>.<attribute> is Unique
```

Our first test for validation is to count the number of records and then count the number of distinct attribute values. Those counts, retrieved using these SQL statements, should be the same.

```
Select count(*) from <table>;
Select count (distinct <attribute>) from <table>;
```

The two numbers returned from these two statements should be equal. If we actually want to extract those multiple record occurrences with the same set of values that should have been unique, there is a separate known primary key.

```
SELECT <table>.<attribute>, <table>.<attribute>
FROM <table> AS t1, <table> AS t2
WHERE t1.<attribute> = t2.<attribute> and t1.<primary>
   <> t2.<primary>;
```

In this case, it is helpful to have a predefined primary key, which can then be used to extract out the offending pairs more easily than in the earlier case of defined keys.

17.1.20   Foreign Key

A foreign key represents a relationship between two tables. When the values in field f in table T is chosen from the key values in field g in table S, field S.g is said to be a foreign key for field T.f. A foreign key assertion must indicate that a field in one table is a foreign key for a field in another table.

We specify that a set of attributes is a foreign key by specifying the attributes that act as the foreign key and the attribute that the key indexes.

```
(<target table>.<attribute>) foreign key for
(<source table>.<attribute>)
```

The referential integrity constraint, which is implicit in the definition of a foreign key, indicates that if table T has a foreign key matching the primary key of another table S, then every value of the foreign key in T must be equal to the value of some primary key in table S or be completely null. Therefore, a foreign key assertion specifies a consistency relationship between tables — for all non-null foreign keys that appear in table T, there must exist a primary key with the same values in table S.

We test this assertion by making sure that all values that appear in the foreign key field of the source table exist in target table.

```
Select * from <source table> where <attribute> not in
(Select distinct <attribute> from <target table>);
```

This SQL statement pulls out all the values that are supposed to be used as a foreign key but do not appear in the target table. These are violating records, and the question is whether the violation occurred because the foreign key value in the source table was incorrect or whether the foreign key is really missing in the target table and should be there.

17.1.21 Alternate Implementation — The Rules Engine

In this section, we have explored the use of SQL as a way of both executing and representing data quality and business rules. We should not feel obligated to only use this mechanism as a tool for databases. Even though a rule is described using SQL, the implementation need not be restricted to an environment where the data sit in a relational database. The use of intermediate data representations, the use of standard data structures such as arrays, linked lists, and hash tables, and other programming tricks will allow for the execution of these rules in a runtime environment separated from a query engine.

We like to think that the kinds of rules engines that we saw in Chapter 12 can be called upon to create intermediately executing rule validation objects. We can encapsulate the interpretation and operation of a validator as an operational execution object that can be inserted into a processing system, and we use this idea in the next section.

As long as the rules engine can be handed a "map" of the data that pass through it — either through the use of metadata for table schemas that can be provided into the rules engine or a data type definition and message format schema, such as that which can be described using markup systems like XML — the rules engine can manage the testing and validation of data quality rules when integrated into the processing stream. In this way, coordinating with actions that can be linked in together with the rules engine, a content-oriented workflow system can be enabled.

17.2 OPERATIONAL DIRECTIVES

In Chapter 8, we also looked at a number of operational directives that were used either to specify the model of the information chain or an insertion of an operational procedure into the operation. In this section, we look at the relation of these directives to an actual processing environment.

17.2.1 Information Chain Specification

The specification of an information chain is embodied through the identification of the stages of processing within the system and the information channels between these stages. The actual benefit of this kind of specification occurs when the specification is in much greater detail, incorporating inputs and outputs that can be fully specified using a data model or a data interchange definition. This benefit allows for the insertion of a validation engine at specific points in the information chain, as will be described in Section 17.2.2.

Suffice it to say, the information chain specification defines a data flow model for information throughout the system and an interface specification for data transfer. The directives specify either a processing stage or an information channel, as well as a qualified name describing the effects of information passing from one point in the model to another.

Each location in this graph can be identified as a source for data, a target for data, a processing stage for data, or a communications channel. The implementation of this model is the construction of a runtime model of the information flow, where each named object is incorporated into a full map of the system. Each location refers to the corresponding actual location in the information chain, and at any point where data is written or read, the data model is maintained. The rest of the directives in this section will refer to the actual processing locations, as referenced via this information map.

We will store the information chain in a metadata table. First, we have a small data domain specifying the kinds of information chain objects.

```
Define infochain_objtype {"SOURCE", "TARGET", "CHANNEL",
   "STAGE"}
```

We then have a table describing the objects in the information chain. Each record contains a type, a name, a source and a target (if it is a channel), and an assigned object id. In addition, each record has a description field, which will cover the description of the actual location in the processing system that corresponds to this information chain object.

```
Create table infochain (
    Objtype      varchar(10),
    Objname      varchar(50),
    Desc         varchar(1000),
    Source       integer,
    Target       integer,
    Objid        integer
);
```

Actually, this is a good opportunity to specify some of our data quality rules.

```
Infochain.objtype belongs to infochain_objtype;
If (infochain.objtype = "CHANNEL") then complete with
   (infochain.source, infochain.target);
If (infochain.objtype <> "CHANNEL") then exempt
   (infochain.source, infochain.target);
```

17.2.2 Measurements

Our goal of a measurement directive is to (1) create an opportunity to insert a rule validation engine at a specified point in the information chain, (2) take a measurement, and (3) record the measurement to a separate data resource.

To this end, we must define another set of data tables, which describes measurements taken based on a rule set executing at a location within the information chain. These tables can be used for as simple a process as collecting conformance percentages to one as complex as maintaining a reference to all violating records (or messages).

This database is used to keep track of the date and time the measurement was taken, the location in the information chain where the measurement was done, the number of records (or messages) tested, the rule set referenced, and the number of passes and fails per rule being measured. The first table maintains the record of which measurements are being taken and their location on the information chain. This corresponds to the location for the measurement and the rule being measured.

```
Create table measures (
    Measureruleid    integer,
    Locationid       integer,
    Rule             integer,
);
```

The next table models each actual measurement.

```
Create table measurements (
     Measurementid             integer,
     Measurementdate           date,
     Ruleset                   integer,
     Numtested                 integer,
     Passed                    integer,
     Failed                    integer
);
```

For the details, we refer to a more descriptive data set.

```
Create table measurementdetails (
     Measurementid             integer,
     Rule                      integer,
     Numtested                 integer,
     Passed                    integer,
     Failed                    integer
);
```

The measurement identifier refers back to the governing measurement in the `measurements` table. Each record in `measurementdetails` refers to a particular rule in the referenced rule set, the number of records or messages that were tested, and the numbers of passes and failures.

A measurement directive indicates the location where the measurement is to take place and the rule that is to be tested. The implementation of this is the creation of a rule tester, integrated with the specific rules and inserted in the information chain at the named location. The rule tester will execute this pseudocode for each record.

```
Passed[1:num_rules] = 0;
Failed[1:num_rules] = 0;
Tested[1:num_rules] = 0;
For each record do
   For each rule do
        If this record applies to this rule, then {
             Tested[this rule]++;
             If this rule passes then
                passed[this rule]++;
             Else
                     Failed[this rule]++;
        }
total_tested = sum(tested[1:num_rules]);
```

```
total_passed = sum(passed[1:num_rules]);
total_failed = sum(failed[1:numrules]);
Insert record into measurements table;
For each rule,
    Insert detail record into measurementdetails table;
```

17.2.3   Triggers

A trigger directive indicates the invocation of a named operation at some point in the data-flow chain. We may include a condition to trigger the operation, or the operation may take place specifically when a record or a message hits a certain point in the data-flow chain. A trigger directive is implemented similarly to the measurement directive: an operational object inserted into the actual processing system, as mirrored in the placement in the information chain.

```
Create table triggers (
    triggerid           integer,
    Locationid          integer,
    Rule                integer,
    action              integer
);
```

Note that we have glossed over the details of the actions being taken. We assume that a separate system can be created to manage described actions, and we are referring to those actions.

The operational object, when integrated into the actual processing system as mirrored by the information chain, will test the rule, and if the rule evaluates to true, the action is taken.

17.2.4   Transformations

Although we have specified transformations as separate directives, we can treat them as a syntactically different but semantically equal version of the derivation rule as described in Section 17.1.16.

17.2.5 Updates

Updates refer to the initiation of an ongoing process and the restarting of a process, as related to both triggers and measurements. We might want to integrate a rule-oriented reload of a data mart from a data warehouse, based on a trigger indicating that the conformance to a data quality rule set has finally measured above the acceptance threshold. These update directives can be integrated as inlined code or as periodic refreshes using the system's timer and scheduling utilities.

17.2.6 Approximate Match

In Chapter 16, we defined two additional rules. The first of these rules, the approximate match definition, defines a similarity score between any two values, along with a threshold indicating whether two values are assumed to match. The formal definition of an approximate match rule must include a defined function, which should evaluate to a real value between 0.0 and 1.0 and a threshold value above which a score indicates a match, which is also a real value between 0.0 and 1.0.

```
APPROXIMATE MATCH
(<real function>(<value1>, <value2>)):threshold=0.75
```

The definition of the function can include predefined operators (such as the same ones used for expressions) as well as user-defined functions (which of course, must be provided to build a working application). The actual implementation of this rule converts the rule definition into a function. Here is an example of the conversion of this rule

```
match_def1: approximate match (1 - (ABS(Value1 -
    Value2)/MAX(Value1, Value2))):threshold=0.75
```

into C code:

```
#define MAX(_a,_b) (_a > _b ? _a :_b)

int match_def1(float _val1, float _val2) {
    if (1 - (abs(_val1 - val2)/MAX(val1, _val2))) >= 0.75)
          return(1);
    else
          return(0);
}
```

We can instead implement this rule as a function returning the score itself and testing the score outside of the function. This in fact is more interesting, since the function can then be used with the next rule.

17.2.7 Approximate Aggregate

The approximate aggregate rule collects a sum of scaled results associated with approximate match scoring. An approximate aggregate associated with a pair of records will be a sum of a set of weights applied to a collection of approximate matches, divided by the sum of the weights, along with a threshold indicating a score above which the two records are assumed to be a match.

```
Approximate aggregate ((<matchA>(<valueA1>, <valueA2>) *
    <scaleA>
    [ + <matchX>(<valueX1>, <valueX2>) * <scaleX> . . .])
    / (sum (<scaleA> [, <scaleX> . . .]))) : <threshold>
```

This rule is implemented also as a function, which incorporates the approximate match rules used within. The result is always a floating point number between 0.0 and 1.0.

17.3 DATA QUALITY AND THE TRANSACTION FACTORY

Now that we have a clearer story of how these data quality and business rules can be used in an executing system, let's look at some specific implementation paradigms. Our first is using data quality rules to help guide the execution in a transaction factory.

In a transaction factory, a transaction, such as a stock trade or a product purchase, takes place, and the factory processes the transaction so that a desired result occurs. The transaction factory takes transaction records as well as other data as raw input, produces some product or service as a "side effect," and perhaps may generate some output data. Each transaction factory can be represented as an information chain, with individual processing stages taking care of the overall transaction processing.

Data quality and business rules are integrated into the transaction factory in two ways. First, transaction factories are built assuming that the data being inserted into the process is of high quality and meets all the expected requirements. Second, the actual processing that is performed is based on the content of the inserted data. Together, we are presented with three opportunities to use data quality and business rules.

17.3.1 Input Validation

Because the factory is built assuming that the input meets a high standard, problems in continuing operations occur when the input does not meet that standard. If a bad record can adversely affect the streamlined processing, then it is beneficial to capture, remove, and correct offending data before it ever reaches the internals of the factory.

In this instance, data quality rules would be defined to match the input requirements. A validation engine would be inserted at the entry point for all data inputs. In addition, we must also define a reconciliation process to direct the way that invalid records are treated (see Figure 17.2).

The implementation consists of these steps:

1. Define the data quality rules based on the input requirements.
2. For each rule, associate a degree of criticality, which will dictate the action taken if the rule is violated.
3. For each rule and degree of criticality, determine the action to be taken. Typically, we can make use of at least these actions.
   a. Ignore: If the violation is not business critical, we may want to log the error but let the value pass.
   b. Auto-correct: We can define a derivation rule that uses the current value of a field to determine the actual value, if that is possible. If a record is auto-corrected, it can then be gated through into the system.
   c. Remove for reconciliation: If the violation is severe enough that it will affect processing, and it cannot be (or should not be) auto-corrected, the record should be shunted off to a reconciliation database, enhanced by the rule that was violated, the data source, and a timestamp.
4. An implementation of a rule validator is built and inserted at the appropriate entry points of data into the factory.
5. The reconciliation database needs to be constructed and made operational.
6. A reconciliation decision process is put into effect.

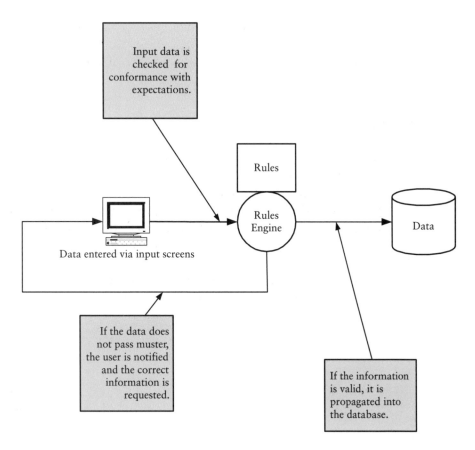

FIGURE 17.2 Using rules for input validation

17.3.2 Supplier Management

Inserting a validation engine at the source of input data also generates a benefit of logging the errors coming from each information supplier, as well as calculating the compliance percentage each time data passes through the engine. By augmenting the validation engine with a measurement directive, we can also accumulate statistics about data quality conformance, which can be presented to the supplier if the data does not meet the requirements. Through the implementation, we can build an automated means for generating a compliance report (see Figure 17.3).

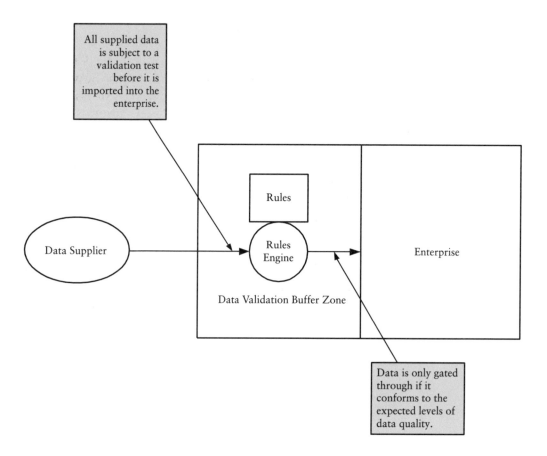

FIGURE 17.3   Using rules for supplier management

17.3.3   Content-Directed Processing

Last, at each decision point in the processing, it is possible that the decision is based on the content of the data record as it passes through a point in the information chain. Again, we can associate actions for data routing based on the values embedded in the records (or messages) as they pass through locations in the information chain. We can then create rule application engines that make use of these rules (and their associated actions) at the corresponding location within the information chain, directing the information flow.

17.4 DATA QUALITY AND THE DATA WAREHOUSE

We have already discussed how complex and pervasive the data quality problem is with respect to data warehousing. In Chapter 3, we looked at an example where we would use data quality and business rules for what we call "data warehouse certification." Certification is a means for scoring the believability of the information stored in a data warehouse. We certify a data warehouse as being fit for use when the data inside conform to a set of data quality expectations embodied in a set of rules. Given these rules, we assign a score to the quality of the data imported into a data warehouse for certifying warehouse data quality.

In this chapter we can see how this can be implemented. A set of rules is developed as a quality gate for data imported into the data warehouse. We will associate with each rule a validity threshold (as a percentage) based on the users' expectations of quality. An engine is configured to incorporated those rules and execute the validation tests as data is prepared to be entered into the warehouse (see Figure 17.4).

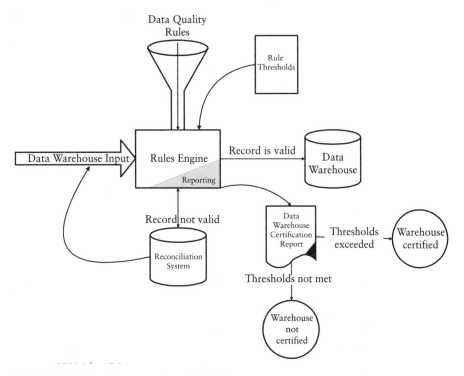

FIGURE 17.4 Data warehouse validation

As records are fed into the engine, any relevant rules (that is, any rules that refer to values of attributes defined within the record) are tested. We create a measurement object, which tallies the successes and failures associated with each rule and outputs the results to the measurements tables. We incorporate a trigger to notify the users whether the warehouse has been certified or not.

For any record, if no rules fail, the record is said to be valid and is successfully gated through to the warehouse. For each rule that does fail, a record is generated to be inserted into the measurements tables with the information about which rules were violated. The record is then output to a reconciliation system, as we described in Section 17.3. The violating record can also be passed through to the warehouse, but now it should be timestamped and marked as having not conformed to the users' expectations, and this information can be used when performing analysis.

After you've imported the data, each rule's validity value is computed as the ratio of valid records to the total of records. A data quality certification report delineating all validity percentages is generated. If all validity percentages exceed the associated thresholds, the warehouse is certified to conform to the users' data quality requirements. Otherwise, the warehouse is not certified, and until the percentages can be brought up to the conformance level, the warehouse cannot be said to meet the data quality requirements.

Since we have integrated the measurement process into the warehouse loading system, we will have a periodic (or as periodic as the warehouse is loaded) measure of how well the database conforms to the data quality requirements. In order to qualify the warehouse after a failed certification, the records output to the reconciliation system must be analyzed for the root cause of the failures, as explored in Chapter 15. After reconciliation, the data is resubmitted through the rules engine, and the validity report is generated again. This process continues until certification is achieved.

17.5   RULES AND EDI

In Chapter 3, we discussed some of the issues associated with electronic data interchange (EDI) and data quality. We focused on the use of XML (the Extensible Markup Language) as a framework for both structure definition (for the definition of data standards) and rules for validating messages based on defined standards. We discussed well-formedness and validity within the XML environment.

In the context of XML, a document is well formed if it conforms to the syntax of XML. This means that an XML parser can successfully parse the document. Also, in order to be well formed, a document must meet a number of other conditions. For example, no attribute (a name-value pair that attributes a tag) may appear more than once on the same start tag, all entities must be declared, and nonempty tags must be nested properly. Another condition is that neither text nor parameters may be directly or indirectly recursive. An XML parser can determine whether a document is well formed or not.

An XML document is valid if it is well formed and it contains a DTD and the document obeys the rules specified in the DTD. This means that element sequence and nesting conforms to the DTD, all attribute values that are required are present, and their types are correct.

What is still needed for information validation within an EDI environment is content-based validation. This can be achieved when using our data quality and business rules to specify content-oriented assertions about the information contained within the messages. We can direct the processing of XML statements via processing instructions within an XML document, and that is the hook through which we can integrate the data quality rule engines.

17.6   DATA QUALITY RULES AND AUTOMATED UIS

One of the major goals of a data quality program is the enforcement of strict rules conformance before information passes into the system. Since many data collections are populated through manual data entry, it would be preferable to create a framework that limits the kinds of errors that can be introduced at data entry time. We can use our data quality rules to help automate the generation of a user interface (UI) based on maintaining a high level of data quality.

17.6.1   Selection Criteria

The definition of data domains, mappings between those domains, and the assignation of rules associating attributes with domains and mappings prove to be an invaluable resource in UI generation. When we declare that an attribute draws its values from a defined domain, we automatically limit the possible values that the user may enter. If we already have those valid values, why not integrate those as the selection choices within a drop-down box when filling in an online form?

17.6.2   Dependence-Based Data Entry

More interestingly, when we have declared that two attributes' values must conform to a predefined mapping, we impose a dependence on the values that can populate the target attribute based on the selection for the source attribute. We can create the drop down for the source attribute's value, and when that value is selected, only those values for the target attribute that are valid under the mapping are presented to the user for selection.

This introduces a more interesting concept associated with the use of data quality rules for UI generation. The definition of a set of data quality rules may create a hierarchical arrangement of dependence between the different data attributes within a database table or a message. For example, associating two attributes with a domain mapping creates a dependence for the target attribute on the source attribute. In other words, we can ensure that the relationship between these two attributes as expressed by the data quality mapping membership rule can be enforced from the data entry point if the value for the target is not collected until the value for the source has been provided!

This simple statement is actually quite profound. It covers all the relationships expressed within data quality rules and basically states that we can ensure a higher level of data quality from the start if we abide by the dependences embedded in the data quality rules. In any rule that incorporates a conditional assertion, we can infer a dependence. For example, the completeness rules defines that if a condition that involves the value or values of data attribute(s) is true, then that record is complete only if other attributes are non-null. This means that there is a conditional dependence on the attributes referenced in the condition. The same holds true for exemption rules, consistency rules, and so on.

To carry our example a bit further, let's presume that there is a completeness rule indicating that if the data attribute OWNS_CAR is "y," then the record is complete with the CAR_REGISTRATION_NUMBER attribute. From our discussions, we know that if the user enters a "y" in the OWNS_CAR field, then the record will not be complete unless the other attribute is given a value. This tells us when the field must be filled in and when it doesn't have to be filled in. This is shown in Figure 17.5.

17.6.3 Building the Dependence Graph

The insight we gain from the idea of dependence is that when many attributes in a table depend on other attributes in the same (or another) table, we can group our requests for data by what is called a *dependence class*. All attributes are assigned into a dependence class with some integer-valued degree. The zero-th degree includes all nondependent attributes. The first degree includes all attributes that depend only on zero-th degree attributes.

More formally, a dependence class of degree *i* is the set of all attributes whose values depend on attributes of a degree less than *i*. At each stage of data collection, we only need to ask for data for the current dependence class, and we can impose our rules on the attribute values being collected at that point because all the conditions for our rules are known to be able to be examined. The relation between different dependence classes can be summarized in a dependence graph.

1	productCode DOES NOT ALLOW NULLS
2	If (substr(productCode,1,1) != 'X') then exempt {color}
3	If (color == 'GREEN' OR color == 'RED') then (size != 'XXL')
4	If (substr(productCode,1,1) == 'A') then (qty >= 100)

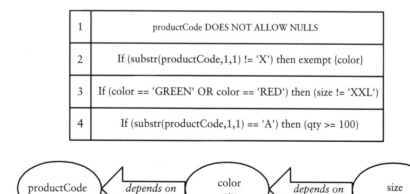

FIGURE 17.5 Examples of data dependence

17.6.4   Creating the UI

To create a user interface, we will generate input forms that are data-directed. The first form to be presented asks for all zero-th degree attributes. Each subsequent form can be crafted to incorporate only those attributes in the next dependence class and can be attributed in format with the data attributes associated via the data quality rules.

To continue our previous example, if the user did indicate that he or she owned a car, the next form could explicitly say, "You have indicated that you own a car. What is the registration number for that car?" and then prompt for the answer. This offers more context to the user than the traditional form of empty fields. Figure 17.6 shows this process.

17.7   SUMMARY

In this chapter, we have examined the ways to create executable systems driven by the data domains, domain mappings, and data quality rules discussed in Chapters 7, 8, and 16. We have seen how the rules can be turned into SQL queries, and we have opened the discussion for how the rules can be integrated into a rules engine such as the kind discussed in Chapter 12.

We also have a notion as to how we can integrate approximate matching and scoring rules into "fuzzy" cleansing applications through the combination of approximate rules with other rules. Including measurements and triggers allows us to describe a full-fledged data quality application before writing a stitch of code.

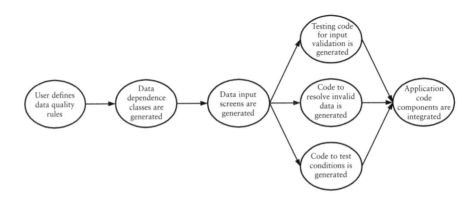

FIGURE 17.6   Data dependence–driven UI creation

Finally, we looked at some implementation paradigms of data quality rules. This chapter brings the story full circle — from the beginning, where we first learned about the quantification of a data quality, assessing the cost of low data quality, the dimensions of data quality, through domains, mappings, rules, and measurements. At this point, we can make use of our analysis tools to completely assess, develop a return-on-investment model, specify, and implement a data quality improvement program. The next chapter provides a complete overview of the entire process from start to finish.

18

BUILDING THE DATA QUALITY PRACTICE

In Chapter 1, we talked about the ideas of knowledge management and how data quality management is the basis of a successful knowledge organization. Our goals in this book have been to elucidate the topic of enterprise knowledge management from first principles: building a quality core knowledge infrastructure composed of high-quality metadata, data domains, data quality rules, and business rules.

To bring things full circle, we must provide a concise guide to the data quality approach to knowledge management. This last chapter brings together the methods and processes that we have discussed in this book, augmented with some of the operational details needed in building a successful data quality practice.

18.1 STEP 1: RECOGNIZE THE PROBLEM

The first step is problem recognition. The problem is only a data quality problem when it becomes clear that some issue associated with data quality has an adverse effect on the business. This boils down to seeing evidence of a data quality problem and finding (at a high level) the areas that are affected by that problem.

18.1.1 Evidence of a Problem

In Chapter 4, we looked at these issues that might indicate the evidence of a data quality problem.

- Frequent system failures and system interruptions
- Drop in productivity versus volume
- High employee turnover
- High new business to continued business ratio (high customer turnover)
- Increased customer service requirements
- Decreased ability to scale
- Customer attrition

When these issues are evident in an organization, it is a good sign that somewhere, poor data quality is having an effect. The next step is to determine what kinds of problems exist and where.

18.1.2   Determining the Problem

Through employee and customer interviews, the analyst's next step is to determine whether the noted evidence points to any particular problems with data quality. Typically, corroborative evidence can be collected via anecdotes, "crisis events," or customer service logs.

Part of this stage involves reconnoitering the management structure. Knowledge of the identity of the senior-level managers with authority over the information resource is important when establishing the need for a data quality program.

18.2   STEP 2: MANAGEMENT SUPPORT AND THE DATA OWNERSHIP POLICY

No data quality program will be successful without the support of senior managers. Because poor data quality affects both the operational and the strategic sides of the business, addressing a systemic data quality program takes on a strategic importance that must be validated by the participation of the management of the business.

There are two parts to this phase. The first is making the proper presentation that highlights the importance of data quality within the organization. The second is the definition of and the securing the enforcement of a data ownership policy.

18.2.1   Gaining Senior-Level Management Support

The best way to win the support of senior management is to cast the problem in terms of how the business is affected or can be affected by poor data quality. A presentation can be crafted that incorporates the following notions.

- The reliance of the organization on high-quality information
- The evidence of existence of a data quality problem
- The types of impacts that low data quality can have
- The fact that managing data quality is the basis of a knowledge organization
- A review of the anecdotes regarding poor data quality
- A review of data ownership issues
- The implementation of a data ownership policy
- A projection of Return on Investment (ROI)

There are two goals of this presentation. The first is to encourage an awareness on behalf of the senior managers of the importance of data quality. The second is the authority to craft a data ownership policy.

18.2.2   Data Ownership Responsibilities

Our data ownership policy will define a set of data ownership roles and assign responsibilities to those roles. Here are some of the responsibilities we discussed in Chapter 2.

- Data definition
- Authorization of access and validation of security
- Support the user community
- Data packaging and delivery
- Maintenance of data
- Data quality
- Management of business rules
- Management of metadata
- Standards management
- Supplier management

18.2.3   The Data Ownership Policy

The data ownership policy is the document guiding the roles associated with information and the responsibilities accorded those roles. At the very least, a data ownership policy should enumerate these elements.

1. The senior-level managers supporting the enforcement of the policies enumerated
2. All data sets covered under the policy
3. The ownership model (that is, how is ownership allocated or assigned within the enterprise?) for each data set
4. The roles associated with data ownership (and the associated reporting structure)
5. The responsibilities of each role
6. Dispute resolution processes
7. Signatures of those senior level managers listed in item 1

18.2.4   Complicating Notions

Keep in mind that there are complicating notions that are working as forces against the smooth transition to a knowledge organization, including these.

- Questions of information value
- Privacy issues
- Turf and control concerns
- Fear
- Bureaucracy

18.2.5   Defining the Data Ownership Policy

These are the steps in defining the data ownership policy (see Figure 18.1).

1. Identifying the interested parties or stakeholders associated with the enterprise data. This includes identifying the senior-level managers that will support the enforcement of the policy.
2. Cataloging the data sets that are covered under the policy
3. Determining the ownership models in place and whether these are to continue or whether they will be replaced or modified

4. Determining the roles that are in place, those that are not in place, assigning responsibilities to each role, and assigning the roles to interested parties

5. Maintaining a registry that keeps track of policies, data ownership, roles, responsibilities, and so forth

18.3 STEP 3: SPREAD THE WORD

Another key factor to the success of a data quality program is evangelism: making sure that the stakeholders (including the users, managers, and implementers) are aware of the value and importance of data quality. Here we discuss two aspects: creating a data quality education forum and what topics should be included.

18.3.1 Data Quality Education

We suggest a training program that can be broken into two parts. The first part covers the "business" aspects of data quality, such as the economic analysis, the cost of low data quality, assessments, and building ROI models. The second part covers the implementation issues, such as data domains, mappings, data quality and business rules, measurements, data cleansing, correction, and enhancement.

18.3.2 Training in Data Quality Systems

A training program in data quality should incorporate at least these concepts.

1. Creation and use of information
2. Storage of information

FIGURE 18.1 Defining the data ownership policy

3. Data ownership
4. Quality concepts and the quality improvement cycle
5. Understanding the economic impact of data quality issues
6. Dimensions of data quality
7. Aspects of reference data domains
8. Data quality and business rules
9. Metrics for measuring and assessing data quality
10. Metadata
11. Data quality requirements analysis
12. Data cleansing and standardization
13. Error detection, correction, and root cause analysis using data quality rules
14. Data enhancement

18.4   STEP 4: MAPPING THE INFORMATION CHAIN

Understanding how information flows through the organization is the next step in improving data quality. The information chain (see Figure 18.2) is a chart describing data movement through the enterprise and is used as the basic map on top of which our other analyses are performed.

An information chain is composed of processing stages and communications channels. To map the information chain, first identify all the processing stages, then the channels of communication between them, and then label each unique component in the map.

18.4.1   Identifying Processing Stages

We look for those stages that create, read, write, send, or process data. Here is a review of the processing stages discussed in Chapter 4.

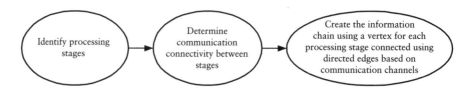

Figure 18.2   Mapping the information chain

1. *Data supply*   Data suppliers forward information into the system.
2. *Data acquisition*   This is the processing stage that accepts data from external suppliers and injects it into the system.
3. *Data creation*   Internal to the system, data may be generated and then forwarded to another processing stage.
4. *Data processing*   Any stage that accepts input and generates output (as well as generating side effects) is called a data processing stage.
5. *Data packaging*   Any point that information is collated, aggregated, and summarized for reporting purposes is a packaging stage.
6. *Decision making*   The point where human interaction is required is called a decision-making stage
7. *Decision implementation*   This is the stage where the decision made at a decision-making stage is executed, which may affect other processing stages or a data delivery stage.
8. *Data delivery*   This is the point where packaged information is delivered to a known data consumer.
9. *Data consumption*   Because the data consumer is the ultimate user of processed information, the consumption stage is the exit stage of the system.

18.4.2   Identifying Communication Channels

An information channel is a pipeline indicating the flow of information from one processing stage to another. A directed information channel is additionally attributed with the direction in which data flows.

18.4.3   Building the Information Chain

The information chain is a graph, where the vertices are the processing stages and the communication channels are directed edges. Every vertex and every edge in the information chain is assigned a unique name.

18.5   STEP 5: DATA QUALITY SCORECARD

The data quality scorecard summarizes the overall cost associated with low data quality and can be used as a tool to help determine where the best opportunities are for improvement.

18.5.1   Impacts of Low Data Quality

Low data quality can have impacts that affect the way the operational and strategic environment run. In Chapter 4, we explored these impacts of low data quality.

- Detection of errors
- Correction of errors
- Rollback of processing
- Rework of work already completed under erroneous circumstances
- Prevention of errors
- Warranty against damages caused by nonconformities
- Reduction of customer activity
- Attrition and loss of customers
- Blockading on behalf of angered ex-customers
- Delay of decisions
- Preemption of decision making
- Idling of business activity while waiting for strategy to be defined
- Increased difficulty of execution
- Lost opportunities
- Organizational mistrust
- Lack of alignment between business units
- Increased acquisition overhead associated with information products
- Decay of information value
- Infrastructure costs to support low data quality

18.5.2   Economic Measures

Each of these impacts must be associated with some economic measure that can be quantified in terms of actual costs. Our starting points for cost estimation for either an impact or the benefit if the impact were removed are the following.

- *Cost increase*   This measures the degree to which poor data quality increases the cost of doing business.
- *Revenue decrease*   This measures how low data quality affects current revenues.
- *Cost decrease*   This measures how an improvement in data quality can reduce costs.
- *Revenue increase*   This measures how improving data quality increases revenues.
- *Delay*   This measures whether there is a slowdown in productivity.
- *Speedup*   This measures the degree to which a process's cycle time can be reduced.
- *Increase satisfaction*   This measures whether customer satisfaction, employee satisfaction, or shareholder satisfaction is increased.
- *Decrease satisfaction*   This measures whether customer satisfaction, employee satisfaction, or shareholder satisfaction is decreased.

18.5.3   Building the Scorecard

To create a data quality scorecard (see Figure 18.3), we follow these steps.

- Map the information chain to understand how information flows within the organization.
- Interview employees to understand what people are doing with respect to data quality issues.
- Interview customers to understand the kinds of customer impacts.
- Isolate flawed data by reviewing the information chain and locating the areas where data quality problems are manifested.

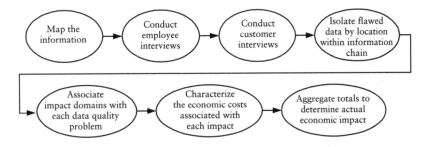

FIGURE 18.3   Creating the data quality scorecard

- Identify the impact domain associated with each instance of poor data quality.
- Characterize the economic impact based on the ultimate effects of the bad data.
- Aggregate the totals to determine the actual economic impact.

18.6   STEP 6: CURRENT STATE ASSESSMENT

The data quality scorecard highlights the effect of low data quality on the bottom line. We must perform a current state assessment to collect enough data to understand the nature of the actual data quality problems (see Figure 18.4).

18.6.1   Choosing Locations in the Information Chain

We begin the current state assessment by picking particular locations in the information chain as targets for measurements. We take into account these characterizations when selecting a location for measurement.

1. *Critical junction*   Any processing stage with a high degree of information load is likely to be a site where information from different data sources is merged or manipulated.
2. *Collector*   A collector is likely to be a place where information is aggregated and prepared for reporting or prepared for storage.
3. *Broadcaster*   A broadcaster is likely to be a processing stage that prepares information for many consumers and, therefore, may be a ripe target for measurement.

FIGURE 18.4   Performing the current state assessment

4. *Ease of access*   While some processing stages may be more attractive in terms of analytical power, they may not be easily accessed for information collection.

5. *High-profile stages*   A processing stage that consumes a large percentage of company resources might provide useful measurement information.

18.6.2   Choosing a Subset of the Data Quality Dimensions

The next stage of the current state assessment is selecting a subset of the dimensions of data quality for measurement. We suggest that at a minimum, selecting at least one dimension from each of our five classes of data quality dimensions.

18.6.3   Measuring Data Quality

In Chapter 9, we reviewed many different ways that each of the dimensions of data quality defined in Chapter 5. The real directive at this point is to choose a way to measure the conformance to expectations associated with the selected dimensions of data quality.

18.7   STEP 7: REQUIREMENTS ASSESSMENT

After completing a current state assessment, we have some ideas of the scope and magnitude of the different problems, and we want to narrow the scope of each specific problem into a manageable unit of work. We can do this by prioritizing each problem, assigning responsibility, and creating data quality requirements.

18.7.1   Distribution of Cost and Impact

At this stage, we combine the result of the data quality scorecard, which attributed the information chain with the impacts and costs associated with low data quality, and the current state assessment, which attributed the information chain with the measured levels of data quality. The result is an assignment of a percentage of the overall cost and impact to each of the problems so that we can order them by an assigned priority.

18.7.2   Assignment of Responsibility

Simultaneously, it is important to refer to the data ownership policy and assign ultimate responsibility for each individual problem. That person will then be tasked with defining the project that brings the level of quality in line with the expectations.

18.7.3   Data Quality Requirements

Each specification of a data quality requirement must include the following.

- A unique identifier for the requirement
- A name for the requirement
- The name of the responsible party
- The location in the information chain where the requirement is applied
- A reference to the dimension of data quality that is being measured
- A description of the measurement method
- If possible, the measurement rule
- The minimum threshold for acceptance
- The optimal high threshold
- The scaling factor as a percentage of the overall system data quality

18.8   STEP 8: CHOOSE A PROJECT

We cannot expect to solve the entire enterprise data quality problem at once, and so the best way to attack it is piece by piece. We have analyzed the cost of low data quality, measured the different problems that exist, determined the source of the individual problems, and assigned a percentage of the cost, impact, and responsibility to each problem. Now is the time to select a problem to solve.

Choosing the first problem to address requires some care, since the results of implementing the first project can make or break the practice. The first project should reflect these ideas.

- The problem to be solved has a noticeable impact.
- Solving the problem results in measurable cost savings.
- There are little or no political issues that need to be addressed.
- There is senior management support.
- Access to the problem space is open.
- The problem can be solved.

Remember: The goal of the first data quality project is to ensure the continued operation of the data quality program. A failure in solving the first project will probably result in the demise of the program, so choose wisely.

18.9   STEP 9: BUILD YOUR TEAM

The analysis is complete. The project has been selected. Now it is time to solve the problem. Each solution project will need to have a team of people that can execute the different parts of the job. In this section, we describe these roles.

18.9.1   Project Manager

The project manager's job is to define the set of tasks to be performed, create a schedule for the implementation, assign the tasks to the different team members, and enable the team members to do their jobs.

18.9.2   System Architect

In solving data quality problems, the role of the system architect is both system analyst and system historian. The architect must be able to understand the way the systems work in the context of the problem and work with the rest of the team members to craft a solution that accommodates the already existing system environment.

18.9.3   Domain Expert

Our choice of a problem to solve was based on the types of impacts and costs associated with the problem. In order to understand how modifications to the process will change the impacts, it is critical to have an expert from the business/analytical side to vet any proposed changes. It is also the role of the domain expert to document the user requirements and work with the rules engineer to transform those requirements into data quality and business rules.

18.9.4   Rules Software Engineer

The rules engineer will work with the domain expert to translate user requirements into data quality and business rules. The rules engineer is also tasked with managing and configuring any automated rules-oriented processing, and this includes evaluation of tools, rule definition, and application integration. This engineer will also implement any software needed for integration with the main system, as well as any standalone applications.

18.9.5   Quality Assurance and Root Cause Analysis

Of course, no data quality team would be complete without a Q/A engineer. This team member is tasked with both qualifying the implementation and performing the root cause analysis to pinpoint problem location.

18.10   STEP 10: BUILD YOUR ARSENAL

While the kinds of tools that exist for data quality were discussed in Chapters 14 and 16, we did not specify or recommend that any particular product. The reason for this is that each problem is slightly different, and different combinations of product capabilities may be needed.

On the other hand, it is likely that the project will need at least some of these components for implementation.

- Data cleansing
- Data standardization

- Database checking/validation
- Rules definition system
- Rules execution system
- Approximate matching

Some of these products may be offered in bundled form — a data cleansing tool may have a rules manager bundled, for example. The important thing is to recognize the kind of application functionality that is needed and plan accordingly.

18.10.1 Build vs Buy

There are many fine products in the market that can make up part of a data quality solution, but that doesn't mean that a solution can be integrated every time. It is possible that much of the componentry needed to configure a solution is available, but sometimes there are reasons why it doesn't make sense to actually buy the product(s). Also, the cost of these products can range from hundreds to hundreds of thousands of dollars. For example, if a cleansing application needs to be run only once before a new data validation system is installed, it may be more cost effective to invest a small amount of money in a simple tool and augment it with constructed applications.

18.10.2 Selecting Data Cleansing Applications

There are different kind of cleansing applications, ranging from name and address cleansing to pattern analyzers and rule-oriented cleansing. The selection of a cleansing application should be based on these factors.

- The kind of data to be cleansed. As we have said, there are different tools that act on different kinds of data. Some products are domain based, which means that they have been optimized for specific vertical applications, such as bank customer data or international addressing. Other products are very general but require a lot of configuration.

- The number of times the cleansing is to be performed. Our premise in this book is that if we can maintain a high level of quality of data that enters the enterprise, we will have lessened the need for static cleansing. On the other hand, if we can determine that it is less expensive to address the symptoms than fixing the problem, cleansing may be more frequent.

18.10.3   Selecting Data Standardization Applications

There may be a question as to the need for a special data standardization application. For the most part, standardization applications are applicable only where there is a recognized standard, such as postal addressing, or where the use of an EDI protocol is required.

18.10.4   Selecting a Conformance/Reconciliation System

As we have discussed a number of times in this book, hooking up a database validation system will require some auxiliary system. This incorporates funneling the results of the rule validation to a reconciliation system, as well as the reinjection of corrected information back into the system.

Frequently, a workflow system is used for part of a reconciliation system. A workflow application allows the user to specify the process through which a nonconforming data record is examined and reconciled. Workflow systems can range in cost quite widely as well, and simple workflow capability can be implemented using relatively traditional technology (such as a database system and e-mails, for example).

18.10.5   Selecting a Rule Management Application

Our intention is to ensure that the definition of data quality and business rules can be entrusted directly to the user. To do this, a rule editing and management interface can be used. This interface should provide an intuitive mechanism for nonexperts to define rules about the information they care about. This kind of application can be integrated with the rule execution system.

18.10.6   Selecting a Rule Execution Application

The rule execution system will take as input the rules defined via the definition and management system and generates executable engines that implement those rules. The rule execution system should conform to the kinds of specifications discussed in Chapter 12.

18.10.7   Approximate Matching

In Chapters 14 and 16, we saw the need for approximate matching as a component of a cleansing and enrichment program. Hopefully, the data quality tools we evaluate will contain some kind of approximate matching component, but if not, it will be necessary to incorporate an approximate matching tool into the arsenal, too.

18.11   STEP 11: METADATA MODEL

The next step to success is to define the metadata model if one does not already exist. Use the guidelines described in Chapter 11 to help set this up. Remember that we can incorporate enterprise reference data into our metadata system, so it is worthwhile to consider the storage of domains and mappings within this framework as well.

18.12   STEP 12: DEFINE DATA QUALITY RULES

We have done our impact analysis and our current state assessment, both of which have fed the requirements definition process. With our application components and metadata system in hand, we are now ready to define our data quality and business rules.

18.12.1   Identifying Data Domains

Either through interviews or automated algorithms, it is time to identify and register data domains. We have defined data domains in Chapter 7, provided a rule framework in Chapter 8, and discussed the discovery of domains in Chapter 13.

18.12.2   Identifying Mappings

As with domains, it is possible to identify mappings through expert interviews or through automatic analysis of the data. The discussion of mappings is also found in Chapters 7, 8, and 13.

18.12.3   Defining Rules

Once the domains and mappings are in place, we can begin to successively build our rule base by collecting the important assertions about the expectations of data quality. Using the current state assessment and requirements as input, we can target those areas that are most amenable to rule definition. We use the rule editing and management application (see Section 18.10.5) to define the rules.

18.13   STEP 13: ARCHAEOLOGY/DATA MINING

Without a comprehensive "archaeological analysis" of the data, we may not be able to get the complete story of embedded data domains, mappings, and rules. We can use data mining applications to explore and discover this kind of embedded knowledge. We can use these data mining algorithms to look for data domains, mappings, and especially data quality rules that are embedded in data.

- Clustering
- Association rule discovery
- Classification and regression trees
- Decision trees
- Link analysis

The use of these techniques may reveal that there are data quality and business rules that are not consistently adhered to and, because of that, simple discovery techniques will not uncover them. Once these kinds of rules are discovered, they can be evaluated by the domain expert and, if vetted, can be incorporated into the defined rule set.

18.14   STEP 14: MANAGE YOUR SUPPLIERS

We have a set of measurements based on the current state assessment and the requirements analysis stage. For those requirements that are to be imposed on external data suppliers, a supplier management process must be put in place. Again, with senior management support, the execution of a supplier management program begins with the specification of minimum expected measures of data quality for data imported into the enterprise.

As we described in Chapter 15, the supplier management program specifies the rules that are being asserted about the expectations of the data, along with a set of penalties for nonconformance. With our validation system to be implemented at the entry point for data, we should be able to get hard measurements of conformance, which can be used in turn to fuel the supplier management process.

18.15   STEP 15: EXECUTE THE IMPROVEMENT

Finally, we are at the execution stage. At this point, we are prepared to actually determine how to incorporate the solution to the data quality problem.

18.15.1   Architecting the Solution

The solution architecture is an augmentation of the current system architecture. Armed with the information chain, we know how data move through the system. When we focus on solving a particular problem, we isolate that section of the information chain and look at the software architecture at that section.

Assuming that we are integrating some kind of data validation and filtering system, we must determine the best place in the current system architecture to integrate the validation engine and reconciliation system. The validation engine will probably be placed along some set of communication channels within the information chain at the point where data is input into a processing stage. The reconciliation system may be a separate system for each problem or the same centralized system, augmented for each implemented use.

18.15.2   Performing Static Cleansing

If we are creating a data quality application, we will want to make sure that we are not leaving any bad data lying around. To this end, we can run a static data cleansing over the existing data to make sure we have a clean start.

18.15.3   Integrating and Testing the Rules

The rules have been defined and reviewed. Now is the time to integrate the rules into an executable system and build the environment to run tests and validate the validator. A test environment should be created that draws its input from the same source as the application will in production, and that environment may be used for testing. This is the opportunity to evaluate the validity of the rules in an operational context so any necessary changes may be flagged and made before moving to production.

This component will incorporate all validation rules and all prescriptive rules. If rules are being used to perform a data transformation, the integration must take place at this time also.

18.15.4   Building the Nonconformance Resolution System

The nonconformance resolution system is the application built from the reconciliation management system as the back end to the rule validation system. The governance of the reconciliation process is based on the data ownership policy. Depending on the way the responsibility is distributed according to both the policy and to the requirements analysis stage, the nonconformance resolution system will generate workflow tasks to those in the responsibility matrix.

18.15.5   Integrating the Rules System with the Production System

At the point where the level of acceptance is reached during the testing phase described in Section 18.15.3, the decision to move into production can be made. This means integrating the rules and nonconformance resolution system in with the original system architecture and switching control into that system.

We should also be careful to integrate the production validation system with the measurement methods used during the current state assessment. Any place where we had a well-defined measurement process and application in place should be tied back together with the production rules engine.

18.16   STEP 16: MEASURE IMPROVEMENT

One of the most critical pieces of the data quality program is the ability to demonstrate success at improving data quality. We already have a baseline for measuring improvement — the current state assessment. At that point in the process, we have identified a subset of the particular areas that critically impact the data quality within the enterprise, and we have gathered measurements based on defined metrics.

When we integrate the rules system, we made sure to also integrate these measurements. The reason is that we have successfully built a validation system to improve the data quality. This should be reflected in the locations and metrics we chose for the current state assessment. In other words, we can deliver a strict determination of measured improvement by continuing to perform the same measurements from the current state assessment. If we really have improved the data quality, we can document it with real evidence, not just anecdotal stories about improvements.

We can use the methods of statistical process control, discussed in Chapter 6, to document historical improvement. We can then make use of that method to assign new thresholds for additional improvements by resetting the upper and lower control limits based on user specification.

18.17   STEP 17: BUILD ON EACH SUCCESS

Finally, we have reached the point of success. We have measured, assessed, analyzed, set requirements, architected and implemented a system, and documented improvement. The success of any small project only contributes to the greater success of the entire program. Therefore, each small success should be used as leverage with the senior-level sponsors to gain access to bigger and better problems.

This is the time to address the sponsoring managers, armed with the measurements of success, to declare war on the next set of data quality problems. As the enterprise knowledge is accumulated in the central information repository, the entire system and the users thereof should derive increased benefit. The ultimate victory is when a systemic measurable improvement is achieved. But winning the war involves winning small battles, and reaching a higher level of enterprise data quality requires dedication, perseverance, and a true belief in the value of enterprise data quality.

18.18   CONCLUSION

At the beginning of this book, we talked about data quality as a hazy and ill-defined concept but one that can severely hamper a company's ability to do business. Our goal has been to demonstrate that data quality is not an unclear concept but something that can be quantified, measured, and improved, all with a strict focus on return on investment.

The goal of becoming an organization that leverages its data resource into a source of enterprise knowledge can be achieved but not without a firm base of high-quality data. Hopefully, this data quality approach to knowledge management will become the pedestal upon which the pillar of corporate knowledge will firmly stand.

INDEX

BIBLIOGRAPHY

Berry, Michael J. A. and Gordon Linoff. *Data Mining Techniques*. Wiley. 1997.

Berson, Alex and Stephen J. Smith. *Data Warehousing, Data Mining, & OLAP*. McGraw-Hill. 1997.

Bowman, Judith S., Sandra L. Emerson, and Marcy Darnovsky. *The Practical SQL Handbook,* 3d ed. Addison Wesley. 1996.

Celko, Joe. *Joe Celko's Data & Databases: Concepts in Practice*. Morgan Kaufmann. 1999.

Fayyad, Usama M. et al., eds. *Advances in Knowledge Discovery & Data Mining*. MIT Press. 1996.

Frakes, William B. and Ricardo Baeza-Yates, eds. *Information Retrieval Data Structures and Algorithms*. Prentice Hall. 1992.

Elmasri, Ramez and Shamkant B. Navathe. *Fundamentals of Database Systems*. Addison Wesley. 1994.

English, Larry P. *Improving Data Warehouse and Business Information Quality*. Wiley. 1999.

Huang, Kuan-Tsae, Yang W. Lee, and Richard Y. Wang. *Quality Information and Knowledge*. Prentice Hall. 1999.

Juran, Joseph M. and A. Blantos Godfrey, eds. *Juran's Quality Handbook,* 5th ed. McGraw-Hill. 1999.

Redman, Thomas C. *Data Quality for the Information Age*. Artech House. 1996.

Sunderraman, Rajshekhar. *Oracle Programming: A Primer*. Addison Wesley. 1999.